ADVANCE PRAISE FOR
IN THE SHADOW OF THE ROUND TOPS

"Our knowledge of historical events is often based on a fragile combination of memory, bias, and flawed accounts written long after the fact. This is particularly true in the Gettysburg historiography when considering the controversies around Captain Samuel Johnston's reconnaissance and Lt. General James Longstreet's countermarch on July 2, 1863. Author Allen Thompson combines his knowledge of primary accounts and terrain to methodically deconstruct the myths, misconceptions, and falsehoods surrounding these events. After reading *In the Shadow of the Round Tops*, you will reconsider much of what you think you know and have more apparent answers to the debates that continue to haunt Gettysburg's second day."

–James A. Hessler, Gettysburg Licensed Battlefield Guide, author of *Sickles at Gettysburg* (2009) and *Gettysburg's Peach Orchard* (2019), co-host of *The Battle of Gettysburg Podcast*

"Allen Thompson has compiled the definitive analysis of the march by Longstreet's Corps to strike the Union left on the second day of the Battle of Gettysburg, an event that would generate charges and counterattacks between former Confederate officers to rival the bloody battle itself. This is a must read for those interested in the Confederate command system at Gettysburg and the influence of those who defended their decisions that fateful day."

–John S. Heiser, National Park Service (ret.)

"Few Civil War battles evoke as much emotion and controversy as Gettysburg, particularly in assessing the performance of leading generals such as James Longstreet. The subject of much recent scholarship, Author Allen Thompson

takes a fresh look at Longstreet's countermarch on July 2 and the available military intelligence that influenced the Confederate decision-making that fateful day. Thompson's thought-provoking work is a worthy addition to the historiography of the war's bloodiest battle."

–**Scott L. Mingus, Sr., co-author of *If We Are Striking for Pennsylvania: The Army of Northern Virginia and the Army of the Potomac March to Gettysburg***

"*In the Shadow of the Round Tops* is the definitive exploration of Longstreet's march to the Confederate right at Gettysburg on July 2, 1863—one of the most controversial events in Civil War scholarship. Here, author Allen Thompson provides us with not only a deep dive into what happened that afternoon but also a splendid exploration of human memory, and how 'Longstreet's Fatal Delay' became so important to post-war Confederate mythology in explaining away defeat. This is an excellent addition to Gettysburg literature, and I thoroughly enjoyed reading it."

–**David A. Powell, author of *The Chickamauga Campaign***

"Few episodes of American history have generated more controversies than the Battle of Gettysburg, many of which still rages today. One of the most intriguing controversies is precisely where Capt. Samuel Johnston, the engineer officer assigned to headquarters of the Army of Northern Virginia, went on his late-night reconnaissance of the Union left during the night of July 1-2, 1863. Johnston claimed to have reached Little Round Top, which would have required him to pass through Union cavalry videttes, none of whom reported any contact that night. Johnston's report, in turn, influenced Gen. Robert E. Lee's battle plan for July 2, and also led directly to the lengthy and time-consuming march and countermarch of Lt. Gen. James Longstreet's Corps to the battlefield. Allen R. Thompson's excellent micro-history, *In the Shadow of the Round Tops: Longstreet's Countermarch, Johnston's Reconnaissance, and the Enduring Battles for the Memory of July 2, 1863* addresses these events in more detail than ever before. This deeply researched and well-written volume deserves a place on the bookshelf of any serious student on the second day of the Battle of Gettysburg."

–Eric J. Wittenberg, award-winning historian

"Allen Thompson has done a masterful job of deconstructing all the Soldiers accounts on such a controversial subject. He treats them with consideration and respect. The parsing and sifting of Veteran's memories to make sense of their experiences certainly was a factor about LTG James Longstreet's Countermarch. *In the Shadow of the Round Tops* will be an important addition to a more accurate narrative of the pivotal events on July 2, 1863 at Gettysburg."

–Rob Abbott, Gettysburg Licensed Battlefield Guide, Colonel USMC (ret.)

In the Shadow of the Round Tops

Longstreet's Countermarch, Johnston's
Reconnaissance, and the Enduring Battles
for the Memory of July 2, 1863

Allen R. Thompson

A KNOX PRESS BOOK
An Imprint of Permuted Press
ISBN: 978-1-63758-523-8
ISBN (eBook): 978-1-63758-524-5

In the Shadow of the Round Tops:
Longstreet's Countermarch, Johnston's Reconnaissance, and the Enduring Battles for the Memory of July 2, 1863

Cover Deisgn by Conroy Accord
Cover Photo by Rob Gibson
Interior Design by Yoni Limor

Permuted Press, LLC
New York • Nashville
permutedpress.com

Published in the United States of America
1 2 3 4 5 6 7 8 9 10

To my family, for always believing in me

TABLE OF CONTENTS

PART ONE

PART TWO

"The historian delves into the dust of mouldering humanity, and learns what were its impelling motives, just as the geologist finds in the rocks the traces of the forces that have moulded the surface of the earth."

- Charles Marshall, June 3, 1886[1]

"A tradition may grow and flower surprisingly; but it doesn't grow like a kind of historical orchid. It must have its root in something definite."

- Samuel Francis Batchelder[2]

"By doubting we are led to question, by questioning we arrive at the truth."

- Peter Abelard

INTRODUCTION

ESTEEMED HISTORIAN HARRY PFANZ WROTE THAT THE Confederate First Corps' countermarch on July 2 was "one of the most difficult non-combat aspects of the Gettysburg campaign to reconstruct and to understand."[3] As with most of his observations, he was right. The lack of firsthand information is quickly apparent to anyone seeking to gain a solid understanding of what happened west of Seminary Ridge on the morning and early afternoon of July 2.

Inevitably, when a subject lacks robust documentation, what little information *is* available understandably becomes the standard version of events by default. With only one or two pieces of evidence, it's difficult, if not impossible, to compare, contrast, and challenge that evidence.[4]

This particular subject, the countermarch and morning reconnaissance, is unique in a sense. While there is almost no *contemporary* record of what happened, it generated plenty of later discussion among the battle's veterans, most of whom focused on the effects of the countermarch. That discussion, however, produced the primary accounts relied on by historians.

The veterans' debate was shrouded behind political agendas and character assassination; however, two individuals, Lafayette McLaws and Edward Porter Alexander, emerged and rose above the fray. There were two primary reasons for this. First and foremost, their accounts were *detailed*. For historians craving information, accounts from the people who were there, who were in charge of the situation and privy to all the inside details, these two accounts became invaluable.

Second, the accounts seem at first glance (and even second and third glances) to be reasonable and trustworthy. Neither account bears serious accusations toward other Confederate veterans, something rare in the Southern postwar debates of the 1870s. And both accounts provide (mostly) dispassionate analysis, using little to none of the flourishing language that props up much of the discussion among the veterans.

McLaws and Alexander dominate the footnotes of the histories from Douglas Southall Freeman's southern opus *Lee's Lieutenants* in the 1940s to the most recent studies of the battle.[5] Since their accounts serve as the cornerstone of countermarch historiography, it's important to understand how their accounts have been interpreted.

Harry Pfanz and Gettysburg National Park Ranger Karlton Smith provide the most concise and insightful overviews of the traditional story.[6] In the very early morning hours of July 1, General James Longstreet's two divisions, commanded by Generals Lafayette McLaws and John Bell Hood, marched to the battlefield from their bivouac several miles west of Gettysburg. The divisions arrived soon after sunrise and took their positions along Herr's Ridge, one of the dominant ridges running north to southeast.

While Longstreet's Corps marched up and formed along the ridge, General Robert E. Lee had ordered his engineer, a young captain by the name of Samuel R. Johnston, to reconnoiter the Federal left flank and find a concealed route into position. Johnston rode off at dawn and returned about three hours later. He reported that he had reached Little Round Top without encountering any Federal troops. From the panoramic vista on the hill's summit, Johnston could see no Federal troops along the spine of Cemetery Ridge. He also reported that there were roads available to march Longstreet's Corps around the Federal left flank without being seen. Lee then directed Johnston to ride with Longstreet and lead his men into position.

When the order was given to march into position for the assault, Longstreet's divisions first moved to the west side of Herr's Ridge to follow Johnston's concealed route, masking the movement from the prying eyes of the Federal signal station on Little Round Top. The column followed farm lanes behind Herr's Ridge to Marsh Creek, then followed the creek south until they reached the Black Horse Tavern, an imposing inn along the Fairfield Road, a major thoroughfare to the southeast. Shuffling across the road, they stepped onto the Black Horse Tavern Road where, a mere three hundred yards further, McLaws and Captain Johnston crested a ridge and abruptly discovered they could be seen by the signal station on Little Round Top.

McLaws and Johnston spent some time riding around the area, looking for another route. Unfortunately, none could be found, and when they returned, Longstreet himself had arrived to find out why the march had ground to an abrupt halt. Not happy with the delay, he asked what was going on. McLaws rode to the hill with him and pointed out the signal flags, telling him there was no route around the hill. However, McLaws had performed his own reconnaissance that morning (despite Longstreet's admonition against it) and knew of a way into position without being seen. The only way to get there, unfortunately, was to countermarch back to where they had started. Longstreet agreed, and the column turned around.

Meanwhile, Colonel E.P. Alexander, whom Longstreet had placed in command of all three battalions of the corps' artillery, had led his guns along the same route. He, too, had noticed that continuing along the Black Horse Tavern Road would expose his column to the Federal signal station. But he also realized that by turning off the road to the left and taking a short detour of a few hundred yards through the fields, he could avoid the hill altogether. By doing this, he avoided the need to countermarch and before noon, was able to slowly roll his guns into the assigned rendezvous by a schoolhouse along Willoughby Run.

After waiting a spell, he rode back to see what was taking the infantry so long, only to find the column stopped in the road, waiting for McLaws and Johnston to return. Alexander pointed out the tracks his artillery had left in the soft ground, telling whoever it was he talked to that they could simply follow his shortcut. But for some reason Alexander could never understand, the infantry wouldn't do it. Instead, they countermarched, wasting hours and delaying the attack.

The traditional countermarch route varies in the particulars depending on whose interpretation is being used (did they take *this* road or *that* road?), but the general route has always been the same. After following the initial line of march back to Herr's Ridge, the column cut across the ridge to the Fairfield Road and followed it up to Willoughby Run. When they reached the stream, they turned right (south) down a ravine road that wound along the banks of the run to a schoolhouse (where Alexander waited with his artillery). Another road led from the schoolhouse to the divisions' respective positions on the southern extension of Seminary Ridge, often called Warfield Ridge.

When the column countermarched, McLaws's Division—which was in the lead—got tangled up with Hood's Division, which had been following it. Longstreet asked McLaws if he would let Hood lead the march instead, since his division was now in the rear. But McLaws insisted on keeping the coveted lead and spearheading the assault. Despite the logistical problems, Longstreet acquiesced and McLaws was allowed to move forward, keeping the lead and the honor of spearheading the attack.

Finally on the right route and with the columns untangled, McLaws marched easily along the road and into position on Warfield Ridge. But as the division reached the crest of the ridge, they could see that the Federal line was not in the position they expected. Rather than emerging from the woods on the flank, they were staring face to face with an entire corps of Federal troops. Hood then marched further to the right in order to extend the line far enough to meet the new threat.[7]

Introduction

* * *

THIS IS THE TRADITIONAL INTERPRETATION. THE CON-clusions I've reached are often different from the traditional ones. Sometimes they're drastically different.

I strongly encourage everyone to read the footnotes and endnotes. All of the sources used to piece together my conclusions are noted throughout the text rather than cited in bunches and string citations at the end of paragraphs or sections. That way, the reader doesn't have to guess at, or search for, which source I used for a particular fact.

I've also included the full quote I've relied on from those sources rather than simply referencing which source was used. This allows the reader to see the quote in as much context as possible, without seeking out the source. Some of the sources are obscure and unavailable without ordering collections of papers from archival collections and sorting through them. It also allows the reader to see the particular language I've relied on, rather than simply trust that the citation says what I've said it does.

The notes also further explain the reasoning I've used to reach my conclusions. The narrative is designed to be readable by anyone, no matter the level of prior knowledge. Of course, the more knowl-edge of the battle coming into the book, the more the reader will ultimately get out of it, but I wanted it to be accessible to anyone with an interest in the battle, the countermarch, Johnston's infamous reconnaissance, or how history is made. That ultimately meant that some of the more advanced and nuanced discussion had to occur in the notes, outside the primary narrative (though there's plenty there, too!).

As a final note, this project started as a follow-up to an article I wrote for *Gettysburg Magazine* about Johnston's reconnaissance. The purpose was to simply connect Johnston's morning recon with the afternoon's countermarch, since those are the two places he shows up in the historical record. It seemed like a natural place to go from the first study.

As I started digging into the sources, I realized that, like so many others who ventured into this subject, only a few accounts were readily available and those contradicted each other on some of the major points (and sometimes contradicted themselves). The actual events, though, *couldn't* be contradictory; whatever happened that morning happened. Instead, it was the *memories* that were contradictory. That led to an exploration of human memory, since that was the ultimate basis for all of the recollections.

People wrote the accounts that we rely on. Even if the brown and musty pages give a sense of prestige and authority to the accounts, they were written by someone who sat down with pen in hand, in a real time and a real place to write down their recollections. But they could only write down what they remembered. How memory works is just as important to a work of history as the ability to find and synthesize primary sources.

This is all to say that the project didn't start with a particular goal in mind other than to try to figure out what happened behind Seminary Ridge on July 2. There wasn't a preconceived result. Indeed, for the vast majority of the project, I had no idea what conclusions the research was leading to. Instead, to steal a line from Sam Johnston, "when I thought that I had gone far enough," I took a step back and started putting the accounts in order.[8]

I think the results surprised me just as much as anyone else.

With that, and an open mind, I leave you to read and hopefully enjoy.

PERCEIVING HISTORY

"I need not say how difficult it is to speak positively and accurately after so many years.... Few men can describe these matters accurately, many will not."

- Joseph Kershaw, letter to John Bachelder, Aug. 7, 1882[9]

"My difficulty about Gettysburg is to reconcile what I saw at the time, and what I heard from others after the battle."

- Benjamin Humphreys, Twenty-first Mississippi, to Lafayette McLaws, Jan. 6, 1878[10]

"There has been so much written on the subject that it is getting to be very difficult to reconcile the versions of undoubtedly honest and well-meaning men."

- Henry Hunt, Sept. 4, 1884[11]

MEMORY

OUR VIEW OF THE PAST IS OFTEN BLURRY. IT IS CLOUDED BY bias of one sort or another, hampered by incomplete memories, and frequently softened by nostalgia. Calling the past "history" has a way of formalizing the collection of memories into a sort of canonized historical narrative. Events occur, fall into a fixed chronology, and are left there for observation. History often has a sense of inevitability.

7

History, though, is anything but fixed or inevitable. The events comprising the chronology derive from the memories of the people who were there. But people do not remember the same event the same way. Historical documents, which provide the basis for our view of historic events, are nothing more than personal memories. The collection of these memories becomes "history."

But history is more than just the memory of events; it is the memory of the *perception* of events. Perceptions vary with each individual; biases, experiences, time, physical viewpoint, faulty memory… all combine to create our individual perception. Two people can see the exact same scene in two very different ways, creating two separate primary sources that may contradict each other. Neither memory is wrong and neither memory is right (if a memory can even *be* "correct" since it is, after all, the perception of the event stored in the brain, not objective data).

But the perceptions of the events are all most historians can rely on. Archaeology can prove, disprove, or question some historical "facts." At the Little Bighorn, for example, a wildfire cleared away the grass and underbrush, allowing a full archaeological dig in the early 1980s. The results of the dig questioned the interpretation of the battle.[12] Photographs, paintings, and drawings can provide other clues. But the primary means of interpreting human history has been the written word.

Before the advent of audio recording, film, and camera shutter speeds quick enough to photograph action, there was simply no way to capture events in real time. The principal tool of conveying the human experience to future generations was pen and paper. Perhaps those jotted words eventually found their way to a printing press for broader reading. Maybe the family or community passed down local history through stories from generation to generation. Truly extraordinary events were eventually elevated to the status of myth or legend, becoming nearly unassailable. But they all started as memories. A basic understanding of how memory works, then, is vital.

MEMORIES ARE AFFECTED BY AN INCREDIBLE NUMBER OF factors. For example, the place the person stood when he experienced the event affected what he saw. His past experience affected how he perceived it. Was he scared, determined, anxious? Was this a familiar experience or the first time? Was he numb to the sight or bright-eyed and more receptive to the sights, sounds, and emotions? How far from the event was he writing? Were the memories fresh in his mind? Was he still at the site where he could see the hills, trees, and ridges, or was he writing a nostalgic letter to a comrade in an office years later? Was he writing a defense of his actions in a public article or a dedication speech for his regimental monument? Had he compared his memories with others, which then innocently infiltrated his own? Were his own memories really his, or a collection of shared memories that latched onto his own? How do we know if a particular memory is accurate? *Can* we know?

This is not to say that truth is relative. Whatever happened, happened, regardless of how it was remembered. It *is* to say that history is relative. All of these factors (and more) contribute to affecting the memory of the events and the memories that are eventually written down. Historians have to rely on these written memories—primary source material—in order to reconstruct the event. But over half a century of psychological research has determined that memory is a very elusive thing and often quite unreliable.

A study conducted after the 1990–91 Gulf War revealed that veterans of traumatic experiences frequently remember the events differently as time progresses. This can happen within only a few years. The study method was simple: veterans were given a questionnaire within a month of returning from combat deployment and then again about two years later. Nearly 90 percent of the veterans changed at least one response, and almost two-thirds changed more than one answer. A third of the changed answers were initially answered as *I did not experience this.* Two years later, the response was changed to *I did experience this.*[13]

None of this means the individuals were lying. Instead, in many scenarios, especially traumatic ones, the brain only stores parts of the event. On recall, it tries to fill in the missing portions of the memory. In situations where the memory is challenged—say, when a provocateur challenges one's recollections of an old battlefield—a phenomenon known as "confabulation" can occur. In this case, the brain can *invent* memories to fill in the gaps. Often associated with dementia, studies have shown this can occur in healthy brains and probably does frequently.[14]

In another example, a team of British psychologists recorded a formal discussion at a psychology seminar. Several weeks later, the team asked the attending psychologists to write down what they remembered. After comparing the responses with the audio recording, the research team found that the attendees only remembered about 8 percent of the information on average. And only *half* of those points were actually remembered correctly! Some of the seminar attendees—all trained psychologists—even remembered things that hadn't actually happened; some remembered things happening during the discussion that actually happened elsewhere.

As psychologist Elizabeth Loftus cautions, "even in the most intelligent among us is memory...malleable." Indeed, "memory traces can actually undergo distortion. With the passage of time, with proper motivation, with the introduction of special kinds of intervening facts, the memory traces seem sometimes to change or become transformed. These distortions can be quite frightening," Loftus warns, "for they can cause us to have memories of things that never happened."[15] As Loftus concludes, "errors and confusions seemed to be the rule rather than the exception."[16]

Whether created from whole cloth or manipulating existing memories, the brain tends to create the memory in the best light for the individual. This is part of a process called self-deception.[17] The brain developed this interesting evolutionary tool essentially as a power-saving device. Lying takes energy, and the brain already uses more than its fair share of energy in the body. By the subconscious tricking the conscious part of the brain, "we hide reality from our conscious minds the better to hide it from onlookers."[18] This allows us to fool ourselves so we don't use all that brain power lying (bluffing is a big part of survival—just look at a peacock's plumage). Indeed, we're not lying because we actually believe what we're saying, even though the memory is untrue or significantly altered.

Not surprisingly, self-deceit tends to make us look better in comparison to others. The derogation of others appears most commonly as a defensive tactic "when your own image has been lowered—suddenly it becomes valuable to deflect attention onto some disliked group—so that by comparison, you do not look as bad as they do."[19] Putting others down to make one feel better is a part of human nature we all intuitively know and understand, even if begrudgingly. This subconscious memory tool fits the dynamics of the July 2 countermarch debate perfectly. Postwar blame flew as thick as the bullets had on the battlefield—it was only natural (literally) that deflection and derogation would occur.

People also have a tendency to remember their own actions in a more prominent role than they actually played. When a person is actively involved in a scenario—a conversation, for example—he is going to subconsciously focus on himself more than the other person. In addition to listening, he is preparing his own response. He's engaged in both input and output processing at the same time. And because one's own actions are almost always remembered most prominently, he'll remember his own input to the conversation as more important than that of the other person.[20]

When an individual is challenged, his immediate and natural response is to deflect blame, cast it upon others, and produce subconscious memories that put him in the best light. Curiously, when a *group* venture does not go as planned, the participants tend to find blame amongst themselves, rather than with the opponent.

Whether it is a sports team or an army, a particular group is much more aware of its own actions and inner workings than it is of its opponent's. In other words, while there are two sides to the story, the group has the most information about its own actions and is more likely to find the major faults there. This is part of what is called "availability bias." The most readily available information concerns the group, so the focus is there.[21] This is certainly on display when it comes to Confederates explaining the loss at Gettysburg. While the Confederate leadership spent the better part of the last three decades of the nineteenth century blaming each other for losing, George Pickett is famously quoted as saying "I think the Yankees had something to do with it." He may not have actually said it, but the quote shines a light on the Confederacy's availability bias.[22] Thus, we have infighting on the causes of the defeat, which in turn biases our sources.

Internal memory processing causes plenty of issues with recall. But there are external factors, too. What is known as the Misinformation Effect creates "false memories," contaminating existing memories with the memories of other people and other information. The brain does not store memories in neat compartments dedicated to "personal memories" and "other people's memories I've heard." Instead, it tosses them into the same bin, and when recalling them later, it can be difficult if not impossible to decipher which part of the memory was actually experienced and which was added by hearing another person's memory.

The Gulf War study is applicable here. According to the study, the veterans' accounts changed partly due to exposure to other information. For example, media accounts largely emphasized the relative bloodlessness of the Gulf War. The study results showed that veterans tended to minimize their memories of traumatic events after repeated exposure to the idea that the campaign was quick and painless. There is no way to know if the veterans had actually experienced what they said they did—the answers were self-reported with no verification. Whether the veterans enhanced the descriptions of traumatic events in the initial questionnaire or minimized the events later cannot be known. Ultimately, that's not the important thing. What *is* important is that the veterans reduced their answers at least partly based on what others had reported. Public information played a role in altering their memories. At least, it played a role in altering what they told others they remembered.[23] Since all we have of the countermarch—or most Civil War topics—are the memories the veterans shared, this is important.

The idea that external events can create these false memories has been studied for over fifty years. The "growing body of research shows that new, post-event information often becomes incorporated into memory, supplementing and altering a person's recollection." Elizabeth Loftus writes that false memory "invades us, like a Trojan horse, precisely because we do not detect its influence."[24] Unintentionally attesting to this fact, Benjamin Humphreys, who ended up commanding a brigade in Longstreet's Corps by the end of the battle, admitted that "my difficulty about Gettysburg is to reconcile what I saw at the time, and what I heard from others after the battle."[25]

This "misinformation effect" has been shown with a startling degree of accuracy. Where groups of people experience or witness the same event, the effect is even greater. Loftus is well-known for her work involving criminal witness testimony, so crime scene witness testimony produces a good deal of the examples. Crime scene "witnesses tend to talk to one another in the immediate aftermath of the crime," she writes. "But because different witnesses are different people with different perspectives, they are likely to see or notice different things, and thus remember different things, even when they witness the same event. So, when they communicate about the crime later, they not only reinforce common memories for the event, they also contaminate each other's memories for the event."[26] This is not far removed from the situation Civil War veterans would have encountered. Having participated in, rather than simply observed the events, their personal experiences were limited. They frequently describe the emotions and a cacophony of sights and sounds, but times and details they admit are fuzzy.

Abner Small, an adjutant in the Sixteenth Maine Infantry, succinctly summarized this in his history of the regiment. "Any member of a regiment, officer or private, can have but little knowledge of movements outside his immediate command." The soldier "has a specific duty to perform, and no time to look with a critical eye upon his comrade's conduct." The lay of the land, "the wooded slopes and deep ravines, the fog, the dense smoke, and the apparent and often real confusion of troops moving in different directions under different orders, utterly precludes the possibility of a correct detailed observation of a battle of any magnitude." Because of this, the soldier "must draw upon his imagination, or from the experience of others."[27] "Like the knight in the story, each one sees the shield from *his* point of view," confirmed Charles Pickett, brother of the more famous Pickett.[28]

Civil War soldiers belonged to individual groups of friends, called "messes," within companies, which then comprised regiments, brigades, divisions, corps, and armies. They talked about the battles, the loss of friends and family, their feelings. They read the official reports after the war, accounts of other veterans in veterans' periodicals like the *National Tribune, Southern Historical Society Papers,* and *Confederate Veteran.* Veterans' groups like the Grand Army of the Republic (GAR), the Military Order of the Loyal Legion of the United States, and numerous Confederate veterans' associations flourished after the war. War stories—memories—were shared over the next few decades. Not until the 1880s did memoirs start to become profitable or desirable (for many, they understandably wanted to simply go home and move on with their lives in the immediate aftermath of the war). All of these things influenced the memories of the men who fought the war. A great many of the accounts that historians rely on were published well after the memories were contaminated.

Events like the First Corps countermarch and Samuel Johnston's reconnaissance are prime examples of how false memories permeate Civil War primary accounts. The more people talked about them, the more they turned into the proverbial fish, the length and struggle to reel it in increasing by the telling. An undefined delay in 1873 turned into a delay of several hours by the 1880s. Though in hindsight it may seem like lying, the continual collection of others' memories simply snowballed into a false individual "memory." As the research team conducting the Gulf War study concluded, "entire scenes of stressful events can be fabricated and then inserted into memory. These scenes are often believed to be true, even after the subject has been informed that the memory is actually false."[29] The story of Longstreet's countermarch is a particularly good historical case study.

The scale on which these false memories can occur is astounding. It should also give us pause when researching historical events. For example, in a mid-1990s study, college students were told that family members had provided stories from the students' childhoods. The stories were fake but were often traumatic in nature: getting lost in the mall, almost drowning, being attacked by vicious animals. Fully 25 percent of the students later recounted the event as an actual memory. While one in four subjects may seem small enough—after all, 75 percent did *not* falsely remember these things—the fact that a quarter of test subjects falsely, but honestly, remembered something as traumatic as nearly dying should be something to take serious note of. Other study subjects have been convinced they met Bugs Bunny at Disney World (an impossibility, given the different brands) and have earnestly remembered fake events after being shown a picture of the event photoshopped to include the participant.[30] It is not far-fetched to assume that a good portion of Civil War recollections are not entirely accurate. Quite the opposite.

According to Loftus, "eyewitness testimony is probably the most persuasive form of evidence presented in court, but in many cases, its accuracy is dubious." This should be particularly concerning to historians who must, out of necessity, rely primarily on eyewitness accounts. Photographs of the war can show us what the uniforms looked like, how an army could devastate the landscape by scouring it of trees and digging zigzagging entrenchments to the horizon. They can show us the awful wreckage of battle, bloated corpses, stiff-legged horses, rows of wooden headboards, and even the flies feasting on the results of the carnage. But photographs and sketches say little as to *how* all of that happened. For that, we count on history's witnesses and hope that they are both honest and accurate.

The level of stress and anxiety during the event and how much interference *immediately* after the event plays a major role in memory storage, too. Studies have shown that sleeping immediately after an event, so as to prevent interfering events to cloud the memory as it is being stored, drastically increases the accuracy of remembrance. According to one study, people who slept within two hours of the event remembered nearly 80 percent of the details, while those who were awake for even five hours after the event barely remembered 20 percent. Likewise, the level of stress and anxiety during the event affects how much detail is stored to begin with—the more stress, the less level of detail being observed while one focuses on the event in a sort of tunnel vision.[31] Needless to say, battle conditions, stressful marches, lack of sleep, and reconnaissances behind enemy lines (or at least near enemy lines) are less than ideal and reliable environments to collect accurate memories.

Campbell Brown, one of General Ewell's aides (and son-in-law), repeatedly surprised himself when he compared his memories with an actual visit to the battlefield more than a decade later. "As to [the] height of Cemetery Hill," he jotted, "it is much less than I thought." Likewise, Round Top is much further from as high as I thought it, but the rise is more gradual + it is hardly so steep as I imagined." He found there were several names for the same road and noticed a significant bend in the main road (Baltimore Street) that hadn't been stored in his memory.[32] This should be of interest to us, as most of the accounts written about the countermarch were at least ten years old—some even several decades old.

The distance from the events has a way of lending a sense of sagacity to the documents. But they were created in a real time in a real place by real people responding to real situations. Many of the writers understood the historical importance of what they wrote and tried to give us the necessary pause. For example, Joseph Kershaw, a brigade commander in Longstreet's Corps, cautioned historian John Bachelder about giving too much credence to individual recollections. "Few men *can* describe these matters accurately," he wrote. "Many *will* not."[33] John Bassler, a member of the 149th Pennsylvania, thought it "a herculean task to separate the truth from the falsehood in the multitude of reports that have rained down…since 1863."[34]

"I know how much our memories of events that took place so many years since fail, each and all of us," Charles Pickett acknowledged. "All that we can…do now is to give our recollections and they are as a usual thing, rather poor reliance." But "by getting the individual recollections of these gentlemen as well as my own, we may be able to get a more intelligent view."[35] This is, of course, how history is created. Comparing sources is a way to "weed out errors or reconcile discrepancies."[36] Joseph Kershaw agreed, telling Bachelder "you can't have true history but by comparing [and] *sifting—especially sifting*."[37]

But some events have limited sources. Events like Longstreet's countermarch and Johnston's reconnaissance, for example, have a single "star witness" who tells the vast majority of the story. If they are wrong, we are back to having nothing but a large gap in the historical record. The temptation to believe the witness, especially if the story is engaging and detailed, is overwhelming. There is nothing quite like a well-written human-interest story that also fills in major gaps in the historical record. When it comes to the countermarch, McLaws's accounts fill that role in every major history of the battle. But in order to truly understand what happened at any point in history, we must be able to separate fact from fiction, even if that results in being left empty-handed.

All of this means that every source has to be intensely scrutinized for accuracy. This is not to confuse scrutinization for dislike, favoritism, or character assassination. All of our memories work this way, and we are all subject to these limitations. We should be grateful that people like McLaws and Johnston eventually did write down their reminiscences even if the details were not entirely correct. As Kershaw told Bachelder, McLaws's account "is valuable if not wholly accurate." [38] Sources are scrutinized here simply because they offer the central pieces to the countermarch story; if their memories are inaccurate, then so is the history.

There is no judgment of the character of the officers here. Being wrong is not the same as lying, and one wrong memory does not negate *all* of a participant's memories. Likewise, being correct about one aspect of the fight does not mean the entire account is credible. For the most part, the soldiers did the best they could with the training they had in absolutely unique circumstances and deserve immense credit for that. Life and death decisions were made quickly in conditions that were quite terrible for decision-making. Not only did men die immediately because of those decisions, but the commanders then came under lifelong scrutiny for them. Most students of the war have studied it many times longer than the soldiers ever served, having the benefit of numerous studies on nearly every aspect of the war. In many cases, it takes longer to read a chapter about the fighting than the fighting actually lasted.

Casting blame for particular decisions is not the purpose here. Nor is it to chastise any participant for their beliefs, faulty memories, or inaccuracies. The biases and factors affecting the memories will be pointed out to show whether the memories are reliable or not, but the accuracy of memory should not be taken to reflect on the character of the veteran himself.

THE WORD "HISTORY" COMES FROM "HISTORIA," THE GREEK word for *inquiry*. Historical inquiry is not only in searching for sources. Once the sources are found, Kershaw's sifting takes place, comparing and contrasting the sources to determine their veracity. Only by comparing the accounts can we begin to get a glimpse of what actually happened.

There are some things we will never know for sure. For example, we simply will not know exactly where Samuel Johnston went on the morning of July 2 or the precise route Longstreet's two divisions took onto Seminary Ridge that morning. Even if the participants came back to the battlefield to give a personal tour, it would not be precisely accurate. They would have been the first to say that.

Ultimately, that's not the important part. What's important is that we try to find the truth, or at least try to catch a glimpse of it. To do that, we have to understand that every account is partly right and partly wrong—how much of each will depend on a variety of factors. These were human beings remembering their personal experiences years later, often in the middle of heated political debates. It was hardly the environment to honestly extract fragile memories. Indeed, battlefield conditions are hardly the environment to form accurate memories to begin with. Even before the bullets started to fly, stress, anxiety, and exhaustion interfered with accurate memory storage. To expect fully accurate recollections of a battlefield is a tall order. To hope for accurate and unbiased details emerging in the tumultuous postwar environment is simply unreasonable.

Even accounts of the battle that were not sparked by accusations of losing the war or wrapped up in discussion of "the cause" have their flaws. By the time many accounts were written, nostalgia had kicked in. Speeches delivered at the dedication of regimental monuments drip with sentimental prose as the survivors, now elderly men with canes and white hair, remembered the defining moments of their generation. One can hardly blame them for being proud of themselves; their defining experience was also very much one of the nation's defining moments, too. It was neither the time nor the place for critical military analysis; it was a time to remember their comrades, their deeds, and their sacrifices.

"Historiography" is defined as "the writing of history based on the critical examination of sources, the selection of particulars from the authentic materials, and the synthesis of particulars into a narrative that will stand the test of critical methods."[39] The term is typically used to describe works that study how a particular event is remembered rather than strictly what happened, i.e. social history versus military history. But really, *all* history is historiography; in order to know what happened, we need to know how the event was remembered in the first place.

A book compiling, sorting, and analyzing memories—a history book—*has to be* historiography because any history book is simply organizing the memories of the people who lived through the event. As we've seen, those memories will be biased, which means leveling out that bias is necessary to figure out the who, what, where, when, and especially the why of a particular recollection.

To put it simply, there is no such thing as unbiased history. Watching unedited film from the 1940s with no commentary is about as close as we can ever get; it is raw footage left for us to interpret without any filter from the person filming it.

Or is it? Even though the image is unfiltered, the camera was still deliberately pointed at the subject for a reason determined by the photographer. The vantage point of a picture taken by an Allied

19

soldier in World War II will necessarily give us a different point of view than one taken by a German photographer even though the image is untouched. Similarly, a letter written by one Confederate officer to another twenty years after the battle defending his performance against criticism from yet another Confederate officer is not pure, unfiltered history. It is the perception of events told through the lens of the writer's memory at the time it was written. Even the author's perception can change over time (for example, Lafayette McLaws had a different view of Sam Johnston's reconnaissance after he spoke with him in 1892 than he did when he gave a speech in 1878).

None of this is bad. It simply means we have to be careful about what sources we use. That means performing a diligent inquiry: doubting the accuracy of every source at first, questioning them, looking for inaccuracies, comparing them against other sources, then repeating the process with *those* sources. Then, we can step back and take a look at the results. They are often surprising.

KEEPING TIME IN THE CIVIL WAR

IN THE SPRING OF 1853, BARELY TEN YEARS BEFORE THE Battle of Gettysburg, an exasperated Vermonter calling himself Inquirer asked a question of the *Burlington Daily Free Press*: "What is the time of day in Burlington, Vermont?!"

"The other day I went to church," he began. "I was in my seat at 11 o'clock." But the "clock in the church said it was 20 minutes past 11 o'clock." Another attempt at piousness resulted in the same frustration. "Again, I was in church, by my watch, at 10 minutes past two. The Minister came at 25 minutes past two, and *his* clock and my watch were 20 minutes apart." Inquirer "determined to keep my watch right—had it cleaned, regulated, all in excellent order—called every day to see that it agreed with the 'true standard.'" But the "'true standard' and the town clock I found did not agree as to the church time; and the clock in the church did not agree with either!"

Inquirer took his watch back to the watchmaker and demanded a refund. But the watchmaker said it kept perfect time, in line with the true standard. He pointed to the clock in his shop, which was the same as Inquirer's watch.

"But who regulated the town clock?" Inquirer demanded.

"Why, sometimes the Sexton," answered the watchmaker. But "sometimes Mr. A. orders it according to his watch; sometimes Mr. B.; and sometimes a Committee in Church Street."

So, Inquirer was back to square one. Determined to answer "What is the time of day in Burlington?" he headed to the train station. The railroad, he was assured, "is always regulated according to the 'true standard.'" Inquirer arrived at the train station "twelve minutes before" the scheduled departure time "by my watch." But the cars had left five minutes earlier. "Pray, what time is it by your Rail Road time?" he asked. Inquirer "looked, and was ten minutes too slow, of Rail Road time." But his watch—which had been verified as the "true standard" time of Burlington—"was then three minutes faster than the Burlington 'true standard!'"

The hotel down the street, purportedly operating by railroad time too, told Inquirer that the train had left five minutes later than the station's clock reported. *Don't the railroad clocks agree around here?!* cried the exasperated Burlingtonian.

The hotelier's answer was illustrative of the problem: "Yes, Sir, they all agree, always *agree to differ*, in time as well as in everything else."

Inquirer was about to give up: "What is the time of day in Burlington? Is there any way of knowing? Or have the people come to believe, with certain philosophers, that there really is no such thing as time at all?"

The editors of the *Free Press* had as much answer as the hotelier. "Mr. Inquirer, if we could help you we would." They, too, had "been hoping, for a long time, that the *chaos*, which, so far as time of day is concerned…might clear away, and something like *order* come in its stead." If the various clock regulators could agree on a standard time, "it would be news indeed."[40]

Twenty-three years later, the editors of the *Leavenworth Weekly Times* complained about the same thing. The patchwork of localized timekeeping standards was *still* causing too many problems. "Our jewelers give us 'sun time,'" the editors explained, "and our hotels and ticket offices keep 'railroad time,' while the market house bell rattles around promiscuously between the two, and the town clock tries to give us all sorts of time at once, and generally succeeds."

Like the flustered Vermonter, the Kansas newspaper editors were not talking about a matter of seconds or even a few minutes. The railroad engineer's "chronometer, which does not vary a second, tells him it is nine forty-five, but the jewelers can prove to him by their 'regulators' that it is only nine-twenty. Under some circumstances this is a small matter," the *Weekly Times* acknowledged. "But when a man goes to the depot at five minutes before ten, and finds that the ten o'clock train has been gone twenty minutes, the thing assumes to him a very serious aspect." Historians trying to piece together a timeline for a particular Pennsylvania morning in 1863 can easily sympathize with the inquisitive Vermonter and Leavenworth's confused commuters.[41]

During the Civil War, and prior to standardized time's general institution in the 1880s, time was generally kept by the town clock. Times between towns could vary (indeed, they were generally *not* in agreement). Local time was kept, logically enough, by a local regulator, who recorded time according to the position of the sun. Local noon—when the sun crosses the meridian—was the benchmark. To an observer without any astronomical tools, this was the highest point of the sun in the sky.

Local noon, however, does not necessarily happen at the same time every day. The rotation of the Earth, its position in orbit, and the fact that the Earth's orbit is elliptical, not perfectly circular, affects the time the sun crosses the meridian.[42]

Because of this, local noon is not necessarily the exact same time every day. Thus, if a soldier were to set his watch based on a precisely accurate reading of local noon one day, it would be no guarantee that his watch would be accurate the next day. Local noon might not be precisely 12:00 p.m. The sun may crest a few minutes later or earlier, meaning his watch would be incorrect by those few minutes when the sexton set the clock again.

As if all this wasn't confusing enough, local time meant the clock was only applicable to that locality; every ten to fifteen miles east or west and the time changed by a minute due to the curvature of the earth. Someone standing fifteen miles west, for example, experiences sunrise a minute later than an eastern counterpart.[43] But like the Burlington watchmaker explained, the accuracy of the town clock depended on who set the time on a particular day. Was the clock tower set by an actual observation of the solar position? Or was it set by the watch of an influential citizen—or even worse, a whole committee of them?!

Exactly how the position of the sun was judged was a question, too. Did the sexton make a best guess as to whether the sun was at its highest point? Or was he using a tool like a sundial to help him measure? Given the variations of local noon, combined with human error and self-interest (Burlington's "Mr. A.," for example, not wanting to reset his own watch or a railroad executive insisting *he* had the true time), clocks set by local time alone can vary significantly.[44] As we saw in Vermont, two people in the same town could be off by nearly a half hour!

In Civil War accounts, we add yet another wrinkle. Soldiers set their watches, if they had them and if they were trying to keep accurate time in the first place, by clock towers, market squares, or railroad stations in the towns they passed through on the march. As we saw in Vermont and Kansas, there was no guarantee the town would have any sense of a standard time within its own town limits. Expecting one town to be even relatively synchronized with another town's clock tower was simply unreasonable. Heading into the battle at Gettysburg, each soldier would be relying on a watch set according to any number of individual timekeepers.

The effects on historians are the same as those for a Burlington churchgoer or Leavenworth traveler. Chambersburg to Gettysburg is approximately twenty-five miles, so local time is two minutes different based on the longitude. Gettysburg to York is approximately forty-five miles, a difference of about three and a half minutes. Assuming the clocks in Chambersburg and York were precise, a Confederate setting his watch by the clock tower in Chambersburg would show a five-minute difference from a Confederate who set his watch by a completely accurate clock in York, all else being equal. But there was certainly no guarantee that the times were accurately set in the first place (Were they set according to a reading of the sun's position on the same day? Did "Mr. A" demand his own timepiece be used? Did York use railroad time while Chambersburg used an erroneous local time?).

A veteran who had set his watch in York could have observed the same event as a veteran setting his watch in Chambersburg. But due to the various factors involving local time-setting, the York observer could have noted the time as 12:00 p.m., while the Chambersburg soldier wrote "1 p.m.," or even "11 a.m." Both soldiers could be right in their recollection if that's what the watch reported, but both could also *technically* be wrong if the clocks were both inaccurate.

This is assuming the soldiers recorded a precise time at all. Understandably, but still frustratingly, many soldiers simply wrote "some time in the morning" or "after sunup," or something similar.[45] Many didn't have watches, so one man's "1 p.m." was another's "about noon," which was "late morning" to another and just "midday" to someone else. Even for soldiers with watches, precise times were usually not at the top of the priority list. They were fighting a battle, after all.[46] (We'll ignore, for the moment, the fact that the Federal army saw many of the same events and recorded their own times, setting *their* watches by different towns and railroad stations, adding even more time confusion into the mix.)

Soldiers in the same company or regiment, standing within yards of each other and witnessing the same events, could have recorded times more than a half hour apart, even if they had looked at their watches at the same moment and precisely remembered the time later. Add to this the fact that the soldiers were several days removed from timepieces that had *any* pretense of regulation and the idea that times can be precisely measured on the battlefield becomes absurd. There is simply no way for a historian 150 years later to know what the exact time was for a particular event.

In order to determine the order of events for a particular day, then, we have to compare accounts. We can look at what else was happening at the same time to determine where in the chronology the event happened. For example, we know there was a sharp skirmish between Wilcox's Confederate brigade and Berdan's Federal sharpshooters, supported by the Third Maine Infantry. Wilcox reported that his brigade encountered Berdan's Federal sharp-shooters before 9:00 a.m.[47] Berdan, on the other hand, reported the fight started well after 11:00 a.m. (Moses Lakeman, commanding the Third Maine, didn't report any time at all).[48] Who was right?

In order to figure this out, we have to look to other witnesses. Confederate artillery chief William Pendleton mentioned the "sharp contest" between Wilcox and the sharpshooters in his official report. But *he* reported it happening after midday while he and E.P. Alexander examined the Confederate front.[49] Wilcox, Berdan, and Pendleton all witnessed the same event but recorded markedly different times. While we don't know precisely what time that happened, we *do* know where Wilcox's brigade, Berdans' detachment of sharpshooters, and Pendleton and Alexander were at that particular moment. From there, we can backtrack to another recorded event, like Wilcox taking his place in the Confederate battle line or the movement of Longstreet's artillery, plug this event into the chronology, and continue on.

NONE OF THIS MEANS THAT WE CAN'T FIGURE OUT WHAT happened on July 2, 1863. But in order to sort it all out, we have to know our limitations and face the reality of the sources we are dealing with. The people who left their recollections did not simply record their story for posterity's sake. While some wrote for their families as a written legacy, others wrote in journals to keep busy, keep a memento of what they knew was a historic era in their country's history, or as a catharsis. Others wrote letters home to battle loneliness, keep family members informed, or to provide their own take on events. After the war, veterans spoke and wrote with an audience and purpose in mind; often, it was to defend or actively blame another party for a certain action taken (or not taken). In all cases, the story was not objective history, but the author's take.

Subjectivity is not a bad thing at all. Their experiences are important—invaluable, really—but none of them are infallible, objective pictures of what happened. They are not so much a snapshot of history as they are an artist's rendition; the memory only paints the picture recollected by the artist, which is not the same as a photograph, which captures things even the artist didn't notice.

As Peter Abelard said in the Middle Ages, we must approach the subject with a sense of doubt as to its accuracy. That leads us to ask questions. Answering those questions brings us closer to the truth, which is, after all, the goal. Questioning a source and doubting its ultimate veracity does not mean we're calling the writer a liar. We're all subject to the same memory problems, especially when the event is traumatic and the post-event discussions so controversial and ubiquitous. McLaws, Early, Pendleton, Alexander, Johnston, Longstreet…all were human, subject to biases, rivalries, and faulty memories. Questioning their memories and comparing—sifting, as Joseph Kershaw would put it—merely recognizes that they had no superhuman powers of observation or memory recall. They were people in extraordinary circumstances. But in the end, they were people.

Not one of the soldiers or citizens in Gettysburg in July of 1863 ever forgot how those days felt, even if some of the chaotic details were blurred by time and memory. Many of us have lived through defining moments and can relate: *Where were you when Kennedy was shot? when you got the news a loved one was killed in Vietnam or Iraq? when you watched the Twin Towers collapse on 9/11?* Everyone remembers the feeling, but the details can be fuzzy…who said what to whom, did I do that the day after, or a few days later…was that me, or am I remembering what a friend told me? Rather than confusing the matter, this can make the soldiers and citizens *less* distant. We can all relate.

The purpose of this inquiry is not to make villains or heroes. It is not to prove a point or a personal theory. No one is above the science of memory or the tug of human nature. There was no hypothesis when beginning the research, no predetermined result or favored person. This is not a pro-Longstreet inquiry, nor does it seek to vilify him or anyone else. The project started as a question: *what happened before the fighting started on July 2, 1863?*

Throughout the process, trying to answer each question spawned entire lines of new questions. Definitive answers are few and far between, but there's one thing anyone researching the activities west of Seminary Ridge on July 2 can attest to: there was much more to the countermarch than a simple mix-up in directions or a botched reconnaissance.

The countermarch became a symbol of all that went wrong with the Confederate army at Gettysburg. Gettysburg, in turn, became the fountainhead of all of the wrongs suffered by the South after the war. As we'll see, Jubal Early and William Pendleton quickly saw the need to shape Southern memory. They jumped into the project immediately after Lee died and with exceptional enthusiasm and vigor. Early especially seems to have understood the power of collective memory and made a concerted effort to create it and foster it in future generations. Pendleton, through a national speaking tour and with the benefit and fervor of his sermonizing career, carried the message throughout the South.

Early and Pendleton were deliberately creating an origin story for a stillborn nation. Early was not shy about his intentions, either, freely proclaiming that his goal was to "furnish…an enduring witness of our fidelity to our cause and the memory of our great leaders."[50] He intentionally framed it as a "holy crusade" and treated it that way in his speeches and writings throughout his life.[51]

The story of the defeat, of *why* the Southern nation had never taken its first independent breath, took on the hallmarks of most origin stories. Lee became the father of the Confederacy, much as Washington had become the father of his country. Both were apotheosized and elevated to the realm of mythology the moment they departed the earth (though the process had begun even before their respective deaths).

But there were villains, too…traitors, snakes in the grass. In the American Revolution, there was Benedict Arnold, a trusted subordinate of Washington before turning coats and joining the British to feed his insatiable ambition. In the Bible, the traitor was Lucifer, an angel of God who became convinced of his own superiority and jealous of God's glory. His pride caused his fall from Heaven and with it, created all the wrongs of the world.

In Early's history, Longstreet played the role of traitor. Like Arnold and Lucifer, his hubris convinced him of his own superiority. He violated orders, delayed the attack, and the delay caused the loss of the battle. Longstreet's fall at Gettysburg took with him the hopes of the South and created the evils and humiliations they suffered after the war. After the war, Longstreet provided his detractors plenty of fuel for this view by publicly siding with the Northern administrations' goals, aligning himself with Republican causes, and publicly criticizing Lee (to Northern publishers, no less).

Initially, Early's statements were confined to a few speeches. Pendleton's evangelistic tour spread the word throughout the South. Eventually, the speech reached Lafayette McLaws in Georgia. As the lead division in Longstreet's column, McLaws became worried that Longstreet would respond and blame *him* for being the true culprit. McLaws and Longstreet suffered a volatile relationship in the Confederate First Corps, and McLaws's reputation had not been stellar among his colleagues in the Army of Northern Virginia. So, he made a quick decision to preempt any blame. McLaws got his account public and made sure Longstreet knew about it. *His* would be the first word on the subject.

In his account, McLaws deflected the blame for the delay back to Lee's staff—engineer Samuel Johnston. He had performed the reconnaissance that morning, led the march, and got the First Corps turned around. If the delay in the July 2 attack had caused the loss at Gettysburg, then the First Corps had nothing to do with it.

This, of course, prompted a heated debate that generated nearly all of the documentation of the countermarch, its causes, and its dire effects. Later efforts by John Bachelder and Edward Porter Alexander to objectively document the battle were frustrated by a campaign of silence from the First Corps commanders. The only voices left for history to hear were those of McLaws, Early, Pendleton, and a few other biased accounts published in veterans' magazines.

So, the record the soldiers and citizens left us can be tough to sort out. But if we listen closely, shutting out the political noise and avoiding the distractions of blame-mongering, we can begin to hear the authentic voices of the men who were there and begin to put together their stories. The process of figuring it out is both rewarding and enlightening.

From this point on, we'll jump into the sources, the controversies, the biases...the *people* who gave us history. My hope is that the answers are as interesting and surprising to you as they were to me. And hopefully, even more questions are raised.

PART ONE

The Fatal Delay: Longstreet Loses the Cause

KNIGHTS OF THE QUILL

"It is necessary…that we should take charge of the history of the war on our side—we who have a greater interest in it than all others living."

- Jubal Early, Address to Survivors' Association for the State of South Carolina, November 17, 1871[52]

"If there be any, in all the land, who have proved renegade to their comrades and our holy cause, let them go out from among us with the brand of Cain upon them!"

- Jubal Early, Address before Washington and Lee University, January 19, 1873 [53]

"Knights of the quill have consumed many of their peaceful hours in publishing, through books, periodicals, and newspapers, their plans for the battle, endeavoring to forestall the records and find a scapegoat."

- James Longstreet, *From Manassas to Appomattox,* **1896**[54]

January 19, 1872

THE DAY WAS AS DREARY AS THE MOOD IN THE SOUTH. Outside the simple chapel at Washington and Lee University, an icy storm whistled and howled, sleet clattering against the windows, rain pounding on the thick wooden doors. Inside, a large crowd, shaking off beaded raindrops and melting ice from their top hats and rubberized ponchos, gathered to hear one of Robert E. Lee's old generals commemorate his birthday.[55]

Lee would have been sixty-five years old that Friday, but he had succumbed to ill health on the morning of October 12, 1870.[56] Southern hyperbole matched its sorrow at the loss of its patriarch that autumn: "The Potomac—overlooked by the home of the hero… conveys to the ocean a nation's tears," wailed one Southern eulogy.[57]

Throughout Southern cities, "the busiest streets were almost deserted." The former Confederate capital had also shuttered its businesses as a "token of sorrow," replacing open signs with mourning badges, photos of Lee, and a simple note: *Closed in consequence of the death of Robert E. Lee.* Houses were draped in laurel wreaths, flags flew somberly at half-mast, the doleful wail of church bells rang from sunrise to sunset, and all public buildings were closed. The whole city had shut down to mourn the loss of its most beloved citizen, "the dispensation of Providence so painful, but so hard to realize."[58] Special church services were held to honor and memorialize "the departed Hero, Soldier, Patriot and Christian." Lee's "high moral qualities and manly virtues…have caused his name to be famed abroad, to the admiration, if not the envy, of the nations of the world." Indeed, the very "land which gave birth to Robert E. Lee may hold its head aloft among the greatest nations in their palmiest days of chivalry."[59] Such was Robert Edward Lee revered throughout the Old Dominion.

Prayers for Lee echoed off the chamber walls of the Virginia Assembly. Reverend George Peterkin, who had traded in his lieutenant's braid for a bishop's mitre after the war, opened the legislative session the day after Lee died. Methodist Reverend John Edwards apotheosized Lee the following day. Lee was "that highest type of humanity," Rev. Edwards declared, "a Godly man…. His goodness paralleled his greatness, and surrounds it (as it still surrounds it) with a holy halo." Southern hearts "are indeed sad, and our tongues refuse to give forth the feelings of our souls."[60]

Monuments would be needed to commemorate Lee's life and achievements. Living up to his surname, Jubal Early quickly organized a convention to erect a fitting monument to Lee's memory.[61] The committee brought in heavy hitters from northern Virginia and Maryland. Reverdy Johnson, a former U.S. senator and attorney general, noted in private practice for his eclectic defenses of slaveowners (*Dred Scott v. Sandford*), a Union general (Fitz-John Porter's court-martial), and a Lincoln assassination conspirator (Mary Surratt) sat on the committee. Johnson had also been a pallbearer at Abraham Lincoln's funeral, making him seem an odd choice to aid in commemorating a Confederate of the stature of Robert E. Lee. Nonetheless, Reverdy Johnson accepted the invitation "to show his appreciation of the character...of the late" general.

Alongside Johnson, former Confederates such as General Isaac Trimble and Colonel William Norris attended with other prominent attorneys and politicians rounding out the committee.[62] Thirteen years later, the Lee mausoleum and memorial would be inaugurated in the same building Early was now speaking.[63]

Robert E. Lee was the patriarch of the postbellum South, the quiet and aloof *paterfamilias* that everyone loved and no one really knew, the "Marble Man." He had guided the army through the choppy turbulence of war and now stood as a beacon for the South in this new storm of reconstruction. As Dabney H. Maury, a former Confederate officer and founder of the Southern Historical Society lamented, "I feel reluctant to suffer anything to detract from Gen. Lee's fame. It is all we have left to us out of the great shipwreck we have suffered."[64]

Now that the light had flickered out, the South was left to navigate the tempest of Reconstruction without their Polaris. Not only would the storm wreak havoc on the culture, both North and South, it ripped giant holes in the history of the war, patched together to help the nation survive the ordeal. In most cases, the patches woven through the turmoil of Reconstruction have not been replaced.

BY THE TIME THE CROWD SETTLED IN TO AWAIT JUBAL
Early's commemoration speech, the reconstruction of the South had
begun in earnest. Ulysses S. Grant, who had committed the unforgiv-
able sin of defeating Robert E. Lee's Army of Northern Virginia, was
now president of the United States. Self-styled Radical Republicans,
intent on wiping away all remnants of antebellum Dixie, seemed
to be running the show. "Old Jube," however, had no intention of
"[surrendering] our cherished traditions" and refused to "adopt
the progressive civilization of the age."[65] The societal and cultural
upheaval in the country was always going to be difficult, especially
in the South. The Southern states were very proud of their traditions, as most cultures are, and were not willing to give them up
just because their armies had surrendered. The war may have been
lost—for now—but the fighting spirit of the South had not.[66]

With a zeal even more fiery than on the battlefield, Early
launched into a fight for the memory and meaning of the war.
Unlike the one that ended with the weary stroke of a pen in a parlor
in central Virginia, this war would take place within the gaudy pages
of magazines, the tightly pressed serifs of newspapers, and between
the busy wallpapered partitions of meeting halls.[i] In this contest,
the Confederacy would have a more meaningful victory than it had
achieved on the battlefield.

The South's traditions, its romantic self-image, history, heroes,
and sense of honor lived on. As far as Jubal Early was concerned,
he would pick up the banner to preserve the memory of the war in
the manner he thought their deeds deserved. "It is necessary…that
we should take charge of the history of the war," he exhorted fellow
veterans the prior November, "we who have a greater interest in it
than all others living."[67]

The South would not—*could* not—forget and simply give up its
way of life. Never would the South "turn our backs on the graves of

---

i   The war, of course, did not end at Appomattox, but the surrender
     of Lee's army certainly served as the symbol of the South's defeat,
     especially for those who surrendered there.

our fallen heroes," Early promised. Southerners would "cherish the remembrance of their deeds, and see that justice is done to their memories."[68] No matter how "gloomy and dark everything may now appear around us," Early soothed, he had "a firm and abiding faith that the time is coming when it will be a higher and more honorable title for a man to be able to say" that he was descended from Confederate soldiers.[69]

Now, at Washington and Lee University, he called upon Southern women to keep the spirit of the South alive in its memory. "In you, my fair countrywomen," the entire South would rely "to instill the sentiments of honor and patriotism into the hearts of the rising and future generations, and teach them to venerate the memory, emulate the virtues and cherish the principles of those who fell fighting for your homes."[70] The "noble and true women of the South will," he promised, always "strew flowers" on the graves of the fallen, "and teach their fair daughters to perpetuate the pious custom." The entire South, he promised, "will adhere to the principles for which Lee, Sydney Johnston and Jackson fought and died."[71] Remember, he cautioned, "a people who forget or discard their traditions, are unworthy and unfit to be free." It is not "proper to run the ploughshares over the graves of our fathers, in order to conform to the utilitarian spirit of this age."[72]

The traditions and principles were more than just political positions. They were the very heart and soul of the South. Their preservation required the utmost care and dedication. "Let every Confederate soldier jealously guard his reputation and honor," Early counseled. "Let us then foster and extend our fraternal associations and perpetuate them."

To do this, the former Confederates had to remain united in this fraternity. Those who disagreed were a threat. The Northern press was all too quick to snatch up dissenting Confederates and plaster their names throughout their campaign columns. As the *Philadelphia Press* noted several years earlier, letters from an "ex-rebel leader are the best campaign documents yet issued. If they had been written for the very purpose of being used in Pennsylvania this Fall they could not be clearer or more telling."[73]

What was more, both Northerners and Southern opportunists were seeking to alter the history of the war. Northerners, of course, had a "view of casting odium on our people and damning our cause in the estimation of the world and posterity." That would certainly make their own cause seem nobler. Southerners could find themselves contributing to this, perhaps unwittingly. "Some mere literary tyros and adventurers" who had never set foot on a battlefield tried to profit off of the popularity of war stories. Both hurt the cause of preserving the true memory. "We must weed out all this trash," Early demanded, "and it can only be done by concert and united action."[74]

"The plan is to have divisions in all the States from which any part of that army came," Early announced. "I hope, also, to see associations formed of all the other armies, and that there may be a general association of the whole.... This will be the means of bringing together, in one grand Confederate Association, all those who fought and suffered for the same cause."

The purpose of this pan-Confederate association was not merely fraternal. "The ends to be accomplished by these associations will be two-fold," Early instructed. "First, to bring into harmonious intercourse the defenders of our cause from all parts of the country." Second, and even more important, "to secure the materials for a history of the whole struggle, without the risk of its being disfigured by jealous bickerings or discordant views."[75]

Punishment against these "bickerings" and "discordant views" had to be swift, harsh, and overwhelming. "If there be any, in all the land, who have proved renegade to their comrades and our holy cause, let them go out from among us with the brand of Cain upon them!" Early howled.[76]

Some Confederates had already earned their mark of Cain. "By their conduct since the war," these soldiers had "forfeited all claim to an honorable association with their former comrades."[77] Early did not name names yet, but he had Confederate Generals James Longstreet and William "Little Billy" Mahone in mind.

Mahone had made the mistake of criticizing the military prowess of one of the members of the Confederate fraternity—none other than Jubal Early. In an article published in June 1870, Mahone was the subject of a "memoir" written by one of Early's "literary tyros and adventurers," the Northerner J. Watts de Peyster, who fancied himself "General," despite having only served in a local militia. De Peyster's memoir quoted Mahone as quipping "although his name was Early, he was always Late," a running joke since Early's West Point days. Mahone went on to say that he "did not like to fight under him...Early was always hesitating whether to fight or not; he would ride up and down his line, from fifteen to twenty minutes, debating whether or not to begin; whereas the battle was to be lost or won, meanwhile."[78]

Early didn't come across the article until March, but was furious. He scribbled a jeremiad to Mahone and waited. Hearing nothing back, he wrote to Walter Taylor, Lee's former aide-de-camp, and instructed him to get the message to Mahone. "I will wait just one month patiently," he warned.[79]

Mahone eventually got back to Early and after a series of letters, Mahone agreed that he could understand, "through a careful reading...where inferences may be taken, however justly or imaginary." Early accused Mahone of giving an interview to a northern officer, "a bitter enemy of the country and cause to which you professed devotion." Early made sure, through back channels and mutual acquaintances, that Mahone was aware their entire correspondence would be published. Mahone eventually conceded and re-published a revised article without the insulting language, along with a partial exchange between Early and Mahone.[80]

Longstreet, who had a much higher national profile than Billy Mahone, did not repent. Longstreet would continue to commit sins against the canons of the united history of the war. He would be dealt with, and harshly.

Jubal Early (left) and William Pendleton (right). Library of Congress.

PRECISELY ONE YEAR LATER, REVEREND WILLIAM NELSON Pendleton stood before an equally adulatory (but less frozen) audience at the Lee Chapel. Serving as Lee's artillery chief during the war, Pendleton took Early's place as keynote speaker at the 1873 birthday commemoration in Lexington. For fans of Early's speech, "Parson" Pendleton would not disappoint.

Pendleton's speech mimicked Early's, if longer and more sanctimonious. Early was a lawyer, after all, and his speech followed the logical progression of his argument. Pendleton was a preacher, and his address overflowed with evangelistic hyperbole. Lee, for example, was a "great man," "sublime in his career," possessing a "halo that will forever encircle his name." An "almost peerless man," Lee "was borne with such consummate ability, practical wisdom and unsullied virtue as to attach to him forever the admiration of mankind."[81] The Episcopal priest left no stops in his apotheotic descriptions of Lee.

The Southern commander was, quite simply, infallible. "Again and again," Pendleton preached, "our army, so small by comparison, defeated and slaughtered day by day thousands upon thousands" of Federal soldiers.[82]

But in defeat, perhaps, Lee's grandeur gleamed even greater. The "non-achievement of results popularly expected" (Pendleton's cumbersome term for "loss") "was simply proof of [the object] being impracticable."[83] Or, of course, incapable subordinates.[84] Infallible people did not lose battles, after all.

"Our chief, even under grief and disappointment, appeared grander, if possible, than ever," Pendleton proclaimed from his pulpit on the dais. "With a magnanimity well-nigh unparalleled in history, [Lee] shielded from blame all under him, and took its whole charge upon himself." As far as the "non-achievement of results" at Gettysburg was concerned, "this was not strictly just. Not at all was he responsible for disappointment here." But such was the character of Lee.[85]

The proper memory of the war relied heavily on the deification of Robert E. Lee. The memorial addresses were filled with references to halos, sublimity, and Providence. Pendleton was not the only one engaging in godly rhetoric.

If Lee was godlike, then he was unconquerable. But the South had, of course, lost the war. Since Lee could not be both invincible *and* have been defeated, something else, something outside of his control, must be to blame. Exactly what caused the defeat occupied considerable breath, ink, and pages.

Both Early and Pendleton outlined the history of the war in terms of numbers of men and materiel. Early's two-hour speech deliberately, though not always spellbindingly, laid out the case. Northern armies had not exactly *defeated* the Southern armies as much as ground them down. The year before, Early had reminded the audience that Lee "had not been conquered in battle." Rather, he was forced to surrender because his army had been whittled away. "What he surrendered" at Appomattox was "the skeleton, the mere ghost of the Army of Northern Virginia."[86]

Lee had been in an unwinnable contest from the beginning, Early insisted, facing "not only...the mere brute power of man, but against all the elements of fire, air, earth and water." Nothing less than the "thunderbolt of the gods" stood between the Confederacy and its independence.[87] Those were formidable odds even for Robert E. Lee.

Indeed, no one in the annals of history could have prevailed against these odds. Homeric Greeks, Leonidas, Alexander the Great, Hannibal, Caesar...none of them could hold a flickering candle to Lee's prowess. The Crusaders did not compare. Napoleon and Wellington came close, but ultimately fell short. Not even George Washington quite measured up to Lee. Though he won his war, Washington had needed the help of European powers, something Lee couldn't count on. No, "our beloved chief stands, like some lofty column which rears its head among the highest, in grandeur, simple, pure and sublime, needing no borrowed lustre; and he is all our own."[88]

But no matter how great the odds, something other than vindictive bolt-hurlers had to be to blame. Divine thunderbolts did not defeat armies. Certainly, the lopsided mathematics played a part. The lack of adequate supplies from the Confederate government and the outcome of the fighting in the other theaters of operations contributed, too.[89]

But the primary cause of the Army of Northern Virginia's defeat was the inadequacy of Lee's commanders. They just could not keep pace with Lee's abilities (except for perhaps Thomas "Stonewall" Jackson, who *did* possess the necessary "unselfish patriotism, Christian devotion and purity of character").[90] Time after frustrating time, Lee's subordinates let him down. At the end of the Peninsula Campaign in the summer of 1862, the Union army could have been utterly "annihilated, had General Lee's orders been promptly and rigidly carried out," Early lamented.[91] Shortly after, at the Second Battle of Manassas, Longstreet dithered while Jackson continued collecting rays of glory.[92]

But it was at Gettysburg, only two months after Jackson died, that Longstreet's true colors were revealed. On the ridges west of town, Longstreet lost The Cause. Unlike Longstreet, Pendleton issued Generals Richard S. Ewell and Jeb Stuart only mild rebukes. Stuart simply made a "miscalculation," and Ewell suffered from a "want of decision" likely chalked up to a severe wound the previous summer. Early, being a division commander in Ewell's Corps, was conspicuously quiet when it came to laying blame on anyone other than Longstreet.

According to Early, Longstreet was ordered to attack the Federal army at daylight. But the assault didn't step off until late in the afternoon. "Had the attack been made at daylight, as contemplated, it must have resulted in a brilliant and decisive victory," Early concluded. As it were, "General Lee saw his plans thwarted by the delay on our right."[93]

Pendleton agreed with Early, telling his audience that Lee had ordered Longstreet "to attack [the Federal left] at sunrise" on July 2. Lee had explained this to Pendleton personally, along with orders for Pendleton to "reexamine the ground as early as possible in the morning." Pendleton rushed out "as soon as light at all appeared," reconnoitering quite a way and even capturing a few Federal soldiers. No time at all was to be wasted so that the attack could begin as soon as possible that morning.[94] (How Longstreet was supposed to attack at sunrise and simultaneously rely on a reconnaissance Pendleton conducted at sunrise was not clarified).

The attack did not, of course, begin at sunrise. Not until 4:00 p.m. did Longstreet's guns open. In the meantime, "hour after hour slowly dragged on" while the Federal army adjusted and strengthened its position. By the time Longstreet *was* in position, the Federal line looked nothing like it had that morning, and more time had to be taken for the Confederate attackers to adjust to the new situation. "The golden opportunity passed," lamented Pendleton to his audience in 1873.[95]

The delay "was at the time known to be lamentable and…will probably be always judged wholly inexcusable." Lee suffered "mental anguish" as the hours ticked by and Longstreet's guns remained silent on the southern end of the battlefield. Indeed, according to Pendleton, Lee "elaborately discussed" this in his official report of the battle written over the winter of 1863–64. (Though the report was published in both northern and southern outlets, Pendleton was either deliberately disingenuous or didn't bother to read it; Lee does not so much as hint that the attack was designed to take place earlier than it did.)[96]

Longstreet's "violation of explicit orders" caused "the loss to us of that battle, and with it the cause of constitutional government."[97] If only the attack had been made in the morning, "as intended… General Meade and his force would with comparative ease have been swept away," judged Pendleton. Then peace terms would have been issued and the South would have gained her independence.[98] Losing the Battle of Gettysburg "eventuated most probably in our ultimate ruin," Pendleton insisted.[99]

Lee was certainly not to blame for the loss of southern independence. In fact, "never were General Lee's genius and power more signally displayed" than at Gettysburg. "Yet through the errors of others…his admirably planned combinations failed."[100] "The vigor on which" Lee should have been able to count on "under circumstances so imperative" was utterly lacking.[101]

To attendees of last year's speech, this would have all sounded very familiar. "A commanding General cannot do the marching and fighting of his army," Early had explained to the audience inside the chapel. "These must, necessarily, be entrusted to his subordinates, and any hesitation, delay or miscarriage in the execution of his orders, may defeat the best devised schemes." Success required "the utmost dispatch, energy and undoubting confidence in carrying out the plans of the commanding General." Longstreet did not do this. Doubting the wisdom of Lee's plan for July 2, he balked, failing to execute his orders "with that confidence and faith necessary to success."[102]

* * *

THOUGH NOT WIDELY PUBLISHED, PENDLETON'S SPEECH *was* widely written about. After his presentation at Washington and Lee, he went on a speaking tour of the South. Newspapers published reviews and notable quotations of the speech where Southerners first read of Longstreet's betrayal.[103]

Longstreet had clearly been cast as Judas in Confederate memory. But why? Certainly, others had made mistakes during the war, if Longstreet's actions on July 2 were indeed faulty. Early himself was fired by Lee in March of 1865 after Lee determined he had lost the confidence of both the Confederate army and the Southern public.[104] What made Longstreet's actions on July 2 the "fatal failure" of the Confederacy?[105]

The answer is not military, but political, cultural, and personal. Barely a year after the war ended, a journalist named William Swinton published *Campaigns of the Army of the Potomac*, a full history of the most prominent Federal army. Swinton had traveled with the army during the war and had earned a reputation for his way with words and influential reporting. His insight on matters ranging from detailed battle accounts to courts-martial were eagerly anticipated and reviews appeared in nearly every major newspaper (and most minor ones), both in the North and South.[106]

The book was very well received. Even in the South, reviewers agreed that Swinton "writes as impartially as we had expected to see any Northern historian write twenty years hence." The *New Orleans Crescent* agreed that Swinton's history "appears to be by far the most impartial and the most able publication in regard to the recent war that has yet been issued from the American press."[107] It certainly didn't hurt Southern reviews that Swinton had the good sense to praise Lee, as the *Richmond Dispatch* noted in its May 2, 1866 issue.[108]

Most reviews touched on the 1862 campaign on the Virginia Peninsula and Richmond, Second Manassas, and the Overland Campaign, which pitted Lee against Grant in 1864 and produced horrific numbers of casualties. Perhaps surprising to modern readers, most reviews glossed over Swinton's treatment of the Battle of Gettysburg, if they covered it at all.

While the reviewers may not have discussed the battle much, *Campaigns of the Army of the Potomac* spent sixty-four pages covering the campaign and battle, just over 10 percent of its 610 pages. On page 340, Swinton wrote that Lee, "[having]…gotten a taste of blood in the considerable success of the first day…seems to have lost that equipoise in which his faculties commonly moved." In staying and fighting at Gettysburg, Lee "committed a grave error." What was more, his primary reason for doing so—the inability to withdraw through the mountains with his wagon trains—"can hardly be considered valid."[109]

What *should* Lee have done, according to Swinton? "There was open another and still bolder move," he wrote. Longstreet, holding the Federal left flank on the Emmitsburg Road (and therefore blocking Meade's route south to Washington), could have maneuvered southeast to Frederick and "could undoubtedly have manoeuvred [*sic*] Meade out of the Gettysburg position." Longstreet, said Swinton, "begged in vain" for Lee to let him move to the right. But Lee would not budge, despite having *promised* his Old War Horse that he would not commit to offensive tactics on the battlefield.[110]

"This, and subsequent revelations of the purposes and sentiments of Lee," Swinton divulged, "I derive from General Longstreet, who, in a full and free conversation with the writer, after the close of the war, threw much light on the motives and conduct of Lee during this campaign."[111]

A small portion of Longstreet's information was revealed in a few of the reviews, but given the backlash that eventually swept away Longstreet's reputation, there was little commentary on it. Indeed, the *Richmond Dispatch* passed over the whole subject with a derisive dismissal of Meade and his abilities, sneering "So little have we in regard to General Meade and the battle of Gettysburg that we are inclined to think that Mr. Swinton does not regard the result as the great Federal victory which the most of writers on that side represent it to be."[112]

The reviewers may have been willing to pass over Longstreet's criticism, but not Early. "If Mr. Swinton has told the truth, in repeating in his book what is alleged to have been said to him by General Longstreet," Early told his audience at the Lee Chapel, then "there was at least one of General Lee's corps commanders at Gettysburg who did not enter upon the execution of his plans with that confidence and faith necessary to success." That was, remember, vital to *any* commander's success. "Perhaps," Early mused, that is why "it was not achieved."[113]

DESPITE THE ATTENTION IT LATER RECEIVED, LONGSTREET'S opinion of Lee's "equipoise" at Gettysburg had no immediate effect on his reputation. The *Richmond Dispatch* concluded its review of Swinton's book with a short list of "our gallant Confederate Generals," a list that included Longstreet.[114] Just ten days later, Louisiana's *Opelousas Courier* recounted a toast at a Texas picnic that Longstreet attended. After the party drank to Robert E. Lee (who was not present), a toast was raised to Longstreet, "the hero of forty-nine pitched battles, and the idol of every true lover of Constitutional Liberty." Three cheers were then given for the old First Corps commander "as a testimonial of the high esteem in which [the soldiers] of our community hold the General."[115]

Just seven months after the Army of Northern Virginia's surrender, British correspondent Francis Lawley wrote of the "last and saddest" conversation between Lee and Longstreet before the surrender, when Lee arrived at "the headquarters of his 'old war horse.'" Lawley had spent his time in America reporting with the Army of Northern Virginia and remembered the "sacred" scene was indescribable. He marveled at the "sustained heroism with which Lee and Longstreet, for four years bore up and stood erect under such a burden as never yet was laid upon man."[116] He would change his opinion later, but in 1865, Lawley found Lee and Longstreet to be a nearly biblical pair, heroes to the South.

A South Carolina paper, announcing Longstreet's new business venture as a partner in a cotton merchant company, was impressed with his stoicism and the example he was setting. "A great deal has been said concerning the attitude of the Southern 'leaders'," the paper reported, referring in part to the habit of some former Confederates to flee the country after the war (Jubal Early, for example). Longstreet had stayed put and tried to go about his business, rebuilding himself after the war. It was "a great satisfaction to see that one who has occupied so prominent and important a position as General Longstreet, has determined to meet the difficulties of the situation fairly and without flinching in thus devoting himself to the accustomed paths of commerce." Longstreet, as the second in command of the Army of Northern Virginia, set a fine example by remaining and trying to push through the difficult transition. His example, and hopefully others like it, "will do more than all else to dissuade the young men of the South from any scheme of speculative emigration, and they will soon come to the conclusion that home, with all its troubles, is better than even a peaceful foreign land."[117]

Had Longstreet merely focused on his new business venture and acted the stoic, if somewhat repentant, Confederate, he may well have tumbled into the same sort of iconoclastic status of Stonewall Jackson or Jeb Stuart. No one could compare to Lee, but Stuart and Jackson were demigods in the Confederate Pantheon. A wounded Confederate leader, especially one who had served the duration with distinction and had been with Lee at the surrender, could easily find himself inducted into this immortal hall.

But Longstreet went beyond mere pragmatic stoicism. Everything began innocently and harmlessly enough. On March 2, 1867, Congress passed the first of its Reconstruction Acts. The March 2 statute divided the former Confederate states into five military districts to be governed by U.S. generals tasked with protecting *all* people in the district, "[suppressing] insurrection, disorder, and violence, and to punish…all disturbers of the public peace and criminals." The district commander had complete discretion whether to allow the local judicial system to adjudicate these matters or to set up military tribunals. Only the death penalty required approval beyond the district commander.

The only way for a Southern state to be rid of the district commander and tribunals—for all intents and purposes martial law—was to accept the Radical Republican agenda. In order to be eligible for political restoration, Southern states would have to ratify a new state constitution acknowledging and authorizing suffrage for any male who had lived in the state for at least a full year aged twenty-one or older "of whatever race, color, or previous condition."

The other requirement was to ratify the Fourteenth Amendment, which mandated state citizenship to those individuals residing in the state and born in the U.S. This was a long way of stating that former slaves were now citizens of both the state in which they lived *and* the United States simply by virtue of their birth within the jurisdiction of the United States. The amendment gutted the prior United States Supreme Court decision *Dred Scott v. Sandford*, which only four years before the war began had decreed Black people (even those who were free) had no citizenship or civil rights in *any* state. What was more, the Fourteenth Amendment explicitly forbade any state from depriving anyone in its jurisdiction "of life, liberty, or property, without due process of law" and mandated "equal protection of the laws."[118]

Only a few days after the passage of the Reconstruction Acts, the *New Orleans Times* sought the opinions of eighteen Southern leaders, including former Confederate generals P.G.T. Beauregard, John Bell Hood, Simon Buckner, and Longstreet.[119] Longstreet responded with a letter to the editor, W.H.C. King, the next day and the letter appeared in the March 19, 1867 issue.[120]

Though he needed no introduction, the *Times* praised Longstreet as a "highly respected and honored...chief" and that no former Confederate "was more distinguished for earnestness, zeal and tenacity" than Longstreet. Longstreet "never applied myself to politics," he cautioned, but "can only speak the plain, honest convictions of a soldier." His advice: "We are a conquered people. Recognizing this fact fairly and squarely, there is but one course left for wise men to pursue. Accept the terms that are offered us by the conquerors!" There was no shame in this. "There can be no discredit to a conquered people for accepting the conditions offered by their conquerors," nor was there any reason to feel "humiliation." The South made an "honest" and "creditable fight, but we have lost. Let us come forward then and accept the ends involved in the struggle."

As much as anyone, Longstreet wanted to shed the government imposed under the new military districts and re-establish a constitutional state government. "The only means to accomplish this," he reminded his readers, was "to comply with the requirements of the recent Congressional legislation," as unpalatable as it may have seemed at the time. Addressing the skeptics who counseled that Congress would refuse to accept the Confederate states back into the nation *even if* they allowed Black suffrage and citizenship to former slaves, Longstreet counseled to "accept the terms as we are in duty bound to do, and if there is a lack of good faith, let it be upon others."[121] For now, that seemed like good advice.

Longstreet found himself in good company, as Lee himself had expressed similar thoughts. Lee, however, religiously confined his views to private correspondence (as Longstreet had prior to this letter). Writing to John Letcher, Virginia's wartime governor, Lee said in August 1865 that "the questions which for years were in dispute between the State and General Governments, and which unhappily were not decided by the dictates of reason, but referred to the decision of war, having been decided against us, it is the part of wisdom to acquiesce in the result, and of candor to recognize the fact." Lee counseled that "the interests of the State are therefore the same as those of the United States. Its prosperity will rise or fall with the welfare of the country."[122] The sentiments would be difficult to distinguish from Longstreet's views published in March two years later, though the political situation would be markedly different.

Lee also counseled that there was no shame in accepting the outcome of the war, even though it had not been the one they had hoped for, and Southerners should do what was necessary to move on. In discussing the application for amnesty and restoration of rights, Lee wrote that "in order to be restored to their former rights and privileges," former Confederates "were required to perform a certain act, and I do not see that an acknowledgment of fault is expressed in one more than the other."[123] Lee was referring to a presidential proclamation from May 1865, issued by President Andrew Johnson, granting full pardons and restoration of rights to former Confederates by taking an oath swearing never to own slaves or take up arms against the United States.[124]

General Beauregard, the influential South Carolina cavalier Wade Hampton, and the wartime governors of Georgia and Virginia all agreed. South Carolina's *Columbia Daily Phoenix* published Longstreet's letter on March 28, advising its readers to follow its advice. "No Southern man…with whatever disfavor he may reward the requirements of the present law, can be humiliated or dishonored by following the counsels and examples of such tried and trusted men as Robert E. Lee, Wade Hampton and James Longstreet," wrote the editors of the *Phoenix*. The paper counseled the "advice of such men must have a large and controlling influence over the sentiments of their fellow citizens," since they "enjoyed the confidence of the Southern people in their most trying day."[125]

Beauregard's response to the *New Orleans Times'* solicitation also counseled submission to the law in order to get back to normal as quickly as possible. Like Longstreet, he first stated he was unqualified for political discourse, but having been asked numerous times for his thoughts, "I shall not shrink from the responsibility of expressing them." They had fought and exhausted their military capabilities. Continuing the struggle on the battlefield was simply not an option. "We must, therefore, submit; but with that calm dignity becoming our manhood and our lost independence." They had to "adopt the least of the two evils" before them.

Although Black suffrage was regrettable, Beauregard wrote, it could become a valuable resource to defeat the Radical Republicans. Black people were born in the South, after all, and their prosperity would rise and fall with the South. On issues like tariffs and "internal improvements," southern Black voters "will side with the whites of the South and West." Black voters would therefore "contribute to give us back the influence we formerly had" in Congress.[126]

This was certainly the approach Wade Hampton was taking in his "miraculous" conciliation in South Carolina, astounding many in the North. At a convention of local Black citizens celebrating their new voting rights on March 19, 1867, Hampton "spoke of the vast importance of the present movement," encouraging the recently emancipated Black workers "to give their friends at the South a fair trial…for as the country prospered, so would they prosper."[127] The *New York Daily Herald* marveled at this. "Has the age of miracles returned?" it mused. "Short of some miraculous agency [how] can we account for the extraordinary fraternization…of whites and blacks at a political colored meeting for the celebration of the enfranchisement of the colored race."[128]

Longstreet privately agreed. In a letter to R.H. Taliaferro that summer, he wrote that since Black people had been granted the right to vote anyway, "it is all important that we should exercise such influence over that vote, as to prevent its being injurious to us, and we can only do that as Republicans." Since the Republicans controlled Congress, they required "reconstruction upon the Republican basis. If the whites won't do this, the thing will be done by the blacks, and we shall be set aside, if not expatriated."[129]

Longstreet expounded on his own thoughts in a second letter to the *New Orleans Times* on April 6. He acknowledged that the South lost the right to secede, lost the "former political relations of the negro," and surrendered the Southern Confederacy in its entirety. Like so many Southern soldiers, those ideas died on the battlefield. It was time to perform "the last funeral rites of the Southern Confederacy" and "deposit in the same grave the agony of our grief, that we may the better prepare ourselves for a return to the duties of this life."

It was "too late to go back to look after our rights under the law and the Constitution," he acknowledged candidly, if naively. Whether the loss of the rights was "by lawful or unlawful process" was irrelevant. The rights were gone and even if the South had the power to fight on (it didn't), it would be futile. If, as Jubal Early would later claim, the principles of the South had never been at stake, what exactly had the South been fighting for?

"When a people resort to the violence of war they should be prepared to show to the world just cause of war," Longstreet reminded the proponents of violent resistance. "What cause can we claim unless we say that we did not know what we were fighting for...?" To Longstreet, it was absurd to argue the South had fought so passionately and arduously, had given up the lives of its young men, had sacrificed its cities to the ruins of war, and had faced deprivation for nearly half a decade over something as seemingly trivial as an abstract political principle. The right of secession alone was barely worth arguing over. It was what the South wanted to preserve by secession that had brought the men into the armies and fueled them through their hardships.

As it now stood, Longstreet saw two options: return to the federal government as states in good faith as quickly as possible or seek shelter with a foreign government. It certainly didn't seem as though the second option was viable, so speeding up the political restoration process was the only practical course. This was against his own personal interest, he reminded the readers, for as a high-ranking Confederate general, he would be among the last to receive restoration of his rights—if they were restored at all. In a published correspondence with John A. Campbell, a former Southern attorney who had mediated unsuccessful peace talks between the Lincoln Administration and the Confederate commissioners before the war, Campbell agreed whole-heartedly with Longstreet's assessment. The concurrence appeared alongside Longstreet's letter in the April 7 issue of the *New Orleans Times*.[130]

James Longstreet. Library of Congress.

HAD LONGSTREET STOPPED THERE, HE WOULD HAVE remained in good company. But Longstreet published one more letter to the *New Orleans Times*. The letter was intended as an open reply to the *Times*, who had taken a turn away from its initial conciliatory approach. The turn was likely fueled by continuing legislation from Congress that more and more Southerners felt was purely vindictive.[131]

In the June 6, 1867 issue, the *Times* printed a piece buried on page four under the heading "The World Upside Down." The two-paragraph snippet highlighted two "perplexing tangle[s]" in postwar politics. The first involved a controversy between the military commander, former Union General Philip Sheridan, and the Louisiana governor. The second paragraph referenced "a letter from one of the bravest and stoutest of the late Confederate generals, who gives in his adhesion to a party whose whole policy seems to be one of vindictive persecution and abuse of his late confederates in arms."[132]

Longstreet surmised he was the brave and stout former Confederate general, and the letter was one he had written to Republican attorney John M.G. Parker on June 3, which evidently ended up in the hands of the *Times*. He immediately wrote the *Times*, demanding the full context be provided. Longstreet's letter to Parker and his reply to the *Times* were both published in the June 8 issue.[133]

At some point between March 18 and June 8, 1867, Longstreet seems to have visited his uncle Augustus Baldwin Longstreet in Mississippi. Augustus was a well-respected politician, judge, minister, and writer. While he agreed with Longstreet's sentiments, he discouraged his nephew from publishing them, especially as Republican policies were viewed as more and more vindictive in the South. According to a biography of Augustus nearly sixty years later, Augustus cautioned James Longstreet against publishing any further letters supporting Republican policies. "It will ruin you, son, if you publish it," he prophesied as to one of the letters Longstreet proposed to write. The account may be apocryphal, the only source being a "Ms. L.B. West" in the 1924 biography, but if it *is* accurate, it could not have referred to the March 18 or June 8 letter, as both of those were immediately printed and submitted to the *Times*. Although Ms. West was confident Longstreet ignored Augustus's advice, it is also possible James listened to his uncle and scrapped any further effort to clarify his beliefs, even though the damage had been done.[134]

On June 8, apparently anticipating some negative reaction to his thoughts, Longstreet sought the public support of Robert E. Lee. This was asking a big favor from Lee, since Lee had yet to make any public pronouncement regarding the current politics. Lee eventually responded at the end of October, citing various reasons for the delay, but he ultimately declined any public support. Though a wise move on Lee's part, it would not help Longstreet. Lee reminded Longstreet of his position regarding public statements but also issued a rebuke of Longstreet's politics. "While I think we should act under the law…imposed on us, I cannot think the course pursued by the dominant political party the best for the interests of the country," Lee replied, "and therefore cannot say so, or give them my approval."[135]

Against all advice, Longstreet published the letter to Parker, earnestly believing it would do some good. But the mood had so drastically changed in the South since March and April that even objectively sound advice seemed radical. Longstreet continued to counsel as he had earlier that year, wildly miscalculating the shift in the public mood.

In his letters to the *Times* and Parker, Longstreet readily admitted that the South's principles had been defeated on the battlefield. The "sword has decided in favor of the North," Longstreet wrote. "What [the North] claimed as principles cease to be principles, and are become law." The "views that we hold cease to be principles because they are opposed to law. It is therefore our duty to abandon ideas that are obsolete and conform to the requirements of law."[136]

Longstreet was naïve if nothing else. He was no less a Southerner than Early or the editors of the *Times*. He wrote his letters in an unsteady hand and spoke in a rough, hoarse voice after taking a bullet in the neck fighting for the South. But his frank analysis was entirely unwelcome in 1867; the wounds of the war were too raw, the politics still hot to the touch.

Longstreet, who had admitted he had little political acumen, proved himself correct. As hatred toward Republicans was boiling over, Longstreet wrote "the war was made upon Republican issues, and it seems to me fair and just that the settlement should be made accordingly." While making it clear that he believed it to be "practical advice" in order to "relieve the distress of the people, and to provide for their future comfort," the language about acceding to Republican principles was italicized and would be what people remembered.[137]

He said the same thing to Mr. Parker in his June 3 letter, reprinted just below his June 7 letter to the *Times*. "Practical men can surely distinguish between practical reconstruction and reconstruction as an abstract question…. I shall be happy to work in any harness that promises relief to our distressed people and harmony to the nation."

But then Longstreet, continuing to speak in "the plain, honest convictions of a soldier," as he had said in March, reverted to his belief that defeat on the battlefield settled *all* questions. "I shall set out by assuming," he wrote Mr. Parker, "a proposition, that I hold to be self-evident." His assumption? "The highest of human laws is the law that is established by appeal to arms." After years of debate, the political questions yielded to physical force and the north won that fight. Thus, might made right and the Northern principles became the law of the land, regardless of whether the South agreed with it. Like it or not, the South had an obligation to accept it.

As if that weren't bad enough, Longstreet saw the Reconstruction Acts as "peace offerings" by the North, and the South "should accept them as such." Longstreet then explained that the Democratic party had no platform other than opposing Black suffrage and citizenship, which was a lost cause. Those things were already here, and they would just have to live with it.[138]

This is where Longstreet departed from the more politically attuned Southerners such as Lee. Most had been on board with practical reconstruction, but Longstreet had jumped headfirst with reckless abandon into the *abstracts* of reconstruction, admitting that the South's principles were defeated on the surrender of the last Confederate army. This was something no Southerner would abide, not while its cities still had piles of rubble, its valleys were still ripped and torn from battle, and its homes scarred with the loss of fathers, brothers, and sons…all while the generals who had defeated them on the battlefield were given increasing political power over their governments.

Historians have cited Longstreet's call to cooperate with Republicans as the reason for the scorn of his former comrades.[139] But Southern hostility stemmed from something much deeper than mere political affiliation, policy disagreements, or even criticism of Lee.[140] Longstreet had accepted the fact that the South and her principles had fundamentally lost—not because they were wrong or immoral but because they had not withstood the brutality of the battlefield.

As a result, those Southern principles were called "obsolete," and the defeated Southerners were obligated to "conform" to Northern principles, dictated by abolitionist Radical Republicans.[141] To make matters worse, Southern principles had been defeated in the crassest way possible—by force and force alone.

Not only did the South's cherished ideals lie in a pool of blood in the trampled fields of battle, but the radical U.S. Congress, filled primarily with northerners, seemed to be standing over the carcass of their principles, ruthlessly mocking them. In addition to requiring Southern states to ratify the Fourteenth Amendment and allow Black suffrage, the military commanders of each district were now instructed to keep a registry of all male voters who had taken the oath of allegiance. Only those registered by the military commander were allowed to vote for a convention of delegates to vote on accepting the requirements for readmission to the United States.

Congress also passed a bill authorizing the military commander or the "General of the army of the United States" to remove any official elected by a former Confederate state. The same bill gave the military commander power to determine a Southerner's eligibility to vote.

Back on March 19, Longstreet had declared "if there is a lack of good faith, let it be upon others." It certainly seemed to a good deal of Southerners that there was a lack of good faith from the

U.S. Congress, who seemed to be moving the goalposts (or at least adding unnecessary and vindictive obstacles to burying the hatchet). While accepting the terms may have seemed sage advice at the beginning of March, by June, the situation was different. Unfortunately for Longstreet, he failed to recognize quite how much the mood had changed.

THE HYPERBOLE OF SOUTHERN NEWSPAPER EDITORS WAS hot, the fiery indignation stoked by the perception of betrayal. Column after column made it clear that the South took issue *not* with Longstreet's idea that they reconcile with the North or even his admission that they were a conquered nation. What made Longstreet a pariah was his admission that the *cause* was defeated, that somehow the South had put it all on the table, winner takes all, and they came away empty-handed, the victorious Northerners not only basking in their shiny new principles, but trampling and mocking those forfeited by the South.

Most of Longstreet's contemporaries would vehemently disagree that Southern principles were ever even at stake. "The result of the war settled no question of right," Early had thundered before a crowd of South Carolina veterans two months before his address at the Lee Chapel. The "war of invasion and coercion" so "unjustly and ruthlessly waged...merely furnished another instance of the fact, that in this world truth and justice do not always prevail, and that might is often more powerful than right."[142] Pendleton echoed this in his own speech: "As well claim that any ruffian's knock-down argument against a virtuous though less vigorous citizen proves his quarrel just."[143] Enforcing culture at the point of a gun was no moral victory. It certainly didn't speak to the superiority of any ideal.

The editors of the *New Orleans Times* agreed. "It would be a sad doctrine to prevail...if truth, right and justice were subjected to such an arbitrament as that of mere physical force."[144] The fight between

North and South had been only about the right of secession. Perhaps *that* question had been answered, but certainly nothing else. No one had even put slavery, Black citizenship or suffrage, the Southern economy, or Southern culture on the table.

"The only principle, if principle it can be called, settled by the surrender," Pendleton preached to his Washington and Lee crowd, was "the assertion of the superior power of the North, which maintained intact the geographical limits of the Union." Southern principles had been stolen as postwar spoils, perhaps, but they had not been defeated. To admit as much was akin to medieval heresy with punishment just as harsh, at least in a figurative sense. After four years and roughly three-quarters of a million dead soldiers, the white flag at Appomattox had only proved that the national government would expend extraordinarily massive amounts of blood and money to keep the borders static and intact.[145]

While Early and Pendleton saw treason in Longstreet's letters, others were more generous, chalking it up to political naiveté. While wrong, no doubt, Longstreet had merely been taken for a sucker by the ruthless Republicans. The *New Orleans Times* thought Longstreet a "brave and reliable military chief," but he was "evidently inexperienced, we may say unsophisticated, in the devious ways of politics and politicians."[146] The *Shreveport South-Western* remembered Longstreet as a "patriot and a soldier" through the war, an "honest, unsuspecting soldier," but "politically he is not a well-informed man, either as to general history or to party politics."[147] Longstreet had "simply fallen into a very common error of military men," believing military victory to equate with moral victory. But only the Bible and the Almighty could dictate morality. The war was "led by the wicked one." It certainly couldn't have settled any moral principles.[148]

Republican politicos like John Parker were simply "tricksters" seeking to "entrap and circumvent" Longstreet's influence. As a soldier entering the admittedly unfamiliar realm of politics, Longstreet was warned against the "too intimate recognition of political flatterers." Like highly evolved beasts of prey, these politicians would lure someone like Longstreet, seeking to do good, into their trap. Not only would they destroy his credibility among Southerners, they provided campaign fodder for their own cause. After all, what better prize than Lee's Old War Horse converting to Republican politics and denouncing the Southern principles?[149]

Longstreet's hometown papers were quick to give him the benefit of the doubt. But within the cradle of secession, the Southern press breathed unforgiving fire. By endorsing the reconstruction principles of the Republicans, Longstreet had betrayed the South and his fellow veterans. In doing so, he was worse than Judas Iscariot, who at least had the decency to kill himself after betraying his comrades. "If General Longstreet had been one of [Christ's] disciples, he would not, like Judas, have hanged himself—but he would have joined his murderers, and have helped them to persecute his other disciples and to crush his cause," howled South Carolina's *Charleston Mercury*.[150]

The *Mercury's* editors "had thrown aside General Longstreet's letter, disgusted at the positions he assumed." Because he had been a "gallant soldier," they initially thought to give him the benefit of the doubt. That is, until the northern press got hold of the letter and began flashing it across Republican campaign columns throughout the North.[151] Longstreet's letter quickly became "the best campaign documents yet issued" for the Republicans.[152] The *Mercury* column quickly spread throughout the South, appearing in page after reprinted page that summer.[153]

Before Lee's death and his speaking invitations, Early and his future cabal privately agreed. "All of the Confederates here have been very much distressed at the course pursued by Longstreet," Early wrote his brother from his self-imposed exile in Toronto a month after Longstreet's last letter was published. Despite his war record, "his letters are calculated to throw discredit to our cause. It is for this reason that I regret his course more than any other."[154]

"Longstreet has buried himself," former General Braxton Bragg jubilantly wrote Early a few years later, just after his speech at the Lee Chapel. "In Virginia, you have buried Mahone," Bragg wrote, congratulating Early on the public relations victory. "And so they will go."[155]

Early's postwar Confederate efforts were even effective internationally. Despite riding with Longstreet's headquarters during the war and keeping up correspondence after the war, the British journalist Francis Lawley wrote Early that "I am satisfied that much of the responsibility for that defeat [at Gettysburg] must hereafter rest on Longstreet."[156] Lawley had become a southern sympathizer, though, and despite his postwar words to Early, he had personally marveled at Longstreet's leadership at Gettysburg. Indeed, just a month after the battle, he had exclaimed to his readers that there was a category of men who are "unselfish, and natural men, who seldom attract and care nothing for public applause, but on whom in the direst stress of critical battle the sternest and most hazardous role devolves. To this order belongs a General Longstreet—a man fighting not for praise, or civil or social distinction." Lawley in July 1863 adulated Longstreet's attack: "the advance of Longstreet's two divisions was completely successful" against the first Federal position. It only stalled because "he had not men enough to" press on.[157] Early's strategy was proving most effective, to the point of changing impressions formed by actual observation.

EARLY'S CRUSADE FOR THE MEMORY OF THE WAR WAS ruthless, zealous, and wildly successful. For Pendleton, his speaking tour was nothing less than a "Sacred Mission toward the best commemoration...yet possible, of our late glorious Commander, and revered Christian friend."[158] Within a few years, the Southern canon had all the elements of the best Greek tragedies and Biblical parables. Lee was apotheosized. Longstreet, who had once sat loyally by his side, had betrayed him. Fallen from glory, he would be despised as the source of all that was bad in the postbellum South.[159]

And of course, there was a distinct moment when the soul of the South was tragically lost by one rash decision. At Gettysburg, in a moment of selfishness, Longstreet ate the proverbial apple. His delay, his petulant insubordination, *deliberately* ignoring Lee's command because he knew better, lost the Confederacy its Eden: victory over the North and an independent country.

With staying power rivaled only perhaps by the Testaments themselves, the South's war gospel has driven the narrative on Gettysburg perhaps more than any other factor. Early's self-proclaimed "Lost Cause" narrative is a part of history in its own right. The effort started immediately after defeat was apparent and has continued to this day. As Longstreet and Billy Mahone discovered, there was no room for debate, well-intentioned or otherwise. To do so meant to be labeled a heretic.

Because nearly everything written about the morning and early afternoon of July 2, 1863 was written after the war, the accounts are heavily influenced by Early's canon. What was said was either in support of the accepted view or in defense of accusations of unorthodoxy.

This influenced not only what was said, but just as importantly what was *not* said. Perhaps taking note of Billy Mahone's experiences in criticizing the keepers of Southern memory, almost nobody in a position to know what happened said anything to anyone, publicly or privately (as Longstreet discovered, it was not uncommon for private correspondence to find its way into a newspaper column).

The vast majority of accounts surrounding the arrival, movements, reconnaissance, and countermarch of Longstreet's Corps on July 2, 1863 exist within this melee and were shaped by it. More importantly, the July 2 controversy was entirely *created* by the Lost Cause narrative. By loudly and vehemently blaming Longstreet for losing the battle and the war through his tantrum-induced foot-dragging, Early and Pendleton set the narrative. Because Longstreet failed to initially respond to the charges and due to the frequent reprinting of those charges throughout the country, the only story that was available was the one presented by Early.

Most importantly, the responses from the First Corps commanders accepted Early's premises. Rather than challenge Early's facts, they simply excused the delay as being caused by intervening factors. When accused of wrongdoing, it is human nature to remember facts in the best light possible and to subconsciously fill in lapses of memory with events that may or may not have occurred. While understandable, it adds additional "false memories" to the equation, further obscuring what actually happened.

This is all in addition to the conscious bias inherent in this sort of discussion. Serious blame was being hurled across the pages. Of course the targets attempted to deflect and land counterblows in their articles and speeches. Unfortunately, the accounts of the pre-attack hours on July 2 come almost exclusively from this political battle. Though they would be distinguished by age, ultimately earning the title "primary sources," they were anything but objective accounts.

MCLAWS'S COUNTERATTACK

"[A] faulty reconnoissance making a change of route necessary in order to carry out Longstreet's order, were the reasons why we were so long getting into position."

- McLaws to Longstreet, published in the *New Orleans Republican* **August 10, 1873.**[160]

"If you will write McLaws and ask him I have no doubt he will give you a copy of his address on the Battle of Gettysburg. It is valuable if not wholly accurate."

- Kershaw to Bachelder, August 7, 1882.[161]

June 10, 1873

LAFAYETTE MCLAWS COULD SEE THE WRITING ON THE WALL.

He had just learned of Pendleton's accusations against Longstreet and must have been somewhat startled by them. Longstreet and McLaws had endured a contentious relationship during the war, one that ultimately ended with Longstreet relieving McLaws of his command. McLaws left his service with the First Corps firmly believing that Longstreet had an ugly habit of passing the buck to subordinates when things went wrong and hoarding praise when they went right.

In the spring of 1864, McLaws vented his thoughts on Longstreet in a long letter to a superior. Longstreet "gained reputation…

by blaming others when he commits faults, and claiming whatever is creditable." His "plans and efforts to injure those who cannot recognize his military pre-eminence & will not lend themselves to advance his schemes have been very skillful and executed in the most energetic manner."

On the retreat from Gettysburg, McLaws complained to his wife that Longstreet was a "humbug, a man of small capacity, very obstinate, not at all chivalrous, exceedingly conceited and totally selfish." Throughout the battle, McLaws found Longstreet "very excited, giving contrary orders to everyone, and…exceedingly overbearing.[162]

For example, as the fighting on July 3 at Gettysburg was winding down and it became clear the Confederates would be unable to push Meade's Federal army off of Cemetery Ridge, Longstreet sent his aide-de-camp Major Moxley Sorrel to McLaws with orders to fall back from the Peach Orchard and Rose farm. McLaws was upset at giving up the ground his men had fought so hard to take, but grudgingly obeyed his orders. As McLaws's men approached Seminary Ridge, they came into view of Federal batteries, which dropped several shells near the columns. But by double-quicking up the slope, they were able to avoid any casualties. When he arrived back within Confederate lines, to McLaws's horror, it seemed everyone in the army thought he had *retreated!*

Captain Samuel Johnston was one of the first to ride up to McLaws and extend what he thought was a compliment. "General, you have your division under very fine control," Johnston congratulated. McLaws asked what the devil he was talking about.

"Have you not been repulsed and are retreating?" Johnston asked, apparently under the impression that McLaws had been part of the afternoon assault.

"I have not been engaged to-day," McLaws informed him. "I am but taking up this position by order of General Longstreet." Johnston apologized, telling him it was simply a misunderstanding.

Moments later, though, Moxley Sorrel rode up to McLaws and ordered him back to the position he had just left. Incredulous, McLaws "demurred most decidedly to the suggestion under the circumstances," and asked in no pleasant terms *why* he was being ordered back—he had just been ordered to leave! "General Long-street had forgotten that he had ordered" the movement and now wanted McLaws back at the Rose Farm.[163]

In another version of the story, McLaws was told that Longstreet watched the division move back to the ridge with General Evander Law. Law had taken command of General John Bell Hood's Division when Hood was wounded the day before. "McLaws has abandoned the Emmitsburg road," Longstreet told Law. Of course, this gave the impression that McLaws had "been driven back," rather than ordered to change position against his better judgment. The fact that the division was seen running away from its position under fire only reinforced the idea that the division was retreating. "I would not be surprised," McLaws grumbled, "if Gen'l Longstreet has stated in his report that I retired upon my own responsibility from my advanced position."[164]

AS THE LEAD DIVISION IN LONGSTREET'S CORPS ON JULY 2, McLaws could not have felt comfortable thinking that the only thing standing between him and Pendleton's public wrath was Longstreet's magnanimity. If Longstreet lived up to McLaws's limited expectations, McLaws could expect the blame to quickly roll to his own feet. He certainly wasn't going to wait around to let that happen. Sitting at his desk in Egypt, Georgia in early June of 1873, he began scribbling a letter to his old corps commander.

"The following is a copy of a letter I wrote in reply to one from a friend asking my opinion" of Pendleton's speech, McLaws began. He outlined Pendleton's charge that Longstreet "was directed to attack the enemy at Gettysburg at daylight" on July 2 "and failed to do it." Not only did Longstreet not attack at dawn, according to Pendleton, but "he sat on his horse until about 4 P.M." Longstreet's "failure to assault at daylight was the cause of the loss of the battle."[165]

McLaws disputed Pendleton's memory, sticking up for Long-street. "I do not know that Gen'l Longstreet ever received such an order," he wrote. But if he did, McLaws had "every reason to think that it was recalled." It simply wasn't reasonable to "think Gen'l Lee would have ordered a main assault" at daylight based on Pendleton's "hasty reconnaissance" the night before, especially knowing that "the enemy had concentrated his forces" in the meantime. It was absurd to think Lee would assault a position "about which we could know nothing until" further investigation.[166] A full reconnaissance of the position would have to wait until morning, making a dawn attack downright reckless.

Having put the sunrise order myth to rest, McLaws then gave a full, if unsolicited, description of his division's actions before going into battle. The division started toward Gettysburg at 4:00 p.m. on July 1, after Longstreet ordered it to wait for Ewell's wagon trains to pass. They arrived at Marsh Creek, two and a half miles from Seminary Ridge, at midnight, where they bivouacked until just after dawn on July 2. "I saw Hood's Division next morning," McLaws remembered, while his own division "moved early on the 2nd to the front." Arriving at Seminary Ridge after a short march of perhaps an hour or two, McLaws was summoned to army headquarters. He dutifully trotted up the ridge where he found Lee "sitting on a log with a map before him. Gen'l Longstreet was walking back and forth a few yards off."[167]

Lee pointed to a spot on the map and asked if McLaws "could place my Division in position at a place he designated on the left of the Federal line," parallel with the Federal position. McLaws "told him I knew nothing to prevent me."

Longstreet then strode over and pointed to the position *he* wanted McLaws to occupy, "which was perpendicular to the one marked by Gen'l Lee." Lee intervened: "No Gen'l I wish it placed as I have told Gen'l McLaws."

Lee told McLaws that he had sent a staff officer to reconnoiter "for the purpose of finding out a way to go into position without being seen by the enemy." McLaws, meanwhile, "must hold myself in readiness to move." McLaws asked to go along on the reconnaissance, but Longstreet once again interjected: "No, Sir, you must stay with your Division."

McLaws started to send his own engineer, Lieutenant Thomas Moncure "of Virginia," along with Lee's staff officer, but he was ordered to stay put, too.[168] Frustrated, McLaws "placed my Division under cover of some woods and hills" and then went on his own personal reconnaissance "far enough to satisfy myself that I could march direct from the point where I was to the position Gen'l Lee wished me to occupy without being seen by the enemy."

McLaws did not mention where he went or how long he was gone. But when he returned to his division posted along Herr's Ridge, he "sat on my horse looking at the Federal troops as they came in, hour after hour from the direction of Emmitsburg. At last," he wrote, "came the order to move, and Major Johnson of Gen'l Lee's staff appeared to conduct the head of the column, as he, so I understood, had made the reconnaissance." McLaws would struggle with Johnston's name and rank in each of his accounts. Nomenclatural problems aside, the two rode on ahead of the column as it wound its way along the ridges toward the Federal left flank.

"Suddenly, we arrived on the top of a hill, giving a fair view of the enemy on the Round Top and to the left." It was clear the column would be seen if they kept going this way "and their numbers estimated," so McLaws immediately halted the division. "Maj. Johnson and myself rode around in the vicinity" to see if there was any other way to go without being seen, "but we could find none."

At this point, Longstreet had arrived at the head of the column and asked "what was the matter." McLaws took him to the top of the hill "and pointed out how plainly the enemy could watch our movements if we went on."

"This won't do," Longstreet muttered.

McLaws then told Longstreet that "I had done my own reconnaissance from the position we halted at in the morning." From there, McLaws said he knew how to get to their assigned post without being seen. Unfortunately, he only knew how to get there from the morning's starting point, not from where they were now.

"We will have to countermarch," to get back to the morning's position, Longstreet observed. McLaws agreed and Longstreet gave the order.

At this point, McLaws realized Hood's Division was overlapping the rear of his own, as Hood had "followed me closely" on the march. This made countermarching more difficult, so Longstreet "proposed that Hood should head the movement." McLaws asked permission to maintain the lead and Longstreet acquiesced. "Finally, all the troops were marching in proper order, out of sight of the enemy" and in the right direction.[169]

Around four o'clock in the afternoon, Longstreet's Corps was in position along Seminary Ridge.[170] The "delay in the reconnaissance and the faulty reconnaissance, making a change of route necessary in order to carry out Gen'l Lee's orders," McLaws explained, "were the reasons why we were so long getting into position." Clearly, it was *Lee's staff* that was to blame, not Longstreet, or by proxy, McLaws. Indeed, McLaws was ready to go "between 8 & 9 o'clock A.M. or earlier."[171]

"I go so much into detail," McLaws explained, "to show that Gen'l Longstreet was not to blame for not attacking sooner than he did on the 2nd of July." It was "a grave assumption and error to assert that because Longstreet's Corps did not assault at daylight, the Battle of Gettysburg was lost to the Confederates." If Longstreet wasn't to blame, then there was no culpability for him to pass on to McLaws.

McLaws offered Longstreet the use of any of the information in the letter "should the foregoing be of any use to you in replying to the statement of General Pendleton." On June 12, 1873, McLaws slid the letter into an envelope addressed to his old corps commander in New Orleans, entrusted it to the postal service, and anxiously awaited the reply.

MCLAWS RECEIVED LONGSTREET'S ANSWER A LITTLE OVER a month later. There was little about the War Horse's response to put him at ease.[172]

Longstreet initially thanked him for his information and asked for any more he could remember. "It is not my purpose to reply to the scurrilous remarks made by Gen Pendleton," he told McLaws, "but I think that I may be justified...in publishing an account of the Gettysburg Campaign, and the events leading to and connected with it."[173] The rest of the letter gave McLaws some idea of what Longstreet might include in such an account, little of which was reassuring.

After spending considerable time explaining his thoughts on the "ruling ideas" of the campaign (namely that he and Lee had settled on a tactically defensive fight), Longstreet addressed McLaws's rebuttal of Pendleton's sunrise order claim. "Your remarks about Pendleton's assertions are as conclusive proof of this falsity as anything that may be addressed," he told McLaws. There was no reason to expound on it.

But then he addressed the bitter feelings between them, left over from their experience in Tennessee in 1863 and 1864. In the fall of 1863, just two months after Gettysburg, Longstreet had been sent with Hood and McLaws to reinforce General Braxton Bragg's Army of Tennessee. Bragg's army was situated just south of the Tennessee River along Chickamauga Creek, having been outmaneuvered and forced out of the city of Chattanooga. Longstreet arrived just before midnight on September 19, though Hood's men were already there and had been fighting all day. Longstreet jumped in with both feet, organized the assault, and in the late morning on the twentieth smashed into the Federal right flank and crushed it. Both his contemporaries and historians have considered Chickamauga Longstreet's best day of the war and the fighting earned him the sobriquet the "Bull of the Woods."[174]

But internal politics threatened to tear the army apart.[175] Longstreet became the de facto leader of a coup to remove the universally despised Braxton Bragg from command. The infighting ultimately resulted in Confederate President Jefferson Davis intervening. After several weeks of political intrigue that confirmed Longstreet's later admission that he was inept at politics, Jeff Davis ultimately retained Bragg as army commander. It was agreed by everyone that it would be best for Longstreet and Bragg to keep as much distance between them as possible, so Longstreet was sent to Knoxville to try and dislodge the Federal force there.[176]

If Chickamauga was Longstreet's best performance of the war, then Knoxville was undisputedly his worst. Envisioned as a lightning strike to surprise the Federals, the campaign instead plodded along through muddy roads. It took Longstreet a month to get his army there (though this was more a testament to poor Confederate logistics and infrastructure than poor execution on Longstreet's part).[177] But once he arrived, Longstreet was indecisive. Reconnaissance was poor and Longstreet postponed the attack numerous times. Eventually, he tapped McLaws to lead the assault on the fort (called Fort Loudon by the Confederates and Fort Sanders by the Federals).[178]

Initial reconnaissance by E.P. Alexander, Longstreet, and engineer Lieutenant Thomas Moncure indicated a relatively shallow ditch around the fort's perimeter. But when McLaws's men rushed in, ready to storm the parapet, they found themselves trapped. The berm had been removed, meaning they had no means to climb out of the ditch and up the exterior of the fortifications. In any event, rain from the night before had frozen and turned the parapet into a wall of ice. The attack failed spectacularly. With the news of Bragg's loss at Missionary Ridge a few days earlier, Longstreet and his demoralized force found additional attacks futile and they retired.[179]

In the wake of the failure, Longstreet immediately cashiered McLaws, who demanded an explanation. Through Colonel Moxley Sorrel, Longstreet replied that "throughout the Campaign on which we are engaged you have exhibited a want of confidence in the efforts and plans which the commanding Gen'l has thought proper to adopt, and that he is apprehensive that this feeling will extend more or less to the troops under your Command." Sorrel's note explained that the "public service would be advanced by your separation from [Longstreet], and as he could not himself leave," McLaws would have to.[180]

McLaws was livid and launched a campaign to clear his name, writing other officers and demanding a court-martial to bring all the facts to light. Longstreet's resultant charges revolved around McLaws's preparation for the attack on Fort Loudon. Specifically,

Longstreet charged that McLaws did not arrange his sharpshooters appropriately before the attack, failed to properly select troops to lead the assault, and that he failed to bring ladders or other equipment to scale the parapet.[181]

The tribunal, headed by Simon Bolivar Buckner, included Gettysburg veterans James Kemper and Benjamin Humphreys. Like the Battle of Knoxville itself, the court-martial was haphazard, and Longstreet did what he could to interfere, ordering Benjamin Humphreys and Micah Jenkins, "an important witness," on thirty-day leaves of absence.[182] After numerous delays, the court found McLaws not guilty on the sharpshooter and troop selection charges, but guilty of "not providing means of crossing the ditch, and in this of failing in the details of his attack to make the arrangements essential to his success."[183]

Adjutant and Inspector General Samuel Cooper, though, promptly overturned the conviction as it was "not sustained by the evidence." Longstreet himself had testified that he saw men walk up and down the parapet and cross the ditch with no assistance and had not deemed ladders necessary.[184] How, Cooper wondered, could McLaws have thought it necessary to bring ladders when the commanding general's own reconnaissance showed they weren't needed and didn't so much as suggest them? In any event, the army hadn't been provided with the ladders or the tools to make them; even if McLaws thought them necessary, they simply didn't exist.[185] McLaws was immediately ordered back to his command.[186] But on his way through Richmond, he met with President Jefferson Davis, who told him Lee preferred he didn't return. Instead of sending him back to his old division, Davis ordered McLaws to command the defenses of Savannah. McLaws wouldn't join the Army of Northern Virginia again.[187]

Longstreet also court-martialed two other commanders, Evander Law and Jerome Robertson, for spurious reasons. Longstreet had always admired General Micah Jenkins, who was quickly rising through the ranks as one of the most promising young Confederate officers. When Hood, who seemed to possess a magnetism for Yankee lead, was wounded at Chickamauga, it seemed natural to place Evander Law back in command; after all, he had commanded in Hood's absence during and after Gettysburg. Instead, Longstreet named Micah Jenkins as the new division commander, despite the fact that Jenkins had never served with the division. Law was upset enough that he resigned and was promptly court-martialed.[188] Robertson never received a verdict, but like McLaws[ii], he never served again with the Army of Northern Virginia.[189]

IT WAS NO WONDER LONGSTREET TOOK A "LESS IS MORE" approach to reconciliation with his old friend and subordinate. "I fear that efforts to explain such matters are not likely to improve them," Longstreet wrote, and he was probably right. The wounds were deep, with lasting implications for McLaws. He had lost his command in the vaunted Army of Northern Virginia, been relegated to the undermanned defenses of Savannah, and eventually ended up retreating north through the mosquito-infested swamps of South Carolina as William Tecumseh Sherman's army turned north after it famously reached the sea.[190] At the outset of what promised to be yet another controversy, a few pencil scratches on a piece of paper were unlikely to resolve any past hard feelings.

So, Longstreet forged ahead to more productive ends. He promised he would not go into too much detail for the rest of his letter, as "a full explanation would probably take up more of your time than I have already consumed." The points he *did* make, then, took on much more significance.

"You may remember that I had a conversation with you just before starting on the Gettysburg Campaign," he reminded McLaws, "in reference to your health, and your ability to undertake the

---

ii   In 1892, Longstreet finally admitted to McLaws that the failure at Knoxville was his fault. "I think I now make clear that it was I who caused the failure at Knoxville." Longstreet to McLaws, Oct. 20 1892, in McLaws Papers, UNC Wilson Library.

service." McLaws *had* been ill the winter of 1862–63, but he had recovered and participated in the Battle of Chancellorsville in May.

As if questioning his virility wasn't bad enough, Longstreet dropped another hammer. The conversation had been "prompted by Gen Lee, who insisted that you should be ordered on some other service." Longstreet thought McLaws "should be permitted to select [himself] what course to pursue" and told Lee that the decision should be left to McLaws. Lee wasn't convinced. "It was not until I promised my personal aid and attention to your command," related Longstreet, that Lee agreed to let McLaws stay with the army. "I thus became responsible for everything that was not entirely satisfactory in your command from that day, and was repeatedly told of that fact."[191]

Rumors about McLaws's Division transferring south swirled throughout the fall and winter of 1862. McLaws had also requested a transfer just before embarking on the Gettysburg Campaign. "You spoke of going South the other day," Longstreet wrote in a quick note to McLaws on June 3, 1863. "I expect that I may make the arrangement for you," provided McLaws's troops could be replaced quickly.[192]

McLaws was a Georgian, after all, and he had been thinking about a transfer to be closer to his family for some time. "It is not pleasant for me to tell anyone how soft hearted I am when thinking of my wife & her little ones, far away, longing to see me, and yet constantly disappointed," he wrote home in November 1862. "How lonesome I feel always being away from them." He was hoping the rumors of a southern transfer were true "for one reason & that is to be near my wife and children & for no other."

If he was upset at all about his career, he did not express it, at least not in any document that survived. His homesickness affected his mood, though, and quite possibly his job performance. "My friends say I am much more cross & unsociable than formerly," he confessed to his wife.[193]

WHETHER IT WAS DUE TO LONELINESS, FRUSTRATION WITH his career prospects, or a combination, McLaws doesn't really seem to have fit in with the Army of Northern Virginia. He did not have the decisiveness or confidence required of a division commander in Lee's army. Moxley Sorrel described McLaws as "an officer of much experience and most careful. Fond of detail, his command was in excellent condition, and his ground and position well examined and reconnoitered."[iii] He was reliable, "could always be counted on and had secured the entire confidence of his officers and men." But he was "not brilliant in the field or quick in movement there or elsewhere."[194]

One of Kershaw's men concluded that McLaws "was not the officer to lead in an active, vigorous campaign, where all depended on alertness and dash. He was too cautious, and as such, too slow." He was "not a man for the times—not the man to command such troops as he had."[195] Though no one doubted his capabilities, devotion, and courage, McLaws simply didn't have the knack for being in the right place at the right time. In an army that rewarded luck, pluck, dash, and daring, there was little room for McLaws's steady and deliberate approach to warfare.[196]

A military man educated at West Point, McLaws resigned from the U.S. Army in April 1861 to enter the Confederate service as colonel of the Tenth Georgia, a volunteer infantry regiment. He was not flamboyant except in his beard, which made him resemble a Caribbean Pirate of the Spanish Main in his portraits.[197]

---

iii   As we'll see, McLaws had a preoccupation with reconnoitering, perhaps due to criticism from Lee at Salem Church.

Lafayette McLaws. The cape and beard give him the flair of a Caribbean pirate, which his fellow Confederate officers felt he lacked on the battlefield. Library of Congress.

He was also a Georgian, and non-Virginians had a tendency to believe Lee's army was partial to sons of the Old Dominion.[198] Some have suggested that McLaws was offended at not being offered corps command when Lee restructured the army after the Battle of Chancellorsville. But the career snub, if it really was one, had more to do with Lee's dim view of his job performance. Lee had taken issue with some of McLaws's battlefield performances, most recently at Chancellorsville. In contrast, Lee thought Ewell "an honest, brave soldier, who has always done his duty well," and considered A.P. Hill the best general in the army after Longstreet and the late Stonewall Jackson.[199] With only two positions available, Lee could afford to pick those he had absolute confidence in, which was not something he could say about McLaws.[200] If McLaws's native state played a role in Lee's decision, Lee could at least point to a number of other reasons he chose to pass on promoting McLaws to corps command.

McLaws's reputation for being slow, whether deserved or not, was well-known within the army, as Sorrel pointed out. On September 13 and 14, 1862, for example, Lee consistently pressed McLaws to march his division faster. "General Lee...has not heard from you since you left the main body," Lee's military secretary, Armistead Long, wrote McLaws during the Antietam Campaign. "He hopes that you have been able to reach your destined position. He is anxious that the object of your expedition be speedily accomplished." Long reminded McLaws to "communicate as frequently as you can with headquarters," and hoped "that the enemy about Harper's Ferry will be speedily disposed of," so McLaws's detachment could return to the main body. Later that evening, after receiving word that Federal troops were approaching, Lee prodded McLaws again: "You will see, therefore, the necessity of expediting your operations as much as possible." Once the mission was accomplished, McLaws was to "move your force as rapidly as possible to Sharpsburg." The next day, Lee wrote McLaws yet again: "I desire your operations [at Harper's Ferry] to be pushed on as rapidly as possible." [201]

After the Battle of Sharpsburg, General Lee reported that McLaws and General John Walker were both ordered to leave Harpers Ferry and follow General "Stonewall" Jackson "without delay." Jackson and Walker both arrived at Sharpsburg on September 16, 1862. McLaws, however, did not. His "progress was slow," and his division did not arrive until "some time after the engagement on the seventeenth began."[202] To make matters worse, A.P. Hill, one of Jackson's division commanders, made the same march in only nine hours, arriving just in time to fend off the final Federal attack and save the day for the Confederate army.[203]

It was not just Lee who noticed. General Jeb Stuart wrote in his report to General Lee, "I explained to [McLaws] the location of the roads…and repeatedly urged the importance of his holding with an infantry picket the road leading from the Ferry…toward Sharpsburg." McLaws did not place the picket, allowing the entire force of Federal cavalry at Harper's Ferry to escape that night "by that very road." Stuart reported that the escaped Federal cavalry later "inflicted serious damage on General Longstreet's [wagon] train."[204]

General John Bell Hood also reported McLaws's punctuality problem. "I am thoroughly of the opinion [that] had General McLaws arrived by 8:30 a.m. our victory on the left would have been as thorough, quick, and complete as upon the plains of Manassas on

August 30," the pugnacious Hood opined.[205] Official reports made for popular reading in newspapers and veterans' periodicals after the war. But while the war raged, the reports would only be sent to the government. A negative mention was bad for career prospects, but not bad publicity.

But General Hood didn't limit his criticism to official army reports. The chaplain of one of Hood's Texas regiments published a chronicle of the regiment in April 1863, quoting Hood's report nearly verbatim. The chaplain, Nicholas Davis, hoped "the reasons for [McLaws's] tardiness...will be satisfactory." If not, "the loud condemnation of a country, which had, in part, entrusted him with its destiny, should fall upon him." Indeed, "the strong arm of the law" should remove him from command if Hood's opinion proved true.[206]

On June 3, 1863, as the Army of Northern Virginia took its first steps north to Pennsylvania, Hood scratched a note to McLaws insisting he had nothing to do with Davis's book. "I did not know your name was mentioned in the book until I received your note," he wrote his fellow division commander. While Hood was confident Davis would correct the aspersion, Hood would do so himself if need be.[207] Whether McLaws accepted the apology is unknown; he doesn't appear to have talked to Hood about it anymore. But the allegations left a deep impression on his ego. He spent considerable ink after the war defending his actions at Harper's Ferry and Sharpsburg.[iv]

Later that year, McLaws fought well at Fredericksburg, ensconced behind the famous stonewall on Marye's Heights. There was little room for censure. But at Chancellorsville, in May 1863, McLaws would experience a delay much like the one at Gettysburg.

---

iv   McLaws was still talking about it thirty-three years later. In a letter to former Confederate cavalryman Thomas Munford in 1896, McLaws wrote that "After the Battle of Sharpsburg, the chaplain wrote a letter which was published in Richmond claiming that if my command had not dallied on the way, I allowing my men to halt and bathe in the river, and had come to Hood's assistance his command would not have been driven from the field as it was 'pell mell.' The statements as to my dallying on the way, was a malicious and infamous downright invention and I told Hood so, and in spite of his denial to the contrary, I believe he was the instigator of it, for that was his character." McLaws to Munford, Jan. 6, 1896, in McLaws Papers, UNC Wilson Library.

He had performed ably on May 1, his columns successfully attacking along the Orange Turnpike over an area reconnoitered by Samuel Johnston.[208] He entered a solid performance on May 2 as well. But on May 3, the indecisiveness that nagged Lee's opinion of him emerged again. McLaws was sent to reinforce Early at Salem Church, where Federal troops from Fredericksburg were threatening the army's rear. Early and McLaws hurled back the Federal assaults and, like the situation on the evening of July 1, the Confederate commanders were confronted with the decision to press the attack or wait until morning. Early wanted to attack; McLaws thought the Confederate force was too small to carry the position. In the end, the attack was postponed, allowing the Federal troops under General John Sedgwick time to dig in.

The next day foreshadowed July 2, 1863. Three brigades, arriving around noon, were sent to reinforce McLaws. But the attack did not begin until evening. In his report, General Lee simply wrote that "[s]ome delay occurred in getting the troops into position, owing to the broken and irregular nature of the ground and the difficulty of ascertaining the disposition of the enemy's forces. The attack did not begin until 6:00 p.m."

Kershaw's Brigade was finally thrown forward, but because of the darkness and uncertainty of the Federal position, "[their] movements were consequently slow." Because the attack started so late, McLaws was unable to realize its full success and the Federals "made good [their] escape," picking up their bridges behind them. The opportunity was lost. General Early was left in position and McLaws sent back to Chancellorsville.[209] As the summer approached, Lee and others had repeatedly noticed that McLaws seemed to lack the ability to be in the right place at the right time.

Lee himself had been forced to personally intercede at Salem Church and take command, putting "him in a temper," as Edward Porter Alexander remembered. "A great deal of time had been uselessly lost," he later wrote, and no one seemed to have any idea where the Federals were or what they were doing. "It was somebody's duty to know," Alexander noted wryly, but the ineptness forced Lee to take matters into his own hands. Though Alexander diplomatically wrote that he never did figure out who Lee was mad at, McLaws was the senior division commander on the field. Lee's report, though characteristically understated in his criticism of McLaws's performance, made no mistake about who was to blame. [v]

Only a month after the retreat from Gettysburg, Francis Lawley had criticized McLaws's performance to his London readership. "On Hood's left, hardly with sufficient promptitude, the division of General McLaws" advanced. "Observing some delay in their advance, General Longstreet threw himself at the head" of the battle line and personally "led them under such a fire as has rarely been witnessed."[210]

Another foreign observer, Fitzgerald Ross, noted early on that there was talk in the army that "McLaws was blamed by some people for having been too slow" and that "the men might have been put in position a good deal sooner."[211] Though Ross's account was published in 1864, he was describing what some of the men in the corps thought at the end of July 2. Longstreet personally seems to have thought the wounding of two key subordinates, Hood and Barksdale, were the primary reasons the attack didn't press further than it did, but at least some people thought it was McLaws's delay that cost the Confederates a complete victory on July 2. McLaws may never have seen these written accounts, but Lawley and Ross had both traveled with First Corps headquarters and it's difficult to believe McLaws didn't hear the whispers.[vi]

---

v   Gallagher, ed., Fighting for the Confederacy, 213. Alexander wrote that "it devolved upon [Lee] personally to use up a lot more time to find out all about the enemy before we could move a peg." In his report, he wrote, "The speedy approach of darkness prevented General McLaws from perceiving the success of the attack until the enemy began to recross the river...." O.R. 25.1: 802.

vi   Though neither Ross nor Lawley gave up the sources of the rumors, Longstreet doesn't seem to have been a part of the whisper campaign. Longstreet talked candidly with Fremantle after the battle, telling the British officer that "the mistake they had made was in not concentrating the army more, and [in not] making the attack yesterday [Pickett's Charge] with 30,000 men instead of 15,000." Fremantle, Three Months in the Southern States, 274. Of course, Longstreet could have said something that wasn't recorded, or complained to his staff, who then forwarded the complaints to Ross and Lawley. But more likely, it came from staff officers in the corps.

On top of all this, Kershaw's Gettysburg report indicated yet another delay. "The command was ordered to move at 4 o'clock on the morning of the 2d," Kershaw reported, "but did not leave camp until about sunrise." McLaws would say the order was countermanded and though it really may have been, Kershaw doesn't offer any reason for the hold up. Kershaw's report appeared in the October 1877 issue of the *Southern Historical Society Papers*, about a year before McLaws's first published speech about Gettysburg.[212] Readers of the *Southern Historical Society Papers* were left with the impression that McLaws simply and inexplicably didn't start on time. It couldn't have been lost on McLaws that it was Kershaw who had been given command of McLaws's Division after the Knoxville affair.[213]

Kershaw's published report indicated that McLaws *could have* arrived at Gettysburg earlier than he did. If he left at 4:00 a.m., he could have covered the distance from Marsh Creek to Seminary Ridge in an hour, putting him at the battlefield around 5:00 a.m., just as the sun was beginning to fully illuminate the field. In a brewing controversy about sunrise attacks, delays, and lost causes, this information could prove to be portentous.[214]

ONE CAN ONLY IMAGINE, THEN, THE LOOK ON MCLAWS'S heavily bearded face when he read Longstreet's letter. Not only had the First Corps commander questioned McLaws's physical fitness for field command, he claimed Lee had wanted McLaws out of the army altogether! And the only way Lee would allow him to stay was if Longstreet took him under his wing. What was more, the letter announced loud and clear that *Longstreet* would take the blame for any of McLaws's errors. And of course, Longstreet was now being very loudly blamed for losing the Battle of Gettysburg and, in turn, the war.

So McLaws could be forgiven for thinking that Longstreet would live up to his low expectations. It didn't appear Longstreet would be writing anything soon, but it was obvious what his approach would be when he *did* get around to publishing something: McLaws was going to take the blame for Longstreet's delay. "*I* became responsible for *everything* that" was wrong in "*your* command," Longstreet stressed. It was not lost on McLaws that *his* division led the march that caused the "fatal delay." It certainly sounded like Longstreet was setting up McLaws and his division to take the blame.

Perhaps it's no coincidence, then, that McLaws's account ended up in the *New Orleans Republican* less than three weeks after Longstreet's reply. Though there's no direct evidence that McLaws sent the copy of his letter to the paper, it's hard to ignore the timing and context. McLaws felt he had spent the war answering for others' misperceptions of him. His march from Harper's Ferry to Antietam had been unfairly criticized, leaving him defending himself to his peers. His division's performance at Gettysburg had been micromanaged; when he was ordered to fall back to Seminary Ridge against his better judgment, it was misconstrued as a retreat by Longstreet (and it seemed by the rest of the army, too). Then he had been cashiered in Tennessee, once again playing defense to Longstreet's charges. Though he was vindicated by the court, it was of little comfort, for he had lost his division with the Army of Northern Virginia. Having now caught wind of *another* possible accusation, one could hardly blame McLaws for trying to play offense for a change.

It's true McLaws had given Longstreet "the liberty to use" the letter "in replying to…General Pendleton," so there's the possibility that it was Longstreet who forwarded the letter to the *Republican*.[215] But the paper betrays no hint of this. Instead, the headline blares *LETTER FROM GENERAL MCLAWS,* implying it was McLaws who sent it to the editor. The first line of the introduction tells the reader that "General Lafayette McLaws has written a letter in answer to the statement of General Pendleton," with no suggestion that Longstreet submitted it as an exhibit for his own defense.

Contrast this with Longstreet's infamous letter of June 7, 1867, which the *New Orleans Times* acknowledged was provided by Longstreet. The editorial introduction is focused on McLaws and his credentials, and the tenor of the *Republican's* introduction is delight that someone like McLaws was weighing in. McLaws "narrates with remarkable perspicuity the events of the second day of July," the editors gushed, "which rendered it impossible that the statements of General Pendleton could be true in the unqualified manner in which he presents them." By all appearances, the letter was submitted directly to the *Republican* by McLaws.[216]

But no matter how McLaws's June 12 letter ended up in the hands of the *Republican*'s editors, his account was now public record. Longstreet was sure to see it and McLaws had the first word this time around. McLaws would certainly be happy to know that his recollection of the battle would remain the definitive account for over a hundred and fifty years.[vii]

MCLAWS INSISTED THAT THE LETTER HE SENT TO LONG-street was merely a copy of one he had written to a friend. But really, the letter was a sort of reconnaissance, designed to feel out Longstreet's intentions. McLaws's assertion that it was a copy of a letter sent to a friend was simply a cover, masking his objective like the Pennsylvania ridges had concealed his movements on July 2.

In fact, McLaws had scratched out a very rough draft two days earlier, working out the details of his account and fleshing out the ideas that permeated the final copy. He then drew up a clean copy for his own papers and sent another copy out to Longstreet. It was this

---

vii   The published letter does seem to have deterred Longstreet from writing an account for a few years. In a letter to Thomas Goree in 1875, Longstreet admitted that "an account by me would necessarily be more complete and might bring up old matters that were better left, when they can, to be forgotten." Pendleton's "recent publication or republication has started many friends again in their petitions that I shall fight the old battle over again." This is curious, as it sounds like Longstreet felt there was more to the story, but that McLaws had at least provided an adequate defense. When Longstreet ultimately published an account, he would largely follow McLaws's lead, although he had some substantial differences. Longstreet to Goree, May 12, 1875, in Cutrer, Longstreet's Aide, 157.

letter that laid out McLaws's official version of the story and would serve as the basis for all of his future public accounts, including the one that ultimately served as the traditional narrative.[viii]

Many of his final edits were simply an effort to appear more certain and confident of some events. For example, in his June 10 draft he wrote that he arrived at Lee's headquarters at "Seminary Hill, I think." He crossed out "I think," then scrawled out a few more attempts to remember exactly what time he reached Gettysburg. Struggling to recall the details in his humid Georgia office, he wavered between "no later than 8" a.m., "about 9 o'clock," and "earlier than 9," before finally settling on "between 8-9 o'clock or earlier."

It's entirely reasonable for McLaws to have wanted to appear certain and confident in his recollections. Early and Pendleton were assertive and ruthless. Given his history with Longstreet, McLaws can't be faulted for wanting to appear self-assured. Waffling on important matters like times and places in this case simply wouldn't do, for it was precisely the time and place that were at issue. But the draft shows that there is ample room for interpretation in McLaws's later accounts. Though he may have kept his uncertainty tucked away in rough drafts, even *he* was not quite sure about many of the details.[ix]

---

viii   Both the draft and the final letter state the letter was merely a copy of the reply to the unnamed acquaintance. But there are substantial corrections, with McLaws re-wording and in some cases substantially changing the contents. Apparently he worked on this for two days, for the draft letter was dated June 10, 1873, while the clean copy sent to Longstreet was dated June 12, 1873. Had the letter truly been a copy, there would be no need for the significant markup to the substance of the letter. The June 10 letter is available in McLaws Papers, UNC Wilson Library.

ix   In his scribbled recollection on June 10, he remembered bivouacking at Marsh Creek "about three miles or something over from Gettysburg." He crossed out "or something over" in the final edit. The correction from relative distance to certain distance reinforces McLaws's desire to display a confident front.

There were more serious discrepancies, though, than deleting a few *I thinks* and rough estimates of the time. In his final letter—the one that went to both Longstreet and the *New Orleans Republican*—McLaws wrote that Johnston had been sent out on a "reconnaissance for the purpose of finding out a way for me to go into position without being seen by the enemy." But in his rough draft, McLaws wrote that Lee "ordered the reconnaissance of the *position*" of the Federal left, a very different objective.[217]

This is important, as McLaws's initial recollection corresponds with Johnston's own (more consistent) memory. Whenever he was asked about it, Johnston reported that he had been ordered to reconnoiter the Federal left. Though that task entailed finding *potential* routes into position, Johnston always maintained he had not been specifically ordered to do so.[218] Indeed, he *couldn't* have planned a precise route, for the plan hadn't been fully developed when he was ordered to reconnoiter.[219]

It was important to McLaws that he get the reconnaissance's purpose right. That was the crux of his defense: *if the First Corps was late, it was because Lee's staff officer performed a poor reconnaissance and got us lost.* With the words of Longstreet's letter ringing in his ears ("I thus became responsible for everything that was not entirely satisfactory in your command"), it was absolutely necessary that neither McLaws nor Longstreet were to blame for the delay. Clarifying that *Lee's* staff officer was responsible for discovering both the location of the Federal flank *and* the route into position was critical. Thus, the "delay in the reconnaissance and faulty reconnaissance, making a change of route necessary…were the reasons why we were so long getting into position. I go so much into detail *in order to show that General Longstreet was not to blame* for not attacking sooner than he did" on July 2.[220] If there was no blame on Longstreet's shoulders, then there was none for him to pass on to McLaws.

McLaws also heavily edited his description of the meeting with Lee that morning. When Lee pointed to the map, McLaws first remembered that he "asked me if I could place my Division in position at a place he designated on the left of the Federal line, or where I supposed it was." He crossed off "or where I supposed it was" in his final letter. After all, he would later say he had no idea where the Federal line was. That was Johnston's job and anyway, Longstreet prevented McLaws from any reconnoitering to discover the Federal position. Perhaps it was best *not* to have shown any knowledge of the Federal position. That would just open him up to more blame and pose more questions.

McLaws also struggled to remember exactly how the march into position played out. He havered back and forth trying to remember exactly who led the march. Was it Johnston? Or just McLaws? Or both of them? He eventually settled on "he and I."[x]

It is understandable that McLaws would have difficulty remembering specific times and even the chronology of events. The battle was a decade earlier and he was working almost entirely from memory. Like later historians researching the event, he had no official report, no order book, and no contemporary notes. And he had the added pressure of his reputation and potential public scorn peering over his shoulder as he wrote.

The inaccuracies in McLaws's accounts say little about his character. By all accounts, McLaws was a devoted husband and father, even-tempered, steady, and fair. He was also human and like anyone, fought vigorously to defend his reputation.

But McLaws's letters and speeches are the foundation for most historians' accounts of the countermarch. For accuracy's sake, they must be scrutinized. Glenn Tucker, one of the few who examines the 1873 letter, calls McLaws's Gettysburg accounts "the most penetrating" and "the most unbiased."[221] A recent study of Longstreet at Gettysburg relies heavily on McLaws's 1878 speech.[222] Stephen Sears, Harry Pfanz, Noah Trudeau, and even Edwin Coddington, all cite primarily to McLaws's Georgia Historical Society speech in reconstructing the morning and early afternoon of July 2.[223] It's important to know whether the accounts are accurate or not.

---

x   The June 10 draft shows McLaws's struggle to remember the details: "At last came the order to move, and Major Johnson of Genl Lee's staff appeared to conduct the head of column, as he, so I understood, had made the reconnaissance + he ~~mar + I + myself we marched~~ on ahead of the Command..." McLaws to Longstreet, draft, June 10, 1873. McLaws Papers, UNC Wilson Library.

McLaws's rough draft (top) reveals his thought process. The image shows his first attempt at jotting down his thoughts on the countermarch. The final draft (bottom) is tidy and well-written, with limited corrections for transcription errors. From the Southern Historical Collection, Wilson Library, the University of North Carolina at Chapel Hill.

* * *

TRAINED AS A MILITARY MAN AND NOT A LAWYER (OR preacher), McLaws accepted the Early/Pendleton premises at face value, never challenging the idea that there was a delay by the First Corps. Instead, he tried to deflect blame rather than challenge the accusation's basis. That was fair enough and it seems to have worked both in parrying blame from McLaws and keeping Longstreet at bay, but the truth was simultaneously ricocheted away from the conversation.[224]

Most historians, and even Lee's staff, have rightly dismissed Pendleton's "sunrise order" as hogwash.[xi] But by not questioning the *premises*—whether there was, in fact, a significant delay, much less an unwarranted one—McLaws merely sought to justify it, arguing within the bounds of Early's and Pendleton's argument. McLaws's accounts all accept that the attack started later than intended and that the attack's timing negatively impacted its result. Historians have therefore accepted it, as well.

The idea rode the printing presses through history, becoming an indelible part of the history of the battle. But there is little contemporary evidence that on July 2 anyone, *including Lee, Pendleton, or Early,* thought there was anything inappropriate about the time Longstreet's attack started on July 2.

Early's and Pendleton's occupations certainly gave them an advantage in the postwar battles. Both were trained to convince others of their ideas and to speak authoritatively on a given subject. Longstreet and McLaws, on the other hand, quietly spent their lives in the military. As Longstreet reminded his readers in the *New Orleans Times,* he spoke simply as a soldier, not a statesman, and his philosophy told him that battlefields decided political questions.[225] The same held true for McLaws. Their military credentials were unfortunately ill-suited for this new political war waging in crowded meeting halls and printed columns, a fight in which Early and Pendleton were disproportionately well-armed.

The deficiency is readily apparent in several of McLaws's statements. For example, he was adamant that his division arrived around 8:00 a.m. and that he went straight to army headquarters. But that admits his division didn't leave its bivouac until close to 7:00 a.m., unless the men marched at speeds that would only justify McLaws's reputation for being immune to alacrity. When Kershaw's report appeared in the *Southern Historical Society Papers,* the delay in the morning's march became public information. Mclaws, who had been silent on this fact in 1873, now had to account for his late start. He added a rebuttal in his 1878 Georgia speech, which then found its

---

xi   Further discussion of the sunrise order appears at page 159

way—not coincidentally—into the *Southern Historical Society Papers* in February 1879, barely a year after Kershaw's report appeared.[226]

Hood's Division was also moving before McLaws's that morning. The commanders of the Second and Seventh Georgia regiments, both of Hood's Division, reported that they moved toward Gettysburg at 3 a.m. on the morning of July 2, a full hour earlier than McLaws had ordered *his* division to march.[227] McLaws even noted seeing Hood's Division that morning, an oblique reference to Hood's passing him on the road.[228] If Hood's Division, which had started its march that morning west of McLaws, was on the road first, then McLaws would obviously not be able to use the road until Hood and his wagons had passed (Kershaw noted only "slight detention from trains in the way").[229] Given the recent feud with Hood concerning McLaws's marching prowess, it is understandable McLaws would wish to omit *why* he had to delay his march. Instead, he simply noted that the original order was to march at 4:00 a.m., which had to be adjusted to around sunrise.

McLaws's morning meeting with Lee also has credibility issues. According to McLaws, he was summoned to headquarters immediately on his arrival, "between 8-9 o'clock or earlier." Lee then famously pointed to the map and asked McLaws if he could reach that point without being seen. McLaws assured him he could. This is an odd request from Lee; surely, he knew McLaws could not adequately answer him. He had just arrived on the field and had not even seen the ground he was to occupy. But McLaws's answer in the affirmative, with no qualifications, is even stranger.

McLaws seems to have realized this, too. Ten years after his speech to the Georgia Historical Society, McLaws published an account in the *Philadelphia Weekly Press*, a periodical known for publishing veteran accounts. This time, McLaws wrote that he told Lee "I did not know *if* there was anything to prevent it, but would take a reconnoitering party" and check it out.[230] This is a much different statement than the one he originally reported, one that is considerably less confident and full of qualifiers. It also deflects blame from McLaws; he *wanted* to scout the route, but Longstreet denied it. By failing to override Longstreet, Lee implicitly denied him the ability to reconnoiter, too. And of course, *Lee's* staff officer scouted the Federal position and avenue of approach and got it all wrong. (In his 1878 speech, he ultimately concludes the reconnaissance may have been accurate, but outdated by the time the First Corps was ready to move. Failure to further reconnoiter would be an ongoing complaint for McLaws.)[231]

In his 1873 letter, McLaws wrote that his intended position was parallel to the Federal line, which ran along the Emmitsburg Road. Five years later, he told the Georgia Historical Society that the proposed line was *perpendicular* to the Emmitsburg Road. McLaws did, in fact, line up along the Emmitsburg Road (though it was closer to forty-five degrees, not parallel). But Lee's plan called for Hood and McLaws to cross the Emmitsburg Road, swing their divisions left, and drive in the enemy line, perceived to be in the air. This would place the divisions nearly perpendicular to the road.[232] McLaws was technically right *both* times, for he was to start off parallel and end up perpendicular to the road. McLaws may well have simply conflated his intended position and the starting position.

LONGSTREET, HAVING CONSULTED HIS FIRST CORPS associates like McLaws, charged Johnston—and only Johnston—with the delay in the march. This, despite his initial report that blamed "engineers, sent out by the commanding general *and myself*" for the delay.[233] According to Longstreet in 1877, though, Johnston had been specially assigned by Lee to guide the column into position, effectively taking the matter out of Longstreet's hands. As Longstreet told the *Philadelphia Weekly Times*, "my troops…moved forward under the guidance of a special officer of Gen. Lee, and with instructions to follow his directions."

Even when Longstreet was convinced they had been spotted, he insisted he had no control over the movement of McLaws's Division. When McLaws halted to figure out a new route, Longstreet rode to the front, quite annoyed at the constant delays. Though his column had been seen, "further efforts to conceal ourselves would be a waste of time." Unfortunately, the matter wasn't in Longstreet's hands. "I did not order McLaws forward," he said, "because, as the head of the column, he had direct orders from General Lee to follow the conduct of Colonel Johnston."[234] Longstreet, like McLaws, was implying the fault lay with Lee, since it was *his* staff engineer that led the First Corps astray.

Longstreet's article was reprinted in the *Southern Historical Society Papers'* first issue of 1878. For strategic purposes, the editors had "decided (very much against the grain)" to publish it. Though "he certainly has no claim to our consideration," Longstreet had "some following in the South and West who are anxious for us to give him a full hearing." The editors thought "it may be well to spike that gun." There was nothing to worry about, though. Longstreet's "article is so weak that it will not help his cause." And in any event, Early's response was "so crushing that it may be best to put the two together." A future issue would indeed pair Longstreet's second article with Early's for the desired juxtaposition."[235]

The task to refute Longstreet's first article, though, fell to Fitzhugh Lee, the General's nephew. In his June 1878 reply, Fitz Lee quickly pointed out that there was no *serious* delay caused by the countermarch. By Longstreet's own admission, only "some delay" occurred. Certainly not the several hours he attributed to Johnston. Instead, the delay was caused by Longstreet's dallying *before* the march.

As part of his preparation for his article, Fitz Lee wrote to Johnston for his take. Though loath to get involved in a political argument with former comrades, he answered Lee within a few days. "I read the paper...with some surprise," Johnston wrote on *Ohio and Mississippi Railway* stationary. "The corps was not put under my charge to be taken where I saw fit." Johnston didn't believe Lee would "entrust me with the conduct of an army corps moving within two miles of the enemy's lines," and even if he did, "I had not received any instructions...as to where [Longstreet] was to go."[236]

As for the cause of the delay, he put it squarely back on Long-street. After getting back from the recon and bringing General Lee up to speed on the conditions south of the Federal line, Johnston was ordered to "ride with General Longstreet." According to Johnston, this was about nine o'clock that morning. "After no little delay, the column got in motion," Johnston wrote. "General Longstreet says 'several hours' were lost by his taking the wrong road. The delay of 'several hours' cannot be attributed to General Longstreet's taking the wrong road (whether he or I is to blame for that), but in the delay in starting, the slowness of the march, the time unnecessarily lost by halting McLaws, and the time lost beginning the fight after the line was formed." Clearly agitated at being thrown to the wolves, Johnston pulled out all the stops.

Fitzhugh Lee also took Longstreet to task on his odd inter-pretation of Lee's orders. If Longstreet really wanted to make the argument that the lead division (McLaws) was under strict orders to follow the "special officer," why couldn't Longstreet have simply left the lead platoon and taken control of the rest of the division? What about Lee's ordering Johnston as a guide meant that *only* McLaws's Division was affected? Why was Longstreet free to conduct Hood's Division? Did Longstreet honestly think Lee's direction to McLaws overrode *any* judgment call from the second in command of the army?

And if that was the case, why did he feel he was authorized to revise McLaws's position based on the discovery of the new Federal line? Lee had specifically overridden Longstreet on that particular point—if nothing else, Longstreet was under direct orders to place McLaws in a certain position. But that was the one point on which Longstreet felt he could make adjustments.[237] The *Southern Historical Society* may have led the attack on Longstreet, but Lee's Old War Horse was not making it particularly difficult.

FOR NEARLY TWENTY YEARS, SAM JOHNSTON WOULD HAVE nothing more to say on the matter. Indeed, his only letters on the subject are replies to letters or articles.[238] Then in June 1892, with the embers of the debate still glowing beneath the myriad recollections and memoirs, McLaws finally wrote directly to Johnston. The engineer, now graying and ill, lived in Jersey City, working as a consultant for the Erie Railroad.[239]

McLaws seems to have found Johnston's whereabouts by chance. Mr. J. Roy Baylor, who was "only a boy during the War," happened to be principal of a school in Savannah, Georgia in 1892 and had "seen much of Genl. McLaws here." But he was originally from Virginia and acquainted with Sam's brother, Major George Johnston. The two apparently talked quite a bit about the war and particularly Longstreet's perceived failures at Gettysburg.

McLaws asked Baylor to review the letter he had prepared to "Major Johnston" and the following day, Baylor sent a short note to Johnston, dropping the names of several mutual acquaintances, mentioning that he knew Johnston's brother, and emphasizing his own Virginia roots. In his cover note, Baylor assumed that the former reconnoitering officer felt the same way about Longstreet as McLaws and much of the South by this point: "McLaws is perfectly convinced that he was a traitor at Gettysburg." Then he poked Johnston: "Genl. Longstreet now maintains that you were sent to reconnoitre by Genl. Lee and did not make a report to him till after 2:00 p.m. McLaws thinks that this is untrue, + that you must have reported sooner."[240] Baylor forwarded the letter to Johnston with his cover letter, incorrectly addressing it to an address in East Orange, NJ, instead of Johnston's home in Jersey City. It took over two weeks to arrive, but Johnston eventually got the pair of letters.[241]

Johnston responded directly to McLaws, politely skirting the dispute. "I do not want to be a party to controversy with anyone, certainly not with General Longstreet, who always treated me with so much kindness and consideration." He then matter-of-factly disagreed with McLaws's memory. While the main purpose of his

July 2 assignment was "to make a reconnaissance of the enemy's left and report as soon as possible," Johnston *did* investigate the "roads over which our troops would have to move in the event of a movement on the enemy's left."[242]

Before sending him on his reconnaissance that morning, Lee "said nothing about finding a route over which troops could move unobserved by the enemy." However, that "was not necessary as that was a part of my duty as a reconnoitering officer, and would be attended to without special instructions." After performing the reconnaissance, he relayed his information to Lee, Longstreet, and Hill, discussed the topography of what would become the southern end of the battlefield, and was finally told "to join General Longstreet. No other instructions whatever were given me." Johnston "fully understood that to mean that I was to be with General Longstreet to aid him in any way that I could."[243]

Johnston, of course, had just as much reason to want to deflect blame as Longstreet and McLaws. Nor was it out of the question that Lee would ask him to guide a full division or corps into position. Just a month before, at Chancellorsville, he had led Wilcox's Alabama brigade into line, though that was a considerably smaller number of troops. Longstreet was also not personally at Chancellorsville, meaning Lee's staff was filling in for Longstreet's. But responsibilities grow with consistent performance and Johnston, by all accounts, performed very well in the year leading up to Gettysburg. It's not unreasonable to think Lee would trust him to guide a division into position, especially when Lee was unhappy with the division commander's recent attempt at independent command.

Johnston had plenty of experience reconnoitering. Along the Peninsula exactly one year earlier he had distinguished himself by conducting an overnight reconnaissance with another engineer who had since died, reaching the Federal earthworks on Malvern Hill to determine they were completely abandoned.[244] A few months later he worked with Longstreet and his staff at Antietam. In November and December 1862, he assisted Porter Alexander in placing the devastating artillery line along Marye's Heights at Fredericksburg, in addition to scouting enemy artillery positions and discovering vulnerable batteries. In fact, by the following year, he was considered "beyond question the best reconnoitering officer" with the Army of Northern Virginia.[245] Scouting a route along farm lanes and over a major road or two was not a major undertaking for Johnston.

The question is not *whether* Johnston was up to the task, then, but rather *was* he assigned the task. Longstreet reported that the engineers guiding the column had been sent by both Lee *and* himself.[246] Who else was with the column and what other directions were given for the march? Whose reconnaissance resulted in the First Corps' marching orders? If Major John Clarke or another engineer from Longstreet's Corps was present, then it's certainly reasonable for Johnston to have believed he wasn't leading anyone anywhere. Clarke was a member of Longstreet's staff and outranked Johnston. Why *would* Johnston be leading the march if Clarke was there, too?

It's just as curious that Johnston didn't use that as a defense (not to mention numerous other complexities and ambiguities in the various stories). He consistently made it known he did not relish the debate and had no desire to go public with his version of events. He also remained tight-lipped in his responses to Fitz Lee and McLaws. Lee had to follow up to ask him for more information and he told McLaws he wouldn't offer any opinions, perhaps learning the lesson from his letter to Fitz Lee that anything could be published, with or without permission. Having been thrown under the microscope, was Johnston simply trying to protect others from the same trouble? Did he honestly not remember? As we'll see, Johnston had good reasons for dropping names where he did and leaving them out elsewhere.

Whether Johnston was being evasive, or simply modest, it would not have been inherently far-fetched for Longstreet or McLaws to believe Lee had assigned Johnston as a guide. Perhaps he was. But Longstreet's contention that Johnston was a "special officer" of Lee, effectively neutralizing his own judgment as second in command of the army, is simply unbelievable and not supported by anything other than Longstreet's account.[xii]

---

xii   McLaws contended Johnston was the guide, but he did not argue that he had no authority to override Johnston's suggestions. This suggests McLaws really didn't know where he was going beforehand, despite his later statements that he knew exactly where to go.

Longstreet's postwar writings revolve around the idea that his own ideas were both better than Lee's and repeatedly overridden by the commanding general. McLaws's 1873 letter blaming the whole thing on Johnston seemed tailor-made to fit into his own beliefs. Longstreet and his corps had been hamstrung by *Lee's* engineer, who led them astray. Not only that, but as a *special* officer of the commanding general, Johnston's appointment removed any and all responsibility from Longstreet's shoulders. The idea was ridiculous, but it cast long shadows and obscured both the details of Johnston's involvement *and* the true causes of both the delay and the countermarch.

WORKING WITHOUT NOTES, WITHOUT A COTERIE OF FRIENDS among the prominent officers in the Army of Northern Virginia, and fending off charges he was sure were brewing, it is easy to sympathize with McLaws. He was certainly no liar, he rolled with the punches, and he left the army with a solid, but not stellar, record. And although he repeatedly stated he had no use for public debate, he kept a keen eye on his reputation and made a point to respond to slights as he had with Hood during the war.

This means that his accounts of the battle are specifically crafted to defend his actions and the performance of his division. There is nothing inherently wrong in this, but his accounts are also decidedly not "unbiased." As the author of his defense, he of course inherently turned all inferences in his own favor. McLaws himself admits that the precise reason his reminiscences are so detailed is to rebut charges against him. "I have thought it best to be this minute as to the arrival of my command in the vicinity of Sharpsburg," he wrote Hood in Mayof 1863, "in order that you can judge how maliciously false is the publication" by Davis.[247] Then in 1873, he wrote his "friend" that "I go so much into detail in order to show that Gen'l Longstreet was not to blame for not attacking sooner than he did on the 2nd of July."[248] If the First Corps was not to blame, then McLaws couldn't be either.

This is probably what prompted Joseph Kershaw to write that McLaws's 1878 speech was "valuable, if not wholly accurate."[249] Historian John Bachelder had been desperate for First Corps accounts of July 2. Aside from Kershaw, no one had really been communicative. McLaws's speech would fill that void, Kershaw advised, but Bachelder should proceed with caution. McLaws's detailed accounts of July 2 were tempting fruits, bursting with the missing information. But like the more parabolic fruit of knowledge, indulging often had the reverse effect.

PERHAPS THERE IS NO MORE FITTING SYMBOL OF LAFAYETTE McLaws's career with the Army of Northern Virginia than Longstreet's Gettysburg report. Longstreet devoted six paragraphs to praising his troops and their commanders, his staff officers, and his support staff, including quartermasters and surgeons. He praised Generals Pickett, Hood, and Trimble as "those most distinguished for the exhibition of great gallantry and skill." Trimble was not even a member of Longstreet's Corps! Rather, he took over for the mortally wounded Dorsey Pender in A.P. Hill's Third Corps. Longstreet had simply exercised tactical control over Trimble's Division during the July 3 assault immortalized as "Pickett's Charge."

Yet McLaws was not mentioned at all. His division had brutally smashed through Sickles's line in the Peach Orchard, clawed and scraped through the meatgrinder of the Rose Wheatfield and bloodied the fields around John Rose's iconic stone farmhouse. The remnants of McLaws's tenacity lay in macabre burial rows, twisted bodies of young men immortalized in the haunting glass sepia of Alexander Gardner's photographs, anonymous symbols of the horrors of war. McLaws's men captured Union General Charles Graham and barreled through the Federal line on the Emmitsburg Road, pushing nearly to the Union reserves on Cemetery Ridge.[250]

But the burly, elaborately bearded Georgian, steady and solid, if not pugnacious and flamboyant, simply disappeared beneath the hearty praise of everyone else. He can hardly be blamed for any bitterness toward Longstreet or his former associates in the Army of Northern Virginia.

Lafayette McLaws is quite the sympathetic character. Perhaps this is why he has always been so easy to believe. His writing is not acidic, it is not biting, and it is not petulant. Instead, it is calm, measured, and straightforward.[251] But...it *is* wrong.

THE STRUGGLE TO CREATE HISTORY

*"For every one hundred letters and circulars I send, I get
about ten replies, & of these ten, about six simply say that
they have lost all records & can't remember anything they
think important enough to write."*

- E.P. Alexander[252]

JOHN BADGER BACHELDER HAD TAKEN IT UPON HIMSELF
to write the definitive history of the decisive battle of the war…when-
ever that battle might happen to take place.[253]

A New England landscape painter with impressive and distinc-
tive whiskers, Bachelder initially wanted to create the definitive
painting of the 1775 Battle of Bunker Hill. Frustrated at the lack of
reliable first-hand accounts of the battle, he eventually scrapped the
idea. Instead, he decided to make sure the critical battle of *his* war
was well-documented, with the idea of making an illustrated history
of the epic battle. To make sure he didn't miss it, he followed along
with the Army of the Potomac and waited as the army crawled up the
Virginia Peninsula.

Bachelder was there for the battles around Richmond in the
spring of 1862, witnessing some of the defining moments of the war,
even though no one realized quite yet just *how* important they were.
It was here, with their backs against their capital, that what became
the Confederate Army of Northern Virginia would gain Robert E.
Lee as its commander. With Lee at its helm, the Confederate army

beat back the Federal advance and chased it back down the peninsula, where the campaign ended in humiliating failure for the
northern forces.

After the serious disappointment that summer, Bachelder went
back home to New Hampshire. He had contracted an illness in the
Virginia marshes and sought to recover while the army itself recuper-
ated. Before he left, however, he made sure to secure promises from
several officers to alert him to any movements that seemed likely to
bring about the elusive "decisive battle."[254]

Nearly a year later, his friends delivered. Sort of. Bachelder's
contacts notified him that the battle had already taken place. Though
he may have missed the battle itself, Bachelder insisted on making
the most of the opportunity. He immediately took off for Pennsylvania to document what had happened.

Though he could never quite pinpoint the date he got there,
the horrifically bloated corpses still lay in the trampled fields, and
the nauseous stench of death, clinging to the humid air, was there to
greet him. Despite the hellish scene, the whiskered Yankee immediately got to work, touring the area from south to north and tediously
sketching the roads and terrain systematically, taking note of the
geographical features and topography "as far as the vision extended."
His landscape study pulled in "fields, forests, houses, barns, hills,
and valleys...every object, however minute, which could influence
the result of a battle" for more than four miles.[255]

But above all, he talked to people. He wanted to know the story,
who fought where, what they saw, what it was like. Officers recuper-
ating from wounds acted as tour guides, showing him the areas where
they fought and describing their experiences. With a sincere desire
to get the story right, he spoke to the wounded of both sides, trying
to pluck as much fresh information as he could from the minds of
the soldiers themselves.[256]

Nearly three months later, Bachelder packed up his volumes of
notebooks and the sketch of his isometric map and headed south
toward the Army of the Potomac. He showed the map to everyone
he could find, ensuring every detail was correct. But he was perhaps
even more interested in endorsements. This was a business venture,

after all, and the approval of the army's top brass would both stamp the map with the authenticity he desired and help sell copies. And sell they did. "Many thousand copies of this work have been sold, yet the demand still continues" with "four different styles" available (!) he crowed in 1870, six years after the map was published.

But accuracy remained a point he prided himself on. The whole project started in the first place because he was frustrated by the lack of authentic sources from Bunker Hill. He was determined that the Gettysburg project would not suffer the same problem. "I have traced the movements of *every regiment and battery* from the commencement to the close of the engagement," he boasted. After the Federal army officers reviewed it that autumn (a thousand total, including forty-six generals, according to Bachelder), "*but one solitary regiment* was discovered to be out of position on it."[257]

He released his full color isometric map the following year, complete with facsimile signatures from Generals Meade, Doubleday, Newton, Hancock, Slocum, Sykes, Howard, Sedgwick, Birney, Alpheus Williams, and artillery chief Henry Hunt, all obtained during his fall visit to the army. The Federal army's chief engineer, Gen. Gouverneur Warren and military mapmaker E.B. Cope signed off on its accuracy, too, as did four prominent Gettysburg citizens.[258]

Colonel Bachelder, as he styled himself after getting the honorary rank as principal of the Pennsylvania Military Institute in the 1850s, was insatiable for information on the Battle of Gettysburg. Not only had he interviewed numerous soldiers and citizens immediately after the battle, he kept up the correspondence throughout his life.

Even before the war ended, he had begun collecting official reports from as many commanders as he could.[259] Naturally, most of these were from Union officers, but it was not from any lack of effort on Bachelder's part. In January 1865, for example, he requested a detailed account of the actions at Gettysburg from General McLaws, a task that became Sisyphean.[260]

In the wake of his court-martial, McLaws had taken command of the Confederate forces at Savannah. At the end of 1864, in the face of General William Tecumseh Sherman's march north (after he reached the sea in his more famous march), McLaws had been forced to retreat into South Carolina. He spent the next month strongly entrenched along the only decent crossing of a swampy run known as the Salkehatchie River. That the crossing would be surrendered was a foregone conclusion. McLaws's force was small and an entire Federal corps, fresh off the relatively bloodless victory of the famous "March to the Sea," approached the river. McLaws's job was to make the Federal crossing difficult, and he did an admirable job. The two forces sparred on February 1. McLaws's defense prompted the Federal troops to spend all day on the second building bridges in order to bypass the Confederate outpost, which they ultimately did.[261]

While McLaws had been waiting for the Federals to arrive, he received a curious letter. *Colonel* John Bachelder, a New England resident, had requested McLaws's official report and a detailed description of his division's actions at Gettysburg. While the Federal engineers worked, McLaws took the time to scribble a polite response to the northern historian's request for information.

"I have just received your letter of January 23d," McLaws wrote, "and will, at an early date, send you a report of the operations of my division; so far as relates to the position of my several brigades, and the result of their charge." Curiously, McLaws refers to *a* report, rather than *his* report, a minor point that suggests a major one. Typically, an officer who submitted a report but no longer had access to it referred to an inability to provide *his* report. That McLaws spoke of an intangible report suggests he never wrote one to begin with.[262]

Given the current situation (there was a war on, after all) McLaws did "not think it proper to give an extended account of the operations of my command" at the moment. But he hoped the brief account would be "satisfactory."[263] Nearly ten years, and at least one empty promise, later Bachelder was still waiting for McLaws's account.[264]

DUE TO THE POPULARITY OF HIS ISOMETRIC MAP AND HIS growing reputation as the foremost expert on the battle, in 1874 Bachelder received a commission from the federal government to place troop positions on an existing battlefield map. The survey had been performed between 1868 and 1869 by military engineers working under the auspices of General Gouverneur Warren. Conducted only five years after the battle, and with the assistance of local citizens who could identify houses, farms, fences, and other features from July 1863, Warren's map was considered to be the most accurate to date. The addition of Bachelder's troop placements, gleaned from innumerable interviews and letters from survivors of the battle, promised to make it invaluable.[265]

But there was a glaring problem. Bachelder had almost no information about Longstreet's Corps. This meant that there was little, if any, southern input for some of the most famous fights of the battle: the Wheatfield, Devil's Den, Little Round Top, the Peach Orchard, and of course, "Pickett's Charge." Though Bachelder had received "full and detailed reports" from the officers and men of the other two Confederate corps, he had received only unfulfilled promises from Longstreet's men. Though he had been in touch with McLaws sporadically throughout the past decade, he had not heard from him for some time. Now working on a deadline and in desperate need of information, he wrote to the Georgia general again.

"It is now more than two years since I received your polite note offering to furnish me any data in your possession regarding the movements of your command at Gettysburg," he began. "Until the present time I have not needed it," but now that Bachelder had a government deadline to meet, "I shall be glad of everything I can get." Despite the New Englander's efforts, he had not been able to cobble together much. "I am confined to a very meagre report from General Longstreet, notes of a conversation with Gen. Wofford, and notes of conversations with wounded men + officers at Gettysburg."

For one reason or another, no one in Longstreet's Corps wanted to talk about Gettysburg.[266]

A note from James Kemper, a brigade commander in Pickett's Division wounded in the famous July 3 assault, sheds some light on *why* the men were hesitant to talk. "Ninety-nine hundredths of his material is drawn from northern sources," Kemper complained about Bachelder. Since most southern accounts would be "unknown and inaccessible" to the Yankee historian, Kemper would simply become the token Confederate account, paraded as a novelty to gawking Northerners like "the captives behind the triumphal car of The Roman Imperitor [*sic*]." He must have realized he was fulfilling his own prophecy by refusing to forward his recollections. *Of course* Bachelder's history would be "drawn from northern sources": southerners were refusing to give him any information. But it seemed too soon for southerners to talk about it. "The day for the history of that battle is not yet," Kemper declared. "It will come."[267]

Ten years later, Pendleton echoed similar sentiments. The editors of *Johnson's Universal Cyclopedia* had reached out to Pendleton, among many others, asking for a short biography for their compilation, which promised to be "a universal dictionary of philosophy, history, biography, literature, law" and a host of other noble subjects. Perhaps mistakenly, they included a list of contributors, which abounded in New Yorkers, an instant turn-off for Pendleton.

The Reverend "deems it his duty," a secretary announced to Johnson's editors, "to say, that, were there no other reason for his declining to furnish the particulars asked of him," (if there *were* other reasons, he didn't say what), "he should judge it wrong, in any way to contribute to a publication so thoroughly pervaded by prejudice and truth-perversion, in the form of partizan [sic] Northernism, as he is sure this compendium must inevitably be." How could it be otherwise, given the contributors list? Pendleton "must protest against that destructive ism," he insisted: "John Brown-ism, Lincolnism, Greeleyism, Grantism, Controlism, Anti-State-ism, Anti-Bible-ism, Politico-Religio-Agitationism, Heathenized Mix-School-ism, etc. etc." Like Kemper, Pendleton would not submit his name to such a venture controlled, as it were, entirely by northern interests.[268]

Charles Venable, who had served on Lee's staff, had similar objections to a request for Lee's presence at a commemoration in Gettysburg. It was nothing but "a piece of Yankee vanity and impudence," he seethed, like the British asking French officers to visit Waterloo and mark their positions, altogether "absurd in the last degree." "Histories will fix the matter," Venable assured him. "Yankees who show people the field will always lie."[269]

Southern hesitation was understandable. As Early so adamantly declared just a year before Bachelder received his commission, southerners guarded their memories jealously. A New Hampshire landscape painter was certainly not going to be the gatekeeper.

Understandable or not, without southern input, Bachelder could only locate "general positions" based on his correspondence with Federal soldiers. Naturally, their knowledge of Confederate regimental movements was limited, gleaned only from what they saw and perhaps conversations with prisoners and other intelligence. Though it was his "honest desire to locate and describe every movement with strict historical correctness," the Confederate memory blockade made that nearly impossible. "How is it possible for me to avail myself of this knowledge without being considered partial?" he pleaded with McLaws, perhaps remembering Kemper's note.

Bachelder had been reduced to panhandling for Confederate information, for a lead…anything. He would be happy if McLaws could just provide names and addresses "of as many officers as you can think of" from *any* command. "Could I not with systematic perseverance, by means of circular letters etc gain this knowledge through intelligent officers and men who participated in the battle?"[270]

By early March of 1876, Bachelder's persistence began to show the glimmer of a payoff. He was finally able to track down several First Corps commanders, most of them from Hood's Division. General George "Tige" Anderson responded first, on March 15, and addressed both the fighting and the morning's movements.[271] Evander Law, who took command of Hood's Division when Hood was wounded, responded to Bachelder on March 16, offering to help if he could track down his reports. He had given them to an acquaintance and had not received them back —a common problem among the veterans, it seems.[272] By May, though, he had recovered them, and sent Bachelder a series of letters primarily describing his actions on July 3. Helpfully, he also designated his troop positions on the maps Bachelder had sent.[273] After years of silence, this was all very promising.

Joseph Kershaw followed suit, responding to Bachelder on March 20. He was perplexed at the utter lack of first-hand information from the leadership in Longstreet's Corps. "I am grieved and surprised to learn that no official reports of Division and Brigade commanders of the 1st Corps of the Confederate Army can be had."[274] Twelve years later, Kershaw was still shaking his head at the silence on the part of the First Corps commanders. In a letter praising McLaws for his initiative in "writing and speaking" about the battle, he wondered "what has become of Sorrel?" "Why does he not help you in these matters? Especially why does he not help poor old Gen'l Longstreet, who has been so ruthlessly and wrongfully assailed?"[275]

Perhaps due to this lack of information, the South Carolinian "deviate[d] from my usual custom of declining to enter into a discussion...of the war." Like Law, he could not locate his battle report, having given it to Federal General Samuel W. Crawford (who had charged down Little Round Top into Kershaw's troops on the evening of July 2). Crawford had forwarded a copy of the report to Edward Porter Alexander, who was working on a history of the First Corps at the time. Alexander, in turn, gave the report to the Southern Historical Society, which is how it came to be published the following year.[276]

Kershaw gave a full description of his brigade's actions, including one of the earliest and most detailed descriptions of the countermarch on record (though still thirteen years removed).[277] Perhaps more important to Bachelder, Kershaw provided contacts. He quickly put Kershaw's leads to good use. Several First Corps officers replied that spring, though only a few responses contained helpful information. Longstreet himself replied in April, but offered little help. "I regret to say that I am not prepared to meet your wishes in regard to the position of the troops of my command at Gettysburg on the second day," he recited. Instead, he referred Bachelder to McLaws (he "will no doubt be pleased to give you such information as he can"), Hood, and his old brigade commanders and told Bachelder to keep an eye out for his own articles, soon to be published.[278] It's not hard to imagine Bachelder pulling at his whiskers in frustration with the circularity of the replies.

Jerome Robertson, commanding a brigade of Texans and Arkansans in Hood's Division, responded ten days after Longstreet, providing a detailed account of his fight on July 2. Less than a month after that, Colonel Benjamin Humphreys of Mississippi wrote an in-depth description of Barksdale's Brigade during the battle. Porter Alexander followed with his own detailed recollection on May 3, and even Walter Taylor, Lee's aide-de-camp, wrote Bachelder by the end of the summer. Taylor offered little of substance, but helpfully supplied a list of Lee's staff officers.[279]

Then, as suddenly as it had started, the southern correspondence stopped. After August of 1876, the well dried up. Nothing arrived from the First Corps veterans until the middle of 1882, save a few notes from Kershaw.[280]

Bachelder seemed to have hit an impenetrable stone wall. Since no one would talk, his map could not be as precisely accurate as he had hoped, at least as far as the First Corps went. Working with limited sources, he would have to do the best he could.

* * *

Edward Porter Alexander, tasked by Longstreet with creating the official history of the First Corps, Army of Northern Virginia. The task would take longer than either of them imagined. Library of Congress.

BACHELDER WAS NOT THE ONLY ONE HAVING A HARD TIME getting information from members of Longstreet's Corps. Porter Alexander, who led one of Longstreet's artillery battalions at the battle, had been tapped by his old commanding officer in 1866 to write the definitive history of the First Corps.[281]

There was perhaps no one better suited for the task. Porter was an astute analyst and well-respected among the veterans. After the turbulence of war, Alexander accepted a position as the chair of the mathematics department at the University of South Carolina, a stable job with a steady income. It was certainly better than many former Confederates would do (the postwar letters are replete with references to financial woes).[282]

As time went on, Alexander would prove remarkably adept at ingratiating himself with both northerners and southerners alike. He was active in veterans' circles, and his letters were frequently published in the *Southern Historical Society Papers*, cementing his Confederate credentials among his Southern peers. But he was also asked to contribute to a series on the war *Century Magazine* was producing in the 1880s. The finished product, eventually published as the four-volume *Battles and Leaders of the Civil War*, included both Northern and Southern authors.

All of that was in the future, though. Alexander had a distinguished military career, beginning with his graduation from West Point (third in his class) in 1857. Appointed a second lieutenant in the U.S. Army, he helped develop a signal system, which was demonstrated before a Congressional committee that included Senator Jefferson Davis. Despite his later cosmopolitanism, Alexander was a staunch, anti-Lincoln Southern secessionist in 1861. He would later claim he was just a headstrong youth and "really never realised the gravity of the situation." He simply wanted to defend the "*right to secede*," and when the right was denied, "I strongly approved of its assertion & maintenance by force if necessary." When Lincoln won the election, and his home state of Georgia seceded, Alexander, who was stationed on the west coast, resigned his commission and found his way back home, eager to join the Confederate cause.

Jefferson Davis, reminded of the young Alexander's signal presentation a few years earlier, assigned him as a signal officer to the Confederate army then forming in northern Virginia. Immediately after the first major battle of the war along the banks of Bull Run, Alexander was appointed chief of ordnance and artillery for the army. His work training both artillerymen and signal corps officers, as well as his efforts to improve the Confederate army's ordnance, earned him a promotion to Major in April of 1862, just a few months before Robert E. Lee took command.

Lee, like most of Alexander's superior officers, was impressed by Alexander's engineering and reconnoitering abilities. Along the Virginia Peninsula, Porter Alexander became one of the first people in American history to observe the ground from a hot air balloon. Both sides experimented with the technology, which was scrapped early the following year. Alexander was impressed with the balloon, though, and couldn't fathom why the armies discontinued their use.

Alexander also caught the eye of Stonewall Jackson, who offered him command of a brigade of infantry. Alexander preferred the artillery, though, so the promotion went to John Gordon. Alexander was promoted to a full colonel in March 1863 and would wear the three stars of a southern colonel on his collar during the march to Gettysburg.[283]

Porter Alexander was optimistic about the First Corps project at first, thinking he could get all the information he needed in one summer break. He sent out questionnaires to as many First Corps officers as he could track down, requesting the number of men in the unit, officers, current addresses, where on the battlefield and how long the unit fought, what regiments were around them, what weapons they had, how many rounds they fired, and recollections of the writer. He worked systematically, sending out questionnaires for individual battles and campaigns, instructing the recipients to "Please fill one of these forms for *every Battle and Skirmish* in which your command participated during the war, as a part of Longstreet's Corps. If the command was a Brigade, state the Regiments composing it, and *their Commanders* in the action. When filled, mail to E.P. Alexander, University of South Carolina, Columbia, S.C."[284]

An example of the form Alexander forwarded to as many First Corps officers he could find while he tried to compile the official First Corps history. This one was sent to Pinckney Bowles regarding the 4th Alabama and asked for information regarding the Antietam Campaign. From the Southern Historical Collection, Wilson Library, the University of North Carolina at Chapel Hill.

Like Bachelder, the response was not what he had hoped. By the spring of 1868, Alexander thought the project futile. He vented his frustration to Longstreet's former aide, Thomas Goree, who had just replied with a "most welcome letter" overflowing with information. After "Longstreet begged me" to write the official history of the corps in 1866, Alexander figured he could get it done "in a three-month vacation." But "I have worked at it now two vacations & all the leisure I could possibly steal from my duties day by day for nearly two years & have hardly made a beginning." Like his New England counterpart, he wanted the personal memories, the stories of the men in the First Corps. But "they only exist in the memories of survivors & I have to elicit them by correspondence & you cannot imagine how utterly hopeless a task this seems," he sighed.

No one seemed to want to talk about their experiences, not even to a well-respected and bona fide Southern Confederate. "For every one hundred letters and circulars I send, I get about ten replies, & of these ten, about six simply say that they have lost all records & can't remember anything they think important enough to write," Alexander continued. "About three promises to write something they remember 'as soon as they get time' & about one sends me what I want to get or ought to get from them." He wasn't wrong. The record is filled with the responses of officers who had unfortunately just sent away their notes to someone (if only they could remember who) and though they would try to get something, they couldn't make any promises.[285]

Within three years of the Confederate surrender, former Mississippi brigadier Winfield Featherston thought "the southern people should, at least, take all necessary and proper steps to have correct and authentic histories written of the late war and especially of the part taken in it by the soldiers."[286] But most also seemed to agree with Kemper. As far as they could tell, the victors were indeed writing the history. The time for the Confederate history of the war had not arrived. It didn't help that the Confederates were still trying to sort out that history amongst themselves.

Alexander's history would not appear until 1907, forty-one years after he began. Even then, it was not because his southern comrades had been cooperative. Rather, it was only "since the publication by the War Department of the full Official Reports of both armies…that it has become possible to write this story, even approximately." Ironically, it took the United States government to provide Alexander with the necessary information to complete his Confederate history.

BACHELDER HAD WRITTEN MCLAWS AT THE END OF 1874 practically begging for information. Two more years of persistence paid off, resulting in the wellspring of the summer of 1876, but the success proved fleeting. Six years later, heading into the summer of 1882, Bachelder had no appreciably new information on Longstreet's Corps. So, he sent another circular to his First Corps connections, summoning them to attend a reunion in June. Most declined again.[287]

Colonel Wyatt Aiken, a South Carolinian in Kershaw's Brigade, did accept the offer to attend a reunion of the 140th Pennsylvania. He took it as an opportunity to revisit the field and discuss the actions of July 2 with what Bachelder supposed was one of the regiments facing Kershaw that day. Aiken explored the field with the likes of Union Generals Dan Sickles, John Brooke, and a handful of other Federal soldiers who had been at the battle. The group toured the ground they had fought over nearly twenty years earlier, engaging in lively discussion about who did what and trading war stories. "To say that it was an interesting day is but a meagre method of describing it," Wyatt enthused.

While Wyatt, Sickles, and Brooke were "investigating that memorable spot"—the Rose Farm—they quickly came to the realization that they had very different recollections. The group of veterans spent a good deal of time in the now serene fields and woods "attempting to reconcile what appear from Mr. Bachelder's map to be very conflicting maneuvers." Wyatt discovered that much of what Bachelder had attempted to reconstruct based on Union observations was quite different from what he remembered himself.[288]

Aiken also realized that perhaps Bachelder, despite his reputation as being the preeminent scholar of the battle, did *not* have all the answers, especially when it came to Confederate actions. "I asked the historian where McGowan's [South Carolina] Brigade fought? And he replied he was unable to give a satisfactory answer." McGowan fought nowhere near Aiken's men; they were in Pender's Third Corps Division and fought along Seminary Ridge on July 1. Whether Aiken knew it or not, Bachelder thought he had Hill's Corps well accounted for, so this must have come as a surprise to the New England historian.

As far as the fighting in the Rose Woods was concerned, Bachelder's map showed General Brooke's position behind a stone wall. Aiken couldn't recall fighting any northerners protected by a wall and so the group set about traipsing through the woods to find one. The search was in vain. After an earnest discussion between them, Bachelder and Brooke believed they may have been mistaken. At least, that's the way Aiken remembered it.

The trip was enlightening, if somewhat concerning. Aiken quickly realized that while Southerners were understandably reluctant to share their memories with a northern historian, it was becoming a necessity if they had any intention of contributing to its history. He had just seen firsthand how the battle was to be presented. As Bachelder had been quite honest about, his was a necessarily northern-centric history. After all, most of the willing contributors were from the Union army.

Aiken quickly penned an open letter to his old brigade commander, urging everyone that remembered the battle to speak up now before it was too late. *This* was the opportunity to have their voices heard. He published his letter in the *Charleston News and Courier* on June 21, 1882 as a clarion call to preserve the southern memory. "One of the objects of this letter is to stimulate the South to take steps to secure a full, fair and just record of the Confederate troops" at Gettysburg. "Mr. Bachelder has been very solicitous to have Southern officers and men to visit the battlefield with him," but none seemed to want to make the trip. Other papers picked up on the call and included snippets within their "miscellaneous columns."[289]

Though Bachelder was from New Hampshire, he was never-theless "untiring in his efforts to induce Southern generals, colo-nels, majors and other officers and men to visit this battlefield and give him the benefit of their experience. But he most signally failed," Aiken lamented. Because none of the men in the old First Corps shared their stories, Bachelder "consequently had to rely in many cases upon the reports of Union officers as to the location of Southern troops." Bachelder had admitted as much to Aiken. "I am flooded with information concerning the Union troops," the bewhiskered historian frowned, "but my knowledge is exceedingly limited concerning the positions or engagements of many of the Southern brigades."[290]

This was simply unacceptable to Aiken. "The people's money is to pay for [Bachelder's] history of this battle," Aiken reminded his southern friends. Whether they liked it or not, a significant sum of their tax dollars was being sent to produce the "official" history of the battle. As it stood, the southern perspective would not be included, *could not* be included.

The history (and its maps) should be "absolutely correct, and impartially given. But how can this be the case if the publication is to be made upon ex parte statements?" Former Confederates had to step forward. "If we desire to perpetuate the gallantry and courage of our Confederate troops," as Early had been advocating for the past decade, "it behooves us to send representatives from every regiment of Gen. Lee's army of Gettysburg…and see to it that [Bachelder] has as accurate description of the movements of the Confederates as he has of the Union troops during those three days of carnage and death…. [W]e need only furnish him with a correct statement of the movements of each Confederate brigade during those three days, and he will be compelled to publish a history that will indeed be a truthful narration of the facts."[291]

Like Bachelder and Porter Alexander, though, Aiken's attempts to stir First Corps memories was fruitless. In what seemed like desperation, Bachelder went back to the one quarry that reli-ably produced, hoping for any straggling information. He wrote

Joseph Kershaw shortly after Aiken's appeal, apparently asking for any information he had.

"I presume you are still at sea about McLaws," Kershaw winked. "If you will write McLaws and ask him I have no doubt he will give you a copy of his address on the Battle of Gettysburg. It is valuable, if not wholly accurate." Aiken's letter, too, was "tolerably correct." But he insisted Bachelder study his own official report, which was now available in the *Southern Historical Society Papers*, a publication Kershaw strongly suggested Bachelder look into. It was "filled with accounts of Gettysburg from high sources," and he could easily obtain copies from editor J. William Jones.

As for Kershaw's own report, "it was written soon after the event in correspondence with officers engaged and with the reports of Regimental commanders before me." The ground, the movements…all were fresh in his head at the time he wrote the report. In general, he considered the official reports the "best data" and thought his own was "accurate" as far as it went. But they were certainly not flawless.

This underscored the difficulty with memory that permeated Bachelder's entire project (and everyone else who has tried to put together a history of the battle since). "I need not say how difficult it is to speak positively and accurately after so many years," Kershaw admonished. "Few men *can* describe these matters accurately, many *will* not." Official reports may have been the best someone like Bachelder could hope for, "but even these are not always reliable, indeed are mostly not."[292]

To his credit, Bachelder persisted, publishing the third volume of his four-volume history (complete with six maps) two and a half years later in March 1885. The history was not well received. In an effort to avoid wading into major controversies, he simply reprinted the accounts and left the reader to sort it all out.[293] He remained "at sea" about a good many controversies, not least of which was the Confederate First Corps.

Spring, 1893

PORTER ALEXANDER MAY HAVE LOST MOST OF HIS HAIR and all of its color, but neither his age nor his tenure as an academic had reduced his athleticism. His "lithe figure" strode easily up the slopes of Little Round Top, even when the carriage horses gave up. Alexander marched alongside Pennsylvania's Governor Robert Pattison, a stream of Gettysburg "celebrities" trailing behind. James Longstreet and Billy Mahone remained on their horses, but most of the rest had dismounted. Even the portly and one-legged General Sickles had dismounted and hobbled up the second half of the slope on his crutches.

As the group reached the top of the famous hill, Alexander paused, then stepped out onto one of the large boulders erupting from the ridge's bare western face. Governor Pattison watched as the old Confederate took in the view for the first time. The horizon was crisp in the warm spring air, a welcome change from the cold gray drizzle from the day before. Though he had helped assault the Union position anchored on this hill thirty years earlier and had been carping about the signal station here for nearly as long, he had never actually stood on the famous crest. For Alexander, the sight was nothing short of awesome, in the oldest and truest sense of the word.

His head slowly turned from right to left, taking in the panorama of the battlefield he had once helped to orchestrate. "His eyes wide," he stared at the governor. "By George! How grand!" he said, his astonishment suppressing the exclamation into a whisper. "What a position!" A reporter asked if he had ever been to the top of Little Round Top. "Never, never," Alexander stuttered. "But I wish I had been up here on that day and they had been down there."[294]

The gathering had been organized by John Russell Young, president of Philadelphia's Union League and a Gettysburg enthusiast. In addition to Alexander, Longstreet, Sickles, and Mahone, Young had managed to convince Longstreet's staff officer Osmun Latrobe, one-armed Union General Oliver Otis Howard (and his brother and son), veteran and War Department Park commissioner John Nicholson, cavalryman Lewis Merrill, and prominent economist and journalist Henry George, to attend the gathering. Members of the Union League and a few New York friends rounded out the tourists.[295]

As they left the Springs Hotel and headed east along the Fairfield Road, one of the former Confederates quipped that the last time they were on this road, they were headed the *other* way and in a much greater hurry. The little reunion was reportedly the first time Alexander had been back to the field which had brought him so much grief.[296] It wouldn't be the last.

Alexander had made quite an impression on John Young. The following year, Young organized a smaller trip to Gettysburg for a group of New York editors and artists, along with a few of the regulars from the Union League. Alexander met the group in Philadelphia and they boarded a train for the famous little town in Adams County. They enjoyed lunch on the train and were able to immediately depart in their waiting carriages for their exclusive battlefield tour.

Alexander and Captain James Long, a noted battlefield guide and Union veteran, led the group along a tour of the first day's fight. Long pointed out the positions of both armies and explained the campaign to the guests, most of whom were here for the first time. Alexander nodded along and confirmed the guide's descriptions. After rustling through the first day's battlefield, the tourists headed back to the Springs Hotel, nestled along the banks of Willoughby Run. Alexander, meanwhile, went to Nicholson's office and "went over the Maps...having in view the location of his Battalion of Artillery upon the field." It was fully ten o'clock that night when Alexander made his way back to the Springs Hotel.[297]

The next morning, they embarked on a condensed tour of the second- and third-days' battlefields. Alexander shined as he took the reins, charming the northern bohemians with his electric narrative. Even those "more familiar with the historic scenes had their knowledge and interest quickened by the wonderfully clear explanations of General Alexander." The old artillerist and engineer was "a most charming and gallant man" and his "vivid intelligence" spellbound the guests. St. Clair McKelway, editor of the *Brooklyn Daily Eagle*, was captivated by Alexander's tour, writing up a column for the May 31

119

issue of his paper. McKelway closed out the excursion with a stirring rendition of the Gettysburg Address (if he did say so himself). Walking the fields with men who had actually struggled there and witnessed the last full measures of devotion of which Lincoln spoke "intensified" the speech's natural "force of literature."

After the short two-day trip, the journalists, artists, and Union Leaguers climbed back onto the train and steamed back east. But Alexander stayed. Twenty-two years after Jubal Early's call for Southerners to grasp their history tightly, the Confederate lines at Gettysburg remained all but unmarked, the southern stories suppressed by their own hands.[298]

Though there was no National Park Service yet, there *were* National Parks. Given the significance of the battle, an association had sprung up almost immediately. In April of 1864, the Commonwealth of Pennsylvania chartered the Gettysburg Battlefield Memorial Association (GBMA) to provide an orderly means to preserve what were considered to be important parts of the battlefield. By the late 1800s, the War Department authorized five national military parks, including Gettysburg. The transfer of property from the GBMA to the War Department was set to happen in 1895, the year after Alexander's tour with the Union League.[299]

As with Alexander's First Corps history, it was the Federal government that ultimately provided the means to begin preserving southern history on a national scale. Though its accuracy would be hampered by the limitations Alexander and Bachelder encountered, the War Department forced at least some sort of public interpretation of the battle from the Confederate perspective. Commissioner John Nicholson, and possibly cartographer E.B. Cope, perused battlefield maps with Alexander, which resulted in a report to the War Department later that year.[300]

It would take a few more years, but by the end of 1898, Iron plaques marking Confederate positions dotted the fields along the tourist avenues and the park was "much gratified to notice an awakening of interest in influential quarters among the people of the Southern States concerning this battlefield and the importance of erecting monuments to commemorate the heroism of their soldiers here." Indeed, the primary difficulty *now* was obtaining the land that Confederate positions sat on, as most of it was still privately owned.[301] Though not the only one, Porter Alexander had played an important role in preserving one aspect of Confederate memory to the best of his ability. But Alexander's advice was only as good as the information he gathered from his former Confederates.

In a way, it had all come full circle. In 1872, Jubal Early had declared the South would "take charge of the history of the war on our side." Indeed, they had. And by casting the "brand of Cain upon" those who dissented from the approved history, who "proved renegade to their comrades," that history was strictly enforced. Like Kemper knew early on, there would be a time and a place for the history of the South to be shared with the world. Thirty-five years after the battle, it seemed that time was starting to come.[302]

LIKE THE PROVERBIAL FISHERMAN'S TALE, THE IMPORTANCE of the July 2 countermarch grew with each retelling. Not until Early and Pendleton blamed Longstreet's tardiness for the downfall of the Confederacy did the march occupy much more than a sentence or two. The countermarch was only briefly mentioned in the reports from Kershaw's brigade. Longstreet himself spent precisely one sentence on the subject. Pendleton did note a delay caused by the turnaround and characteristically offered that he and his staff were "dispatched to remedy, as far as practicable, the delay."

But the timing of the July 2 attack was far from a devastating blow to the Confederates. In fact, Pendleton acknowledged in his report that the only real success of the day was by the First Corps on the Federal left. Even Robert E. Lee, who was agitated at Longstreet's delay on July 3, failed to note any irritation with his War Horse on July 2.[303]

The reason for this is simultaneously simple and complex. Fundamentally, the countermarch legend was merely a defense mechanism against the attacks of Early and Pendleton. But the reason for the accusations against Longstreet are much more complicated. As humans have done even before recorded history, Early began the process of spinning a mythology tale to explain the unexplainable. If Lee was invincible, then there had to be another explanation for the loss. This explanation involved both the tragic hero and the villain. Lee was of course the tragic hero, since he knew from the beginning success was impossible but fought honorably against impossible odds. The villain was Longstreet.

The myth quickly took on religious overtones. Lee was apotheosized and granted a "holy halo." Longstreet became the South's Lucifer. The right hand of Lee throughout the bitter struggle of the war, he ultimately fell from grace when he betrayed Lee after the war in a spiteful attempt to steal his glory. The Fallen Confederate was responsible for all the evils they were now suffering. Lee had been the light; evil and imperfection were incapable of emanating from him. Longstreet, by his selfish betrayal at Gettysburg, became the fountainhead for the South's suffering. So it was that Stuart and Ewell (whom Lee was personally on record as blaming) received a small swat on the hand, while Longstreet's perceived delay on July 2 became apocalyptic.[304]

But if Early and Pendleton were wrong—if the timing of Longstreet's attack on July 2 was *not* caused by biblical betrayal or was not the death knell of the Confederacy—then Longstreet and his corps were blameless. As we saw, the First Corps commanders did not attack the premise of the argument, accepting the charge that the attack *did* start later than expected. Instead, McLaws utilized a preemptive strike, seeing that he was in the line of fire from two potential attacks (one from Longstreet and a corresponding one from Early and Pendleton).

McLaws's 1873 letter was well positioned to fend off both attacks. By admitting that the delay existed, but was only due to the countermarch, he exonerated Longstreet, ensuring Longstreet would not attack him in turn. But by admitting there was a delay, he accepted Early's and Pendleton's premise that the battle was lost on July 2. And so, the reason for the delay had to lie outside the First Corps.

The blame was deflected back to headquarters in the form of Sam Johnston, Lee's engineer. Better yet, the only way the attack went off at all was because McLaws happened to know the way, thanks to his morning reconnaissance. At least, according to McLaws. His letter to Longstreet and the *New Orleans Republican* was perhaps his best defensive performance to date. Not only would he create the foundation of the countermarch story for over a century and a half, he would entirely salvage his reputation for posterity.

Longstreet eventually weighed in with his own story, which prompted McLaws to offer a more detailed account (his speech published in the 1879 *Southern Historical Society Papers*). Then a response from Early's crowd, and so on and so forth. As the debate ricocheted among the former commanders, the countermarch's legacy grew from a slight inconvenience meriting brief mention in the official reports to the primary reason the South lost the war and their independence.

By the 1880s, like any great fisherman's tale, the fish had grown to monstrous proportions. The level of detail in each retelling grew as the memories faded; the further from the event, the more minutiae could somehow be recalled. This was no accident, but neither was it lying. Human memory can be disturbingly malleable and subject to a whole host of influences. The stark silence from former Confederates in the years after the war meant that historians like Bachelder and Alexander had little to work with. The few accounts available set the foundation for all the later stories. Memories of an event that did not seem to be all that important at the time became infiltrated; the natural gaps in veterans' recollections were filled in by what they had heard from others, their brains often telling them that they had, in fact, experienced those things. Others' memories fused with their own, and the process occurred exponentially. Eventually, the veterans truly remembered things they had not experienced. They weren't lying. But they *were* wrong.

EVENTS, EVEN MONUMENTAL ONES LIKE THE BATTLE OF Gettysburg, don't unfold according to a narrative. The narrative is created after the fact in order for us to make sense of the chaos. We look for patterns, themes, chronology, causes, and effects to organize events into a story that makes it easy (or at least easi*er*) for us to follow along.

But there aren't always patterns or readily discernible causes for events. Often, several things contribute to one effect, which in turn causes another set of possibilities, and so on. But the human mind craves logic, order, categorization, and continuity. Thus, the narrative is created and, like memory, the gaps are filled in with things that make sense, whether they are true or not.[305]

So, the answers to the countermarch, or any part of the series of July 2 attacks, are not easily or definitively yanked out of the tangle of accounts. There is no single thread to unravel the knot and no "black box" with all of the answers to be found. Instead, the answers come as pieces to a jigsaw puzzle. Unfortunately, we don't have many of the pieces, for a variety of reasons. The best we can do with a historical puzzle like the countermarch is to gather as much of the evidence as we can before trying to piece it back together, without a preconceived notion of what the answer is.

Casualties are a big part of the problem; the people who saw and knew the most about the events often didn't survive to tell us what happened. Hood was seriously wounded shortly after the battle started and his replacement, Evander Law, may or may not have written a report. If he did, it didn't survive (or at least hasn't been discovered yet).[306] Two of McLaws's four brigade commanders were mortally wounded on July 2. No reports exist from *their* replacements, either. Only Kershaw's report is known to exist. And only one regimental report seems to have survived, giving us a total of three reports—Longstreet's, Kershaw's, and Major Maffett's—pertaining to McLaws's Division.[307] Two mention a countermarch (Kershaw and Maffett) and Longstreet mentions a delay due to taking a road allowing them to be seen. A total of five official sentences are expended on McLaws's march into position on July 2, three of which come from Kershaw.[xiii]

Other reports may well have been written and lost (many Confederate records were destroyed with the collapse of Richmond). It's also quite possible they were never written in the first place. Longstreet submitted his official report on July 27, a mere three weeks after the battle, before anyone in his command submitted a report to him. The standard procedure for submitting a post-battle report was that the regimental commanders handed in reports to the brigade commander, who then used those to draft his own report to the division commander, who in turn wrote a summary based on the brigadiers' reports. But the regimental reports weren't even tendered by the time Longstreet's staff completed the report for the entire corps. Only Pickett is known to have even submitted one, though it was famously rejected and has not survived, much to the chagrin of more than one historian.[308]

Aside from missing an unknown number of pieces to the puzzle, the evidence we *do* have is far from perfect. The recollections we have to work with are often more concerned with the preservation of the narrator's own reputation or the destruction of someone else's than they are with leaving a true, unbiased account for posterity. They were, after all, human. The purpose of the majority of primary sources was to tell *their* version of the story, which of course is all they could know firsthand. Most of the time they believed their stories were true; they often admitted when they were uncertain of things. But they were not objective historians (if there is such a thing). We should not expect them to be.

What we are left with is the scattered debris from the postwar battle for memory and reputation. The fights often seem petty, especially from the detached view of history. But it was not about simple politics. The cause of this written war was about maintaining some semblance of control and grasping onto a strand of normalcy after

---

xiii   Pendleton reported that Longstreet had to take an alternate route, but wasn't part of the First Corps' march and didn't witness the countermarch firsthand. O.R. 27.2: 350.

the foundation of Southern culture had been utterly demolished. Whether leveling the Southern economy, culture, social hierarchy, and politics was ultimately a good thing or not is beside our point. Resetting a culture is not something that is done quickly, easily, or without resistance. Right or wrong, it would be unreasonable to expect the South to have simply admitted defeat, picked itself up, and carried on.

The war was devastating to the country as a whole, but especially to the South. After so much hardship, the people who fought it and suffered through it argued deeply and passionately about what the war's sacrifices meant. Northerners could attempt to ease their losses with the comfort of ultimate victory. Both the unionists and abolitionists got what they wanted, though the cost was unspeakably high.

The South did not have that luxury. The fierce, personal, and very public struggles for the meaning of the war were the result. *Why* had they fought so long and so hard, sacrificed their homes, livelihoods, culture, and a tragically large number of their youth, now lying beneath Southern clay in row upon eternal row of glimmering tombstones? The dialogue was difficult and intensely personal for the South. There was never really a chance that the debate would be anything other than loud and passionate.

It is directly out of this conversation that we get the primary documentation of the countermarch (and from that, Johnston's morning reconnaissance). In a way, the enigma of the countermarch is a microcosm of the war. There are quite literally two opposite memories of the event and diametrically opposed interpretations of its meaning. The resolution, in the form of McLaws's story, tried fusing the pillars of the opposing viewpoints. The story was enough to satisfy both the "knights of the quill," as Longstreet described the *Southern Historical Society Papers* crowd, as well as the First Corps leadership.

In a sense, it was fitting that McLaws would be the one to create the standard and accepted version of the story. He was neither a Virginian nor endeared to the First Corps. Despite its obvious flaws, both sides seem to have been able to accept his story without conceding any ground to the other. Kershaw seemed to be saying as much when he told Bachelder that it was "valuable, if not wholly accurate." So it is with so many of the veterans' stories. They all offer something and none offers everything. By following Kershaw's advice to sift through the accounts we can separate the flakes and nuggets of gold from each account.

With all of this in mind, we can begin to reconstruct the morning of July 2, 1863. The result presents a picture of the battle very different from the ones we've seen so far. But this picture also removes the familiar players from rigid characters in a historical drama. There are no heroes or villains, no protagonists. There is no narrative to drive. Instead, the story of the countermarch is fundamentally the story of real people reacting to real events, both along the ridges of Adams County and in the battle for its memory.

PART TWO

1863

JULY 1

*"Every effort was made to ascertain the numbers and
position of the enemy, and find the most favorable point
of attack."*

**- Robert E. Lee, Report of the Battle of Gettysburg,
July 31, 1863**[309]

THE DEEP, ANGRY GROWL OF THE ARTILLERY GREW LOUDER,
each shot becoming more distinct as they trotted toward the battlefield. Pendleton rode alongside Lee as the pair traveled east over the
crushed stones and mud of the Chambersburg Pike.

They had started the morning on the west side of the mountains, not far from Congressman Thaddeus Stevens's Caledonia Iron
Furnace.[310] At least, the remnants of it. Early's men had burned
the furnace when they passed through the mountains just five days
earlier, one of the few examples of retributive justice against northern
civilian property sanctioned by the Confederate army that summer.
But Thaddeus Stevens was an ardent abolitionist and a leading
Radical Republican, so the exception had been gleefully made.[311]

Lee was not in a particular hurry as he wound through the
mountain pass. He was well aware that an entire division of General
A.P. Hill's Third Corps, already across the mountains, had marched
east toward Gettysburg to investigate conflicting reports of Federal

131

troops there. The day before, a brigade from Hill's Corps had marched to Gettysburg to reconnoiter and gather supplies. They returned mostly empty-handed. The brigade commander reported the presence of Federal cavalry and had turned back before they entered the town, rather than get caught in a fight.

No one at headquarters was convinced that it was Federal cavalry, but Hill decided to send a full division into Gettysburg and investigate the next morning. Thus, the flattened *thuds* that occasionally punched the air in the mountain pass were not alarming…at first. "It might be only a passing skirmish," Pendleton thought. Then again, "it might be more serious." So, through the mountains they went.

But by the time Lee and his entourage emerged at the Cashtown pass, the rumblings seemed to be intensifying. That was worrisome. Lee "moved rapidly forward," Pendleton and the headquarters staff trailing behind. It seemed something "more serious" was, indeed, going on and Lee needed to find out what.[312]

PENDLETON THOUGHT IT "WAS, PERHAPS, TWO O'CLOCK" when they started up a steep ridge crowned with two thundering battalions of Confederate artillery. "Perhaps" should be emphasized. Based on what Pendleton described, it was probably closer to one o'clock that afternoon.[313]

The ridge, one of many "which form the peculiar feature of the country round Gettysburg," was known as Herr's Ridge for the owner of the tavern perched on top.[314] The slope masked their ability to see much as they approached, but the crackling musketry, excited shouts of men in combat, and rising gray smoke revealed what was happening on the other side. Leaving their horses with the staff officers tucked safely away on the western side of the ridge, Pendleton and Lee made their way up the hill.[xiv, 315]

---

xiv   Pendleton's movements are illustrated on the map on page 135. Herr's Ridge is Point 1.

Landscapes change through the years as erosion gnaws at the soil, new trees sprout, and human development alters elevations and sightlines. A visitor to Gettysburg today will not see what Lee and Pendleton saw. The modern visitor would find themselves several feet lower than Lee and Pendleton with a farm complex and quite a few more trees blocking the panorama.

Pendleton's view from Herr's Ridge, on the other hand, offered several critical feet of elevation and was impeded only by the Confederate artillery that was "posted in front of our lookout," methodically blasting away at the Yankee troops before them. Through squinted eyes and field glasses, Pendleton watched the fight "raging with considerable violence" below.[316]

The battle was unfurling over otherwise scenic pastures and rows of crops, the focus being the Federal line extending north along the spine of another ridge (two ridges east of Herr's). This one was called Seminary Ridge for the immaculate brick red seminary building regally watching over the fields below. Between Herr's Ridge and Seminary Ridge was yet another ridge (this one known as McPherson's Ridge, since a part of it was owned by Congressman Edward McPherson).

A crop of Federals had clung to a foothold on McPherson's Ridge, attracting the attention of nearly all the Confederate cannon. Lee and Pendleton were witnessing the attempt of these Yankees to squirm out of the precarious position, while the Confederates tried to dislodge the rest of the Federals from their line on Seminary Ridge. "Observing the course of events," Pendleton reported, "the commanding general suggested whether positions on the right could not be found to enfilade the valley between our position and the town and the enemy's batteries next [to] the town." Lee tapped Pendleton to find a position to launch shells into the left flank of the Federal line on Seminary Ridge.[xv],[317]

Herr's Ridge rippled roughly north and south, curling to the southeast the further it went. A mile south of the Herr Tavern sat

---

xv   Cross-referencing what Pendleton says he did with what his aides said *they* did, references to Pendleton would be best read as "Pendleton or his staff."

another inn, the Black Horse Tavern. Owned and operated by Francis Bream for over twenty years by the time the armies showed up, it hugged the banks of Marsh Creek where the creek and the Fairfield Road met. A towering, bare hill bore Bream's name; its shadows cast not only upon the tavern but would ultimately shroud the memories of some very important Confederates who, on July 1, had no idea it even existed.[318]

Pendleton's mission didn't take him quite that far, though. He headed south with his aide Lieutenant George Peterkin and Sam Johnston, probably along the Herr's Ridge Road, a byway that would be log-jammed the next morning but for now was empty. A number of farm lanes peered out from the woods to join Herr's Ridge Road. Pendleton likely veered off into the woods to his left along one of these lanes, for he soon reached a point "where the Fairfield road crosses one range of hills" along Willoughby Run. There, Pendleton found "some guns that had been sent for from McIntosh's battalion… under Capt. [Marmaduke] Johnson."[xvi] They had moved up from their position near Bream's Hill, unlimbering on the high ground between Herr's and McPherson's Ridges, but had no opportunity to fire. The Confederate infantry were closing fast on the Yankees holding onto Seminary Ridge, and it's likely their shells would have fallen among their own troops, as well.[319] So they remained silent.

From Pendleton's perspective, this was "the farthest to the right admissible, as there was no infantry support near." The majority of the infantry had advanced as part of Heth's effort to shove the Federals off Seminary Ridge. For a time, there had been a line of skirmishers where Pendleton now sat astride his horse, but they, too, had moved forward with the main assault. For the moment, Pendleton, Johnson, and his artillerymen were the end of the Army of Northern Virginia's line.

As if to emphasize that point, "a wooded height a few hundred yards beyond seemed occupied by the enemy."[xvii] The Eighth Illinois Cavalry, part of the force Hill's Corps had run up against that morning, had since been posted on the Federal left to protect the

---

xvi   Point 2 on the map.
xvii   Point 3 on the map.

flank. The line of Confederate skirmishers that had recently advanced had in fact been sent to guard against just this threat. The Illinois cavalry's line had been anything but static, making it difficult to determine exactly where they were when Pendleton reached the road. But there's little question they were in the vicinity.

The cavalrymen probably weren't in the woods, though from Pendleton's angle it may well have seemed the line extended that far. The point mattered little to Parson Pendleton, though; he had no intention of finding out just how many Federals were there or what they were up to. His job was to see if he could bring artillery farther to the right to fire down the Yankee line. The troops in front of him blocked his path and effectively ended his search for the enfilade position.[320]

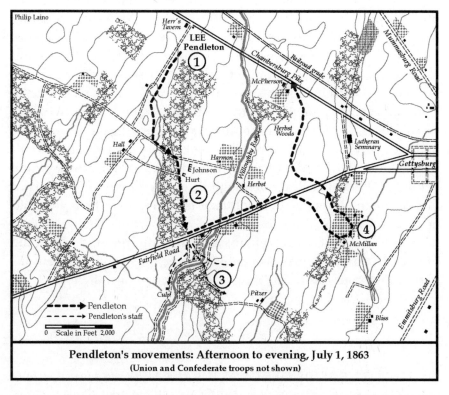

Pendleton's movements: Afternoon to evening, July 1, 1863
(Union and Confederate troops not shown)

Pendleton's reconnaissance on the afternoon of July 1, 1863. Map by Philip Laino.

While Pendleton was off to the right, "the enemy yielded ground on the left." The Confederate infantry swept up into the town, chasing the Federals onto the large open plateau south of Gettysburg, called Cemetery Hill. The Confederates had won the day, crushing two corps of Federal infantry.

But they had also driven the Army of the Potomac into a sort of Gibraltar. Even now, as the blue-clad infantry scrambled through the town, the Federal artillery was creaking into position, ringing the hill with barrels glaring down at the Confederate pursuers. Moving the Yankees from their new position would require delicate planning. That meant thoroughly reconnoitering the new Federal position, repositioning troops, and coordinating the attack among the corps commanders that evening.

For Pendleton, it meant supervising the artillery chiefs as they brought up their guns from the afternoon positions and scouting out new positions. With Seminary Ridge cleared of Federal troops, he busied himself observing the placements of Third and Second Corps guns, all in the shadow of the Lutheran Seminary.

The wooded height was now free of cavalry and accessible to Confederates. Pendleton found it offered extensive views of the surrounding area (though modern views are again deceptively limited). Perched on what would become one of the more important hills the next day, Pendleton noted a road winding along the tree line behind McPherson's Ridge. Though he granted himself undeserved prescience in his report, Pendleton certainly realized the road could be a useful means of moving artillery to the right. That had been the whole point of his reconnaissance that afternoon. Perhaps the sought-after artillery platform could now be discovered. He sent his staff out to scout this ravine road and headed toward the town.[321]

ON THE OTHER SIDE OF TOWN, JUBAL EARLY WAS PREPARING for action, at least as *he* told it. While Pendleton had been looking for the enfilade position, Early's Division had helped sweep the

Federal right wing off a small knoll north of Gettysburg, driving the Yankees into the town. Though they captured a host of prisoners in the process, occupying the town began to feel like more of a burden than it was worth. The number of Federal prisoners was "so great as really to embarrass us," Early reported after the battle.[322]

Moving through the town proved difficult, too. From a bird's eye view, the town seemed to be a relatively simple gridded layout. But the view was quite different from the ground. Alleyways abruptly turned into dead ends that gave the term a gruesomely literal meaning. Fences marked off small grazing plots for farm animals and family vegetable gardens, slowing down both the fleeing Yankees and their Southern pursuers. Linear combat formations were not well suited for this sort of fighting, so keeping order was difficult.

In the center of town, the streets converged into a square, sometimes more prestigiously referred to as the Diamond. Until recently, the Diamond had hosted the county courthouse. But a new one, the pride of the town, had recently been completed on Baltimore Street and the old courthouse had been razed. Now, the square was empty, save for muddy wagon ruts crisscrossing in every direction...and a mass of confused soldiers.[323]

By the time Early trotted into the streets, the fighting had pushed through the town to Cemetery Hill. But the town was still an active combat zone. Sharpshooters took advantage of numerous second- and third-story roosts. "There were some sharp-shooters in the upper end of the place, firing on us apparently from the houses and now and then hitting somebody," Ewell's staff officer and son-in-law Campbell Brown remembered. Even an occasional artillery shell found its way into the town proper. Federal soldiers hid in any conceivable hiding spot—basements, attics, chimneys, haystacks, woodpiles—desperate to avoid a trip to the dreaded Southern prisons (Southerners didn't fare well in Northern prisons, either). Though many were just trying to avoid capture, enough were still intent on fighting to make the streets of Gettysburg a very dangerous place that afternoon.[324]

Meanwhile, one of Early's brigade commanders, Colonel Isaac Avery, had managed to slip out the east side of the town with his North Carolinians to prepare for an attack on Cemetery Hill. It proved a bad idea. The Federal infantry may have been disorganized, but Avery quickly discovered that the artillery was not. The hill snarled at the Confederates below, baring the iron artillery barrels like the teeth of a cornered dog. Seeing the fresh gray targets, they unleashed a barrage into Avery's men until he managed to find "the cover of a low ridge which…runs through the fields from the town." The message that Cemetery Hill was not to be trifled with rang loud and clear, and his men hunkered down for the evening. At the same time, General Harry Hays, who had joined Avery in pursuing the Federals into town, formed his Louisiana "Tigers" into battle line in the streets and detailed parties to continue mopping things up in town.[325]

ROBERT E. LEE HAD WATCHED THE COLLAPSE OF THE FEDeral line from Herr's Ridge. As the remnants tumbled back to Cemetery Hill, Lee wanted to keep the pressure on. Turning to his staff officer Major Walter Taylor, he gave him a message for Ewell: "It was only necessary to press 'those people' in order to secure possession of the heights," south of the town. "If possible, he wished [Ewell] to do this." [326] Not pausing to jot down the directive, Taylor raced north of town to deliver it to Ewell.

WHILE HIS STAFF INVESTIGATED THE RAVINE ROAD, PENDleton rode along Seminary Ridge to supervise the Third Corps gun placements. Garnett's artillery battalion, which had gotten into the action at the end of the fight, moved up to the seminary and parked, waiting for orders. Another battalion, Poague's, moved to the right of Garnett. In order to unlimber the battalions and place them in line, Pendleton needed to find a patch of ground roughly 600 yards long and over thirty yards deep.[327]

Searching for a suitable platform, he followed the Fairfield Road east toward the town. He hadn't gone far when he bumped into General Stephen Ramseur, one of Rodes's brigadiers. Like Pendleton, Ramseur was looking to get his men into position for the evening, and he asked Pendleton not to open fire with Garnett or Poague; his men were settling in nearby and Confederate fire would invite a Federal reply. Since there wasn't going to be an attack, the artillery duel would be pointless and only cause shells to drop in on his men, killing them needlessly. Pendleton agreed and parked Garnett and Poague behind the ridge.[328]

Pendleton and a member of his staff (probably Lieutenant George Peterkin) continued to examine the ridge, probably just far enough to reach the apple trees of David McMillan's family orchard.[xviii] The ridge at that point offered a view of the open, sloping ground south of Cemetery Ridge and was high enough to face off against the batteries on Cemetery Hill. Satisfied that the ridge offered a suitable artillery position for Garnett's battalion, Pendleton notified Walker and headed back across the field to where he had left Lee on Herr's Ridge.[329]

EWELL AND EARLY CANTERED THROUGH TOWN TO DETERmine how best to attack Cemetery Hill. A brief reconnaissance of the ground and the new Federal line convinced Ewell that an attack was possible, but his men would need help. From his position in the town, he "could not bring artillery to bear on" Cemetery Hill. He also reported that his men were "jaded by twelve hours' marching and fighting." They weren't in any condition to storm the heights. Not alone, anyway.[330]

During their recon, Ewell and Early *had* noticed an "eminence in front of our right" that would "command" Cemetery Hill. The "eminence" must have been Cemetery Ridge, which certainly was advantageous in attacking its namesake hill, if not quite "commanding" it. That was on the other side of the town, though, and would require

---

xviii   Point 4 on the map.

coordination with A.P. Hill's Third Corps. If the remnants of both corps attacked simultaneously, they might be able to squeeze the Federals out of their position on the hill. A message was sent to Lee asking him to order the coordinated assault.[331]

JAMES POWER SMITH WAS NOMINATED FOR THE TASK OF taking the message to Lee, and he galloped off through the town and out the Chambersburg Pike where he had left him. But Lee wasn't there. Looking around, Smith noticed "a road toward the south—I then learned that Gen. Lee and staff had passed that way." So, Smith trotted along that road for a mile or so until "at some woodland on my right," he found "couriers with Gen. Lee's horse—and asking for him, was told that Lee and Longstreet were down in the field to my left." Smith climbed off his horse and headed down the slope on foot until he "found Lee and Longstreet at a fence in the valley—or down the slope—observing with a glass the movement on the hill before them."

The two generals were probably in the vicinity of McMillan's house when Smith found him. Bachelder's isometric map, the one he sketched out during his three-month fact-finding visit in 1863, shows a road running along Seminary Ridge. The road intersects the Chambersburg Pike at the widow Mary Thompson's quaint stone house, since known as "Lee's Headquarters." Nearly a mile south of that, the road intersects the Fairfield Road near the Shultz and McMillan residences. Though the road ends there, a rider continuing along the ridge in the same direction would pass a woodlot to the right (and of course Smith would be able to see the couriers holding the horses about a half mile in front of him). An observer standing by these woods, known as McMillan's Woods, is facing directly opposite Cemetery Hill and, not coincidentally, the area became the southernmost artillery platform of the Confederate army that night.

On foot as he approached Lee and Longstreet, Smith relayed Ewell's question: *would Lee order A.P. Hill's Corps to assist in a coordinated assault on Cemetery Hill this evening?* Lee appeared to mull the idea over for some time; the initiative was with the South today, and he hated giving it up. But the view through the field glass showed the Federals had already turned the hill into a formidable defensive position. The broad, open hill was ringed with the angry mouths of Federal artillery, and the infantry had rallied, posting themselves along the fences and stone walls crisscrossing the hill.[332]

As Smith remembered it, Lee handed him the glass and pointed across the field toward Cemetery Ridge. "I think this is the eminence of which Gen[eral]s Early and Rodes speak as commanding the Cemetery Hill," he said, pointing the glass toward the rise of ground at Ziegler's Grove. "Gen. Longstreet and I have just been examining it and find that some of the enemy's forces are already there." Though Lee was hesitant to let the initiative die, "Gen. Longstreet's people are not up yet, and I have no troops to advance on this point." He then gave the order to Smith: "I will direct Gen. A.P. Hill to support Gen. Ewell—tell Gen. Ewell he must do in his front what seems best, taking Cemetery Hill if he can, and I will do all we can to help him."[333]

The eminence Ewell spoke of was most likely Cemetery Ridge and Zeigler's Grove. The view here is from McMillan's Hill, where James Power Smith found Lee and Longstreet examining the Federal position on the evening of July 1. The Confederate view wouldn't have been obstructed by the development or trees appearing in the modern view. The sloping ground and ultimate elevation of the "eminence" is apparent here. Author photograph.

Cemetery Hill and the eminence commanding it, as seen just after the battle from Seminary Ridge. Library of Congress.

Looking south toward the Round Tops from McMillan's Hill. There is no other "eminence" that would "command" Cemetery Hill between Ziegler's Grove and the Round Tops. Even the Peach Orchard does not appear as "commanding" from this vantage point. Author photograph.

Smith took the message back to Ewell, who was still in the town. The message was nothing if not noncommittal. Though Lee had directed Hill to support, his corps "had halted a mile further away & showed no signs of moving." Rodes's Division had been "pretty well used up," while Early only had two brigades to call on. Ewell's remaining division, commanded by General Edward "Allegheny" Johnson, was only just arriving and would be some time getting into position. Meanwhile, daylight was quickly ticking away.[334] Any attack on the hill from Ewell's direction *had* to be supported, but there simply wasn't anyone in a position to help.

With only two brigades ready for an attack, no support, the light fading quickly, and no real idea if Federal reinforcements were in the vicinity, discretion made a very good case for being the better part of valor. There would be no attack on Cemetery Hill that night. The initiative would have to be followed up in the morning.

A modern view of McMillan's Hill and a part of the extensive orchard, as seen from the direction J.P. Smith approached Lee and Longstreet on the evening of July 1, 1863. Author photo.

BACK IN THE TOWN, A BREATHLESS MESSENGER ARRIVED FOR Early. General William "Extra Billy" Smith's son had galloped into town to deliver the horrifying news that a large force of Yankees was bearing down on them. They would soon be in the rear of the army!

"I don't much believe in this" report, Early sighed to Ewell, "but prefer to suspend my movements until I can send and inquire into it." He may not have had any faith in the reports, but he couldn't ignore them. Ewell agreed and told Early he would try to coordinate directly with Hill for the contemplated attack. Though Ewell and Hill had battered the two corps they had faced that day, there were still five Union army corps unaccounted for. So, he sent two lieutenants, Tom Turner and Robert Early (Jubal's nephew), to investigate.[335]

Early had been having problems getting Smith into position all afternoon. After his first order for Smith to cover the left flank, Smith had replied that he couldn't: Yankees were advancing on the York Road. Early ordered him to go anyway. When Smith's exasperated son reported additional Federal troops near the York Road, Early, with a discernible grumble, sent Gordon "with his brigade to take charge of Smith's also," with orders to "keep a lookout on the York road, and stop any further alarm." With that, 1,600 men went off to block a threat that no one quite believed was there. But with no available cavalry to send to the flanks, *someone* had to check it out. The result was that Early was left with only two of his four brigades for any attack on the very real Federals on Cemetery Hill.[336]

THE RAVINE ROAD RUNNING ALONG WILLOUGHBY RUN, directly behind and parallel to the developing Confederate line, intrigued Pendleton. At least in retrospect, he thought it could "be important toward a flank movement against the enemy in his new position."[337] This may have been a self-serving act of prescience discovered through the clear lens of hindsight, but there's no doubt he thought it deserved a more thorough look on the evening of July 1.

Pendleton's claim of foresight is not entirely unwarranted, though. He had spent the afternoon and early evening looking for artillery positions on the right of the Confederate line. While there's no indication Pendleton met with Lee since he left him on Herr's Ridge that afternoon, Pendleton wasn't wrong in assuming Lee was looking to move reinforcements to the Confederate right. Though he couldn't have foreseen the importance the road would play the next day, Pendleton and his staff would become intimately familiar with it within the next twelve hours.

AS DUSK DRIFTED INTO DARKNESS, MAJOR CHARLES MARSH-all rode toward Ewell with a much more difficult decision than whether to attack Cemetery Hill without support. There was no question whether an attack was feasible on Cemetery Hill that evening: it wasn't. As Armistead Long concluded after scouting the area himself, "an attack at that time…would have been hazardous and of very doubtful success." Lee agreed.[338]

Since James Power Smith had met Lee and Longstreet on Seminary Ridge that evening, the commanding general had come to the conclusion that an attack on the south side of Cemetery Hill was the only acceptable approach. The slope was gradual and open, rather than steep and cluttered like the eastern face. So, unless Ewell's position east of the town could still offer some benefit, the Second Corps was to swing around to the south side of Gettysburg to assist in the next day's attack along the gentler avenue of approach.[339]

In town, Marshall ran into Harry Gilmor, a cavalryman assigned to Ewell's Corps who would act as the provost marshal for the next few days. Rather than grope through the unfamiliar darkness searching for Ewell, Major Marshall asked Gilmor to lead the way. The cavalryman took Marshall to the Second Corps commander, where he sat with Rodes and several other officers in town. Lieutenants Turner and Early hovered nearby, having recently returned from the Confederate left. Marshall delivered his message to Ewell and his commanders: *unless the position east of town could "be used to advantage," move back to the Confederate right.*[340]

Ewell was quiet for a moment, mulling it over. "It was an important matter," he told Marshall. He wouldn't be able to give him an immediate answer. The message was not a direct order and left much room for discretion. *Could* the position be "used to advantage?" He and Rodes began to discuss the issue when Early rode up. Ewell relayed Lee's message to Old Jube, who didn't have to weigh any issues at all. His answer: *attack!* And do it now. As Lieutenant Turner remembered it, Early promised Ewell that "if you do not go up there tonight, it will cost you 10,000 lives to get up there tomorrow."[341]

But Early didn't command the corps and the consequences wouldn't rest with him. Reports of Federals on the left flank, dubious or not, had to be considered. Lee had taken the option of attacking off the table, in any event. An attack from the south the next day would save his men the dreadful prospect of storming the heights. Even now, in the heavy glow of the Pennsylvania moonlight, it was evident that the Federals had backed into a daunting position. Lee's staff, Rodes, and Ewell had all come to the conclusion that an attack up the eastern face of Cemetery Hill would *not* be to the army's advantage.

But there was one very promising aspect to Ewell's position. About the same time J.P. Smith had galloped off in search of Lee with the request for support, Lieutenants Turner and Early had been scouting Culp's Hill, the wooded hill *next to* Cemetery Hill. They reported that Culp's Hill was completely empty. Though hesitant to attack *Cemetery* Hill, Ewell was intrigued by the possibility of moving Johnson's fresh division onto *Culp's* Hill. A large Confederate presence there could force the Federals off Cemetery Hill without a shot. *That* was a decided advantage.[342]

After speaking with Early and Rodes, Ewell decided that he *could* use his corps to advantage where it was. He issued orders to General Allegheny Johnson to put his division on the wooded hill and rode to Lee's headquarters to explain it all in person.[343]

July 1

✳ ✳ ✳

THE FIRST OF JULY HAD BEEN A FRUSTRATING DAY FOR Lafayette McLaws. He and his men had spent all morning and most of the afternoon "ranged alongside" the Chambersburg Pike. The whole division had waited just outside Fayetteville, Pennsylvania, which sat in the lap of the Blue Ridge Mountains on the west side of the pass, eager to cross into another of Pennsylvania's lush valleys. On the road at eight o'clock that morning, they were ordered to stand aside while Allegheny Johnson's Division strode past.

As the tail end of the column began to pass, McLaws rode to the sharp-eyed and immaculately bearded Major John Fairfax, of Longstreet's staff. McLaws wanted to know if he was supposed to follow the infantry or wait for Johnson's wagon train to pass before stepping off. Fairfax wasn't sure, but he galloped off to find out. He quickly returned with instructions for McLaws to sit tight. They would march behind the wagons. McLaws and his men would have nothing to do but sit beside the road and watch as the wagons shook past, disappearing into the mountain pass like ants marching to the top of the hill.

Eventually the last wagon waddled by, and by 4:00 p.m., the South Carolinians, Georgians, and Mississippians of McLaws's Division were able to tip their rifles over their shoulders and stretch their legs. As the men "rose the hills between our camp of the morning and Gettysburg, we heard distinctly the sound of cannon, and a cheer went from the column." They "quickened their pace to the music of the guns," knowing a fight lay just ahead.[344]

But the men of McLaws's Division would have to wait until the next day to join the ball.[xix] The sun dipped behind them as the head of the column wound through the mountain pass, quickly covering them in the glow of the bright moon above. The steady, muffled crunching of leather soles on the crushed stone of the turnpike, the dull clang of tin cups, and the sloshing of water in half-filled canteens broke up the quiet of the summer night. The pass wound

xix   Civil War soldiers often referred to a battle as "the ball." For one
       example, see Hayes, ed., *The Diary of Father James Sheeran*, 197.

147

nearly eight miles through the hills but was not particularly arduous for a mountain road. Within a few hours, the head of McLaws's column emerged from the mountains at Cashtown, just eight miles from Gettysburg.[345]

GENERAL LONGSTREET HAD ARRIVED LATE IN THE AFTER-noon, just in time to "see the enemy retreating up one of the oppo-site ridges, pursued by the Confederates with loud yells."[346] Lee was probably still on Herr's Ridge when his old war horse rode up and together, they watched the latest rout of their opponents in blue.[347]

Sitting atop the ridge with his victorious commander, Long-street was surprised when Lee spoke of "attacking General Meade upon the heights the next day." Longstreet reminded him that he was under the impression they intended to fight a defensive battle.

In a famous response, Lee pointed at Cemetery Hill and thun-dered, "If the enemy is there tomorrow, we must attack him."

"If he is there," Longstreet countered, "it will be because he is anxious that we should attack him—a good reason, in my judgment, for not doing so." He insisted the army would be better served by moving to the right (the South), positioning "our army between him and Washington, threatening his left and rear, and thus forc[ing] him to attack us." Then the Confederates could choose the ground and make Meade attack *them*. The region was "admirably adapted to a defensive battle," Longstreet observed, scanning the ridges, hills, and woods sprouting all over the countryside. It was, after all, "Meade's army, not its position, [that] was our objective."[348]

In Longstreet's mind, finding a defensive position and forcing the Federal army to attack had been the "ruling idea" of the campaign. As he told McLaws, "under no circumstances were we to give battle, but…[instead] force the enemy to do so in a position of our own choosing." The First Corps would receive the attack, while the other two would "then fall upon and…destroy the Army of the Potomac."[349]

Though the idea was probably discussed, and while it may have been the intention to fight a tactically defensive battle, Longstreet ran into trouble when he said that it was "upon this understanding my assent was given." Of course, Longstreet's permission was not at all necessary to begin the campaign. In context of his first article on the subject, though, it appears Longstreet used the term "assent" to indicate he had been convinced, rather than that he *allowed* the campaign to happen. That scenario makes sense, for his opinion did carry weight as second in command of the premier Confederate army. But then, Longstreet's pen did not often make fine points with much clarity.[350]

Lee had "gotten a taste of blood," remembered Longstreet, and was intent on attacking the Federals where they were.[351] "He seemed under a subdued excitement, which occasionally took possession of him when the 'hunt was up,' and threatened his superb equipoise." Longstreet could see there was no point in talking Lee out of an attack. The commanding general "was in no frame of mind to listen to further argument at that time, so I did not push the matter."[352]

For now, anyway. Perhaps he'd change his mind in the morning after a full reconnaissance had been made of the Federal position.

This, at least, is how Longstreet remembered it. The evening probably played out a bit differently. As the Federals retreated through and around the town, Longstreet and Lee made their way east from Herr's Ridge to Seminary Ridge. Longstreet was not entirely wrong that Lee initially intended to keep the initiative that afternoon. He *had* sent Major Taylor to Ewell with the suggestion that he take Cemetery Hill if possible (or practicable). But that was far from a direct order. He made no attempt to drive his forces unyieldingly toward the hill, equivocated on providing reinforcements for Ewell's attack, and eventually decided to wait until the next day to follow up the victory, knowing more Federal troops would almost certainly arrive overnight. That was a far cry from being consumed by the "taste of blood."

Like Pendleton, Lee and Longstreet had to wait until Seminary Ridge was cleared of fighting before moving forward to continue reconnoitering. And like Pendleton, they found the elevation at the

McMillan farm well-suited for observation of the Federal line, which was now curling onto the ridge just south of Cemetery Hill. As J.P. Smith and Armistead Long both noted, and contrary to Longstreet's postwar claims, Lee was not willing to commit to a major battle at Gettysburg quite yet. Hence the "practicable" and "general engagement" language Ewell and Rodes mulled over and Lee's half-hearted response to Ewell's request for assistance.[353]

After the war, Longstreet took quite a bit of credit for the prudence that Lee was already exercising. He remembered cautioning Lee that "if the Federals were there in the morning, it would be proof that they had their forces well in hand" and ready to meet a Confederate attack.[354] Lee knew this, too and remained quite concerned about the position of the Federal army all evening and into the next morning. Despite the victory that afternoon, Cemetery Hill "frowned darkly and menacingly" upon the Confederate lines. It was precisely the prospect of storming these heights that made both Lee and Longstreet seriously consider any other option.

The British correspondent Francis Lawley remembered that Longstreet "shook his head gravely over the advantages conferred by [the Federal position] and thoughts of turning it by flanking were undoubtedly uppermost in his mind *and General Lee's.*"[355] The other foreign observers in Longstreet's camp remembered the same thing. Fremantle wrote in his diary that Longstreet "spoke of the enemy's position as being 'very formidable'" and "that they would doubtless intrench themselves strongly during the night.[356] Fitzgerald Ross, the Austrian observer, remembered that Longstreet arrived in his camp late on July 1 and confirmed the rumors of battle. "The Yankees would probably make a stand tomorrow on the hills south and east of town," Longstreet told them, "as their position was strong, and a general action was pretty sure to take place."[357]

The available cavalry wouldn't suffice to screen the movement of thousands of troops within a mile of the enemy over relatively open ground, nor would they be able to fend off Federal cavalry patrols that would hamper foraging parties. In Lee's mind, that meant they couldn't stay where they were to await a Federal attack, and they couldn't maneuver; they would have to attack even if the conditions weren't ideal.[358]

Lee's aide, Charles Marshall, agreed with Lawley's evaluation. After conferring with Ewell and Hill, Marshall wrote, "General Lee at one time contemplated a movement round the left flank of the enemy, but he abandoned this plan in view of the facts that he was uncertain of the position of General Meade's corps, that in the absence of the cavalry such a movement could not be concealed from the enemy, and that our line of march must have necessarily been so close to the enemy's position as to have exposed us to a very dangerous attack."[359]

Longstreet's claim that he was the only one who saw a downside to fighting at Gettysburg is simply not credible.[360] Lee had seriously considered it, too. And though he ultimately decided against it, the idea of moving around the Federal left (as opposed to attacking it) wasn't rejected out of hand as Longstreet insisted after the war.

BESIDES THE IMPRACTICALITY OF MOVING AROUND THE Federal left, the victory on July 1 had energized an already supremely confident Army of Northern Virginia. That victory was sweetened by the impression that the Yankees had fought better than they ever had before and were *still* driven through the town in a "headlong retreat."[361] Indeed, Lee's was a supremely confident army. The Army of Northern Virginia had earned quite a reputation for itself under his command during the last year, and its self-assurance bred absolute disdain for the fighting ability of the Army of the Potomac. This, along with the July 1 victory, "conspired to induce the belief that little more was wanted than a vigorous onslaught on the morrow to drive the Federals from the heights and open the way without let or hindrance to Baltimore or Washington."[362]

Not everyone was quite as jubilant, though. It was not lost that the Federal soldier was "fighting on his own soil, with his back to the wall, and in a position which for strength and eligibility for defence has not been surpassed during 27 months of warfare."[363] The barrels of the Federal cannon glowering at them from Cemetery Hill grimly reinforced that. But retreating was not a real option, either. There was one road to and through the pass at Cashtown. The army had no opposition getting through the mountains in June and could fan out onto several roads to avoid a bottleneck. Now, in the face of the Federal army, they would be stuck on one road and could expect a fierce attack on their column. Whichever corps was in the rear would be forced to fend for itself. If the other three corps turned around to reinforce it, then they would be in the same spot they were now: forced to fight a battle they didn't want. If a fight was going to happen, it may as well be at Gettysburg.[364]

Despite the strength of the Yankees' position, everything pointed toward one inescapable conclusion: attack. Lee would have to "float with the current, and to trust the enthusiasm of his troops to carry him triumphantly on the morrow over the heights."[365] Lawley's observations are supported by Lee's own report. "It had not been intended to deliver a general battle so far from our base," he began, but "to withdraw through the mountains with our extensive trains would have been difficult and dangerous." What was more, they "were unable to await an attack…. A battle had, therefore, become in a measure unavoidable, and the success already gained gave hope of a favorable issue."[366]

Resigned to an attack, Lee spent the evening getting as much information on the Federal position as possible. Lee, Longstreet, Ewell, Early, Pendleton, and Armistead Long all reconnoitered the Federal position, the roads available to the Confederates, artillery positions, and potential troop positions on July 1. The resulting intelligence convinced Lee that although a strategic flanking maneuver wasn't possible, a tactical strike on the Federal left flank most certainly was. From the south, the ground sloped gently toward the Federal position on Cemetery Hill, while the hills near the McMillan farm presented good artillery positions to pound the Federal line and support the attack.[367] It's no coincidence that both Pendleton and Lee spent a good amount of time at the McMillan farm that evening. Indeed, that's exactly where J.P. Smith had found Lee and Longstreet when he delivered Ewell's request for reinforcements that evening. And of course, the Confederate artillery spent the night rolling into position there, preparing for an attack the next day.

The only remaining question, then, was when to attack. Lee wondered if it might be better to wait until Friday, July 3, when he would have his entire army up and hopefully Stuart's cavalry. Armistead Long, if his postwar recollection is correct (and in this case, there's no real reason to suspect that it's not), suggested they attack on July 2. There was no reason to let the Federals concentrate and dig in while the opportunity to hit them piecemeal presented itself.[368] Lee, who was already thinking the same thing, made up his mind that his army would attack on July 2. He sent Marshall to the left with the message to bring Ewell back to the south side of town, unless he thought he could better assist where he was.

All this suggests the threat to Lee's equipoise was probably much greater in Longstreet's mind a year after the war than it had been on the fields of Gettysburg in the summer of 1863. Nothing about Lee's orders or actions that evening smacked of recklessness or bloodlust. Rather, the majority of the evening was spent cautiously and deliberately investigating the Federal position to find a weakness (and debating whether to fight there at all).[369]

SOME TIME AROUND TEN O'CLOCK THAT EVENING, ON HIS way back to his headquarters at Cashtown, Longstreet found McLaws and his column trudging through the darkness toward Gettysburg. The First Corps commander instructed McLaws to get his men to Marsh Creek, which wasn't far in front of them, and to let the division rest. Orders were to be back on the road by "daybreak." Around midnight, Hood's Division sidled up along the creek and McLaws's troops, and they all got what rest they could before marching to the battlefield in the morning.[370]

EWELL AND MARSHALL RODE THROUGH THE DARKNESS toward Lee, guided by Marshall's memory of the terrain and splashes of moonlight.[371] When he arrived at army headquarters, Ewell dismounted, and he and Lee disappeared into the tent.

Marshall waited outside. There's no transcript of the conversation, but Ewell remembered that he told Lee "[Culp's] hill…was unoccupied by the enemy, as reported by Lieutenants Turner and Early, who had gone upon it, and that it commanded [the Federal] position and made it untenable, so far as [he] could judge."[372] Early and Ewell had discussed a separate "eminence" south of Cemetery Hill that commanded it during their initial reconnaissance of the position as the Federals reformed. Culp's Hill, on the other hand, "commands" Cemetery Hill from the east.

The "long conference" with Ewell convinced Lee to let the Second Corps remain where it was, concentrated in the town and along the eastern base of Cemetery Hill. Johnson's Division would occupy Culp's Hill that night. Ewell rode back to his corps, reaching his own headquarters around midnight "with orders to be ready to attack at daylight."[373] Ewell then sent Lt. Turner with a message for Johnson ordering him "to take possession of this [Culp's] hill, if he had not already done so."[374]

By morning, the Federals on Cemetery Hill should find themselves trapped, fish in the proverbial barrel.

CONTRARY TO HIS OWN POSTWAR NARRATIVE, LONGSTREET was not sulking or apathetic when he left army headquarters, as even his own staff officers had been convinced by the turn of the century. Moxley Sorrel, for example, remembered Longstreet's "sullen inactivity" on the morning of July 2 and that throughout the battle "there was apparent apathy in his movements. They lacked the fire and point of his usual bearing on the battlefield."[375]

Contemporary observations and Longstreet's own actions don't suggest any ambivalence at the plan of attack for July 2, however—at least as it stood on the night of July 1. It wasn't until after the war that Longstreet's temperament, tactical preferences, and motives were brought into focus.

Longstreet left army headquarters under the impression he would probably be attacking the Federal left at some point the next day, but the particulars hadn't been determined. Before he left, Lee instructed him to have his two available divisions up and in a position to attack as "early as practicable," as Armistead Long remembered it.[376] By all contemporary accounts, Longstreet did exactly that. McLaws and Hood were both within three miles of the battlefield by midnight, with orders to move the rest of the way starting before dawn. Hood was on the march by 3:00 a.m. McLaws moved right after him.[377]

If the men writing before any controversy broke out are to be believed—and there's no reason they shouldn't be—Longstreet wasn't in any sort of foul mood that evening, much less a traitorous one. Of course, he was serious, perhaps even somber. He had seen the Federal position that had to be taken the next day, and any lucid observer could see the day promised to be a bloody one. It had been precisely one year since he had laughed off the difficulty of taking a similar position at Malvern Hill and been proven gravely mistaken (in every sense of the term).[378] He certainly wasn't going to repeat the mistake of arrogance *this* July.

But a "sly undercurrent" of discontent with Longstreet's performance did leak into the press in late July of 1863.[xx] Almost certainly

---

xx   It may well have been this "sly undercurrent" that William Youngblood, a courier assigned to Longstreet, remembered after the war. In a letter to Longstreet in 1892, Youngblood (formally a member of the Fifteenth Alabama) wrote that while Lee was standing on the Virginia side of the Potomac, "Fairfax rode up by [Lee's] side and told him that 'blame was being put upon Gen'l Longstreet' for failure at Gettysburg. Gen'l Lee replied, 'Gen'l Longstreet is in no wise to blame. It all rests upon me.'" Youngblood to Longstreet, Sept. 5,

stemming from McLaws, the grumbling in the papers echoed his complaints home to his wife on July 7, which pinned the battle's loss on Longstreet "for not reconnoitering the grounds and for persisting in the assault when his errors were discovered."[379]

Perhaps it's mere coincidence that the *Savannah Republican* reported that McLaws and Hood, both "excellent officers," had "desired that a reconnaissance of the ground should precede the assault, in order to ascertain, if possible, whether the enemy occupied the high hills in their front, and in what force; but the decision of Generals Lee and Longstreet was against it, and the assaulting column was ordered to move forward." The correspondent then threw a not-so-veiled jab at Longstreet: "It is a fact not generally known, and which it may not be improper to state in this connection, that in all his famous flank movements General Jackson was careful to examine the ground, and to learn the exact position of the enemy, and hence his blows were always well aimed and terrible in effect."[380]

Even before his 1873 letter to Longstreet, it seems McLaws was trying to get out in front of the story. He must have heard the *other* undercurrents of dissatisfaction with his own alacrity as the undertow continued to pull his reputation further underwater. McLaws could not, however, be criticized for lack of zeal or agility in responding to slights against his reputation. Indeed, he seems to have been much more adept at that than Longstreet ever was, for McLaws's reputation survived the postwar fighting in much better shape than his old commander's.

The *Savannah Republican* also made a point to note that "in no single instance that now occurs to me did our troops retire except under orders." (Recall McLaws's complaint that Confederate officers believed his division had retreated on the evening of July 3, when Longstreet had in fact ordered them back). Even more interesting, correspondence from the *Republican's* reporter dated July 14 seems to be the first documented charge that had the attack begun

---

1892, in Longstreet Papers, UNC Wilson Library. Youngblood's story of being a courier checks out according to his National Archives file. NARA M311, RG 109, Roll 0250.

earlier on July 2, the battle would have been won: "if the attack had been renewed early on the morning of the 2nd, instead of at a quarter to four in the afternoon," the Confederate army "might have dispersed, captured or destroyed the three Federal corps engaged on the first day [*sic*]."[381] The *Savannah Republican* did not, however, blame Longstreet's temperament for the delay; rather, it was due to *Hood's* column being exposed to enemy observation, which caused the infamous countermarch.[382]

McLaws certainly had a reasonable sense of indignation toward Hood, given the winter controversy about McLaws's timeliness, Hood's leapfrogging of McLaws's column that morning, and then his leading the attack on July 2. It may be much less than a coincidence that the Savannah newspaper blamed Hood's marching prowess on the delay, rather than McLaws's, an accusation that doesn't seem to appear again.

It's curious that the one paper negatively reporting about Longstreet's performance at Gettysburg happened to be from McLaws's home state and just happened to sound all of the same complaints McLaws would voice for the next thirty years. Indeed, McLaws's gripes seem to have found a way into the papers one way or another, both during and after the war.

It's worth noting that other newspapers didn't seem to share the sentiment. Contrast the *Republican's* coverage with the *Richmond Dispatch's*: "General Longstreet...succeeded in driving before him the enemy's left, after hard fighting for the remainder of the day and during a portion of the night."[383] Numerous reports of Longstreet's death circulated, prompting the *Memphis Bulletin* to reprint bios of the fallen general (among several others presumed dead). "Since Stonewall Jackson's death he has been considered the best subordinate officer in Lee's army," the paper noted.[384] The only battlefield performance Longstreet had put in since Jackson's death was Gettysburg. Only the Georgia paper brought up McLaws's complaints about the battle.

Longstreet picked up on this grumbling, as did his uncle Augustus, who (coincidentally?) lived in Georgia. According to Longstreet, Augustus suggested he publicly reply to these "accusers."

Longstreet wrote back that though "the battle was not made as I would have made it"—that is to say the army stayed and fought rather than maneuvered south—Longstreet's duty as a soldier was "to express my views to the commanding general." If he then decided on a different course, "it is my duty to adopt his views, and to execute his orders as faithfully as if they were my own." As to a public response, "as General Lee is our commander, he should have the support and influence we can give him. If the blame, if there is any, can be shifted from him to me, I shall help him and our cause by taking it. I desire, therefore, that all the truth will be known in time, and I leave that to show how much of the responsibility of Gettysburg rests on my shoulders."[385]

In what would become the driving theme of the First Corps narrative at Gettysburg, Longstreet and McLaws were at odds before ever leaving the battlefield (indeed, McLaws's adjutant remembered Longstreet and McLaws engaged in "*very earnest* conversation" during the placement of troops on July 2).[386] And just as he would be ten years later, Longstreet was content to let McLaws's version of the battle remain publicly uncontested, though Longstreet *did* make sure to submit his official report within days of the column's publication (that a corps commander would submit his campaign report before any regimental, brigade, or division reports were submitted is odd and this is as good an explanation as any as to why Longstreet broke protocol).[387]

It seemed to suit him, in any event. He parlayed the perceived dissatisfaction into his own persona of prescient dissident; he knew it would fail, his story went, and so he did everything he could to stop it. That dovetailed perfectly with Early's crowd, who believed Lee was infallible. Longstreet was a self-made scapegoat, admittedly violating Lee's plan, which would have worked perfectly if he had simply sucked up his pride. Longstreet, of course, maintained Lee's plan went off as ordered and was demonstrably flawed, resulting in the loss. Longstreet did all he could, but couldn't prevent the doomed attacks. Since neither proposition was tethered to the truth, they quickly drifted to opposite and antagonistic ends.

* * *

MCLAWS WAS CLEARLY UPSET AT THE HANDLING OF THE battle from the get-go, but what about Pendleton? Was he simply lying, making up the whole sunrise order out of thin air after the war? Or is there a more charitable explanation, some shred of truth in which Pendleton began to spin his ultimate yarn?

There is, in fact, some reason to believe Pendleton honestly believed Longstreet was supposed to attack at daylight on July 2. That Pendleton was wrong—that Longstreet was *not* supposed to have attacked at dawn—is one of the few things that is known for certain. Long, Taylor, and Marshall, none of them Longstreet supporters, all went on record as saying there was no "sunrise order" issued. And yet Pendleton insisted there was, both publicly and to Longstreet during a letter-writing spat in the mid-1870s.

In April 1875, after his speaking tour had ended and the speech had been published in *Southern Magazine*, Pendleton received a coldly formal letter from Longstreet. "You have seen fit to arraign me before your audience and before the world," Longstreet glared. He demanded answers and names. *Describe the reconnaissance that would have prepared for a sunrise attack. Where, exactly, was the sunrise attack supposed to be made? Who was supposed to be guiding the First Corps into position at sunrise? Which officers gave Pendleton this information?* "It can hardly be necessary to assure you that my purpose in seeking to have you put your statements in more definite shape is to attempt an account of the Gettysburg Campaign," he abruptly ended.[388] If Pendleton was going to make the accusations, Longstreet wanted the evidence, and he wanted it public.

Pendleton was furious at the response. His clenched grip on the pen can be seen in the dark and deliberate strokes of his words. The address wasn't about slandering Longstreet, he insisted. "My theme," Pendleton began, "was Gen'l Lee, not Gen'l Longstreet.... If my evidence comes in conflict with your statements, your interests, or your reputation, that is your misfortune."

If anything, Longstreet had brought this upon himself. The whole point of the statements on Gettysburg, according to Pendleton, was "in vindicating the military reputation of Gen'l Lee" from "the writings of an eminent author, Mr. Swinton, based upon an account...derived from you." If Longstreet hadn't tried to tarnish Lee's reputation in the first place, in a Northern publication, no less (recall Pendleton's thoughts on the northern press in his reply to *Johnson's Cyclopedia*), then Pendleton wouldn't have had to defend it.

Pendleton didn't "perceive the necessity or propriety of entering into controversy with you. When you attempt an account of the Gettysburg Campaign, doubtless the whole truth will come out." Pendleton had simply given his personal account "as a witness, not an accuser; and my testimony will stand or fall before your impeachment, which," he might add, "I invite."[389] If Longstreet wanted to set the record straight, he could write his own account.

Longstreet quickly fired back. "You flatter yourself in presuming that your evidence comes in conflict with my interests or reputation.... School-boys may be misled by you," but "anyone who is at all familiar with the operations of the late conflict, and anyone who may hereafter be as readers of its records" wouldn't believe a single word "that you have written about myself."[390] Longstreet's instincts and faith in public opinion were once again remarkably off the mark. But then he never claimed to be able to read a room.[391]

That ended the personal correspondence between Longstreet and Pendleton. But despite the fiercely defensive stance toward Longstreet, Pendleton was earnestly surprised at the "tenor" of Longstreet's "quite...insulting private letter" and the offense that Longstreet had taken.[392] So much so, in fact, that he wrote to Armistead Long later that year to see if there might be more to the story.

Though Pendleton was "thoroughly satisfied that the statement which I made and published on the basis of such remembrance is altogether faithful," Longstreet's reaction had him second-guessing himself. "I cannot more than men in general claim absolute infallibility of memory after the lapse of ten years," Pendleton privately admitted. "My sense of duty as well as my self-respect requires me to get all the evidence possible, to substantiate the actual truth of the case."[393]

Pendleton could, of course, be lying and simply trying to get more evidence to build his case. But liars don't generally seek out independent confirmation of the lie; instead, they discourage it. Pendleton probably remembered *something* that made him truly believe Longstreet received an order to attack at sunrise. And there *was* an order to attack at daylight given by Lee to another corps commander on July 1: Richard Ewell.[394] Pendleton may well have simply heard the order for Ewell to attack at daylight and assumed it was for Longstreet.

Charles Marshall, responding to Longstreet as the First Corps commander was gathering information for his first public riposte, suggested Pendleton overheard the early morning attack orders for July *third*.[395] Campbell Brown's immediate recollection supports this. He wrote in his diary that "Longstreet was to have attacked at daylight" on July 3, but was "not ready till 10 a.m."[396] Lee noted in his report, which was penned by Marshall, that "Longstreet's dispositions were not completed as early as was expected."[397] Writing at a distance of nearly ten years, and with strong bias against Longstreet buried in his memory, it's certainly possible Pendleton simply—and honestly—confused the dates.

Charles Venable, another of Lee's staff officers Longstreet called on, thought Pendleton's phantom sunrise order was the result of "an absolute loss of memory said to be brought on by frequent attacks resembling paralysis." Venable went so far as to suggest that was the reason Washington and Lee University didn't publish the address at the time. "It is a sad pity it ever got into print," he lamented. As far as Venable was concerned, Pendleton's postwar account of the battle was worthless. Armistead Long had the better information.[398]

So, Longstreet wrote to Long, who played the middle ground.[399] He answered Longstreet's inquiry in the spring of 1875, telling him, "I do not recollect having heard of an order to attack at sunrise or at any other designated hour…. As my memory now serves me it was Gen Lee's intention to attack the enemy on the 2nd of July as early as practicable."[400] "The only feeling I have on the matter," Long sighed in another letter the following year, "is that of regret at beholding a controversy among such distinguished members of the Army of Northern Virginia."[401]

Pendleton's opinion of Longstreet had already deteriorated to a point of no return by 1873 and any ambiguity in his memory would certainly not fall in Longstreet's favor. Stereotypes, in this case applying to one particular individual rather than a large group, affect the memory.[402] Not having an accurate idea of what happened in the first place (the orders to Longstreet would be either second-hand or overheard, not issued directly to Pendleton), Pendleton's memory filled in the gaps of what he didn't actually observe with inferences: *someone* was ordered to attack at dawn on July 2, and since Longstreet ultimately did attack, that order must have been for him. His negative opinion of Longstreet certainly helped fill in the memory gaps with inferences against Longstreet.[xxi] He may well have truly believed what he was saying and honestly believed his memory was accurate. The fact that it was *not* an accurate recollection only makes him human.[403]

Though Pendleton was probably simply mistaken or suffering from the effects of ill health, his comments lit the fire of controversy. Ironically enough, his own actions on July 2 provided the kindling for the fire, a fact that would be buried within the silence of self-deception. The postwar controversy bred a web of very tangled stories, all of which probably had origins in the truth. But the sheer volume of personal stories quickly clouded memories already strained by adrenaline, the passage of time, and the strain of adjusting to life after their abject defeat. Though understandable—the narrators of the events are all *people*, after all—it's not an auspicious place to start for an historian.

But by following Kershaw's advice, by mining archives and sifting through memories, we can eventually discern a much clearer picture of what happened on July 2 in the shadow of the Round Tops.

---

xxi   Pendleton was by no means the only Confederate whose memory affected the history of July 2.

JULY 2

"There spring to the surface so many 'ifs,' any one of which would have secured a different result, that on an occasion like this it would fill columns of this journal to give expression to them in language."

- Francis Lawley[404]

The Plan Begins to Unravel

DAWN, IT HAS BEEN SAID, IS THE "HOUR OF SILENCE."[405] THE early morning twilight has always been associated with peace, with quiet, with self-reflection. And indeed, in the fields north and west of Gettysburg lay the bodies of hundreds of souls now at eternal peace, those who had seen Plato's fabled "end of war."[406]

But for those who survived the fighting on July 1, the war would continue. Those tasked with orchestrating the killing had been busy planning its continuation that evening. Only a few hours earlier, with Lieutenant Tom Turner's information that Culp's Hill was utterly bare of Federal troops, Richard Ewell had convinced Robert E. Lee to let him leave his corps east of town. When dawn turned to daylight and the sun rose over the eastern hills, they expected the Federals to be both literally and figuratively in the shadow of the Confederate line.

Though short of poetic, it was at least apropos, then, that Lieutenant Turner was the one to ride into Ewell's headquarters at dawn

163

with news that would change everything. Not only had Johnson *not* taken the hill, but another Federal Corps (the Fifth) was scheduled to begin its march to the battlefield at that very moment. In his report, Ewell wrote dryly that "General Johnson stated…that after forming his line of battle this side of the wooded hill…he had sent a reconnoitering party to the hill" to report on the enemy's position. Johnson said he'd stay put until he got further orders.

Turner also showed Ewell the captured dispatch from the Fifth Corps commander, Major General George Sykes, that he would begin his march to the field at 4:00 a.m. from his bivouac only four miles away. That could put him on the field by 6:00 a.m., just under two hours from now.[407]

Ewell didn't record his thoughts for posterity, but they can easily be imagined. He had "supposed until near daylight," when he received Turner's message, "that the hill had been taken possession of, as he had directed."[408] But "day was now breaking," Ewell lamented, "and it was too late for any change of place."[409] The one-legged Second Corps commander immediately ordered Johnson to "be ready to attack" and to take the hill "if possible" (qualifiers seem to abound in the orders for Culp's and Cemetery Hill).[410] He'd have to explain to Lee that the lynchpin of the day's plan had come loose and they were flatfooted.

WHY WASN'T JOHNSON IN POSITION THAT MORNING? There's no reason to think Ewell issued a vague order; both his acting artillery chief, Colonel J. Thompson Brown, and Jubal Early spent the pre-dawn hours preparing for the attack, believing Culp's Hill would be occupied by Johnson overnight. Brown reported that he was "under the impression and hope that the wooded hill on the enemy's right would be taken that evening." In anticipation of the morning's attack, he "sent an officer to move on with the division and endeavor to find a road for the artillery." But "the attempt to take the hill was not made, however, that evening," Brown noted in a discouraged afterthought.[411]

Early too, had "been informed that a large portion of the rest of our army would come up during the night, and that the enemy's position would be attacked on the right and the left flanks very early next morning."[412] At that point, the Federal right was inching up the western face of Culp's Hill and the left was just starting to spread out onto Cemetery Ridge; not until late the next morning would the Federal line even begin to resemble the well-known "fish hook." General Harry Hays, one of Early's brigadiers, reported that around 2:00 a.m., in preparation for the attack, "I moved my troops into an open field between the city and the base of a hill…between us and Cemetery Hill, throwing out skirmishers to the front."[413]

Ed Johnson seems to have heard a different order, though, or at least interpreted it differently. None of his brigade commanders reported attack preparations that night, nor did they mention any orders to occupy the hill. Instead, they invariably reported forming a line near the base of the hill and sleeping on their arms. Pickets were thrown forward, which suggests an intent to stay put for the night.[414] No matter the reason, Campbell Brown remembered that Ewell "held [Johnson] not altogether free from blame in the matter."[415]

So, what of the reconnaissance mentioned by Ewell in his report? This was probably the encounter between four companies of Virginia pickets and several companies of the Seventh Indiana. Both the Federal and Confederate commanders had an eye toward Culp's Hill as the sun set on July 1. General Wadsworth, commanding a division of the Federal First Corps, ordered the Seventh Indiana to the far right of the line in order to "hold the crest of a hill to the right."[416] Colonel Ira Grover, the Seventh's commander, then sent several companies further along the flank, in case any Confederates were "also looking in that direction, with a view to turning our flank, and getting in rear of us before morning, and had also sent out a scouting party to learn if that position was occupied by us."[417]

Of course, the Confederates *were* looking toward Culp's Hill, perhaps more closely than even Grover thought. Late that night (or early on the second), the Twenty-fifth Virginia moved through the darkness of the woods on Culp's Hill toward their picket post. "On nearing the summit," the Virginians were "met by a superior force of the enemy, which succeeded in capturing a portion" of the party.[418]

Colonel Grover's recollection of the event was similar. After deploying on the right, the Hoosiers had "immediately commenced the construction of a temporary breastwork." That way, if "a force of the enemy attempted to penetrate our lines" that night, they "were easily supposing themselves confronted by a heavy force."[419] That's precisely what happened.

According to one account, two Hoosiers on picket heard noises "as of men moving cautiously in the timber some distance to our right" and went to check it out.[420] Then "the two scouting parties met." Colonel Grover shouted *Halt! Surrender!* and the Confederates, "supposing they had got into our lines," obeyed. The rest of the Virginians fell back in a hurry.

Orville Thomson remembered capturing a captain and a lieutenant, though he thought they were in the Forty-second Virginia, which was also sent forward onto Culp's Hill that night.[421] Lieutenant Turner, writing years later and on second-hand information, was under the impression that Johnson's picket (or reconnaissance) "had been fired upon by a party of the enemy on the summit and with the loss of one or two men, had retired."[422]

The Twenty-fifth Virginia's report is threadbare, though the quick reference to being placed on picket, rather than performing a reconnaissance, is significant. Despite the one-sided story, there is support for Thomson's memory. Second Lieutenant William Striet Dryer was listed as captured on July 2, the only officer in the Twenty-fifth that was captured *during* the fighting. The rest of the regiment's captured officers were all formally taken prisoner while lying in hospitals after the Confederates retreated.[423]

Presaging how the rest of the day would develop for the Confederates, the first (and perhaps most important) order for the day's attack seems to have simply been misunderstood. Nothing about the actions of Johnson's brigade commanders that evening suggests they were preparing for imminent movement. Instead, they seemed ready for a daylight attack. Even Johnson's message to Ewell indicates the misunderstanding: he would "refrain from attacking the position until [Ewell] had received notice of the fact that the enemy were in possession of this hill."[424] Johnson clearly knew the hill was supposed to be empty, but his message suggests his timing was off, that he was under the impression he was supposed to move onto the hill in the morning, *not* overnight.

Perhaps Johnson wasn't aware of the urgency, which could be both his fault and Ewell's for not relaying it. Campbell Brown sheds some light on this. In a note sketched out for work on his memoirs, Brown jotted that "in order to get possession of Culp's Hill, Johnson had to move by the route actually and necessarily taken by him to be out of the fire of the Cemetery Hill guns, fully 2 miles" out of the way.[425] Jubal Early thought the same thing. Johnson's Division "arrived at a late hour," he reported, "its movement having been delayed by the report of the advance on the York road"—another consequence of the "phantom force" Billy Smith had seen that afternoon. Thus, "no effort to get possession of the wooded hill on the left of the town was made that night."[426]

After a long march, maneuvering in the dark, and uncertainty to what was in front of him, Johnson hesitated, waiting for clarification of his orders before moving forward. This was not fundamentally different from Ewell's own situation in front of Cemetery Hill the evening before. And though both Ewell's and Johnson's decisions may have been eminently justified, they were undoubtedly momentous.

IT ISN'T KNOWN WHO HAD TO DELIVER THE MESSAGE TO Lee and tell the commanding general that the first thread in the day's plans had begun to unravel. No one could know yet just how far the thread would pull, but it was concerning, a poor start to a situation Lee hadn't wanted in the first place. Reporting after the battle, Lee dispassionately explained that Johnson hadn't taken Culp's Hill and that more Federal troops were arriving near Cemetery Hill. "Under these circumstances," Lee lamented, "it was decided not to attack until the arrival of Longstreet, two of whose divisions…encamped about 4 miles in the rear during the night."[427]

If Lee's report is accurate, then he never intended Longstreet to initiate the attack that morning. And if that's the case, then the attack wasn't delayed by Longstreet or his dragging feet. Rather, it was the change in circumstances—more Federals and the loss of Culp's Hill—that caused the postponement of the planned sunrise attack. (It's also another indication that Pendleton confused his officers when he remembered hearing orders for a daylight attack.)

By now, the sun was just beginning to glimmer over the trees on Culp's Hill. Daylight would prevent Ewell from moving back to the Confederate right. Anyone standing on Cemetery Hill could see a number of reasons why, not least of which were the shimmering barrels of Federal cannon keeping watch over the open ground between Culp's Hill and the town. A full division of Confederates marching across the farm fields would present irresistible targets. And even if they managed to move out of the range of the guns, the movement would announce the abandonment of the flank, inviting an attack on those who remained, like Early.

With Ewell stuck east of the town, Lee sent Charles Venable to ask Ewell if he thought an attack was still possible.[428] Ewell took Venable with him to investigate the situation before answering. In the meantime, Lee would find out what the prospects of an attack from the South were.

Like it or not, Lee was stuck with Ewell on the eastern side of town without possession of the hills. Until he had more information, the attack would have to wait.

THE INAUSPICIOUS START TO THE MORNING ALSO PROVided the roots of the day's controversies. We saw how Pendleton's prejudices affected his memory, filling in gaps with negative inferences toward Longstreet. He wasn't the only one. Reuben Lindsay Walker, the Third Corps artillery chief, also wrote a letter about his experience at Gettysburg, which appeared in the *Southern Historical Society Papers* in 1878. "I have a *strong impression*," Walker wrote, "that I heard General Lee say that evening that he wished the battle opened at the earliest possible moment the next morning by a simultaneous attack on both flanks." Walker remembered Longstreet and A.P. Hill at the meeting, and maybe even Ewell.[429]

Like Pendleton, Walker was probably right in his facts, but wrong in his conclusion. The attack *was* supposed to start first thing in the morning. Jubal Early was ready at the base of Cemetery Hill. Johnson, seemingly mistaken as to his orders, was in position for an attack on Culp's Hill. Ewell and his staff fully expected an attack to begin that morning. When Lee delayed the assault, he ordered Ewell to wait for Longstreet's guns, apparently postponing the start of the attack several times.[430] The natural conclusion was that *someone* wasn't where they were supposed to be. Since Ewell's orders revolved around responding to Longstreet's attack, it was a short logical leap to deduce that Longstreet was the cause of the delay. Coupled with Longstreet's fall from Southern grace and his post-war insistence that he didn't want to attack in the first place, Confederate heuristics naturally concluded that it was *Longstreet* who wasn't where he was supposed to be, and that was the cause of the delay.

But that wasn't the case on July 2. As the battle was shaping up, it was *Johnson* whose arrival time precluded a dawn attack (not that it was necessarily his fault). And as it turns out, none of Longstreet's later accusers happened to be in a place to know what transpired at headquarters on the morning of July 2, and so none of them could speak from personal knowledge. The accusations were simply derived from reasonable lines of logic in an attempt to link the unconnected events in their memory. Much of the time, the brain connects the dots accurately, since the lines are drawn using past experience. But in this case, there *was* no personal experience to draw on, and so they inaccurately drew on others' memories.

Pendleton, for example, was not at headquarters at dawn but was out with his staff and Lindsay Walker placing artillery on Seminary Ridge.[431] Campbell Brown was close enough to Second Corps head-quarters that morning to know "all was ready at daylight," but wasn't anywhere near Lee when orders were issued to the First Corps.[432] Both Ewell and Brown remembered receiving the order postponing the attack, but neither mention being told *why*.[433]

Armistead Long, Charles Marshall, Charles Venable, and Walter Taylor, on the other hand, *were* in a position to personally know Longstreet's orders and none of them remembered any orders for the First Corps to attack at daylight. The closest any of them came was Long, after years of communication with Early and heavy involvement in the postwar correspondence and publication spree. In his memoir, he wrote that Lee told both Hill and Longstreet that they would "attack the enemy in the morning as early as practicable."[434] That's a far cry from "attack at dawn."

Even Jubal Early admitted that he had only heard Lee's statement that the attack was to be on the Federal left and right flanks at dawn on July 2. "I do not know what were the specific orders given to Longstreet," Early conceded. Since Lee's "orders were manifestly given in person...no living man can say precisely what they were, except General Longstreet, if he indeed recollects them." [435] Longstreet *did* remember what was said, but his memory wasn't consistent. Depending on when he was telling the story, Longstreet either went to Lee's headquarters to receive his orders for the day or to protest them, two very different purposes.[436]

That he went to see Lee around sunrise isn't in doubt. Fremantle remembered that Longstreet was up at 3:30 that morning and left for army headquarters before it was light. John Logan Black, commanding a hodgepodge of cavalry and artillery, reported to Lee's headquarters "at daylight." Lee was busy talking with Hill, but Black remembered that "Lt. Gen. Longstreet soon came up and joined Gen'l Lee."[437]

Longstreet would quickly learn that the situation had changed drastically since he left the field the night before. Now, his First Corps would be making the attack, probably on the Federal left. Since Ewell's assault was canceled for the time being, Longstreet would await further instructions and place his troops, who were just coming up, where they could be used for whatever the day's plans were. Since it looked like the attack would be on the Federal left, he would shade his corps to his own army's right. For now, reconnaissances needed to be sent out, information gathered, and decisions made. The silence of dawn was over. There was work to be done.

Reconnoitering

WILLIAM PENDLETON RODE ALONG SEMINARY RIDGE IN THE calm twilight, still and quiet save for groaning artillery carriages, the muffled grunts and curses of the men wheeling them into position, and the stamping and snorting of the horses tasked with hauling them. Pendleton and his staff were busy placing the guns for the attack that morning, which as far as he knew was still on schedule. Years after the war, Pendleton's staff officer, Coupland Page, recalled the morning poetically. "The stars were shining in all their brilliancy and glory," he wrote, "not the slightest indication of day-dawn, save the twinkling stars as they blushed before the Morning Star."

Riding slowly down the spine of the ridge, Pendleton, Lindsay Walker, Coupland Page, and a collection of staff officers, began placing the artillery that Pendleton had kept in reserve the night before. In Page's recollection, Pendleton would select a spot, leave a staff officer there to guide the artillerists into position, and then continue down the line, repeating the process for each battery.[438] One of the first to roll into position that misty gray morning was David McIntosh's battalion, which Pendleton had left in reserve the night before. The gunners pushed their cannon into David McMillan's expansive orchards on the eastern slope of Seminary Ridge, staring barrel-to-barrel at the Union guns on Cemetery Hill, less than a mile away. Pegram's Battalion leapfrogged McIntosh, rolling down the ridge a full mile to a dogleg in the tree line known as the Point of Woods.[xxii]

---

xxii   The Virginia Monument marks the point today. McIntosh's batteries were placed from the Fairfield Road through McMillan's Orchard. See Bachelder's Isometric Map and the Warren/Bachelder Map for July 2. McIntosh didn't report the time. O.R. 27.2: 675. Captain E.B. Brunson, reporting for Pegram's Battalion after the battle, noted that "at an early hour" on July 2, the battalion "took position a mile to the right of the pike…and opposite the Yankee center, about 1,400 yards." O.R. 27.2: 678. McMillan's Orchard is well documented on Bachelder's Isometric Map, as well as the Park Service's Record of

The artillery wasn't the only branch of the army moving at that early hour. Brigadier General James Lane reported that his left "was a short distance from the Fairfield road," while his right passed through the woods, "beyond the stone fence and into the peach orchard near McMillan's house," where General Dorsey Pender ordered him to stop.[439] His men would be sheltered in the woods just behind McIntosh's guns.

To Lane's right, Colonel William Lowrance's North Carolinians marched into position, shuffling from north to south along the ridge. They had had quite a day on July 1, getting caught in an artillery crossfire and losing their brigade commander, Brigadier General Alfred Scales.[440] Now they found themselves holding down the extreme right of the Confederate line. They were alone in the unknown twilight, which unsettled Colonel Lowrance. "Being an important point on the immediate right of our artillery," he reported, "we its only guard, and with no support, I considered it hazardous in the extreme." To keep watch for any Yankees trying to move around the flank, Lowrance "threw out a strong line of skirmishers…fully one-half mile to the right," which drifted back toward the rear.[441]

As the sun began to creep into the sky, the Confederate line stretched from the base of Culp's Hill, through the town, bent south at Seminary Ridge, and inched across the Fairfield Road, ending at the Point of Woods. From there, Lowrance's skirmishers leaned back to the south and west to guard against any sudden Yankee movements.

ALL THIS HAD BEEN DONE BEFORE LEE DISCOVERED THAT the plan needed to be changed. Three fresh divisions would be available first thing that morning for an attack on the Federal left: Richard Anderson's Third Corps Division and Longstreet's two divi-

---

Treatment Maps. ROT Maps, 7A, 9, 10. Frank Haskell, among others, remembered that the morning was "thick and sultry, the sky overcast with low, vapory clouds.…Men looked like giants there in the mist." *The Battle of Gettysburg*, 19–20.

sions, Hood and McLaws. Before he could place them, though, he'd need to get a closer look at the Federal line.

Almost everyone involved had a different take on what happened next. At first glance (and in fact, after many glances) the accounts appear irreconcilable, hopelessly muddled in murky memories, ego, and controversy.

Pendleton, Page, Johnston, Long, Longstreet, George Peterkin, Lafayette McLaws, Joseph Kershaw, and Robert E. Lee all left accounts for posterity and some left many. None of them say quite the same thing. Of course, *everyone's* version of the story can't be entirely true. Though everyone may have remembered things slightly differently, only one particular sequence of events took place south of the town that morning. Ultimately there's one truth lurking out there.

But in order to find it, or at least come close to it, we have to look through the many different lenses of the many different people who experienced it. Those people witnessed the events from various vantage points. No single person saw everything, but everyone saw something. The stories they tell are the only real windows we have into the events, but each window only grants us so much of a view.

Like looking out a physical window, we can only see so far to each side, and we only get a fixed angle. In order to get the full view, we not only have to change positions and look through every window, we have to understand that each view can only be a limited one. None of them tell the whole story, but each of them tells an important part of the story.

Fortunately, there are a number of windows available to us, giving us a good look at the scouting done that morning.

OUR FIRST LOOK IS THROUGH THE FOGGY GLASS OF CONTRO-versy. Only a few months after the battle, Pendleton submitted his report to Lee. Pendleton spent an inordinate amount of time discussing the morning's activities, including a sunrise reconnaissance on Seminary Ridge with Sam Johnston, Armistead Long, and Lindsay Walker.[442] The report was only printed once, in the fifth volume of the *Southern Historical Society Papers*, in 1878.[xxiii] For most of the rest of the nineteenth century, it remained just another report of the battle. Compared to his dramatic (and lengthy) speech, the report didn't garner much attention.

But in November of 1895, newspaperman Leslie Perry reignited a quick burst of flame between the aging Confederates when he wrote a long column that appeared in the *New York Sun*, using Pendleton's report as a *defense* of Longstreet. If Pendleton conducted a sunrise reconnaissance with Johnston on July 2, Perry argued, then Lee couldn't possibly have expected Longstreet to attack at daylight.[443] William Jones, the editor of the *Papers*, fired off a response a month later. As part of his argument that Lee *did* order Longstreet to attack at daylight on the second, he quoted Pendleton's aide George Peterkin.[444]

The exchange caught the eye of sixty-two-year-old Samuel Johnston, then living in northern New Jersey. Johnston noticed his name in the excerpt of Pendleton's report, which prompted a letter to George Peterkin. This proved to be the last known letter written by Johnston on the subject. He was polite, but frankly disagreed with Pendleton's recollection, primarily the claim that Pendleton accompanied Johnston on the reconnaissance.

"As so much in this controversy between General Lee's friends and General Longstreet depends upon whether or not General Pendleton is correct," Johnston wrote, "and as I am the captain Johnston referred to," he thought it was "most important indeed" to give his thoughts on the subject. As the Federal forces fell back on the first day, he remembered, he rode with Long, Walker, and Pendleton to investigate the right "to be ready for a flank movement on the part of the enemy." Then, he said, he and chief engineer Colonel William Proctor Smith made another reconnaissance, returning after dark.

The following morning, "about four o'clock...General Lee called me and directed that I go at once and make reconnaissance

---

xxiii   Pendleton's report was only printed once prior to the publication of the *Official Records* in 1889.

as far as practicable on our right." Johnston briefly recounted his reconnaissance, mentioning Clarke again, and figured he was gone for maybe three hours, at the most.

"As I started from headquarters at 4 a.m....and did not return till about 7 A.M., and then joined General Longstreet and remained with him till the battle of the second day was over, it is very evident that I did not make a reconnaissance with Gen'l Pendleton on the second." There simply wasn't time.

But not one for controversy, Johnston gave Pendleton the benefit of the doubt. He "most probably...did make a rec[onnaissance] on the 2nd," Johnston thought, but that reconnaissance must have been done "in order to more thoroughly understand the country with a view to locating his batteries." Unfortunately, Johnston thought it would be "necessary to say something for publication" and when he did, he "will have to say that the reconnaissance referred to by General Pendleton was made on the first, instead of the second." Like Charles Marshall, Johnston figured Pendleton just mixed up his days.[445] (It doesn't appear that Johnston ever got around to saying anything publicly. Nor does it seem Peterkin replied to his letter. If either happened, they're currently lost to history.)[446]

AT FIRST GLANCE, THERE APPEARS TO BE A GLARING CONTRA-diction. Pendleton and Johnston either conducted a reconnaissance together or they didn't. They can't *both* be right; someone must be wrong.

But counterintuitively, both *are* correct. For the most part, at least. They were just looking through different windows at different times. Pendleton was on Seminary Ridge placing artillery that morning, then "surveyed the enemy's position" with Long, Walker and Johnston. Pendleton considered this observation a reconnais-sance; indeed, it was important enough to Pendleton's battle experi-ence that he included it in his report.[447] But Johnston, who was about to embark on a closeup investigation of the Federal line, well beyond the protection of his own lines, did *not* consider a distant "survey" of the Federal line a reconnaissance. The same event was simply viewed and remembered two different ways by two different people.

Part of the confusion may have stemmed from Pendleton's speech. In it, he mixed and confused the events of July 1 and 2. He remembered that on July 1, the "ground further south of [Cemetery Hill] was…carefully examined by myself, and…found encouragingly less difficult than the steep ascent fronted by our troops." According to his report and nearly everyone else's recollection, though, this was done on the morning of the second.

In his speech, Pendleton thought he reported back to Lee around 9:00 p.m. on July 1. Lee then ordered him to conduct another reconnaissance on the morning of July 2 in order to "reexamine the ground as early as possible." So "as soon as light at all appeared" on July 2, the "reconnaissance was accordingly made through a long distance."[448] Though it's not how Pendleton initially reported it, this was the most public version of his story.

If Johnston was using Pendleton's speech as his reference point, then it's easy to see the confusion. Since Johnston accompanied Pendleton on his afternoon reconnaissance on July 1, he knew Pendleton conducted that reconnaissance in order to find an artillery platform, *not* to scout the Federal left in anticipation of an attack the next day. He also knew that he didn't go with Pendleton over "a long distance" on the morning of July 2, so he assumed Pendleton must have been referring to a more focused reconnaissance that morning, performed "with a view to locating his batteries."[449] That happened on July 1, so from Johnston's perspective, Pendleton simply mixed up his dates. And since Pendleton *was* placing his artillery on the morning of July 2, when Johnston met him, it was a reasonable assumption to make, even though it turned out to be wrong.

July 2

* * *

ARMISTEAD LONG PROVIDES A HELPFUL CLUE IN SORTING out the confusion. In an 1876 letter to Jubal Early, published in the *Southern Historical Society Papers*, Long wrote that Lee "breakfasted and was in the saddle before it was fairly light. At that early hour, on visiting Hill's headquarters, everything exhibited signs of preparation for action."[450] Of course, everything *would* be in motion, for no one could know the attack had been postponed until Lee and Long arrived.

But more importantly, Long strongly implies that Lee was with him when he went to Hill's headquarters that morning, meaning Sam Johnston probably was, too. John Black's recollection supports this. When Black arrived at Lee's headquarters that morning, he was told the general "had walked off a short distance." Black eventually found him "conversing with Lt. Gen. A.P. Hill," suggesting Lee traveled to Hill's headquarters that morning like Long implied. For if Hill had come to Lee's headquarters, it's unlikely Long was riding to Hill's. Why send Long to Hill's headquarters if Hill was already with Lee? [xxiv]

Johnston always claimed that he was summoned by Lee at daylight. That makes sense, since that's when Lee found out that Ewell wasn't on Culp's Hill and promptly postponed the attack. Needing fresh intelligence as to the Federal left to see if an attack there was a real possibility, he called Johnston and ordered him to reconnoiter the area and report back as soon as possible. Long connects the dots between Lee waking up Johnston and Johnston getting to Seminary Ridge.

By riding to Hill's headquarters, which was at the Emanuel Pitzer farmhouse a few hundred yards behind Seminary Ridge, Long, Lee, and Johnston were also riding straight into Pendleton's report. They arrived at the Pitzer farmhouse "about sunrise," and

---

xxiv   It's more likely that Lee rode to see Hill than Hill traveled to army headquarters. After all, it was Lee that knew the plans had changed; Hill wouldn't have had any reason to stop what he was doing and go to Lee's headquarters at sunrise.

Long was directed to "assist Colonel Walker in disposing of the artillery of Hill's corps." From there, Long "discovered that there had been considerable accession to the enemy's force on Cemetery Hill during the night; but it was chiefly massed to his right, leaving much of his center and almost his entire left unoccupied."[451] This made the Federal left flank well suited for an attack.[452]

Long's letter places him, Walker, and Pendleton on Seminary Ridge observing the Federal position *and* locating artillery batteries "soon after sunrise," just as Pendleton reported. Though Long doesn't specifically mention Sam Johnston, his account suggests Johnston was present, at least when read in conjunction with Johnston's letters. Sam Johnston, remember, had been under the impression that Pendleton's July 2 recon was done with an eye to placing his artillery.

After the sunrise survey, that's exactly what Pendleton did. According to Long, after they viewed the Federal position and discovered the Federals had primarily reinforced their right, "Pendleton offered his services to Walker; and [Long] proceeded to our left."[453]

Johnston's knowledge of Pendleton's recon and its purpose implies he was with Pendleton that morning, too. As Johnston left for his more in-depth reconnaissance, the last thing he would have seen Pendleton doing is setting off with Walker to finish placing the artillery. Since he wouldn't have known Pendleton later went on a separate reconnaissance, he naturally assumed that if Pendleton considered a ride down Seminary Ridge that morning a "reconnaissance," then it must have been simply to find suitable artillery positions.

* * *

The ground covered by the sunrise survey. The Point of Woods is at the far left, marked by the Virginia Memorial. McMillan's Woods is hidden by the trees and development on the right. Author photo.

THE SUNRISE SURVEY TOOK PLACE ALONG SEMINARY Ridge, between McMillan's Orchard and the Point of Woods. This was the "farthest occupied point" of the Confederate line "soon after sunrise," marking the end of Pegram's battalion and the beginning of Lowrance's skirmish line. It also offered a panoramic view of the field, from Cemetery Hill to the Round Tops. From that vantage point, there was one inescapable conclusion: the ground south of Cemetery Hill was much better suited for an attack than on the Federal right.

Besides the fact that the bulk of the Federal troops were on the right flank, the ground on the Federal left sloped gently toward Cemetery Hill, while the northeastern face of Cemetery Hill was steep and jagged. Any attack from the south would also be helpfully guided along by the Emmitsburg Road, which sat atop a ridge leading directly to the base of Cemetery Hill.

The major exception to the Confederate panorama was the ground behind the Emmitsburg Road, between the ridge and the looming Round Tops. That was utterly invisible from the Confederate line. If an attack was to be made along this ridge, the ground on the other side would have to be investigated.

That task fell to Sam Johnston.

Samuel Richards Johnston, the enigmatic engineer who performed perhaps the most famous (or infamous) reconnaissance of the Civil War on the morning of July 2, 1863. Photo courtesy of David P. Batalo.

SAMUEL RICHARDS JOHNSTON WAS THIRTY YEARS OLD when he trotted south along Seminary Ridge that morning. Six feet, two inches tall, with a dark complexion, a thick dark beard, and piercing hazel eyes, Sam Johnston was a blue-blooded Virginia gentleman from the ranks of a prominent (but not elite) northern Virginia family.

Johnston grew up along the banks of the Potomac River, a stone's throw from George Mason's Gunston Hall and a silver dollar's throw from George Washington's Mount Vernon estate. His obituary, still decades away in 1899, would remember that he was "a typical Virginia gentleman," and even though he was the last son of his father's second marriage, he was properly "educated in classical schools."[454] That ultimately led to the first step of what would become a long career on the railroads.[xxv]

The Johnston family played important parts behind the scenes of momentous events, but like Sam, didn't catch much notice of the quill pens and printing presses. His grandfather, George Johnston, had served as part-time legal counsel for George Washington. As a Virginia legislator, he also served alongside Patrick Henry and helped draft the Stamp Act Resolutions in the 1760s, one of the first steps toward the revolution the following decade.[455]

George Johnston's son, also named George, served on General Washington's staff, but perished in the cold winter encampment at Morristown, New Jersey in 1778.[456] The elder George's daughter married a man who became one of the first United States Supreme Court justices and also happened to be a friend of George Washington (unfortunately she wouldn't live to see the new nation; she died in 1775).[457]

By the time Sam was born in 1833, the Johnston family had created a strong name for themselves in Fairfax County. A perusal of land records shows they often served as trustees in property trans-

---

xxv   By the age of twenty-four, he was working at the regional Alexandria, Loudon & Hampton Railroad. *Alexandria Gazette*, Feb. 15, 1858. The railroad took out a help wanted ad for a "a negro girl, about 13 years of age," with direction to apply to "Sam'l R. Johnston."

fers.[xxvi] His father, Dennis, was considered "a highly respected citizen of the County" and served as a magistrate. He "died leaving a large circle of relations and friends to mourn" him.[458]

Dennis Johnston also left behind large land holdings, which were distributed among his heirs. Sam received a sizable tract of land, but sold it to another family member two years later. Eventually, he purchased his brother John's half interest in a 350-acre colonial estate known as West Grove (another brother, George, owned the other half). The estate sprawled along Little Hunting Creek, a scenic offshoot of the Potomac, nestled against his family's other estates.[459]

With a budding new career as an engineer in the growing railroad industry and a beautiful estate along the river, Sam soon married Mary Galbraith Ege, the daughter of one of Pennsylvania's most successful iron foundry magnates, in a ceremony at West Grove.[460] Mary and Sam had three kids together, but tragically two died by the age of three. Sam rode off to war when his namesake, Sam Jr., was only a year old. He may never have seen his son again, for young Sam, Jr. died in December of 1863. Alexandria was occupied by Union forces throughout most of the war, so getting a furlough home wasn't an option, though Mary probably headed further south at some point. By early 1865, his second son was born, named after Sam's military mentor, Robert E. Lee.[461]

Johnston's thoughts on the political causes of the war aren't recorded, but as a native son of Virginia, he jumped headfirst into the war when his state seceded. According to his obituary, which may have simply picked up on a dramatic tale, Sam was traveling south on a train when he received the news that Virginia had voted to secede. He "pulled the bell cord, stopping the train," and imme-

---

xxvi   At the time, it was common for a wealthy individual to loan money for the purchase of property through a Deed of Trust. Rather than owe a bank for decades through a mortgage with the property as collateral, the Deed of Trust created a trust for the property. The purchaser was granted possession (but not ownership) of the property, and when the full price was paid, the trustee drafted and recorded a new deed conveying the property from the trust to the buyer. Dennis Johnston and his family often served as the Trustee, meaning they had a degree of respect, trust, and prominence in the community.

diately headed back to northern Virginia.[462] Whether he impulsively stopped the train or not, he did help raise Company F of the Sixth Virginia Cavalry, earning the rank of Second Lieutenant for his efforts.[463]

Barely a month after the secession vote, Johnston led a team of men ordered to seize the property of the local Federal tax collector, Josiah Millard. Millard was a northern transplant, moving from Massachusetts with his wife and father-in-law in 1854. A prominent local citizen and U.S. government official, Millard was also an ardent and vocal unionist, making himself a ready target for retaliation by zealous young rebels in crisp uniforms.[464] Johnston and his team seized Millard "with great force and violence...[dragging] him from his house" as a prisoner of war, hauling him and his property south "to a rebel camp at Centerville" and then on to Culpeper Courthouse. That night in Culpeper, Millard was "bound...hand and foot" with "cords and ropes," and "otherwise injured and mistreated for at least 20 days." He was "greatly injured in his health, and property, and his feelings most cruelly outraged."[465]

In Johnston's mind, he was acting as a lieutenant in a legitimate military organization. As a Unionist who was actively helping the war effort, Millard and his property were subject to confiscation by the Confederate army. Millard of course saw it differently. He sued Johnston and won a hefty default judgment (Johnston was with the Confederate army and could hardly make an appearance in court to defend himself). The charges would come back to haunt him and nearly leave him homeless after the war.[466]

For now, Johnston was focused on military matters. He served in the Sixth Virginia Cavalry until assigned to General Jeb Stuart as the Acting Inspector of Outposts.[467] Johnston impressed Stuart and by the end of March, he was officially serving on the flamboyant cavalier's staff. Describing Johnston as "sober, indefatigable, and capable," Stuart thought he had "remarkable qualifications for the post of military engineer" and quickly recommended him for promotion to the Engineer Corps.[468]

Johnston's enlistment in the Sixth Virginia expired on May 1, before his lieutenant's commission in the Engineer Corps was official, but he stayed on for a "special assignment" along the James River building earthworks at Chaffin's Bluff until the paperwork came through. (Only days later, General Lewis Armistead's son Keith would join the Sixth Virginia Cavalry as a private in Company A, then served on detached duty with Stuart until the Gettysburg Campaign began.)[469]

Johnston spent the summer of 1862 working at Longstreet's headquarters, continuing to impress the generals in the Army of Northern Virginia during the Peninsula Campaign. After the bloodletting had subsided at Malvern Hill one year before his most well-known reconnaissance (almost to the hour), Johnston and another rising star in the engineer corps, Major Richard Kidder Meade, were sent to reconnoiter the Federal lines. In a drenching rain, the two young engineers made it up to the Federal works. To their surprise, they were completely empty; the Federals had retreated overnight. Johnston and Meade raced back to headquarters and, sopping wet, reported the news to both Stuart and Stonewall Jackson.[470] Johnston ultimately earned a position as the only engineer on Lee's staff, reporting for service in August of 1862.[471]

During the Second Battle of Bull Run and Antietam, though officially on Lee's staff, he was frequently sent to assist Longstreet. This is perhaps one of the reasons he was so hesitant to speak poorly of the First Corps commander after the war. Johnston's service with Longstreet also helps explain why he readily came to mind as the engineer leading the way when actual memories became hazy.[472]

At Fredericksburg that winter, Johnston "untiringly aided" Armistead Long, Pendleton, E.P. Alexander, and Colonel Henry Cabell "in posting and securing the artillery" both before and during the battle.[473] Lee was pleased that the "earthworks were constructed on [the hill's] crest at the most eligible positions," and were "judiciously chosen and fortified."[474] Even Longstreet agreed.[475]

Alexander remembered things a little differently. With a wry smile and perhaps some rosy nostalgia, he related a story about placing the guns on Marye's Heights with Sam Johnston. Being a trained military engineer, Alexander had been instructing the civil engineer Johnston on some of the finer points of artillery, now that

Johnston had proven himself a trusted reconnoitering officer. Alexander told Johnston that it was better to place the artillery on the brow of a hill, rather than the top. The elevation lost was more than made up for by the ability to cover the approach against attacking infantry.

When Lee arrived to examine Johnston's gun placements, he chided him for placing them too low, losing the elevation necessary to more effectively counter the Federal artillery across the river. Johnston, who had just been instructed by Alexander to place them there, trotted along the ridge to find him.

"You made me put them here," he told Alexander, presumably lightheartedly. "Now you come along and help me take the cussin'."

As Alexander approached, Lee called out: "Ah, Colonel Alexander, just see what a mistake Captain Johnston has made here in the location of his gun pits, putting them forward at the brow of the hill!"

"General," Alexander answered, "I told him to put the pits there, where they could see all this canister and short range ground this side [of] the town. Back on the hill they can see nothing this side [of] the river."

"But you have lost some feet of command you might have had back there," Lee argued.

Alexander explained he had already considered that and commanding the infantry's approach more than made up for any lost elevation. Whether Lee agreed with Alexander or not, the guns stayed where they were and famously blasted shot and shell into the attacking Yankees. There was little need for counter-battery fire during the assault.

Several days after the artillery's ghastly but shining performance, Alexander strode into headquarters and saw Sam Johnston sitting at the campfire. Alexander "took the opportunity, when the general was near enough to hear, to say loudly to Johnston, 'Sam, it was a mighty good thing those guns about Marye's were located on the brows of the hill when the Yankees charged them!'"

Alexander "could not resist the temptation to have one little dig at" Lee, though he was nervous he had gone too far. Fortunately, Lee "took it in silence and never let on that he was listening to us."[476]

By the spring, Johnston was receiving independent assignments.[477] Then the army finally received a designated chief engineer, Colonel William Proctor Smith. A talented young West Pointer, Smith looked at Johnston as an assistant, as he "had been for some time the only representative" of the engineers on Lee's staff.[478] They soon became acquainted with one another under fire; on April 30, as the Battle of Chancellorsville erupted, both were sent to General Richard Anderson's Division to examine the position and establish a line of entrenchments.

The next day, May 1, 1863, Johnston was sent to reconnoiter the Orange Turnpike before Jackson's attack (Smith took the Mine Road with another engineer).[479] As it turned out, it was McLaws who attacked up the Turnpike, driving the Federals back. After scouting the Turnpike, Johnston guided General Cadmus Wilcox's brigade into position.[480]

Sam continued his reconnoitering work throughout the battle. Sent to investigate whether the Federal army was reacting to Jackson's famous flanking movement around its right, Johnston found he was unable to get close enough to the Union lines to get the information he needed. He was seen by the Federal pickets and chased away by "bullets passing uncomfortably close." Discouraged and heading back to headquarters to report he couldn't complete his assignment, Sam spotted a large oak tree "very much higher than any other tree near it." He climbed the tree and "with the aid of a strong glass telescope," had a good look at the Union line.

Settling in, he "began writing to General Lee. Folding my notes, so that they would drop and not be seen," one of his couriers would pick them up and take them to Lee. Johnston spent a good deal of time in the oak branches taking notes before being noticed by Federal troops. He watched nervously as the Union officers called up a battery to try shooting him out of his perch. The first shot nearly hit him, smashing through tree branches just below him. Johnston decided he had seen enough and scurried down the tree in a hurry.[481]

During the fighting on May 3, Johnston "discovered large parks of the enemy's wagons and the camps of some of his troops" across the river. He pointed this out to the artillery commanders, who trained their guns on the "point indicated by Captain Johnston" and unleashed "a hot fire upon" the stationary Federals.[482]

After the battle, Johnston and E.P. Alexander reconnoitered "a position whence the line of battle of the enemy beyond Mine Run could be reached.[483] The engineers spent the rest of May designing and preparing works in the area, and in "tracing maps and making reconnaissances."[484]

The record is relatively silent as to what Sam Johnston and Proctor Smith were up to during the march to Pennsylvania, but most likely they were scouting routes, making maps, and assisting with water crossings. On June 29, as the impending battle drew near, Sam Johnston, Major Clarke, and Captain Henry Richardson of Ewell's Corps, headed to Harrisburg to meet with fellow engineer Jed Hotchkiss. The four engineers met a few miles outside Harrisburg and began to reconnoiter in preparation for the army's anticipated move to the Pennsylvania capital.[485]

When the army was recalled and ordered to concentrate near Gettysburg and Cashtown, Johnston most likely rode south with Ewell, for he was already on the field when Lee and Pendleton arrived.[486]

As he rode down Seminary Ridge that morning, Johnston had a crowded years' worth of experience, having served on the staffs of Jeb Stuart, James Longstreet, and Robert E. Lee. This was his sixth campaign overall and the fifth one serving on Lee's staff. He had been up to the Federal lines on more than one occasion, been shot at with rifles and cannon, and had consistently provided fresh and reliable intelligence. This morning, Lee needed someone to disappear over the Emmitsburg Road Ridge, into harm's way, to quickly gather critical information. Sam Johnston was just the man for the job.

JOHNSTON DIDN'T HAVE A WATCH AS HE RODE ALONG THE ridge that morning after the sunrise survey, but if he did, the hands would have told him it was about 5:30 or maybe even 6:00 a.m. Traditionally, Johnston's recon is thought of as a *dawn* reconnaissance, which lends an air of drama and intrigue, but it actually took place a bit later.[487]

The mistake in time originates with Sam Johnston himself. In a letter to Fitz Lee in 1878, he related that "early on the morning of the 2d" he was "ordered by Gen'l Lee to make a reconnaissance of the enemy's left."[488] Given the controversy over sunrise orders and delayed attacks, Fitz Lee was interested in a more specific time and asked Johnston to clarify. Johnston responded that he frankly didn't remember what time he left, but he took a guess to humor him. "I purposely avoided fixing the time of day in my letter to you," he told Lee, "because I did not have a watch at that time and any notice that I took of the time would be too unreliable to be of any use to you." After all, "amid the excitement and anxieties of such an occasion one would form but a very incorrect idea of the passage of time."

But he decided, perhaps unwisely, to "give you a few thoughts that may help you, by comparing them with what others have written." Those thoughts included his best guess that he "left HdQ. about sunrise—say 4 o'clock."[489] Notably, Johnston initially wrote that he left *headquarters* "about sunrise." That's not necessarily when the reconnaissance began in earnest. There was an important intervening stop on Seminary Ridge, which both Armistead Long and William Pendleton corroborate.

But Johnston gave an exact time and history latched onto it, hungry for precise information. From then on, it became nearly canonical in the Gettysburg gospel that Johnston left on his reconnaissance at dawn, since sunrise wasn't until after 4:45 (4:48 to be exact).[490] Part of that is Johnston's fault, for when he wrote about it later, he didn't reiterate his uncertainty.[491] Daylight and 4:00 a.m. became synonymous, despite the forty-five-minute separation. And of course, Johnston didn't immediately begin his reconnaissance when he left headquarters, at least in the way we understand it. He stopped on Seminary Ridge to view the line first. The misunderstanding has caused more than its fair share of misinterpretation about the reconnaissance and, since Johnston was the only one telling the story, about his credibility, character, and abilities.[xxvii]

Fortunately, a lot was going on in the Confederate army at sunrise, and other people wrote down their own reminiscences, giving us a few other windows to look through.

THE DISTANCE FROM LEE'S HEADQUARTERS TO HILL'S HEAD-quarters is just over a mile, a shade under a fifteen-minute horseback ride. If Lee, Long, and Johnston left army headquarters at sunrise (4:48 a.m.), then by the time they arrived at the Pitzer farmhouse, moved up the western slope of Seminary Ridge to meet Pendleton, and viewed the opposing lines, it would be just after 5:00 a.m. The sun would be visible in the sky and could be fairly described as *after* sunrise, just as Pendleton reported.

As their individual assignments all included determining the size and location of the Federal force, they probably moved up and down the ridge from the Point of Woods to McMillan's Orchard. Not only does the Point of Woods offer a substantial view of the field, a farm lane led directly from Pitzer's house to the observation point, making it a natural place to begin the survey.[492] Likewise, McMillan's property, which sits on a deceptively high portion of Seminary Ridge, provided an important, and much closer, view of Cemetery Hill. That made it a reasonable vantage point for the group to conclude the

---

xxvii   For example, if Johnston left at 4 a.m., there is a much higher chance that he would have encountered Gen. Geary's men on Little Round Top that morning. This is often cited as one of the reasons he couldn't have made it to Little Round Top and, as Stephen Sears wrote, he either "embellished his role rather than confess his failings" or he "unwittingly went somewhere else." Sears, *Gettysburg*, 253. National Park Ranger Karlton Smith notes the presence of the Second Corps, Buford's cavalry division, etc. as a reason Johnston couldn't have reached Little Round Top. Smith, "To Consider Every Contingency," *Papers of the 2006 Gettysburg National Military Park Seminar*, 104–105.

sunrise survey. And, as we'll see, there's other evidence to suggest this is where they ended up.

How long the survey took isn't known, but it was more than a few minutes. The distances between the Pitzer farmhouse, Point of Woods, and McMillan's Orchard are not far, but they do take time to traverse. Had they headed directly toward McMillan's house from the Point of Woods, they would have expended nearly another ten minutes (which meant another ten minutes back). With stops to view portions of the line with field glasses, discussions of the situation, and a gait designed to allow observation, a simple "survey [of] the enemy's position" could easily have occupied a half hour or more of their time.[xxviii]

By "comparing" Johnston's thoughts "with what others have written," we can discard the 4:00 a.m. guess he shrugged at Fitz Lee. Between Ewell's realization near sunrise that the plan had already gone awry, Long's recollections, and Pendleton's report of a sunrise survey with Long and Johnston, it's clear that Johnston wasn't even called to headquarters until nearly 4:45 that morning. After spending time reviewing the field from Seminary Ridge before heading out into no-man's land, Johnston wouldn't leave Confederate lines until 5:30 or 6:00, almost two hours later than his initial guess. Though a dangerous and important assignment, it wasn't a dawn reconnaissance.[xxix]

---

xxviii   Hill's headquarters was a quarter mile from the Point of Woods. The woodline extends another quarter mile toward the Emmitsburg Road. From there, it's roughly a quarter mile to McMillan's house.

xxix   While we have to be hesitant in taking precise times at face value, markers like sunrise and sunset are more reliable (indeed, many reports and recollections include solar positions like daylight, noon, etc. rather than specific times, as they were both more reliable and discernible). We can also reliably convert Johnston's estimate of "sunrise" to a specific time, even at a distance of over 150 years, where a watch face was dependent on the many factors affecting mid-nineteenth century time.

The view from the Point of Woods where Johnston, Pendleton, Long, and Walker began their sunrise survey on the morning of July 2, 1863. Author photo.

JOHNSTON SET OFF TOWARD THE ROUND TOPS WITH TWO primary goals: investigate the Federal left and do it quickly. As he told Fitz Lee in 1878, he "was ordered by Gen'l Lee to make a reconnaissance of the enemy's left and report as soon as possible."[493]

He also told Lee that he "made the reconnaissance accompanied by Major J.C. Clarke of the Engineers (Longstreet's Staff)." Johnston got Clarke's middle initial wrong, but he was referring to Major John J. Clarke, who was indeed an engineer on Longstreet's staff. xxx

---

xxx   Clarke's middle name has been something of an enigma. Johnston referred to him as John C. Clarke, while the National Archives and Virginia Military Institute records show John J. Clarke. John J. Clarke, NARA M331, RG 109, Roll 0057.; John J. Clarke Papers, VMI. He is also noted as John J. Clarke in an 1870 petition to remove his political disabilities due to his service in the Confederate army. "Disabilities," *Richmond Dispatch*, April 30, 1870. But Clarke became a prominent bridge contractor after the war and was invariably known

Though Clarke was relatively new to Lee's army, he had spent a long time working on fortifications at Richmond and earned a promotion to Major by the spring of 1863.[494]

Clarke was with Johnston on the reconnaissance to Harrisburg on June 29, but whether he went back to Longstreet's headquarters or with Johnston directly to Gettysburg isn't known.[495] Regardless of where he was on July 1, he was decidedly at First Corps headquarters on the morning of July 2, as Arthur Fremantle remembered Clarke finding a horse for him that morning.[496]

More than thirty years after the reconnaissance, Johnston wrote that he "did not know [when he received his orders at headquarters] that another engineer officer was to accompany me but I was joined by Major J.C. Clarke of General Longstreet's staff."[497] Though Johnston's description conjures up an image of Clarke galloping after Johnston, trying to catch up with him on Seminary Ridge, Clarke probably joined him near the Point of Woods after the meeting with Long, Pendleton, and Walker.

Longstreet had just come up and met Lee around sunrise.[498] Though traditionally they met at Lee's headquarters, the timeline suggests it was probably at the Pitzer farm, or perhaps just up the ridge at McMillan's Hill. Fremantle remembered that Longstreet

---

professionally as John Graham Clarke. Perhaps he thought it would help his career prospects if his name was not linked to Confederate service, for immediately after his political disabilities petition, he seems to have exclusively used the middle initial "G." *Richmond Dispatch*, Feb. 28, 1871; "To Contractors," *The (Alexandria) Daily State Journal,* June 10, 1872. In the December 20, 1870 *Richmond Dispatch,* just eight months after petitioning for restoration of his political rights, he was referred to as Colonel John G. Clarke. And his obituaries all use the middle initial "G." "Richmond and Allegheny Railroad," *The (Staunton, VA) Valley Virginian,* Dec. 16, 1880; *The Brooklyn Daily Eagle,* Sept. 17, 1880. But since we're following him during his time with the Confederate army, we'll call him by the name he used during his Confederate service: John J. Clarke.

A John *C.* Clarke lived in Alexandria in the late 1860s. Johnston only knew John J. Clarke briefly. Perhaps he remembered the name of John *C.* Clarke from his hometown when he compiled his recollections later. *Richmond Dispatch,* Aug. 7, 1869.

was already on the field when he arrived around 5 a.m. John Black also remembered Longstreet joining Lee around sunrise. If Black and Fremantle are right, then Longstreet met Lee near the Pitzer farmhouse that morning.[499] And since Clarke was with Fremantle earlier that morning, it's likely Clarke rode with him to Seminary Ridge, arriving as Johnston was surveying the Federal line. When Longstreet ordered him to go on the recon as well, he would have to catch up. Given the timing, he either caught up with Johnston as he was with Long, Pendleton, and Walker, or as Johnston was headed back down Seminary Ridge or Willoughby Run.[500]

Clarke didn't leave any surviving account of the battle or the reconnaissance. He died in a gruesome and freak train accident in New Jersey in 1880, just three years after Longstreet published his first article blaming Johnston for the delay. Johnston didn't name anyone else in his account, so why bring up Clarke? Though it's certainly possible Johnston was looking for someone to "help take the cussin'" here, Longstreet had already blamed his own engineers for leading them down the wrong road. More importantly, Johnston doesn't mention Clarke's presence during the march, which is where contemporary criticisms of Johnston lay. So, it's unlikely Johnston was looking for his own scapegoat.[501]

Instead, he was probably giving Fitz Lee another source. Clarke was a popular officer, was later promoted to chief engineer of the Army of Tennessee and became a very successful bridge contractor after the war, not to mention "one of the largest iron contractors in the country."[502] He was also well known in the veterans' circles. Two former Confederate engineers served as pallbearers after his untimely death on the New Jersey railroad tracks, as did Lindsay Walker. George Peterkin's father, the Reverend Joshua Peterkin, conducted the funeral service and "one of the largest funeral processions ever seen in Manchester" brought Clarke's body to Hollywood Cemetery.[503] Not coincidentally, Peterkin, Walker, and the engineers were all part of the countermarch controversy. In the debate with this crowd, Clarke's account would be taken seriously.

Though Johnston would eventually have a very successful career, in 1878, Clarke was much more prominent in the South. Having a respected engineer and someone of Clarke's stature in the postwar South support his recollection would certainly lend credence to his statement. Curiously, and probably not coincidentally, Johnston didn't mention Clarke at all to McLaws, who would not be impressed with his status among the Virginia officers, but once again brought him up to George Peterkin in 1895, who by that time was a bishop in his own right.

Though Johnston wasn't looking to pick a fight with Longstreet, he *was* protective of his reputation (especially in 1878, as his life was just starting to turn a corner after more than a decade of relative hardship). Corroboration of the reconnaissance by Clarke could add an air of legitimacy to his reconnaissance among his circle of peers.

Of course, this is conjecture, but it is not without evidence. A cursory perusal of the *Southern Historical Society Papers* and the numerous Southern periodicals and speeches shows just how capricious reputations could be in the postwar South. Johnston was in massive debt when he returned from the war and in serious legal trouble. He owed thousands of dollars in judgments from creditors that had called while he was serving on Lee's staff. Josiah Millard had since won his case against him, winning a judgment of $3,000. Johnston's West Grove estate had been confiscated by the U.S. government due to his service in the Confederate military. As a final insult to his substantial injury, Millard bought West Grove at the U.S. Marshall's sale and haughtily lived there while the Johnstons fought the confiscation in court.[504]

A few years after the war, Johnston was able to land a temporary contract job as a surveyor for a county project, then worked a brief stint as an engineer for the Potomac Mining Company followed by a short-lived tenure with a firm associated with the Columbia Turnpike.[505] A promising railroad job was cut short when a competitor bought the surrounding land, blocking its expansion.[506] Johnston suffered another setback when he was seriously injured by a kick to his leg from his horse.[507] Finally, in July 1877, he was hired as the Master of Roads for the Ohio and Mississippi Railroad and moved to Cincinnati. He had been at the job less than six months when Fitz

Lee sent him Longstreet's article blaming him for losing the Battle of Gettysburg.[508]

Sam Johnston could be forgiven for being protective of his reputation. For more than a decade, he had been trying to pick up the pieces of the career and status he had left behind when he rode off to war (not to mention grieving the loss of two children). Now that things were looking up, the old second-in-command of the Army of Northern Virginia had very publicly blamed him personally for losing the battle. Dropping the name of the popular and successful Clarke was understandable given Johnston's circumstances.

Though Johnston would go on to success and professional esteem by the time he wrote to McLaws, at the beginning of 1878, he could use all the help he could get.

WHO ELSE RODE WITH JOHNSTON AND CLARKE THAT morning? Though McLaws later claimed he provided two hundred men from his division to accompany the reconnaissance, there's no corroborating evidence to support it. Lee told Johnston that as a young engineer in Mexico, he "found that he could get nearer the enemy and do more with a few men than with many." Johnston himself "found that to be true in every instance."[509] If Lee wanted a quick and quiet reconnaissance that morning, sending nearly a full regiment of infantry wasn't practical. (McLaws may have confused sending Wofford's sharpshooter battalion out as skirmishers in advance of his column during the march).[510]

Instead, Johnston remembered that he had only "three or four men." One of those was Clarke, but he didn't mention any names to McLaws (why would he? McLaws didn't seem to be on a friendly fact-finding mission).[511] It's possible that Johnston took a courier or two with him, as he did at Chancellorsville, so he could send real time messages back to Lee.

But just because it's possible doesn't mean it's likely. His assignment at Chancellorsville was to observe the Federal line for a long period of time, alerting Lee in case anyone spotted Jackson's attack. It was important that he had the couriers to send the messages back while keeping his eye on the Federal line. But Johnston's July 2 assignment wasn't to stay in one place and relay a continuous stream of intelligence; it was to find particular pieces of information and bring them back quickly. There was little need for a coterie of couriers, though it's reasonable to think he brought *someone* to send back a particularly important and urgent message (say, if infantry was advancing at that very moment or if some members of the reconnaissance were captured).[xxxi]

If the balance of the party wasn't made up of anonymous couriers, then who went? If Johnston's estimate is even partially correct, *someone* went with him and Clarke that morning. If it wasn't a courier, then it was a staff officer. And there is a very finite selection of people to choose from.

William Pendleton reported that the army's chief engineer, Proctor Smith, joined Johnston after the Seminary Ridge survey. After the morning's meeting and placing the artillery, Pendleton took several staff officers on a reconnaissance of the Ravine Road. When he was done, he sat on a hill where Willoughby Run intersects the Fairfield Road, looking over the ground "between this point and the Emmitsburg road." Union cavalry prowled the fields and Pendleton could see infantry, artillery, and wagon trains moving up the road.[xxxii]

---

xxxi   Couriers also meant more people that could be captured with the intelligence Lee sought, which would tip off the Federal command of Lee's intentions.

xxxii   There is no proper name for the hill. We'll refer to it from here on out as Pendleton's Hill. It may be tempting to conclude that the high ground along the Fairfield Road was Bream's Hill, but that would be stretching Pendleton's report too far. He was clear that he reconnoitered the Ravine Road and he returned to an elevated point. He started his reconnaissance very near Pendleton's Hill, so retracing his steps would have brought him back to that point. Even if he went to Bream's Hill at some point during the morning (though there's no evidence he did), it would be quite a generous reading of his report to conclude he returned there at the end of his reconnaissance.

"This front," Pendleton reported "was, after some time, examined by Colonel [William P.] Smith and Captain Johnston (engineers)."[512]

Proctor Smith was a West Pointer, graduating in the class of 1857 alongside E.P. Alexander, Richard K. Meade (who scouted the Malvern Hill line with Johnston), and Marcus Reno (who led the charge ahead of Custer at the Little Bighorn).[513] While Johnston was getting his feet wet as a reconnoitering officer on the Virginia Peninsula in 1862, Smith was designing and building fortifications around Richmond (and collecting promotions). By April of 1863, when he was assigned to Lee's army as the chief engineer, he had reached the rank of Lieutenant Colonel.[514]

One of Smith's overarching jobs as chief engineer of the Army of Northern Virginia was to organize the First Engineer Troop, designed to be a consolidated engineer unit for quicker deployment and more efficiency. But the momentous events of the summer precluded any work on it, and General Lee specifically ordered Smith to put the Engineer Troop on hold.[515]

At Chancellorsville, Smith performed a good deal of reconnaissance work, and there, as well as at Richmond, he had the trust of his commanding officers to select battle lines. "We selected a line of battle at Tabernacle Ch. and put the troops in position," he reported, "afterwards selecting two other lines in the direction of Fredericksburg, it being the intention...to allow the advance of the enemy to come close together."

The next day, as Johnston reconnoitered the Orange Turnpike in advance of McLaws's attack, Smith scouted the Mine Road. Then as Sedgewick overran Early's position at Fredericksburg, Proctor Smith was sent to scout positions for McLaws's men at Salem Church.[516] It was at Salem Church, remember, that Lee had uncharacteristically lost his temper, blaming McLaws for his reconnaissance failures.

But while he wrote extensively about the minutiae of the engineers' activities at Chancellorsville, Smith was frustratingly tight-lipped about their activities at Gettysburg. "All the officers displayed energy and ability in selecting positions and placing the troops in line of battle, Longstreet on the Right Wing, Ewell on the left wing and A.P. Hill in the centre." Aside from reporting on Captain

Henry Richardson's wounding and the reconnaissance through the mountain passes for the retreat, that was the extent of his report on the battle. (In contrast, he spent the next paragraph offering more characteristically detailed accounts of the fortifications and bridges during the retreat.)[517]

It wouldn't have been at all out of the ordinary for Proctor Smith to accompany Johnston, whom he regarded as a sort of assistant and now recognized as a more than capable reconnoitering officer. But if the chief engineer of the army was on the reconnaissance, why didn't anyone—especially Sam Johnston—mention it?

According to his obituary, Smith was "very reticent as to the part he took in the war, except to intimate friends, and even they had to exercise considerable tact in order to draw him out."[518] If Johnston intended to give Fitz Lee additional sources, Proctor Smith wouldn't have been much of a wellspring.

Johnston similarly remained relatively guarded about his wartime activities. There are only four surviving letters, one of which was published against his wishes. He only wrote one unsolicited letter about the battle (that we know of), and there's no evidence he had much interest in veterans' affairs, especially after leaving Virginia in 1877. (He only happened to see Leslie Perry's article because it was printed in a local New York paper.)

He seemed hesitant to drag anyone else into the argument. Most of his correspondence on the subject takes great pains not to implicate anyone or further the controversy. Despite the direct accusation from Longstreet, for example, Johnston wrote Fitz Lee that "I do not know whether the distinguished Lieutenant General intended that the compliment or his censure should outweigh" and "while I am confident that I have given a correct statement, I do not want my letter published."[519] Fourteen years later, he told McLaws that "I do not want to be a party to controversy with anyone, certainly not with General Longstreet, who always treated me with so much kindness and consideration" during the war. "Therefore, I will confine myself to answering your questions as nearly as I can, avoiding comment."[520] (His self-imposed confinement may have had something to do with

Fitz Lee publishing the paper against his wishes. In any event, it was wise, as McLaws published Johnston's letter, too.)[521]

Proctor Smith was not only his superior officer but a popular officer in the circle of former Confederates who subscribed to the *Southern Historical Society Papers*. Less than six months before Johnston wrote his letter to Fitz Lee, Proctor Smith had attended the Lee Monument Ball at the prestigious White Sulphur Springs in his home state of West Virginia.[xxxiii] The Ball saw such notable attendees as General Joseph E. Johnston, S.D. Lee, General and Governor James Kemper, General DuBose (commander of the Fifteenth Georgia), Wade Hampton, and Robert Toombs. Proctor Smith was considered an important enough Southern son to be included in the list of dignitaries in the *New York Times*' report on the Ball.[522] Two years earlier he had been a staff member at the inaugural ceremony of the Stonewall Jackson monument in Richmond.[523]

But true to his obituary's memory of him, he did not often don his Confederate colors or speak of his service, nor did he travel far to do so. There doesn't appear to be any correspondence available to or from wartime comrades and many didn't always know where to find him. He seemed content to live out his life in relative quiet as an engineer in West Virginia.[524]

Pendleton's lone statement in his report provides the only window showing Smith's involvement, but it's an important view. Despite Pendleton's later reputation for inaccurate memories of the Battle of Gettysburg, in 1863, he had no reason to make up the fact that Smith accompanied Johnston. And there's no evidence at all that Johnston went on an afternoon reconnaissance (nor could he have gone on the other side of the Emmitsburg Road Ridge). If Proctor Smith was with Johnston when he examined "this front," then it was during the morning reconnaissance.[xxxiv]

---

xxxiii   West Virginia seceded from *Virginia* in 1863, so it's slightly inaccurate to say Smith was a native West Virginian. But he was native to western Virginia, which ultimately became annexed as part of the state of West Virginia.

xxxiv   Pendleton also wasn't in a position to know exactly when Johnston and Smith reconnoitered and returned, for he was on his own reconnaissance that morning.

* * *

IF BOTH CLARKE AND SMITH JOINED SAM JOHNSTON ON his reconnaissance, then at least half of Johnston's party has been accounted for. That is, if he remembered correctly when he told McLaws he had "only three or four men." At least one other engineer was on Longstreet's staff, though.

Captain Henry Judson Rogers is mentioned by Longstreet in the usual litany of praise at the end of his July 1863 report.[525] Rogers was also noticed by John Logan Black, the South Carolina cavalryman who witnessed the "council of war" that morning. Black arrived "at daylight" and saw Lee "conversing with Lt. Gen. A.P. Hill.... Capt. Rogers, a Virginian I knew & had known well at Adams Run had accompanied Gen'l Lee & was sitting some paces off. I rode up and dismounted, sat down by Capt. Rogers, waiting for Gen'l Lee to be unengaged." Longstreet soon rode up and joined the conversation with Lee and Hill, while "Capt. Rogers and I were out of ear shot & ourselves talking in a low tone."[526]

Henry Rogers was the nephew of Confederate General Asa Rogers, who commanded the Second Division, Virginia Militia near Middleburg. General Rogers had written his nephew a recommendation letter that helped land him a spot on General P.G.T. Beauregard's staff early in the war.[527] Captain Rogers also served for a time on A.P. Hill's Division staff in 1862 and then on Longstreet's staff at the beginning of 1863, when he was captured during Longstreet's foray at Suffolk, South Carolina. Fortunately for Rogers, he spent just a shade over a week in captivity and was paroled at the end of April.[528]

Henry's cousin, Arthur Rogers (General Rogers's son) may actually have been an acquaintance of Sam Johnston. Both were engineers and both were classically schooled in Alexandria, which meant they were enrolled in classes with a tutor. Young Arthur Rogers was sent to Alexandria to study with Benjamin Hallowell, perhaps the most prestigious tutor of the day.[529]

July 2

Hallowell had established a boarding school in downtown Alexandria in the 1820s, within miles of where Sam Johnston grew up on his family estate. Hallowell's students included the children of Virginia's elite families, including a young Robert E. Lee, who studied math with Hallowell in preparation for his enrollment at West Point.[530] Rogers and Johnston were both from prominent Virginia families and were both at least in the same social and educational circles. Given the importance of the social network in antebellum Virginia, it's hard to imagine the Johnstons and Rogers weren't at least nominally acquainted. That would be just one more reason not to mention him in the increasingly hostile and public debate.

There *is* some question as to whether Rogers was at the battle. Though no longer a Union prisoner, some of his paperwork suggests he was at Richmond while the army was fighting in Pennsylvania. For example, a request for promotion was submitted on July 4, 1863, just a day after the famous (or infamous) assault on Cemetery Ridge. Sitting in the rain as the army prepared to retreat seems an odd time to send in for career advancement, especially since the engineers were employed in a variety of logistical activities. But ten days later, he was with the army on the Virginia side of the Potomac, for he submitted a receipt for harnesses, saddles, bridles, and other tack required to move a depleted and retreating army via horsepower.[531] Regardless of the strangely dated promotion request, both Longstreet and John Logan Black remembered Henry Rogers at Gettysburg and they did so entirely independent of each other. It's more likely the promotion request was either backdated or submitted by someone on his behalf, meaning he was present on the field on July 2.

If he was with Lee and Longstreet at sunrise on July 2, it's possible (but by no means certain) he accompanied Longstreet's other engineer on the reconnaissance that morning. He wasn't a high-profile figure like Clarke or Smith. Even if he *had* gone out on the recon that morning, Johnston may not have remembered it, and if he did, there's a good chance he wouldn't have mentioned it. But Black remembered talking with Rogers "in a low tone" throughout the famous meeting between the generals, making it unlikely he had gone with Johnston, Clarke, and Smith. So, Rogers will have to remain a possible, but unlikely, member of the July 2 reconnaissance.

JOHN CHEVES HASKELL HAS ALSO BEEN SUGGESTED AS ONE of the riders that morning.[532] Haskell was second in command of Major Mathis Henry's artillery battalion, assigned to Hood's Division.[533] Haskell wrote a memoir, published in 1903, detailing his experiences at Gettysburg.

"On the evening of the [first] of July," he began, "we heard firing just across the mountain and were ordered in that direction and marched all night across the mountain, reaching the plain of Gettysburg about daybreak." As they neared the battlefield, Haskell remembered the dreadful scenes of the first day's fighting and "passed through the field hospital of Pettigru's [*sic*] brigade, which I had last seen in North Carolina." The artillerists continued "only a short distance and halted to rest and feed just on the Emmetsburg [*sic*] pike where we opened the fight later that same evening."[xxxv]

Haskell's memory has some flaws, of course, and he meshes the pre-battle activities together, but his manuscript is easy enough to follow. "We lay there till about four o'clock [p.m.]," he continued, "when we [were] ordered to take a position not more than a hundred yards from where we had been since early morning and open[ed] on the mountain opposite (Little Round Top). About an hour earlier I had, with several couriers and one of our officers, ridden over the top of Round Top, finding only a picket of two or three men, one of whom we captured."[534]

Without the rest of his memoir for context, a ride "over the top of Round Top" with another officer (*Captain* Sam Johnston, perhaps?) with a handful of couriers and "no body of the enemy…in sight" certainly sounds like Johnston's reconnaissance. But Haskell was clear that this all happened in the afternoon. His ride "over the

---

xxxv   Haskell probably meant the Fairfield Road, as they were already marching on the Chambersburg Pike.

top of Round Top" was at 3:00 p.m., according to his memoir, and it was "about one or two o'clock" in the afternoon when he noticed the fields were devoid of Federal troops. In the nearly obligatory commentary on Longstreet's culpability, Haskell remembered that Lee and Longstreet rode up around noon to observe the Federal position, *before* Haskell went on his own recon.[535]

If Haskell made his reconnaissance in the afternoon, he would have run into more than just a handful of Federals and undoubtedly would have become *their* prisoner, rather than vice versa as he described. Union General Hobart Ward's Third Corps brigade had moved into position in and around Devil's Den by that point and the area was covered by a regiment of Federal sharpshooters.[536] There's simply no way he could have conducted the reconnaissance even close to the way he described it.

But Haskell remembered *something* that afternoon. Though his memoir clearly confuses details, like the names of roads and chronology, that's understandable given forty years had passed by the time he put pen to paper. He also seems to include remnants from other people's stories (the captured cavalrymen, riding over Round Top), another common occurrence in later postwar accounts.

Rather than Johnston's reconnaissance, Haskell probably remembered riding with E.P. Alexander to place his own battalion as Hood was arriving. In his initially unpublished memoir, Porter Alexander remembered that he brought "a courier or two with me" when he went on his own reconnaissance that day.[537] Though Alexander remembered one long reconnaissance, he was also writing several decades after the war and, like Haskell, probably conflated several shorter and more defined recons. Alexander's memoir mentions looking for artillery placements, including Henry's Battalion, that afternoon; likewise, Haskell remembered his own recon occurred just before taking position, coinciding much more closely with Alexander's brief reconnaissance to find artillery placements than Johnston's early reconnaissance.[xxxvi] So while it's tempting to read

---

xxxvi   It has also been suggested that Johnston may have "enlisted" the assistance of local citizens. Of course this is possible, but there's nothing to suggest he did. To draw an inference, there must be at least

Haskell's memoir and conclude that he rode with Johnston, it doesn't appear that he did.

WHEN JOHNSTON LEFT THE SUNRISE SURVEY, HE HEADED south. But where exactly he ended up, how he got there, and what he saw hasn't been agreed on by historians. Johnston claimed that he reached Little Round Top and had a "commanding view" of the surrounding area. While none of Johnston's contemporaries disputed his account of the reconnaissance, modern historians tend to dismiss the idea that he reached Little Round Top and conclude the intelligence he brought back was wildly incorrect.[538]

The details of Johnston's reconnaissance only survive in fragments of the four letters we have from him. He was the only member of the recon to write about it and even then, he did so grudgingly and guardedly.[539] Keeping in mind the purpose of the reconnaissance, along with the inherent biases and problems with memory, we can follow Sam Johnston, John Clarke, and Proctor Smith on their famous, and misunderstood, reconnaissance that morning.

"MY GENERAL ROUTE WAS ABOUT THE SAME THAT GENERAL Longstreet took when he made his march," Johnston wrote Lafayette

---

some connection to documentary evidence. The inference acts as the connection between the points of documentation. Without the evidentiary endpoints, the inference is just conjecture or speculation. So while the possibility certainly remains open that a southern sympathizer, or even a scared Unionist trying to curry favor with the occupiers to save one's self and property, guided Johnston's party on their reconnaissance, for the time being it must remain speculation. (The Wentz and Culp families famously had southern connections, for example, but even in those cases, there's no evidence their knowledge of the area was utilized).

McLaws in 1892, almost twenty-nine years to the day from the reconnaissance. Johnston and his team "crossed the creek on the same bridge that [Longstreet] did and turned to the left at once and got on the ridge where you [McLaws] subsequently formed your line, following along that ridge in the direction of the round top across the Emmitsburg road and got up on the slopes of round top, where I had a commanding view, then rode along the base of round top to beyond the ground that was occupied by General Hood, and where there was later on a cavalry fight."[540] To Fitz Lee, he recalled he "had to ride about (4) miles" and "more than half this distance was covered by our pickets."[541] Then in 1895, he told George Peterkin that he "assured" Lee that he reached Little Round Top.[542]

Johnston didn't take much of a breath describing his route to McLaws, so it's helpful to break it down, keeping in mind that distances and details were often distorted when recalled later. Campbell Brown, for example, scratched down some "impressions on my mind" as he toured the battlefield on its fifteenth anniversary in 1878, just a few months after Johnston wrote his initial thoughts to Fitz Lee. Brown was surprised at how his memory had played tricks on him. "Round Top is much further from as high as I thought it," he scribbled into his notebook. "As to [the] height of Cemetery Hill, it is much less than I thought."[543] As Johnston reminded Fitzhugh Lee, the "excitement and anxieties" of the moment affected one's perception during the battle. It was the perception, the initial imprint, that the soldiers recalled later. If the initial imprint was distorted by excitement and anxiety, then the recollection would naturally be inaccurate, even before any external factors affected it.[544]

Johnston remembered that he rode about four miles to get to the Round Tops, roughly half of which was covered by Confederate troops. The distance from Lee's headquarters to the Round Tops, following Johnston's route, is about four and a half miles. From McMillan's Hill, it's about 3.8 miles. Even with the help of a map, giving Johnston a margin of error of a half mile seems fair, given the length of time that had passed. (He was also referring to the distance to get *to* the Round Tops, not the round trip.)

When Johnston began his recon that morning, the Confederate line extended two miles south of Lee's headquarters to the Point of Woods. Lowrance's skirmishers covered another half mile, meaning over half the distance from Lee's headquarters to the Round Tops was within Confederate lines, just like Johnston remembered. Though Johnston remembered the route being covered by pickets, he more likely remembered Pender's Division and Lowrance's skirmishers that morning.

Johnston described his "general route" as "about the same that General Longstreet took." Johnston qualifies his statements twice: his *general* route was *about* the same as Longstreet's. Ultimately, Longstreet's two divisions marched along the Ravine Road west of Seminary Ridge, so any route that traced Willoughby Run to the Eiker's Mill Road would qualify as being "about the same" as Longstreet's route.[xxxvii]

If Johnston stuck to farm lanes, he could have followed the Pitzer farm lane back to the Ravine Road, as he was familiar with both roads after his afternoon reconnaissance with Pendleton the day before. It would also help justify his later statement that he did, in fact, examine some of the roads the infantry would have to take into position.

But he could also have followed the farm lane through Spangler's Woods, which is the woodlot that creates the "point" in the Point of Woods. That lane leads to a road known appropriately as the Spangler-Pitzer Lane, which also leads back to Willoughby Run and the Ravine Road.[545] Either of these routes follows the rough outline of Longstreet's march into position and are entirely possible based on Johnston's description and his whereabouts that morning.

It may be tempting to place Johnston on the Black Horse Tavern Road that morning, as that's the road McLaws initially started on when he was forced to countermarch. But only one brigade of Long-

---

xxxvii   Eiker's Mill Road is now called the Millerstown Road, which becomes Pumping Station Road. The road has been called other names, such as the Millerstown Road and even the Fairfield Road. To avoid confusion, it's referred to as Eiker's Mill Road as the National Park Service Record of Treatment Maps refer to it.

street's men set foot on the road and even then, only marched along it for a few hundred yards.[546] Longstreet's men spent so little time on that road that it's not accurate to say it was the route Longstreet took.

Likewise, it wouldn't make sense for Johnston to have scouted the road. When he left, McLaws's Division hadn't arrived, so there were no troops anywhere near the Black Horse Tavern or the road that bore its name. To scout the road would have taken him at least a mile and a half out of his way (three miles round trip), and at 5:30 a.m. there was no need to scout it. Rather, the Ravine Road, which was less than a mile behind the Confederate line, captured the attention of the Confederate planners that morning.

Johnston then remembered crossing "the same bridge" that McLaws did before turning left and getting onto the ridge where McLaws's Division formed that afternoon. Based on his description, there's little doubt that Johnston crossed Willoughby Run near Pitzer's school house. There was a crossing at the small building and the road intersects with Eiker's Mill Lane; a traveler heading south could make a left and ride along the road to the top of Seminary Ridge.

Johnston's reference to a bridge has caused its fair share of consternation. In notes he took while preparing his 1896 article, McLaws noted that "my command did not cross any creek on a bridge."[547] None of the contemporary maps show a bridge in the vicinity, either. Though Bachelder's isometric map clearly shows the Ravine Road running through Willoughby Run, there's no indication it was anything but a ford.[548] More likely, there may have been a makeshift bridge to allow the schoolchildren to cross when the creek was high, but which was removed as an obstacle by the infantry or considered so insubstantial as not to warrant a mention.

Some have speculated that the reference to a bridge indicates Johnston crossed Sach's covered bridge, which crosses Marsh Creek a little over half a mile west of Pitzer's school house. Sach's bridge is a substantial bridge and would indeed be memorable even thirty years later. But there's nothing else to suggest that's the bridge Johnston is referring to.

Johnston described crossing the same bridge as Longstreet (or Longstreet's infantry) and then getting on the ridge McLaws later deployed his troops. If Johnston's general route was even remotely close to the one Longstreet took, and if he's relatively accurate that he got to Warfield Ridge shortly after crossing the bridge, then the bridge can't be Sach's bridge.

In order to end up on Warfield Ridge shortly after crossing Sach's Bridge, Johnston would have to have crossed from west to east. That means he would have had to have crossed Marsh Creek already. Otherwise, he would be on the western side of Marsh Creek, a full mile from where McLaws was positioned. The only reasonable place to have crossed would be the stone bridge on the Fairfield Road, which is substantially out of Johnston's way. Even if he traveled cross-country, the bridge on the Fairfield Road was nearly two miles in the opposite direction of the area he was supposed to be scouting. From the Fairfield Road bridge, Johnston would have had to ride nearly another three miles to reach Sach's Bridge, a total detour of five miles.

Johnston's assignment was to cover a defined area in the shortest amount of time possible. Despite the alluring reference to a bridge, there's nothing in Johnston's (or anyone else's) accounts that suggest he crossed over Sach's Bridge.

Johnston's "commanding view" from Little Round Top, captured by Alexander Gardner's photographers several days after the battle. The Taneytown Road is to the far right with Zeigler's Grove and the "eminence" visible in the center left background. Library of Congress.

* * *

BRIDGE OR NO BRIDGE, AFTER JOHNSTON AND HIS PARTY crossed the creek and turned left onto Eiker's Mill Lane, they "follow[ed] along that ridge in the direction of the round top across the Emmitsburg Road." Eiker's Mill Lane forked a few hundred yards beyond the creek, with the right lane leading through a patch of woods until it emerged at the residence of Philip Snyder. Just 150 yards south of there, on the other side of the road, was another farm lane, used by farmer John Slyder. Slyder's lane led straight to his farmhouse along Plum Run, at the foot of Round Top.

The Slyder Lane entrance on the Emmitsburg Road. Note that the lane leads directly toward the Round Tops. Author photo.

The terrain changes dramatically just a few hundred yards down the lane, and one quickly becomes isolated in a large ravine between the ridge and Round Tops. If Johnston followed John Slyder's farm path, then not only would he be heading "in the direction of the round top," but he would be nearly invisible to anyone not already in the ravine. Since "to see and not to be seen" was how Johnston described his role as a reconnaissance officer, the Slyder Farm Lane offered a perfect route through the ground he was supposed to scout.[549]

Though the Slyder Lane matches Johnston's description and accomplishes all of the goals of his reconnaissance, other routes are possible, too. For example, he may have continued along Warfield Ridge further south, riding along the general path of modern day South Confederate Avenue. From there, he could have taken the Bushman farm lane, which starts out nearly parallel to the Slyder Lane. Or he simply could have followed the ridge as it curled toward the southern slope of Big Round Top, guided by the contours of the ridge, rather than farmers' paths.

The view north from the Slyder Lane. Only a few hundred feet down the lane, Johnston would have been invisible to anyone north of him. Author photo.

Looking toward the Emmitsburg Road from the Slyder Lane. The white building is the Snyder farmhouse, only about fifty yards beyond the Emmitsburg Road. The bend in the Slyder Lane would conceal Johnston from any cavalry patrols along the road. Author photo.

The view from the bottom of the ravine along the Slyder Lane. From the lane, Johnston would be able to confirm there were no Federal troops in the ravine. He could also see that the terrain was not good for maneuvering troops and maintaining command control, both facts he almost certainly reported to Lee. Author photo.

No matter the precise route he took, once he crossed the Emmitsburg Road, he had a good view of the wrinkled topography south of the Peach Orchard. More importantly, he could see no Federal troops in the ravines, swales, and marshes. It must also have been abundantly clear that the ground was not ideal for maneuvering infantry.

Johnston remembered that he eventually "got up on the slopes of round top, where I had a commanding view." The term "round top" was used freely in the nineteenth century and described any large conical hill (there were at least two other "round tops" in the area). Though today, the two hills are delineated as Big and Little Round Top, in 1863 locals often referred to the entire area as "Round Top." In addition to referring to the specific hill, the term was often used for the series of ridges that emanated from the larger hill. While there *are* references specifically to Little Round Top before the hill gained its historical prominence, it was more often known by any one of a variety of other names: Granite Spur, Rock Hill, Spur of Round Top, Rocky Hill, or Sugar Loaf Hill.[550]

211

In 1892, Johnston simply wrote that he got on the slopes of "round top." Three years later, when he wrote to George Peterkin, he was more specific, telling the bishop that he had reached *Little* Round Top. The view from the northwestern slope of Little Round Top certainly qualifies as "commanding." More than one photo, then and now, has been taken of the vista. The panorama had even caused a wide-eyed Porter Alexander to remark "How grand!... What a position!" when he first climbed the summit in 1893.[551]

More important than a grand view of the pristine countryside, Johnston could clearly see all of the ground he had been sent to investigate. Every nook and cranny of every ridge and ravine was laid out before him. He could see all the way to his own army's battle line a mile and a half away and had a clear view all along the spine of Cemetery Ridge. The impressive view is in fact the precise reason modern historians don't believe he got there.

Though none of his peers questioned his account, what if those historians are right and Johnston *didn't* get to Little Round Top? Where was his commanding view?

One possibility is that Johnston's party reached Big Round Top and found an impressive view there. But the tree coverage on the hill makes this unlikely. Perhaps, like at Chancellorsville, Johnston climbed a tree on Big Round Top. That would solve the problem of foliage obscuring the view, but Johnston doesn't mention that he climbed any trees. Of course, just because he didn't explicitly say he climbed a tree doesn't mean that he didn't; but his description implies it was the "slopes of round top" themselves that offered the "commanding view," not an arboreal perch.

To assume Johnston didn't get to Little Round Top also assumes that he was either lying or incompetent. Both hills, including the bare western slope of Little Round Top, are visible from nearly everywhere on the field: the Point of Woods, McMillan's Orchard, Warfield Ridge, the Slyder Lane, Bushman's farm lane.... The hills dominate the horizon south of the Federal position and were noticed by nearly everyone in the Confederate army.

It stretches the imagination to assume that Johnston, one of the best reconnoitering officers in the army, confused Little

Round Top for another hill. For if he wasn't *on* Little Round Top, he would be able to *see* Little Round Top, which of course would tell him that he wasn't there. Indeed, the whole point of Johnston's reconnaissance was to investigate the ground between the Emmitsburg Road Ridge and the Round Tops. The hills were fundamental to his reconnaissance, if not as a vantage point, then at least as a landmark. If professors and historians can orient themselves to the battlefield using Little Round Top, certainly Johnston could.

But just because he couldn't have *confused* the hills doesn't necessarily mean he actually made it onto Little Round Top. As Stephen Sears suggests, he could have been lying "rather than confess his failings."[552] That's true, but there was little reason for him to do so in the 1890s. Johnston was accused by his contemporaries of leading the First Corps down the wrong road, not for providing bad intelligence. Even if the reconnaissance didn't make it to the top of either Round Top, it wouldn't have been considered a failure, so there would be nothing to confess.

Indeed, Johnston told Peterkin that Lee was surprised at how far he got, meaning Lee didn't even expect him to be able to get to Little Round Top in the first place. There's nothing about the sunrise survey that suggests Johnston's goal was to get to the top of Round Top, either. With the help of a field glass, the slopes of Little Round Top are visible from Seminary Ridge; the hill was empty that morning and they all could see it. Lee's pleasant surprise was more likely caused by Johnston's ability to get there without running into Federal troops.

What was more, Johnston didn't initially mention where he went at all—his route and reconnaissance simply weren't an issue. The only reason we have any idea *where* he went is that McLaws asked about it nearly thirty years after the fact. There was no reason for Johnston to have mentioned reaching either Round Top, except as part of his honest memory.

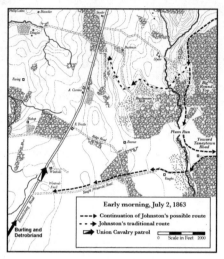

Johnston's probable route, showing potential alternatives and the more traditional return trip. Map by Philip Laino. See full sized maps on pages 465–466.

ACCORDING TO JOHNSTON'S LETTER TO MCLAWS, ONCE he viewed the field from his "commanding view," he "rode along the base of round top to beyond the ground that was occupied by General Hood, and where there was later on a cavalry fight."[553] The precise route Johnston took when he left Little Round Top isn't known, for he didn't leave an account any more detailed than the letter he wrote McLaws. But he did reveal that wherever he went was later occupied by Hood's Division and hosted a cavalry fight.

Hood's Division occupied the ground from Devil's Den to Big Round Top, staring down the Federal troops on Little Round Top and Big Round Top after the July 2 attack. During the night, the line extended further south, from the southern base of Big Round Top, across Plum Run, and onto the neighboring hill known as

214

Bushman's Hill. Skirmishers extended across Bushman's Hill to the Emmitsburg Road, with the line ending around the Kern house. As the day progressed and the Federal cavalry threat grew, Evander Law (who had taken over for the wounded Hood) shuffled a few more regiments that way.[554]

Law told Bachelder that he eventually decided the whole thing was a diversion designed to lengthen and weaken his line. The sight of cavalry forming closer to Big Round Top convinced him and he decided to attack the dismounted troopers on the Emmitsburg Road first. Having driven them back, he turned his attention back to the hills, where the Federal cavalry, led by General Elon Farnsworth, had begun its attack.[555] The charge became infamous when the young Farnsworth was killed. The dashing cavalier became a sort of martyr (even though his side won in the end), and the attack, framed as a tragically romantic suicidal charge, became decidedly more famous than the cavalry fighting on the Emmitsburg Road.[556]

Johnston's mention of a cavalry fight could have referred to either of these attacks, though Farnsworth's charge naturally comes to mind. Farnsworth's more famous attack *did* take place in the area Johnston was known to have scouted; Hood's men *did* occupy that ground for a much longer period, and the attack garnered enough publicity for Johnston to have known about it. Both Law and his men wrote about the attack extensively and it takes up a fair amount of space in their reports, second only to the July 2 assault.[557]

To reach the area occupied by Hood's Division from his vantage point on Little Round Top, Johnston probably retraced his steps along the western slopes of the Round Tops back along Plum Run, toward Bushman's Hill. If he curled along Bushman's Hill, the adjoining ridge (the southern end of Warfield Ridge) would have led him back to the Emmitsburg Road, loosely following along what would become the road bed of South Confederate Avenue. The modern park road, which leads the eyes and mind to conclusions as easily as it leads cars to tourist stops, subliminally suggests this, too. If he went this way, then he reached the Emmitsburg Road on the higher ground near the intersection with South Confederate Avenue, near the modern picnic facility.

But Johnston wasn't confined by tour roads or park boundaries. The only limits were his judgment and Federal soldiers. And it's clear from his recollections that he remembered riding *past* Hood's position and the scene of the cavalry fight.

Johnston wrote McLaws that he continued "*beyond* the ground that was occupied by General Hood and where there was later on a cavalry fight."[558] By all accounts, Farnsworth's charge crashed right into Hood's line and even passed behind it, into the rear to threaten the artillery. If Johnston stopped in the vicinity of Bushman's Hill and Plum Run, then he didn't pass *beyond* Hood's lines *or* the scene of the cavalry fight. Instead, he would have stopped *at* Hood's line. It may sound trivial, but words mean things and Johnston said what he said. If he stopped within Hood's lines, he was articulate enough to have said what he meant. If he went where he said he did, he must have traveled further south, past the Round Tops.

Johnston also wrote that he continued his reconnaissance until he "thought that I had gone far enough."[559] That suggests that he went a considerable way further than Hood's line and the scene of Farnsworth's charge. He didn't stop there, but instead continued past it until he had investigated the area to his satisfaction.

This all begs the question *why* he would continue further south if he had spotted the Federal line from Little Round Top. It seemed he had arrived in the rear of the army, after all, and could report both the position of the Federal left *and* the topography between the Round Tops and Emmitsburg Road. What more could there be to the south to justify spending more time? Speed *was* a priority, so Johnston must have had a reason to think his reconnaissance wasn't complete after riding through the ravine and to the top of Little Round Top.

In addition to Sickles's bivouacking Third Corps, Johnston had seen a division of Second Corps infantry arriving along the Taneytown Road. The night before, the Confederates could easily observe two brigades of the Third Corps marching up the Emmitsburg Road. The two other Third Corps brigades arrived well after midnight, considerably less visible to Confederates on Seminary Ridge. Without all seven Federal corps accounted for, there was an important question left open: *were any other Federal troops marching up either road from the south that morning?*

It's hard to imagine Johnston's reconnaissance being considered complete with these two questions unanswered. *He* certainly didn't think so. And if he had an intuition that there might be more Federal troops coming up either the Taneytown or Emmitsburg Roads, he was right. He spotted Federal infantry marching up the Emmitsburg Road, maybe a mile south of him, close enough that he worried about being stuck on the east side of the road.

The approaching Federal columns would be difficult to see through the foliage on Bushman's Hill, though. And the contours of the Pennsylvania farmland make it difficult to see long distances to the south from Warfield Ridge. Perhaps he used a glass, but a field telescope or binoculars couldn't see through the ridges. Distance wasn't a problem. Topography was.[560]

Johnston's accounts obliquely suggest this, too. He mentioned that "after examining the roads which our troops would have to move in the event of a movement on the enemy's left, I returned to Headquarters and made my report."[561] Johnston is not immune from the biases and imperfections of memory, so it's possible his memory of scouting roads for maneuvering was *not* for the purpose of finding a route into position, but really a cursory examination of the Emmitsburg and Taneytown Roads. There's little evidence he investigated any roads other than these and the Ravine Road. But he was also being accused of getting lost; a reasonable defense to that charge would be to claim that he *did* scout the roads, and it was the delay in getting the march started and the attack underway once the troops were in position that were the real culprits. It just so happens that's the defense he presented.[562]

SO WHERE ELSE COULD HE HAVE GONE? NUMEROUS FARM lanes meandered through the woods along the southern base of Round Top and along Plum Run. Johnston could have followed any number of them to work his way south from Little Round Top. There were ample farm paths to take him to the Taneytown Road along the southern base of Big Round Top in order to quickly take a look down the road. Unlike the view from Warfield Ridge along the Emmitsburg Road, the view south along the Taneytown Road is wide open, allowing Johnston to see for miles. The road was empty, for most of the Federal wagons had been left behind in Taneytown. Determining that there were no more Federal infantrymen tramping up the road, he decided he had "gone far enough."[563]

Whichever path south he took, he eventually would have run into a more substantial road known as Knight (or Wintrode) Road. This east-west road no longer exists in its entirety, but at the time Johnston was there, Knight Road ran from the Taneytown Road to the Emmitsburg Road, passing over the top of a ridge owned by Samuel Wintrode.[xxxviii], [564]The road gradually climbed the ridge through Wintrode's property, ending up on a hill appropriately called Wintrode Knoll where it intersected with the Emmitsburg Road. In the summer of 1863, the knoll was bare, offering a view some distance down the Emmitsburg Road.[xxxix]

Sam Johnston remembered that after he thought he had "gone far enough," he "turned back, of course moving with great caution, and when I again got in sight of Emmitsburg Road I saw three or four troopers moving slowly and very cautiously in the direction of Gettysburg." The Federal cavalry was moving so slowly, "I was afraid that I would be detained too long and finally cut off by a large force coming up."[565]

Two brigades of the Federal Third Corps had been left in Emmitsburg on July 1 and were now marching north to rejoin their

---

xxxviii The entrance to the modern Battlefield Bed and Breakfast roughly follows the path of the Knight Road.

xxxix This area is all private property today. No NPS surveys have been done and none of the contemporary battlefield surveys ventured that far south. Today, a large stand of trees blocks the view south, but with a little imagination, a visitor to the sliver of NPS property on Wintrode Knoll can remove the trees and take in the view from the nearly 500-foot elevation (the nearest hills are about twenty to sixty feet lower than Wintrode's).

command, escorted by cavalry patrols sweeping the road ahead of them. If Johnston had left on his reconnaissance at 4:00 a.m., then it's hard to reconcile his description of approaching Federal infantry the way he described it. The first of the two brigades didn't arrive until at least 9:00 a.m., meaning they would be too far away to be seen clearly and, in any event, posed no danger to him several miles away.[566], [xl]The danger would have instead come from the Second Corps marching up the Taneytown Road. *If* he left at 4:00 a.m.

But because Johnston left the sunrise survey around 5:30, he approached the Emmitsburg Road on Wintrode Knoll around 7:30 or 8:00 that morning. Wintrode Knoll is about two and a half miles south of the Trostle farm, where the Third Corps infantry reported that morning. If the vanguard of the Federal column reported at 9:00 a.m., it was a little over an hour away when Johnston saw them from Wintrode Knoll. At a normal marching pace, that means they were about three miles from the Trostle Farm, or a mere half mile or so south of Johnston and his team. If the cavalry escort was moving slowly ahead of the infantry, Johnston's fear of being seen was well founded.

Fortunately for Johnston, the cavalry left just enough space to let him slip through, though it was uncomfortably close. "They might have seen me," he admitted to McLaws, "but I do not think they did." Once he cleared the Emmitsburg Road and the Federal troops, he "lost no time in getting back.... I recrossed the bridge and took the most direct route regardless of fences, to where I had left General Lee. There was the usual delay in finding headquarters."[567]

---

xl   If Johnston was gone nearly three hours, like he said he was, then the infantry was more than two hours (or over four miles) away from the Trostle farm. Even if Johnston could have seen them, they presented no danger to him at 6:30 or 7 a.m.

The expansive view looking south along the Emmitsburg Road from Wintrode Knoll. At the time Johnston was viewing the area, the countryside would have been considerably more open. Author photo.

Johnston had left General Lee near the Pitzer farmhouse, but he wasn't there when Johnston got back. He and Longstreet had ridden to the front to "observe the position of the Federals, and [get] a general idea of the nature of the ground."[568] This could have been anywhere from the Seminary proper (which is where tradition places him), McMillan's Orchard, or the Point of Woods. In his final word on the matter, Johnston remembered the three generals were "near the seminary" when he found them. "Near" isn't particularly precise, and it could apply to any location from McMillan's Orchard to Lee's traditional headquarters at the Mary Thompson house.

Lee's exact location isn't particularly important, since Johnston found him relatively quickly. In a famous scene, Lee was sitting on a fallen tree, flanked by A.P. Hill and James Longstreet, a map spread before them. Lee saw Johnston approaching and waved him over.

Either standing behind or next to the generals, Johnston "sketched the route over which I had reconnoitered" on the map, stepping back when he was done. Lee was "surprised at my getting so far, but showed clearly that I had given him valuable information," Johnston recalled with more than a hint of pride shining through the faded ink.[xli]

In his letter to Peterkin, Johnston remembered Lee told Longstreet "I think you had better move on," though that's likely thirty years of the "fatal delay" controversy clouding his memory (it's the only time he mentions Lee telling Longstreet to move). After Johnston made his report, Hill and Longstreet left and Johnston "took a seat beside General Lee and we talked of the topographical features of the country."[569], [xlii]Though his letter to McLaws provides the most detail of his reconnaissance and report, he refers to this private conversation with Lee in all of his letters, none of which contradict what he told McLaws.

Johnston's report has posed a problem to modern historians for decades. Harry Pfanz, in his excellent work on July 2, asked "why did Johnston and Clarke see no Federal troops in the Little Round

---

xli   Perhaps Lee's surprise wasn't that Johnston made it to Little Round Top, but that he traversed so much ground to the south without any additional Federals in sight (other than the two brigades in plain sight marching up the Emmitsburg Road). The assumption has always been that Lee was surprised that Johnston made it to Little Round Top, but that's not a necessary interpretation. Johnston also recalled Lee's surprise nearly thirty years later, when Little Round Top was firmly established in the battle's historiography.

xlii   Johnston's letter to Peterkin, thirty-two years after the battle, is the only time Johnston specifically states that Lee pointed to the map and asked if he made it that far. Johnston "assured him that I did." But Little Round Top probably wasn't delineated on the maps they were using. The most likely map in use was the 1858 Adams County Wall Map, but that only shows roads and properties. Likewise, the map Jed Hotchkiss made shows vague hills and ridges, but no specifics south of Cemetery Hill (which makes sense, given he was the Second Corps engineer). More likely, Johnston used a combination of tracing his route on the map and pointing to physical locations across the way. Johnston to Peterkin, Dec. 1895, in S.R. Johnston Papers, VHS.

Top area?"[570] Stephen Sears, in his bestselling *Gettysburg* in 2003, wrote that "if Johnston's party went where he told Lee it went, there was no way it could have failed to see or hear at least some trace of the better part of two Yankee infantry corps and two brigades of Yankee cavalry." Because he didn't report any Federals near Little Round Top, Sears concluded Johnston provided "utterly false intelligence."[571] Likewise, Allen Guelzo thought Johnston delivered "the very best news Lee could have desired: there were no Federal troops anywhere south of Cemetery Hill."[572]

But Johnston never claimed he told Lee there were no troops nearby. In fact, he didn't mention the contents of his report at all. He simply said he gave his report to Lee, Longstreet, and Hill, traced his route on the map, and then discussed the topography with Lee.[573] The implicit assumption is that if Johnston had reported that there were Federal troops at the Trostle and Weikert farms, Lee wouldn't have ordered the attack where he did. But as we'll see, Lee's plan that morning *does* seem to have considered the presence of the Third Corps on Cemetery Ridge. And though it turned out quite differently for a variety of reasons, the plan was a sound one.

WHAT *COULD* JOHNSTON HAVE REPORTED TO LEE THAT morning? Unless more documents surface, we can't know exactly what Johnston told Lee when he returned. But we can at least reconstruct the Federal position to know what he was *able* to see.

The Federal Third Corps was the closest body of troops to Johnston's vantage point on Little Round Top. The corps (minus the two brigades left in Emmitsburg) began to arrive around dark on July 1.[574] Though the Third Corps' report claimed the corps began arriving at 5:30 that evening, General David Birney (who took over when Dan Sickles was wounded) had good reason to push up his arrival time. On June 30, Meade "noticed with great regret the very slow movement of [the Third] corps yesterday.... Considering the good condition of the road and favorable state of the weather," the

Third Corps' march "was far from meeting the expectation of the commanding general," delaying the troops and wagons behind it. Army headquarters reminded Sickles that the Second Corps, "in the same space of time…made a march nearly double" that of the Third Corps'.[575] In reporting to Meade after the battle, Birney made a point to address those precise issues, stressing that the Third Corps "marched with enthusiasm and alacrity over the road," which was "rendered almost impassable by the mud" and the preceding two infantry corps.[576]

But the rest of the corps (and, indeed, the rest of the army), remembered the Third Corps arriving around nightfall. General Hobart Ward, commanding a brigade in the corps, reported arriving "about dark." The 114th Pennsylvania remembered arriving around 7:00 p.m., while the Ninety-ninth Pennsylvania's commander recalled arriving "a short time after sunset," where it "bivouacked in a field on the right of the road" a mile south of the town.[577]

The other division of the Third Corps, commanded by General Andrew Humphreys, had a more adventurous evening. By the time his orders to march north to Gettysburg arrived on the evening of July 1, Humphreys's Division was already west of Emmitsburg. He halted the column in its tracks along the Waynesborough Pike, ordered one brigade (Burling's) back to Emmitsburg, and then caught up with the division's adjutant, who was already talking to the locals "for the purpose of pointing out the route the division was to follow." They ultimately decided to march north along a road "nearly parallel to" the Emmitsburg Road "and about 2 miles west of it." That way, they wouldn't have to backtrack through Emmitsburg and they wouldn't compete with the other division for the road.[578]

By the time they reached Marsh Creek, the moon was shining in what was a quiet, peaceful night among the rolling hills of southeastern Pennsylvania. The brigade's guide, a doctor from Emmitsburg, insisted they turn left, so they followed along the Black Horse Tavern Road. In the exact opposite scenario that would baffle the Confederate troops around twelve hours later, Humphreys was halted in his tracks by a warning that they would be discovered by Confederate troops near the tavern a short distance in front of them. With whispered orders, the column quietly turned around and slipped back along the road, eventually making it to the Emmitsburg Road without ever having alerted the Confederate pickets. Exhausted, they finally pulled into the fields near the Trostle farm and collapsed between midnight and 2:30 a.m.[579]

The troops were in no particular order that evening, but had simply bivouacked in fields farmed by Abraham Trostle and George Weikert.[xliii] Major Henry Tremain, one of Sickles's aides, remembered that the "Third Corps had simply gone into bivouac…. Neither the batteries nor the infantry were occupying any special posts selected for defence or offence [sic]. They awaited the light."[580] Likewise, Captain E.C. Strouss of the Fifty-seventh Pennsylvania remembered his regiment "bivouacked for the night in a field to the right and in rear of the Trostle house."[581]

The chaplain of the 141st Pennsylvania recalled they were "bivouacked in the field near George Weikart's [sic] house."[582] There are (and were) several Weikert properties on the battlefield, which can cause confusion. John Weikert owned property along the Wheat-field Road, just south of the Trostle farm. But *George* Weikert's property was northeast of the Trostle farm, about a mile and a quarter south of Cemetery Hill.[583] Another regimental commander, Colonel Calvin Craig of the 105th Pennsylvania, reported that his regiment camped about a mile south of town, which puts it at the northern boundaries of the *George* Weikert farm (if not a little further north).[584] When Humphreys arrived, his tired men slept in their makeshift camp north of the rest of the corps, closer to the main line and filling in the open ground between Birney and Cemetery Hill.[585]

By all accounts, the Third Corps remained in that position until at least 7:00 a.m. Lieutenant Colonel Benjamin Higgins, commanding a regiment in Birney's Division, reported that while he packed his men up at 6:00 a.m., they didn't settle on a position until at least 7:30 a.m.[586] In Humphreys's Division, both Captain Matthew

---

xliii   Peter Trostle actually owned the farm, but his son Abraham lived there with his wife and nine children farming the land. Reardon and Vossler, *A Field Guide to Gettysburg*, 256.

Donovan and Lieutenant Colonel Porter Tripp remembered being awake by sunrise, but staying put until around 8:00 a.m.[587]

Lieutenant Colonel Adolfo Cavada, one of Humphreys's aides, remembered the confusion in the division that morning. After the tense march of the night before, Cavada had simply fallen asleep in the field. He was awakened at daylight by "a rude shake of the shoulder" and a gruff voice telling him to get up. Cavada was told to position his men, but where they were supposed to go and who he was supposed to report to wasn't known. "Daylight had by this time gained on the surrounding gloom" and bugles and drums began their calls. He finally found Humphreys and was ordered to take a regiment to the picket line up by the Emmitsburg Road. Except for the regiment heading toward the road, "the men were being roused and formed."[588]

At full strength, the Third Corps fielded less than 11,000 officers and men. But only four of its six brigades were on the field when Johnston reconnoitered the area. When Johnston looked out from Little Round Top, he could have seen perhaps 7,000 infantrymen sleeping, making coffee, or generally milling about. A few hundred men may have been shuffling from one place to another, like Colonel Higgins's regiment. But the corps was in nothing resembling a battle line or military position. As Henry Tremain put it, the corps looked as though it was in reserve.[589]

The Third Corps, then, was spread out in bivouac from the Trostle farm to the northern boundaries of the George Weikert farm, with a few campfires probably within Nicholas Codori's and Sarah Patterson's farm fields to the north of Weikert's farm.[590] The blue-clad bivouac covered about forty acres, variably in woods and open fields, with the closest troops a half mile north of Sam Johnston as he took in the view from Little Round Top. For comparison, the Third Corps occupied a space about twice as large as the Rose Wheatfield. Even if some of the early morning fog hadn't burned off yet, there's no way he could have missed them.

BUT THE THIRD CORPS WASN'T THE ONLY FEDERAL INFANTRY in the area. The Second Corps marched right past the Round Tops on the Taneytown Road that morning. Surely Johnston (or Clarke, or Smith, or a courier) would have been able to see or hear them?

According to the Second Corps commander, General Winfield Scott Hancock ("the Superb"), the Second Corps "bivouacked for the night about 3 miles in rear [south] of the town. The march was resumed at daylight" and the corps arrived "on the field...about 7 a.m." Hancock reported that his "troops were soon placed in position, the right resting near the Emmitsburg Road, to the west of Cemetery Hill."[591]

Hancock's Second Corps was composed of three divisions, commanded by Generals Alexander Hays, John Gibbon, and John Caldwell. Hays and Gibbon arrived first, with Caldwell bringing up the rear. Members of Gibbon's and Hays's Divisions remembered moving out from their camp three miles south of town at about 3:00 a.m.[592] Caldwell followed about an hour later, making a brief halt behind the Round Tops around 5:00 a.m., where it stayed until 6:00 a.m.[593]

As it arrived on the field, the Second Corps began to deploy in columns. That meant that each brigade was formed with one regiment in line of battle, one in front of the other, so that the brigade was essentially a stack of regiments. This made maneuvering easier and took up less space until the line could be fully formed.[594]

More importantly, most of the corps was facing toward Cemetery Hill, at least when they were observed by Confederates that morning. Years after the battle, the 148th Pennsylvania's Maj. R.H. Forster remembered spending the morning "in the woods to the right of the [Taneytown] road facing to the east, where it remained until sometime in the forenoon."[595] Just after the battle, Colonel Arthur Devereaux reported that Gibbon's Division spent an hour on the eastern side of the Taneytown Road "with its front toward the right of the position held by our army."[596] That meant the brigade was facing northeast, toward Cemetery Hill, and shaded toward the right of the line.

Likewise, Colonel Samuel Carroll, commanding a brigade in Hays's Division, reported that his brigade "was formed in line of regiments…between Woodruff's battery on the left and the Taneytown road on the right."[597] With the Taneytown Road on the right, the brigade would have been facing north, toward Cemetery Hill. To an observer—say Armistead Long or Sam Johnston—the Second Corps would appear to be positioned primarily as reinforcements for the Federal line on Cemetery Hill.

Not coincidentally, this is exactly how it appeared to Armistead Long that morning. In viewing the Federal position from Seminary Ridge, Long noticed that "there had been considerable accession to the enemy's force on Cemetery Hill during the night." Because these reinforcements had been "chiefly massed to his right…much of his center and almost his entire left [appeared] unoccupied."[598] Not until at least 8:00 a.m. would the Second Corps begin its shift to the position typically shown on maps; that is, west of the Taneytown Road facing Seminary Ridge.[599]

At the time Long viewed the Federal position just after sunrise, his assessment was accurate. Johnston viewed Cemetery Ridge from Little Round Top about an hour and a half later, between 6:00 and 6:30 a.m. By then, Caldwell had started his march past Little Round Top.[600] He would form in columns, as well, and wasn't in any sort of defined formation until about ten o'clock that morning.[601]

From his vantage point on Little Round Top that morning, Johnston would have been able to see two Federal divisions in columns facing Cemetery Hill. Some troops may have been facing west, but the bulk of Gibbon's and Hays's Divisions appeared to be supporting the Federal right. Caldwell's men were marching north, past both Little Round Top and the Third Corps. Though not yet in position, they didn't appear to be extending the line south. Instead, they were marching toward Cemetery Hill. Just as Johnston, Long, and Pendleton had observed that morning on Seminary Ridge, the Federal line seemed to be focused entirely on Cemetery Hill.

With the majority of the Federal army facing north, the ground occupied by the Third Corps looked to be the *rear* of the army, rather than the left flank. That seems to be the intelligence Sam Johnston brought back to headquarters. Only five days later, on July 7, Lafayette McLaws wrote a frustrated letter to his wife, peripherally suggesting this was the case. Among aspersions cast at Longstreet, he told her that "the intention was to get in rear of the enemy who were supposed to be stationed principally in rear of Gettysburg, or near it."[602] Though the Federal army would change its position later that morning, and Sickles would famously change his own position that afternoon, when Samuel Richards Johnston looked out over the field an hour after sunrise, the Third Corps occupied the *rear* of the Army of the Potomac.

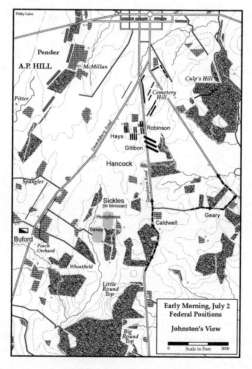

The Federal position south of Cemetery Hill as Johnston would have seen it from Little Round Top on the morning of July 2, 1863. Map by Philip Laino. See a full sized version of this map on page 464.

A modern view of the Second Corps' position on the morning of July 2, 1863. Most of the troops would be to the right of the photo, facing northeast. Author photo.

But what of General Geary's Twelfth Corps troops that had been stationed on or near Little Round Top on the night of July 1? As one bestselling historian has written, "Little Round Top was occupied by two regiments of Geary's Twelfth Corps Division until well after daylight on July 2." Johnston clearly couldn't have been there at the same time.[603] Though noting Geary's presence, other historians have concluded that Johnston and Geary's men must have just missed each other, perhaps by only a few minutes.[604]

Geary's Division of the Twelfth Corps *was* on Little Round Top the evening of July 1 (or at least in the vicinity). Geary reported that when he arrived, he sent two brigades to "a range of hills south and west of the town," which he "regarded as of the utmost importance, since their possession by the enemy would give him an opportunity of enfilading our entire left wing and center."[605] Colonel Charles

Candy, commanding one of the two brigades, reported that he was ordered "to throw forward two regiments to the left, and occupy a high range of hills overlooking the surrounding country, and watch for any attempted advance of the enemy on the left of the army."[606] Colonel John Patrick commanded one of the regiments on the skirmish line that night and remembered deploying "across an open valley to a light strip of woods, and in front of that timber facing an open field."[607]

Though it's possible in the darkness the men mistook another hill for Little Round Top, as many assume Johnston did later, the descriptions match the famous hill. Little Round Top *does* overlook a valley, and a thin strip of woods marks the eastern boundary of Rose's notorious wheatfield. Even in the moonlight, the Round Tops are simply unmistakable.

While there were decidedly troops on or near Little Round Top that morning, the division was "relieved at 5 a.m. on the 2d" by the Third Corps.[608] Colonel Patrick also remembered receiving his orders on the skirmish line at "5 o'clock to return to the brigade."[609] As Geary's men were packing up then, Johnston was riding slowly along Seminary Ridge with Robert E. Lee and Armistead Long on his way to Hill's headquarters. He wouldn't leave his own lines for at least another half hour or so, and then cautiously made his way to Little Round Top. Geary's men didn't need to move particularly fast to be well out of Johnston's way by the time he arrived on the hill that morning. The idea that Johnston and Geary just missed each other is just another consequence of Johnston's off the cuff estimate he gave to Fitz Lee.

JOHN BUFORD'S TIRED CAVALRY WAS ALSO IN THE AREA that morning and could have posed more of a threat to Johnston's intelligence mission than just monitoring the roads. Buford reported to the cavalry corps chief of staff that he "placed my command on our extreme left to watch and fight the enemy should he make another attack." The division spent the night there, "with pickets extending almost to Fairfield," six miles southwest.[610]

Years later, a member of the Seventeenth Pennsylvania Cavalry remembered that they moved "in the rear of the famous Peach Orchard" on the night of July 1, where by sunrise they were "exchanging compliments with the enemy."[611] Newel Cheney, a trooper in the Ninth New York, remembered decades after the battle that they were positioned "three fourths of a mile west of Little Round Top and across the Peach Orchard." And Adolfo Cavada remembered meeting some cavalry videttes "who were notified of our approach" as Humphreys's Division finally arrived after midnight.[612]

Cheney recalled that the Ninth New York "did picket duty on their front" that night. The next morning, one company "patrolled the roads in front of Buford's position" (and gave Sam Johnston a fright?) and Cheney claimed they "discovered Longstreet's corps approaching from that direction." More likely, they encountered Anderson's Confederate Division moving into position, as we'll see.[613]

At least some of Buford's men probably *were* stationed in the Peach Orchard on the night of July 1 and the morning of July 2. But by the time the regimental histories hit the shelves, the contours of the tactical history were already formed and it's difficult to tell whether "the extreme left" really was the Peach Orchard or if that just made sense to troopers trying to remember it years later. The Peach Orchard eventually became one of the battle's grim landmarks and in retrospect could be seen as the left of the line, even though it wasn't part of any defined "left" at that point in the day.

Buford's two depleted brigades had dispatched squads to picket the roads for miles to Emmitsburg and Fairfield. More troopers prowled the fields and woods in the neighborhood, further reducing the number of horsemen in camp. While there may well have been cavalrymen in the Peach Orchard, there certainly weren't two full brigades occupying it that morning. Indeed, at midnight Cavada only remembered the videttes.

The Sherfy Peach Orchard was also substantially larger than it is today. The orchard, which was big enough to make it onto the 1858

Adams County wall map, took up about sixteen acres of land. Even if Newel Cheney was right and the full division did sleep in the Peach Orchard, they weren't confined to the corner of the intersection of the Emmitsburg and Wheatfield Roads.

ASSUMING JOHNSTON COULD HAVE SEEN ALL OF THIS—and there's no reason to think he couldn't—then he could have reported the following situation to Lee. The two Federal corps they fought yesterday, the First and Eleventh, were still in the same place they had retreated to on Cemetery Hill. Another corps (the Second) was just arriving and appeared to be mostly in reserve, for they were in columns facing Cemetery Hill and the Federal right. Yet another corps (the Third) was camped about a mile to the rear. Federal cavalry occupied the high point between Cemetery Hill and Little Round Top (the Peach Orchard), with patrols in various directions.

Not only could Johnston report with confidence the position of the Federal army, he also had a chance to ride over the ground between the Emmitsburg Road Ridge and the Round Tops. After he gave his report to Lee, Longstreet, and Hill, he sat down with Lee to discuss the topography.[614] While Lee may have been happy about the Federal position, he seemed to have been less satisfied with what Johnston told him about the ground.

Thanks to the Gettysburg National Military Park and its supporters, the ground Johnston and his party traversed from the Snyder farm to Little Round Top is immaculately preserved. With the exception of overgrown fields, allowed to run wild without abundant livestock to trim them, the ground looks the same as it did when Johnston, Clarke, and Smith rode over it on the morning of July 2.

Looking out from the ridges south of the Round Tops, the fields look relatively smooth and calm. But riding into the ravine between the Round Tops and Emmitsburg Road Ridge, it's quickly apparent that the eyes are deceived. The ground pitches and rolls toward the

Round Tops and Houck's Ridge, becoming swampy as it approaches the rock-choked Plum Run winding along the base of the hills.

As many southerners would discover only a few hours later, it would be hard to maintain visibility when regiments dipped into the pockets of the earth, much less keep shoulder-to-shoulder contact as they tossed and turned along the waves of the Pennsylvania granite ridges and hillocks. Standing on one side of the morass, it was easy enough to look across the ground to the other side; not so once one became isolated in its many swales. To form two divisions for attack on such ground wouldn't be easy, nor would marching across it.

No one recorded Lee's thoughts on the matter, but after listening to Johnston's topographical report, he sent Colonel Charles Venable to Ewell with a message to delay the attack.[615] As Venable galloped off, Lee climbed into the saddle. He was going to have a look at the east side of Cemetery Hill for himself.[616]

WHILE SAM JOHNSTON AND HIS TEAM RODE SOUTH INTO the ravine beneath the Round Tops, William Pendleton and three staff officers explored the ground behind Seminary Ridge, looking for a way to funnel three divisions into position for the anticipated attack.[617]

After viewing the Federal line at sunrise, Armistead Long told Lindsay Walker that it was important to put artillery on the ridge further to the right. Pendleton "offered his services to Walker," but from Pendleton's account, those services seem to have been rather cursory and simply advisory, for he doesn't mention it at all.[618] Part of the reason may have been because he simply didn't have more artillery to put there. The Sumter Artillery, attached to Anderson's Division, had already been extended down near the Point of Woods. Long doesn't appear to have realized that no more Third Corps guns were available until later that morning.[619]

Instead, when the meeting ended, Pendleton "return[ed] from this position more to the right and rear, for the sake of tracing more exactly the mode of approach," though he wasn't clear whether the approach was for infantry, artillery, or both. He and his staff "proceeded some distance along the ravine road noticed the previous evening."[620]

Pendleton's report suggests the sunrise survey was concluded near McMillan's Orchard. If Pendleton *returned* to a position, the obvious implication is that he was already there. And if he headed to the right and rear, then he was headed in the direction of the Pitzer farm. The Pitzer farm lane, not coincidentally, led directly to the Ravine Road.

Coupland Page also remembered riding south along Seminary Ridge, looking out at the Round Tops framed in "bold relief" in the distance.[xliv] They eventually "left the line upon which we had heretofore been traveling [Seminary Ridge], rode across an old scrub-oak field, and came to what seemed to be a country road, which led in the direction of the two Round Tops." According to Page, Pendleton and his staff "turned slightly to the left, rode on down a hill until we came to a creek crossing said road, and there the General...crossed the stream and as the road ascends on that side, he went a short distance, halted, took out his field glass," and made "some observations of a high point on our extreme right."[621]

Page was awfully specific in his recollections, if not entirely accurate. That being said, the general route he described follows Seminary Ridge south, back toward the Pitzer farm (either taking the farm lane or cutting across now familiar fields). The Pitzer farm lane forks at the base of a wooded hill behind the Pitzer farmhouse. Turning slightly to the left would take the party south, "toward the Round Tops." That lane, known today as the Pitzer-Willoughby Run Lane, leads over the hill and directly down to Willoughby Run and the Ravine Road. A ford leads across the run to the George Culp house.

---

xliv   Though the Round Tops are to the southeast, they are a striking landmark even when heading due south along Seminary Ridge.

Hill's headquarters viewed from Seminary Ridge. The hill Pendleton and his staff crossed over to get to the Ravine Road can be seen in the distance, behind what was the Pitzer farmhouse in 1863. The property is now privately owned. Author photo.

Looking southeast from the vicinity of the sunrise survey, the Round Tops stand in "bold relief," as described by Coupland Page. Author photo.

At the bottom of the hill, Pendleton stopped in the stream so they could water the horses. Page "notic[ed] a farm house on my left with a white picket fence in front facing the road and seeing smoke ascending from the chimney in the rear wing of the house, I said to [my messmate] 'I think I will go over and see if I can get a breakfast.'" The other staff officer asked him to get two, telling Page he had some Winchester Corporation notes "and they are as good as gold."[622]

There were three farms along Willoughby Run: George Culp's, John Plank's, and Samuel Pitzer's. George Culp remembered Confederates coming to his house, offering to pay for milk and bread with gold and silver (possibly taken from Emanuel Pitzer's house, which was hosting Hill and his staff).[623] Although there were thousands of Confederates in the vicinity, most of them wouldn't have had an opportunity to plunder the Pitzer farmhouse, since Hill's staff occupied it before the infantry made it there in any great number. Whichever Confederates visited Culp were probably attached to a general's staff. Which, of course, Page and his messmate were.

But Culp was not the only farmer on Willoughby Run to have Confederate "guests" that day. The next farm south was owned by John Edward Plank and his family, who also tried to stay through the battle. After seeing Confederates approaching and watching in horror as the Harman farm caught fire and burned to the ground during the first day's fighting, they locked their doors and huddled inside. Not until the grim results of July 2 began to appear at their door and the quiet farmhouse quickly turned into a hospital did the Plank family finally leave.[624]

The last farmhouse, and the one furthest south, was the Samuel Pitzer residence, which overlooked the eastern banks of the run. Page remembered that the farmhouse was on his left; if he was riding south, then that would have been to his east. As the only farmhouse in the vicinity on the eastern bank of Willoughby Run, it's a strong candidate for Page's visit. At least at first glance.

But Pendleton was clear that the reconnaissance didn't make it that far south that morning. Not until the woods were cleared by Anderson's men shortly after noon would Pendleton and his staff venture as far south as the Samuel Pitzer farm. And since Pendleton's report is more reliable than Page's undated recollection, it's unlikely Page was referring to the Pitzer farmhouse in his memoir.

More likely, Page had turned around to talk to his unnamed messmate and then noticed the smoke billowing from the chimney of a farmhouse to the west. Facing north, Culp's and Plank's houses would both be on Page's left, as he remembered it. Given what Page described next, he probably decided to get his breakfast at the Plank farm, not the Pitzer or Culp houses.[625]

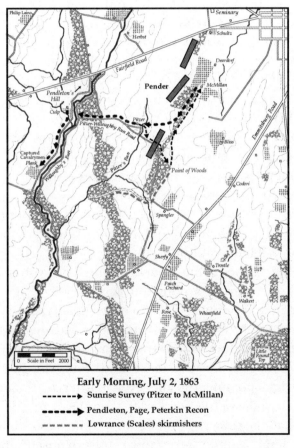

Early Morning, July 2, 1863
------▶ Sunrise Survey (Pitzer to McMillan)
▬▬▬▶ Pendleton, Page, Peterkin Recon
▬ ▬ ▬ Lowrance (Scales) skirmishers

The sunrise survey and Pendleton's subsequent reconnaissance. Map by Philip Laino.

* * *

THINGS SOON GOT EXCITING. THE PARTY WAS "MADE AWARE of having entered the enemy's lines by meeting two armed dismounted cavalrymen," Pendleton wonderfully understated in his report.[626] Page, on the other hand, added all the dramatic flair he could muster.

As he pulled on the reins to get his horse to stop drinking, Page looked up to see that "two Yankee cavalrymen came around from the rear of the house, opened the gate" and began walking toward him. Page asked what they were doing there and if they had been paroled. Their sidearms quickly told him they weren't prisoners. "I threw my right hand as quick as a flash to my hip," Page remembered, "made a motion, still holding my hand out of sight, (as I had no revolver of any kind) and commanded them to surrender." Hopefully the bluff would work, for he was in quite a bind.

"I don't know so much about that, Johnny," the Yankee trooper said. Page didn't write down what was going through his head at the moment, but the sweat on his neck and brow must have been caused by more than just the thick July humidity.

In Page's version of the story, he faked a motion to pull a revolver out from his belt and told the cavalrymen to hand over their revolvers or "I'll blow your brains out."

The bluff worked. One trooper pointed a revolver at him and Page told him to turn it around and hand it over. Page snatched it up, cocked it, and pointed it at the other cavalryman, who handed his pistol over, too. Page left his prisoners with his messmate and rode over to Pendleton, who was surveying the ground.[627]

Though Page's story is tense and compelling, it's hard to believe he had no sidearm and even harder to fathom that two armed cavalrymen would surrender themselves to a lone Confederate they had the draw on. Pendleton, on the other hand, reported that the Federal troopers were "apparently surprised" and "immediately surrendered," contradicting Page's standoff story. They were "disarmed and sent to the rear with two of the three members of my staff present."[628] Pendleton's account is much more believable, though considerably less dramatic, than Page's.

Though the idea of Pendleton and his staff stumbling upon two Federal cavalrymen and taking them prisoner may sound fantastic, it probably happened, even if not quite the way Page told it. Corporal George Barber of the Ninth New York Cavalry was reported captured on July 2, an event important enough to the regiment's memory that it made its way into the unit's history.[629] Though a small contingent of the Ninth New York was briefly engaged alongside Berdan's sharpshooters and the Third Maine Infantry later that afternoon, it's unlikely he was captured then, for there's no mention of any Federal prisoners taken during the short, but intense, firefight. More likely, Barber was captured while picketing behind the Confederate lines that morning.[630]

Of course, Page embellished his story a bit, as did many veterans for the various reasons we've seen, but the basic tenets hold up to scrutiny. Pendleton did reconnoiter the area and there does appear to have been at least one Federal trooper captured that morning. And if the prisoner was captured at a farmhouse, like Page remembered, then it was probably at the Plank family's secured property (perhaps the Federal troopers were looking for a way to get a fresh breakfast, too).

The Pitzer farm was too far south for Pendleton's men to have gone that morning, while the Culp farm was too far north for the captured Federals, for it was obviously close behind Confederate lines. Though possible, given the range of Buford's scouting parties that morning, it's unlikely a pair of cavalrymen would venture that far behind enemy lines with no support. More likely, Page noticed the smoke escaping the Plank's chimney as they cooked breakfast for themselves that morning, probably oblivious to the tense moments between Page and the cavalrymen in their farmyard just outside.

* * *

THE CAPTURE OF THE CAVALRYMEN ENDED THE RECONNAIS-
sance. Believing himself to have "entered the enemy's lines," Pendleton found himself "satisfied...of the course and character" of the
Ravine Road and headed back.

He "returned to an elevated point on the Fairfield Road"—Pendleton's Hill—"and dispatched messengers to General Longstreet
and the commanding general."[631] Peterkin was sent with a message
to Longstreet that "the way is open, (or words to that effect)." Page,
meanwhile, took the cavalrymen straight to army headquarters.[632]

Pendleton's Hill "furnished a very extensive view" of the ground
all the way out to the Emmitsburg Road (but apparently not past it).
Today, the hill consists of buildings and parking lots, with extensive
foliage blocking any real view, though persistence, squinting, and
the slightest imagination provides a hint of Pendleton's view. But
in the summer of 1863, the hill was considerably less cluttered and
Pendleton could see "the enemy's cavalry...in considerable force
and, moving up along that road toward the enemy's main position,
bodies of infantry and artillery, accompanied by their trains."[633]

If Pendleton saw Federal infantry marching along the Emmitsburg Road, then he must have seen Burling's and de Trobriand's
Third Corps brigades arriving near the Trostle farm, for those
were the only Federals marching up the Emmitsburg Road that
day. That meant he had reached his hill by 9:00 or 10:00 a.m. (he
doesn't mention whether he saw the head of the column or the
middle). George Burling didn't report to Third Corps headquarters until around 9:00, and Regis de Trobriand arrived at 10:00.
From his vantage point, Pendleton couldn't have seen them much
further south, so there's a relatively small window he could have
observed them.

Page, meanwhile, rode ahead of Pendleton, taking his prisoners
(or maybe just the one) back to Seminary Ridge. On the way to
headquarters, he passed through Hood's Texans, resting between
McPherson's Ridge and Seminary Ridge. The Texans heckled the

prisoners as they rode through, one of the last laughs they'd have for the day. *Whar's yo critter, boys,* the Texans jeered. *Yu gwine to jine the infants?*

Page rode into headquarters, where he was greeted by one of Walter Taylor's "brightest smiles," and turned his prisoners in. Lee wasn't there, though, "having gone over to Gen'l Ewell's line" to take his own look at Cemetery Hill.[634] According to most accounts, Lee left Seminary Ridge around nine (and returned a little after ten), the same time Burling and de Trobriand were marching up the Emmitsburg Road and Pendleton remembered sending his staff to report.

Thus, as Johnston was waiting for the Federal cavalry to get out of his way on the Emmitsburg Road, Pendleton and his staff were exploring the Ravine Road and gathering exciting stories about quick-drawing cavalrymen. Then, as Johnston was reporting the Federal position and awful topography of the ground south of it, Coupland Page was marching his prisoners up the Ravine Road. Peterkin, meanwhile, was off to report to Longstreet. Neither Johnston nor Pendleton knew exactly what the other was up to, though Pendleton eventually learned that Johnston and Smith investigated the Emmitsburg Road Ridge area that morning (though like the sunrise order mix up, he thought Johnston went out later than he did).

Robert E. Lee, meanwhile, was increasingly unhappy with how the morning was turning out, and through visible frustration, was about to make a very momentous decision.

WHILE JOHNSTON AND PENDLETON RECONNOITERED THAT morning, Longstreet's men began to spill off the Chambersburg Pike and into the fields west of town. Hood's Division, which got the jump on McLaws that morning, reached the field first. Hood personally arrived "in front of the heights of Gettysburg shortly after daybreak." The troops weren't far behind, and they "soon commenced filing into an open field near me." As his troops left the road, Hood went with Lee and Hill to observe the Federal line.[635]

The division poured into the fields between McPherson's Ridge and Seminary Ridge, south of the Chambersburg Pike, ready to move where they were needed for the day's attack. Lee had only just discovered that Johnson wasn't on Culp's Hill, and was beginning the process of modifying his plans, so there wasn't much for Hood's Division to do for the time being. George Anderson, who commanded a brigade in the division, remembered that they "took position with other troops on the right of the road, waiting to be assigned our places for the fight."[636], [xlv]

Coupland Page, of course, remembered running into Hood's men as he brought the captured cavalrymen back to headquarters. Sam Johnston also remembered seeing Longstreet's men in the same general area, across Willoughby Run "at the slope near Head[quarters]."[637] When Evander Law arrived with his brigade later that day, he "found the rest of the division resting about a mile from the town, on the Chambersburg road," not in any battle line.[638] The area between the Chambersburg and Fairfield Roads, Willoughby Run, and Seminary Ridge, is about three quarters of a mile west of the 1863 town limits. With over 160 acres, there was more than enough room to comfortably fit the 5,000 men of Hood's Division that had arrived (Law's 1,900 Alabamians wouldn't arrive until nearly noon).

McLaws had been ordered to march at 4:00 a.m., but when he formed his division, he found the road already occupied by Hood's column. Instead of his division leading Longstreet's Corps to the battlefield that morning, it would be Hood's, leaving McLaws to once again stand idly by, watching other troops pass him by. McLaws always maintained his order had been countermanded, and perhaps it had. But the winter feud between Hood and McLaws had never really ended; McLaws hadn't responded to Hood's apology note (that we know of), leaving the reputational wounds festering.[639]

---

xlv   John Bachelder failed to include Hood's morning position on his famous set of maps. Given the lack of information available even today, with the advantage of numerous repositories of diaries, collections of papers, books, etc., it's not surprising Bachelder didn't feel confident enough to include his position on the map.

Hood may simply have been rushing to the field under his well-known aggressive nature, eager to get to the front. "So imperative had been the orders to hasten forward with all possible speed," Hood remembered, "that on the march my troops were allowed to halt and rest only about two hours, during the night."[640] It's also possible Longstreet ordered Hood to bypass McLaws, not wanting McLaws to set the pace. Hood may also have started later than intended or taken longer to pass McLaws than expected. Or it may simply have been the normal leapfrogging that accompanied a march, which alternated the marching order so one division wouldn't have to march at the back of the column every day, where they would choke on the dust and sink in the churned-up roads from the troops in front of them. There's simply not enough evidence to know for sure, but whatever the reason, McLaws's men would march the last few miles to the field behind Hood's men.

Regardless of *why* McLaws didn't start at 4:00 a.m. (and as we saw, this was important to him, considering his reputation), his division set off for the final two-mile march to Gettysburg just after sunrise, or about 5:00 a.m. The lead brigade, commanded by Joseph Kershaw, probably began to arrive at Herr's Ridge just before six, for the division was less than two miles away. In a letter to Bachelder, Kershaw remembered that his brigade "arrived in front of Gettysburg, about one half hour after sunrise on the morning of the second."[641]

When they arrived, Kershaw reported that they "moved to the right of the Third Corps," most likely referring to Heth's Third Corps brigade bivouacked in the woods on the eastern slope of Herr's Ridge (though Anderson's Division was in the area, too).[642] In his letter to Bachelder, Kershaw went into a little more detail. "We debouched from the main road by a by-road that traversed an open common for a few hundred yards, and there halted, the head of the column having reached the mouth of a lane which the road then entered at Hoss' house." From that point, Kershaw "saw large bodies of troops passing along a road in front of Round Top."[643]

Fremantle remembered that he saw Longstreet "disposing of M'Laws's division for to-day's fight" at around 7:00 a.m.[644] McLaws probably formed a rough battle line on the spine of Herr's Ridge (which is less a ridge than a series of hills), facing east. When the march into position began later that morning, Kershaw wrote that the division "moved by flank from the head of the column perpendicularly to the rear."[645] That was a maneuver allowing a battle line facing one way to quickly get into marching formation facing 180 degrees to the right. The whole battle line would face to the right, "doubling" into a column four men across. Then the head of the column angled to the right.[646] Since the maneuver is performed while the troops are in battle line, it suggests McLaws's Division formed that way on the ridge when they arrived.

Thirty-three years later, McLaws estimated that his line occupied "about one and a half miles of space."[647] Using available numbers, rough calculations support his recollection.[648] That meant his division stretched along the Herr's Ridge Road from the Cashtown Pike to an unnamed farm lane between Dr. Edward Hall's house and Adam Butt's farm.[649], [xlvi]

Hood's and McLaws's two divisions—about 11,000 men, as Law's Brigade had yet to arrive—were only about a half mile apart, well within sight and sound of each other. Hood's men were five hundred yards from the Thompson House on Seminary Ridge and a shade over half a mile from the McMillan Hill vantage point. McLaws was perhaps two thirds of a mile further west of Hood. Despite later recollections obscured by the stains of personal and political grievances, Longstreet's First Corps was on the field shortly after sunrise, ready to move when Lee's critical decisions were made.

[xlvi] The lane is probably an unnamed lane appearing on the Warren Map based on an 1868 survey of the battlefield. There is some debate about which lane Kershaw was referring to, but based on his description of the march and the maneuver he made to get behind the ridge, the unnamed lane seems most likely. Until the early 2020s, the farm plots had remained almost unchanged, appearing the same on the 1868 Warren survey, 1937 aerial maps, and modern satellite imaging.

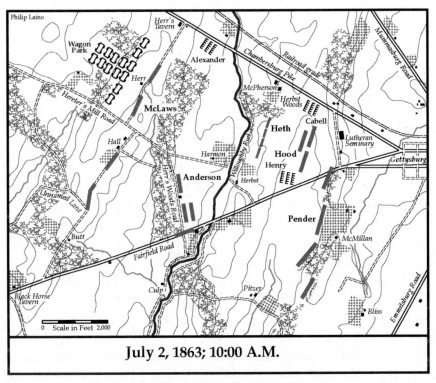

July 2, 1863; 10:00 A.M.

The position of the Confederate First Corps and Anderson's division at about 10:00 a.m. Until Lee determined exactly where to attack, the Army of Northern Virginia's fresh troops couldn't get much closer to the front. Map by Philip Laino.

A New Plan

THE VIEW OF CEMETERY HILL WASN'T VERY GOOD FROM Ewell's headquarters. On its eastern face, the hill is steep, and overlooks a narrow strip of ground between the town and the woods on Culp's Hill. Federal artillery watched over every step the southern attackers would have to take, daring them to march into a crossfire not unlike the one Johnston and Alexander created at Marye's Heights. The long, open approach to the Federal position, crowned with plenty of artillery atop the foreboding slopes must have flashed awful memories of Malvern Hill, one year and a day ago.

From Lee's perspective, there wasn't much question about it. The attack would have to be made against the Federal left. Jed Hotchkiss, who was at Ewell's headquarters while Lee made the decision, saw immediately how heavily it weighed upon him. Lee "was not, in my opinion, very sanguine of its success," Hotchkiss scribbled in his diary, for he "feared we could only take [the Federal position] at a great sacrifice of life."[650] Lee would be visibly uncomfortable and anxious all day.

With the decision begrudgingly made, Lee headed back to his own headquarters to issue the necessary orders. Armistead Long, who had found Lee at Ewell's headquarters while conducting his review of the artillery, rode with the army's commander back through town. They stopped at McMillan's Hill around 10:00 a.m. to take a better look at the Federal line from that side.[651]

Cemetery Hill didn't look much better from this angle. Lee and Long could see the Federal Second Corps beginning to shift, leaning back from its position in reserve into a line along the crest of Cemetery Ridge. Looking out at Cemetery Hill and Ridge, Long saw that "the Federals had considerably increased in numbers and extended their left." Marshall, too, remembered they "found that the enemy had strengthened his position greatly during the night."[652] Three divisions of Federals swung from their position in reserve and rolled over into an active battle line along the spine of Cemetery Ridge.

For Lee, who hadn't wanted to fight here to begin with, the news kept getting worse. The rest of the day wouldn't help his mood.

LEE WAS FAMOUSLY FRUSTRATED THAT MORNING, AND FOR good reason. It was true he hadn't wanted a battle the day before, but his army was nothing if not adaptive. They had fought and won battles in worse spots than this. After surveying the field and receiving the intelligence reports from his staff the night before, he intended to mass his army south of the town and strike a blow on the defeated and depleted Federal force on Cemetery Hill. There had been some accession to the Federal force, but not much, on the evening of July 1. With four fresh divisions within a few miles of the field, the Confederates would have the advantage in numbers for once.[653]

But then he let himself get talked out of it to take what seemed at the time to be a safe gamble, leaving two divisions east of town to crush the Federal line in a vice. Three of the four fresh divisions could exploit any successes from the west, if necessary. But the morning light brought the news that Confederates had not, in fact, gained a foothold on Culp's Hill. Not only were his own troops at the bottom of the hill, Federal troops were reportedly on the top of it, with more on the way. Before the sun was fully in the sky, Lee's plan had evanesced into the morning mist, leaving him back where he had started the night before, but with a major handicap. Two of his divisions were now stranded east of the town, the exact scenario he had hoped to avoid the night before.

Now, the only plausible attack was against the Federal left. Johnston's initial intelligence told Lee that the Federal army was paying little attention to that flank. But as Lee and Long looked out across the swale from McMillan's Hill, they could see this, too, was changing. The Union left was now extending to the south, toward the horrible ground beyond the Rose farm.

But there was no other way. As Francis Lawley related to his London readers, "it struck me that both Generals Lee and Longstreet yielded reluctantly, and *contre-coeur* to the policy of pressing forward at once to this day's attack." Lawley noticed Lee's dour demeanor, too. The general "struck me as more anxious and ruffled than I had ever seen him before, though it required close observation to detect it."[654]

Lee's anxiety may have been easier to observe than Lawley thought, for the British correspondent wasn't the only one to notice it. Armistead Long remembered that Lee was impatient all morning, though he (like nearly everyone else after the war) pinned the anxiety on Longstreet's supposed inertia. Hood told Longstreet directly that Lee was "anxious you should attack that morning."[655] As the postwar debate heated up, Long published a letter in the *Southern Historical*

Society Papers recalling that "Lee's impatience became so urgent" after reconnoitering Cemetery Hill "that he proceeded in person to hasten the movement of Longstreet." But that was at ten o'clock in the morning. Rather than any frustration with Longstreet, Lee's anxiety was more likely the stress of having to choose the best of several bad options and the prescience of hindsight reminding him that he shouldn't have let Ewell stay east of town.[656]

Lindsay Walker remembered Lee's mood, too, though he also blamed it on Longstreet. "Between 9 and 10 o'clock," Walker wrote, "I was lying under the shade of a tree…when General Lee rode up." Lee saw one of Walker's battalion commanders, Col. W.F. Poague, and "mistaking him for one of General Longstreet's officers," reprimanded him "for being *there* instead of hurrying into position on the right." When he found out Poague wasn't a First Corps officer, his tone mellowed and he asked if the artilleryman knew where Longstreet was. Poague didn't know, so he called Walker over.

Walker thought he might know where Longstreet was, so he offered to take Lee there. "As we rode together General Lee manifested more impatience than I ever saw him show upon any other occasion," Walker remembered in the pages of the *Southern Historical Society Papers*. The commanding general "seemed very much disappointed and worried that the attack had not opened earlier, and very anxious for Longstreet to attack at the very earliest possible moment. He even, for a little while, placed himself at the head of one of the brigades to hurry the column forward."[657]

Walker's story is mostly just that: a story. Lee had just returned from Cemetery Hill when he supposedly found Poague resting. At the same time, Long remembered finding Walker and wondering why the higher ground further south on Seminary Ridge hadn't been occupied by the Third Corps artillery yet.[xlvii] Rather than Lee reprimanding Longstreet, perhaps Walker conveniently misremembered *Long's* frustration with *him*.[658]

---

xlvii   Long, remember, wrote that "on arriving at the point where I left Walker a few hours before, the ridge to which his attention had been called in the morning was still unoccupied." Long to Early, April 5, 1876, in *SHSP* vol. 4, 68.

There certainly wasn't any reason Longstreet should have been moving anywhere; Lee hadn't even issued an attack order (and Longstreet hadn't been a part of the original dawn attack plan anyway). Walker had fallen victim to the same mental error that Pendleton had in remembering the sunrise order for Longstreet. In reality, Lee simply had no reason to wonder where Longstreet was, for his Old War Horse was well within sight less than a mile away. And of course, if Lee had no idea where Longstreet or his men were, he couldn't very well hurry one of the brigades to the front.

The periphery of Long's recollections hints at the real reason for Lee's frustration that morning. "After giving General Ewell instructions as to his part in the coming engagement," Long recounted in his memoir, Lee "proceeded to reconnoitre Cemetery Ridge in person." Though the general had been frustrated all morning, "Lee's impatience increased after this reconnaissance."[659]

Lee's well-known irritation that morning wasn't caused by Longstreet. Indeed, Longstreet wasn't ever missing that day. His divisions were on the field before Lee left for his reconnaissance of Cemetery Hill and were within sight of headquarters all morning. If Lee or his staff had a hard time locating him, it was an indication of a much larger communications failure than any grumpy corps commander. (While there *was* a communication problem on July 2, it wasn't primarily with the First Corps).

Rather, the anxiety was a culmination of the entropic events that plagued Confederates ever since they drove the Federals off Seminary Ridge. The hills just south of town, Cemetery and Culps, seemed to have an inexplicable aversion to Confederates. Both hills managed to keep Confederates at bay without any attack on July 1, a specter that eternally haunted the southerners. The early morning bad news was quickly followed by mediocre news from Johnston, followed once again by bad news while reconnoitering the left of his line, and even more bad news as the Federals extended their own left. Nothing seemed to be going right this morning.

With so much going wrong so early in the day, Lee had plenty of reasons for being anxious and frustrated that morning. At the moment, however, James Longstreet had nothing to do with it.

* * *

THE MORNING'S INTELLIGENCE HAD CONVINCED LEE THAT the only reasonable attack was from the south. Longstreet, with his two fresh divisions, was the logical choice to lead the assault. The other two unengaged divisions, Anderson's and Johnson's, were split between two different corps and more than two miles.

The details of the plan weren't written down and were rarely discussed. What *actually* happened provided enough to write about and naturally, that's what filled the pages of memoirs and histories. Very little was written about what was *supposed* to happen. The rank and file would of course have almost no idea what the original plan had been, so their accounts don't provide much insight. And when the generals brought it up later, it was upon the reputation-strewn fields of political warfare, where the mud of politics smeared the truth to the point of imperceptibility.

Nonetheless, it's widely believed that McLaws was supposed to lead the attack, with Hood following up as support to provide the final punch when McLaws's steam ran out.[660] Relying on McLaws's 1878 speech, for example, Harry Pfanz wrote that Lee "explained how he wanted McLaws to attack the Peach Orchard, but we do not know what was prescribed for Hood."[661] McLaws certainly insisted he was to be in the lead. Though his reputation and pride had a lot to do with it, he was probably right.[662]

Though McLaws's aggressiveness and marching prowess may have been questioned at headquarters, he *was* a steady and reliable force in battle. Having his division in front, closely watched by Longstreet, would provide the first blow to the (hopefully) surprised Union infantry. Then, the more aggressive Hood could drive the victory home, supported by Anderson's Division to the left and Ewell's attack to the north. If all went according to plan, the Union line would be engaged on all fronts, precluding its ability to shift troops and plug holes. (That his army was not able to pull off the simultaneous attacks was the primary reason Lee personally thought the battle was lost.)[663]

Kershaw, reporting on the battle that fall, gives a hint as to some of the specifics. Longstreet "directed me to advance my brigade and attack the enemy at [the Peach Orchard], turn his flank, and extend along the cross-road, with my left resting toward the Emmitsburg road."[664] Major R. C. Maffett, commanding one of Kershaw's regiments, reported that Kershaw's orders to him were "to gradually swing round to the left until nearly facing an orchard, from which the enemy were pouring a deadly fire of artillery."[665] McLaws agreed.[666]

One of Alexander's artillery captains, C.B. Manly, remembered similar instructions. When they got into position, they would be "perpendicular to the enemy's line," Manly wrote, "but it was supposed that [the Federal] left did not extend to this point of intersection to which we were moving. My instructions were that if we gained this point, we would be on the enemy's left flank."[667]

McLaws formed along the southern end of Seminary Ridge, with his right flank (Kershaw) nearly touching the Emmitsburg Road. This was *close* to the original plan, but not quite. If McLaws is to be believed at all (and in this case, we have little else to go on), he was directed to form *across* the Emmitsburg Road. This makes sense if the Federal line remained where it was at 10:00 a.m., when the plan was devised. The Second Corps marked the Federal left, with a small corps of Federals (the Third) in reserve. If McLaws formed his division across the Emmitsburg Road, extending through the Rose property, then he would be on the Federal left and maybe even in the rear, as he wrote to his wife a few days after the battle. That arrangement would entirely avoid the rough ground south of the Rose farm, which Johnston discussed with Lee earlier.

General Hood remembered similar, albeit more general, directions. In his letter to Longstreet in 1875, Hood wrote his former commander that "the instructions I received were to place my division across the Emmettsburg road, form line of battle, and attack." Unfortunately, he doesn't say whether this was to be in front of McLaws or behind him. Longstreet's article for *Century* suggests Hood was supposed to be behind McLaws, for he was to be behind McLaws in the march.[668]

As it turned out, Hood formed to the right of McLaws, but that wasn't the original plan. General Jerome Robertson's report supports this. Though it's unknown if Robertson was referring to the initial orders or the modified orders, he echoed Hood's recollection of the instruction to guide the left flank along the Emmitsburg Road. Robertson was ordered to "let my left rest on the Emmitsburg pike" while he kept his right "well closed" on Law's Brigade. He quickly discovered he couldn't do both, suggesting that the instructions to follow the Emmitsburg Road were either too literally interpreted or remnants of the initial plan that no longer worked under the new circumstances.[669]

If McLaws was supposed to line up along the Wheatfield Road, then Hood, lined up with his left resting on the Emmitsburg Road, would be in position to follow McLaws.[xlviii] Hood, who was positioned in the swale between McPherson and Seminary Ridges, would take the Ravine Road to his assigned position, following Anderson. Hood had to wait for Law before moving, so his column would catch the tail end of McLaws's as it swung around the Black Horse Tavern Road.

Longstreet recalled that Hood marched with Alexander and as we'll see, Alexander took the Ravine Road.[670] It also makes little sense for Hood to follow McLaws, for he would be adding two miles to his march. His division was already near the Ravine Road (perhaps half a mile once it formed into columns). If Hood's men followed McLaws, they would have to march a mile to the rear to reach Herr's Ridge, then over another mile and a half along that ridge and behind Bream's Hill. When it was over, a route following McLaws would be five miles. Following the Ravine Road, it was only three.

McLaws, on the other hand, was already positioned along Herr's Ridge Road, so following that road to the Black Horse Tavern Road made sense. Since Anderson moved first, simultaneous with McLaws, and McLaws was supposed to be the lead division, Hood could await

---

xlviii   The modified plan, which called for Kershaw to push the Federal troops out of the Peach Orchard, then directed Kershaw to align along the Wheatfield Road, so he would end up in the same position, but with a brief fight first.

the arrival of Law without losing any additional time. Not coincidentally, that's what happened.

Once Anderson was in position, Law would have (hopefully)
arrived and Hood could get his division onto the Ravine Road.
The time waiting for Law would also allow McLaws to move around
Bream's Hill and cross the valley onto Seminary Ridge. Contrary to
some opinions, such as Lee's staff officer Walter Taylor, there was
good reason for Longstreet to have waited for Law before getting
Hood into position.[671] As we've seen, though, Longstreet was much
more adept at defending a military position than a reputation.

IT WAS AFTER 10:00 A.M. WHEN LEE REACHED HIS DECISION
and perhaps fifteen minutes later when the couriers arrived at the
various corps headquarters with orders. Anderson, whose men were
in reserve in the shade of the Herr's Ridge Woods, was to move to the
right of Pender, extending the line south along Seminary Ridge.[672]
Longstreet would move to Anderson's right, positioning himself to
attack the left of the Second Corps and the Third Corps.

Exactly where Anderson's Division was when he received his
orders is a sort of enigma, for there's a vast discrepancy in the recollections. Captain Charles Moffett, part of Wright's Brigade of Anderson's Division, remembered getting into his line of battle on Seminary Ridge around 11:00 a.m. His brigade was third from the right,
meaning it was one of the last to form.[673] Only the small Florida
brigade and Wilcox's Brigade would file into line on their right and
Wilcox's arrival on the ridge is well documented to be after 11:30,
for he encountered resistance from several Federal units.[674]

Other writers also remembered a late morning or even early
afternoon march into position. General Lowrance, whose brigade
had been the far right of the line when Pendleton and Johnston
surveyed the field at sunrise, reported that Anderson's men finally
relieved him around 1:00 p.m.[675] That's a bit late, but it does

suggest Anderson moved to Seminary Ridge later in the morning. John Purifoy, a veteran turned historian, estimated Anderson "was ordered to extend Hill's line…about noon."[676] Likewise, Porter Alexander thought it was 11:00 a.m., at least when he sat down to write his analysis at the turn of the century.[677] (In his official report, he remembered arriving on the field around 10:00 a.m., at which point the troops were already moving.)[678]

But some of Anderson's commanders reported a much earlier movement. Wilcox, whose brigade had been stationed near Black Horse Tavern that night and had almost surprised Andrew Humphreys's men, wrote that "at 7:00 a.m.…the brigade rejoined the division, then in front, and advanced, bearing to the right, for the purpose of taking position in line of battle."[679] Ambrose Wright also remembered moving early that morning. Though he had remained behind with "severe indisposition" during the move to Gettysburg the day before, he caught up with his brigade at 7:00 a.m. "Just after assuming command, I received orders to move my brigade…immediately in rear of Major-General Anderson to a position already occupied by a portion of the troops."[680]

Anderson certainly didn't move into the same position twice. But men in the same division on the same field remembered moving to the same place hours apart. How to reconcile the difference?

Anderson, as it turns out, was in two different places that morning. His division spent the evening of July 1 on Knoxlyn Ridge, about a mile west of Herr's Ridge. Anderson reported that "upon approaching Gettysburg, I was directed to occupy the position in line of battle which had just been vacated by Pender's division."[681] Pender, in turn, spent a portion of July 1 on Knoxlyn Ridge before moving up to Herr's Ridge and eventually joining in the final attack on the Union lines on Seminary Ridge.

Hill helps clear up some of the confusion in his own report. Heth and Pender, he wrote, "were bivouacked in the positions won [on July 1], and Anderson, who had just come up, was also bivouacked some 2 miles in rear of the battle-ground."[682] Knoxlyn Ridge is two miles west of the July 1 battlefield.[683]

Anderson reported that he "continued in this position until the morning of the second, when I received orders to take up a new line of battle on the right of Pender's division, about a mile and a half farther forward."[684] Moving a mile and a half would put Anderson between Herr's Ridge and Willoughby Run (and another mile and a half put him in his battle line). Anderson probably marched along Hereter's Mill Road (Old Mill Road today) into position, which is the primary east-west road other than the Chambersburg Pike. This is a logical route, as it runs parallel to the Chambersburg Pike, which when Anderson was moved up, was occupied by the tail end of Longstreet's infantry, his artillery reserve under Alexander, and wagon trains.[xlix]

This is exactly where Armistead Long remembered seeing Anderson around ten o'clock that morning, when he returned from his reconnaissance east of town with Lee. Heth's Division was in and around the woods along the Pike, leaving Anderson's Division about a hundred acres or so to stretch out in. Anderson's first move that morning, then, was from Knoxlyn Ridge to the swale at about 7:00 a.m. The move from there to Seminary Ridge, where the battle line was formed, was around 10:30.[685]

LONGSTREET ALWAYS INSISTED HE RECEIVED HIS ORDERS to march at eleven o'clock that morning. In his first word on the matter, he wrote "it was fully eleven o'clock when General Lee arrived at [his] conclusion and ordered the movement."[686]

---

xlix   Though today the road is called Old Mill Road, the NPS Record of Treatment Maps indicate it was Hereter's Mill Road at the time of the battle. Pfanz came up with two possibilities: either Anderson moved up from Knoxlyn Ridge some time in the morning and then moved onto Seminary Ridge or he moved very slowly all morning, taking up the entirety of the forenoon getting from Knoxlyn Ridge to Seminary Ridge. *Gettysburg: The Second Day*, 114. Given the recollections of those involved, the first option seems the most likely.

But Longstreet wasn't the only one to remember his orders being issued at 11:00 a.m. In his memoir, Lee's aide Charles Marshall wrote that after Lee's trip to Ewell's sector showed that an attack on Cemetery Hill "would have little prospect of success unless it was combined with other attacks of his left and centre," he "returned to Seminary Ridge, and about 11 o'clock issued orders to General Longstreet to begin his attack upon the enemy's left as soon as possible."[687] Porter Alexander agreed with Marshall. In his own memoir, written decades later, after countless discussions, and after digesting nearly ceaseless streams of articles, books, and speeches, Porter Alexander also concluded that Lee issued his orders for July 2 at 11:00 a.m.[688]

Given the problems with exact times, we can't know precisely how close to 11:00 a.m. Lee issued the order. It certainly wouldn't have been something written down at the time. Not only that, but Longstreet, Marshall, and Alexander corresponded somewhat regularly and we've seen how memories rub off on others; one person's memory of eleven could easily have become everyone else's. But given the external evidence, 11:00.a.m is probably close enough to work with.

Alexander's revised report also suggests a late morning order. He explained that when he arrived on the field "about 10:00 a.m. I was ordered by Lieutenant General Longstreet to accompany the movements to the right, *then being commenced* by Hood's and McLaws's divisions."[689] Alexander was never particularly reliable in his time of arrival, so "about" must be interpreted broadly. It seems Alexander relied primarily on his subordinate, Osmond Taylor, for the time, in any event. Taylor remembered arriving "about 10:00 a.m." and "after resting about one hour, we took up the line of march for the left wing of the enemy."[690]

Later writers, including Sam Johnston, would argue that Longstreet did not move promptly. Johnston wrote that there was "no little delay" between the time he was ordered to accompany Longstreet around 9:00 a.m. and the time the march actually started.[691] It was *this* delay, not the countermarch, that Johnston blamed for the late attack. This was understandable, given the controversy swirling about everyone's head and the part McLaws and Longstreet suggested Johnston played in the countermarch. But the fact remains that until at least 10:00 a.m., there was nowhere for Longstreet's Corps to go.

LAFAYETTE MCLAWS REMEMBERED THINGS VERY DIFFERently than most of the other Confederates west of town that morning. As we saw, he took great pains to address any perceived affront to his reputation, which had come under fire by Lee, Hood, and anonymous whispers. Longstreet had even reminded McLaws that Lee wanted him out of the army entirely. Until his dying breath, McLaws sought to right what he saw as the injustices against him. This isn't to say he was wrong, but it certainly preoccupied him and influenced his memory to a large degree. And since McLaws's memory is the most heavily relied upon source for First Corps activities that morning, it has indelibly shaped the way the battle is remembered.

Key to McLaws's story is his personal audience with Lee on the morning of July 2. The meeting sets up most of the major tenets of his account, but the details simply don't support his version of events. Probably unconsciously (that is to say, he wasn't lying), McLaws misremembered most of the important details. Perhaps it is no coincidence that this portion of the rough draft of his 1873 letter to Longstreet is the most heavily edited.[1]

---

1   McLaws to Longstreet, June 10, 1873. McLaws Papers, SHC, UNC. A sample of the editing done in the rough draft: "As I came up, Genl Lee sent for me; he was then sitting on a log with a map before him; Genl Longstreet was walking back + forth a few yards off. Gen Lee pointing to his map asked me if I could place my Division in position at place *he designated* on the left of the Federal line, ~~or where I supposed it was~~ *their left*. I told him I knew nothing to prevent me. Genl Longstreet then came up and remarked that he wanted my division in a position *pointing to it on the map which was* perpendicular to the one *marked by* Genl Lee ~~had designated~~; Genl Lee remarked "No Genl I ~~want~~ wish it *placed as I have told Genl McLaws which was* parallel to the enemy's line."

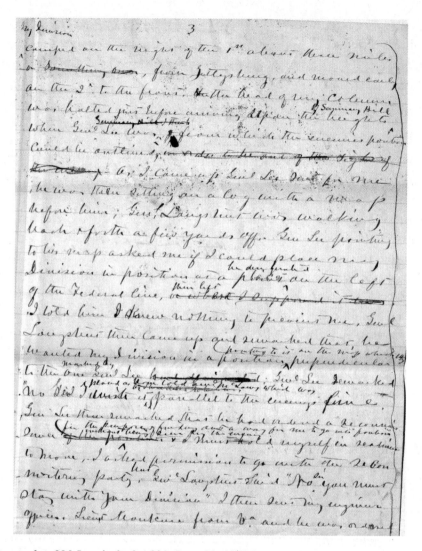

A sample of McLaws's draft of his June 10, 1873 letter to Longstreet, showing his description of the morning's meeting with Lee. From the Southern Historical Collection, Wilson Library, the University of North Carolina at Chapel Hill.

The political melee swirling around him as he tried to reconstruct his memories was the least conducive environment to producing accurate memories. Without any notes and trying to reconstruct the day's events amidst the prospect of ruinous charges, McLaws was trying to access memories he already considered bad. For many reasons, July 2 was a day to forget. It would only be natural and expected for the interpretations of those memories to swing in his own favor as he retrieved them. Natural, understandable, expected... but still inaccurate.

McLaws remembered that "just after I arrived General Lee sent for me...and I went at once and reported." He found Lee in what has become a classic image of Confederate headquarters on the morning of July 2: Lee "sitting on a fallen tree with a map beside him" and his generals surrounding him. McLaws and Lee saluted one another and Lee told McLaws that he wanted him "to place your division across this road" and pointed on the map "to the place I afterwards went to" (the Emmitsburg Road). Lee then instructed McLaws to "get there if possible without being seen by the enemy." When Lee asked if he could get there, McLaws replied that "I knew of nothing to prevent me, but would take a party of skirmishers and go in advance and reconnoitre." Lee stopped him: "Major Johnston, of my staff, has been ordered to reconnoitre the ground," he explained, "and I expect he is just about ready."

McLaws asked to go with him, but Longstreet, who had been pacing within earshot, forbade it. "No, sir," Longstreet said, "I do not wish you to leave your division." Then he pointed to a spot on the map and told McLaws to position his troops exactly opposite how Lee had instructed.

"No, General," Lee corrected. "I wish it placed just perpendicular to that," McLaws remembered. McLaws "then reiterated my request to go with Major Johnston, but General Longstreet again forbade it. General Lee said nothing more, and I left them." From there, he returned to his division and "put it under cover under a line of woods a short distance off."

McLaws then "sent my engineer, Lieutenant [Thomas] Montcure, to go and join Major Johnston...as he was an officer in whom I had confidence, but [he] was ordered back." Frustrated, McLaws decided to go on his own reconnaissance anyway "and was soon convinced that by crossing the ridge where I then was, my command could reach the point indicated by General Lee, in a half hour, without being seen."[692]

This is the story that has made it into the history books and popular memory. But aside from McLaws, no one else remembered seeing him with Lee on the morning of July 2. Quite the opposite. It seems McLaws arrived just after the famous council of war adjourned at dawn. Rather than being summoned immediately to headquarters for orders, he was met by Longstreet as his column trudged along the Chambersburg Pike and down the muddy Herr's Ridge Road.

Arthur Fremantle, who was present for the meeting of the generals that morning, remembered Hood, Longstreet, A.P. Hill, and even the wounded Harry Heth, huddled around Lee. But he made no mention of McLaws. Having traveled with Longstreet's headquarters for over a week by the time the battle started, he certainly knew who McLaws was and could have included him if he were there. In fact, McLaws's Division had been the first of Longstreet's troops Fremantle encountered and he rode alongside them the first few days he was with the army. (For what it was worth, Fremantle was initially impressed with McLaws's Division, which was "well shod and efficiently clothed" and "marched very well" with "no attempt at straggling.")[693]

Hood's presence at the council makes sense, as does McLaws's absence. Hood's Division had just arrived while McLaws's Division was just stepping off from its bivouac along Marsh Creek nearly three miles west of the conference. Fremantle departed the Confederate army just a week later, leaving Hagerstown on July 9 during the army's retreat. He was on a ship bound for home by July 15, and his diary was published the following year, long before any internecine bickering between the Confederate commanders.[694] It's difficult to discern any ulterior motives in Fremantle's exclusion of McLaws from headquarters that morning.

But Fremantle wasn't the only one who observed the meeting. Colonel John Logan Black was quite impressed that he was able to observe three generals in a council of war. He eagerly left the story to his grandchildren in his postwar memoir. His recollections seem to have been written solely for the purpose of leaving them to his family, for they weren't published until a descendent found them in the 1960s.

As we saw, Black arrived on Seminary Ridge right around sunrise and was there when Longstreet rode up shortly after. Black was present for the entire meeting, and when the council ended, Lee introduced Black to Longstreet and assigned Black's services to him. Then Longstreet and Black rode off towards McLaws's Division, which was just arriving.[695]

Like Black, Fremantle remembered Longstreet leaving Seminary Ridge after the council of war and riding off toward McLaws's Division. It was then that Fremantle "rode over part of the ground with General Longstreet and saw him disposing of McLaws's division for to-day's fight."[696] According to Moxley Sorrel, he didn't take notes throughout the day, instead sitting down at quiet times or in the evening to jot down the day's events. Nonetheless, Sorrel marveled at the accuracy of the Englishman's account.[697]

BESIDES MCLAWS, LONGSTREET WAS THE ONLY LIVING witness to the meeting between Lee and McLaws that morning. Perhaps not the *best* witness, at least from McLaws's perspective, he was an important one nonetheless. After the war, Longstreet published four accounts (three articles and a memoir), three of which described the events on Seminary Ridge on July 2 in detail. None of them mention a meeting with Lee and McLaws.[698] In fact, Longstreet's memoirs directly contradict McLaws's account of the morning meeting.[li]

For example, in an article for the *Philadelphia Weekly Press* published about a year before McLaws's account, Longstreet wrote that he arrived at Lee's headquarters at dawn to "renew my views against making an attack." When it became apparent that Lee was set on attacking, Longstreet and Lee rode out to "observe the position

---

li   Though Longstreet is certainly prone to his own biases, when compared to other accounts of the morning and putting McLaws's meeting in context, Longstreet's account seems to be the *more* accurate of the two.

of the Federals, and got a general idea of the nature of the ground." Then Lee sent a staff officer, Charles Venable, toward Cemetery Hill to reconnoiter in that direction, "with a view of making the main attack on his left." Lee, of course, left for Cemetery Hill soon after Venable.

Longstreet's chronology, which is relatively accurate, derails the story McLaws had sent him in 1873. If Lee had not yet determined where the attack was going to take place, he certainly couldn't have shown McLaws his intended position on the map that morning. Indeed, Lee's morning itinerary included meeting with Longstreet, Hill, Hood, and Heth, followed by a briefing from Johnston around 8:30 a.m. or so, and then a reconnaissance of Cemetery Hill at 9:00 a.m. Lee was either talking with other generals or staff officers that morning (none of whom remembered McLaws at headquarters) or off reconnoitering. And if Lee wasn't *at* headquarters at 9:00 a.m., then McLaws certainly couldn't have met with him then.[699]

It's important to remember McLaws's poor reputation in the Army of Northern Virginia, regardless of whether it was deserved. Though Fremantle knew who McLaws was, he makes no mention of him during the numerous depictions of Longstreet's headquarters scene. Even if Longstreet was exaggerating in 1873 when he told McLaws that Lee was ready to transfer him out of the Army of Northern Virginia before the Pennsylvania campaign, Lee *had* expressed official dissatisfaction with McLaws in his prior reports. McLaws had commanded his division since November of 1861, yet he was not promoted to one of the two available corps commands during the army's spring restructuring. Rather, Richard Ewell, absent from the army since August of 1862 while he recovered from the amputation of a leg, received one of the promotions.[700] A.P. Hill, of course, received the other. Though McLaws doesn't seem to have expressed any disappointment, publicly or privately, it's hard to avoid viewing this as a snub, further evidence that Lee was not entirely happy with McLaws's performance.[701]

All of which makes McLaws's account that much harder to believe. If Longstreet was relatively accurate in his 1873 letter to McLaws, Lee had instructed him to keep a close eye on McLaws during the campaign. And if Fremantle and John Black are to be trusted, Long-street left army headquarters specifically to place McLaws in position along Herr's Ridge. In contrast, it doesn't appear Longstreet had much to do with placing Hood's Division at all, either in its morning position or in its ultimate battle line on Warfield Ridge.

When it was discovered that the Federals were not in their expected position, Longstreet rushed Hood to the far right of the new Confederate position. That meant Hood would have to operate nearly independent from the rest of the army, disappearing into the swampy ravine that Lee had wanted to avoid. Perhaps remembering Lee's admonition, Longstreet took additional time and extra pains to make sure *Hood* retained the more independent command, while McLaws was close to the center of the line and easier to keep an eye on. Longstreet then conspicuously stayed with McLaws's Division during the afternoon's assault, even directing McLaws when to send in each brigade and riding out in front of the brigades as they stepped off. Fremantle took this as the bravado of personal leadership, but it may have had just as much to do with command control and personal oversight. If McLaws felt Longstreet was "exceedingly overbearing" at Gettysburg, perhaps that was by design.[702]

This all sheds a very different light on McLaws's July 2 meeting with Lee. McLaws portrayed his conference as a relatively private audience with his commander, in which Lee placed the confidence of the attack in him, asking his opinion as to whether his division could pull off the march unseen, blatantly contradicting Longstreet in front of his subordinate, and sending his personal staff officer to guide McLaws.

In context, though, it seems Lee summoned McLaws for a more condescending purpose. Without faith in McLaws's ability to exercise independent command, Lee wanted to make sure there was no doubt as to what McLaws was supposed to do. "Can you get there?" Lee asked, pointing to a specific location on the map. *Make sure you aren't seen.... This is how you are to position your division.... No, we have already scouted the position, there's no need for further input.* It had only been two months since Lee had felt the need to personally correct McLaws's battlefield at Salem Church. Indeed, had it not been for the initiation of the Gettysburg Campaign on June 3, McLaws may not even have still been with the army![lii]

This all means the meeting was probably much later in the day than McLaws remembered, perhaps 10:30 or 11:00 that morning. By the time he was summoned to headquarters, the attack had already been planned (how else would Lee know exactly where the Federal left was and where he wanted McLaws deployed?) McLaws had been left out of the organization, planning, and decision-making, left alone with his division until Lee called him to headquarters. In this sense, McLaws probably *did* remember sitting astride his horse with nothing to do for hours upon hours. And if he was sitting atop Herr's Ridge around 9:00 or 10:00 a.m., he probably really did see Federal infantry trudging up the Emmitsburg Road.

To McLaws, it may well have *seemed* that he was waiting for no reason and that Longstreet was dragging his feet, just like it *seemed* that no one had spent much time reconnoitering. But that was more of a reflection of McLaws's isolation than anything else. What McLaws didn't know, or at least fully understand, was that Sam Johnston had been gathering intelligence on the Federal left, Pendleton and his staff had been scouting behind Seminary Ridge, and Lee had personally reconnoitered the situation east of the town. That no one thought to explain this all to McLaws isn't surprising (indeed, it wasn't even fully explained to Ewell).

Likewise, when Longstreet refused to let McLaws reconnoiter, he was not being negligent. Nor was Lee simply acquiescing to a

---

lii   Another possible interpretation is that Lee had become accustomed to issuing orders directly to McLaws that year. His was essentially an orphan division at Chancellorsville, as Longstreet and the rest of the First Corps had gone south to Suffolk and were not back in time for the battle. Throughout Longstreet's absence, Lee would have issued orders directly to McLaws, making it seem much less unorthodox to discuss the plan directly with Longstreet's subordinate. However, Longstreet *was* present at Gettysburg that morning and Lee was a career soldier. Not only did he understand the proper protocol, he was very much concerned with it. While it is of course possible Lee breached protocol out of recent habit, it is more likely the past history with McLaws was the primary factor here, especially with Longstreet present.

grumpy subordinate when he allowed Longstreet's denial to stand. Rather, the job was already done and they did not need McLaws's input. Obviously, McLaws did not take it that way.

Though it seems self-evidently redundant, history is written by those who write it. McLaws wrote the account and his interpretation became the standard version of the story, primarily because it was detailed, thorough, and readily available. On its face, it seems like a fair and reasoned account. In McLaws's mind, his meeting with Lee was a critical part of the morning on Seminary Ridge, setting the stage for the near-mythical events later that day. But the fact that no one else even mentioned it in passing is a good indication that it was much less significant outside of McLaws's own memory.

ONE OF MCLAWS'S BIGGEST COMPLAINTS WAS WHAT HE perceived to be the lack of reconnoitering by the army and especially Longstreet. In his letter home to his wife on July 7, he complained that "Longstreet is to blame for not reconnoitering the grounds" before the attack "and for persisting in ordering the assault when his errors were discovered."[703] He let that feeling be known to the *Savannah Republican* correspondent on the march back to Virginia, too. So it's no surprise that he made a point to tell his audience at the Georgia Historical Society (and then the *Southern Historical Society Papers* readers) that he tried desperately to reconnoiter the ground in front of him, but was forbidden by *both* Lee and Longstreet.

But again, McLaws is mistaken. McLaws mentions that his engineer at the time was Lieutenant "Montcure." As with Johnston, he would consistently get the name wrong. But unlike Johnston, there's a strong likelihood that Lt. Moncure was not actually at the Battle of Gettysburg at all.

Lieutenant Thomas Jefferson Moncure (without the "t") came from a prominent Virginia family, the son of a state senator. By 1853 he had graduated from the Virginia Military Institute, worked as a teacher in Fredericksburg, and then as a civil engineer in Virginia and Minnesota. He helped raise a company of infantry at the outbreak of the war and was stationed in Richmond assisting with munitions until requesting a transfer to a more active assignment. Eventually he made his way into the Engineer Corps.

In the nearly one hundred pages available in the National Archives there is no record of T.J. Moncure's actions in July of 1863. In June of that year, however, he was in Richmond performing topographical engineering work, apparently as a contract engineer before receiving an official commission in the Engineer Corps from the Confederate government. Not until September 1863 does he turn up in the records for McLaws's Division, but even then, he was assigned to Kershaw, not division headquarters.[704] It seems he followed McLaws to Tennessee, for he appears in the court-martial proceedings for McLaws, having reconnoitered the approach to Fort Loudon, a reconnaissance with much bigger career ramifications for McLaws.[705]

Army of Northern Virginia records are silent on Moncure, as well. Proctor Smith makes no mention of Moncure when he compiled the list of engineers for his report of the spring and summer campaigns, an odd omission if he was present, as Moncure was a VMI-trained military engineer.[706] Smith's July and August order book entries make no mention of Moncure, either.[707]

Not only does Smith make no mention of Moncure, he reported that McLaws *had* no engineer. McLaws's previous engineer had just been reassigned before Smith arrived, a fact he asterisked above the list of engineers in his report. "McLaws had no Engr. Off. Capt. Collins having been detached from his command to build Germanna Bridge," he scribbled. "The Bridge was not finished, the enemy driving Captain Collins away before it was finished."[708]

Though it is feasible the army sought to provide McLaws with a replacement for Collins, no mention is made of any engineer officer on McLaws's staff, much less of Moncure himself, throughout the Chancellorsville or Gettysburg campaigns. Captains Sam Johnston, James Boswell, and Oscar Hinrichs assisted McLaws in placing troops on May 1 at Chancellorsville, while Proctor Smith himself scouted the route for McLaws to attack Sedgwick (the attack that never happened and allowed Sedgewick to escape).[709] Even McLaws's adjutant, James Goggin, later recalled they had no guide on the march into position at Gettysburg.[710] There is no sign of any engineer on McLaws's staff until the Army of Northern Virginia arrived back in Virginia after the Gettysburg Campaign.

If Moncure *was* available to go with Johnston, why did McLaws not send *him* once he decided to disobey Longstreet's orders and reconnoiter anyway? McLaws had specifically been told not to leave his division and yet he rode quite a way away from it when reconnoitering. Moncure, on the other hand, was only told not to accompany Johnston; McLaws could have sent Moncure off to scout while he sat on the ridge waiting for orders. If Moncure was present, then he strangely sat idly by while McLaws violated Longstreet's direct order to stay put. If McLaws really did reconnoiter that morning, it's just one more reason to believe Moncure was not at the battle.

What's most likely is that McLaws confused the chronology of Moncure's tenure with his division. His memory failing him, without notes to refresh it, and unable to explain why he did not reconnoiter as he tried to reconstruct the morning's events, he filled in the memory lapse the best he could. He assumed that Moncure *must* have been at Gettysburg, and so it was Moncure that he ordered to reconnoiter.[liii] And having been an integral part of the Knoxville debacle, which led to the end of McLaws's tenure with the Army of Northern Virginia, Moncure was someone recognizable to McLaws when he was mining his memory for details.

---

liii   Recall the psychologist seminar in which the psychologists incorrectly placed events that happened elsewhere into their recollection of the seminar. Loftus, *Memory*, 64–65. Indeed, McLaws even questioned himself. In his 1892 letter to Johnston, he wrote that Longstreet "also objected to my sending my engineer 'Montcure'?" McLaws to Johnston, June 8, 1892, in McLaws Papers, UNC Wilson Library.

* * *

MCLAWS INSISTED THAT HE CONDUCTED HIS OWN RECONN-aissance later that morning, despite Longstreet's order to remain with his division. McLaws claimed he was able to discover a concealed route from Herr's Ridge to his assigned position on Warfield Ridge. Of course, Pendleton and Johnston had discovered the Ravine Road the night before and Confederates had continued to scout it all morning. Perhaps McLaws *thought* he had discovered it, for it was new to him that morning, but surely the presence of Hill's Corps a few hundred yards in front of the road suggested it may not have been as big a secret as he later claimed.

And while McLaws *may* have performed a short reconnaissance that morning, time was limited. It certainly couldn't have been done *after* his meeting with Lee, which happened just before he started his march. It's possible his chronology is off and he performed a recon-naissance *before* the meeting, but that recon wouldn't have yielded any epiphanies. The back of Seminary Ridge was well-scouted and the Ravine Road was no secret to the army. McLaws was by no means the only person aware of it.[711] That's not to mention McLaws wouldn't know where he was supposed to be going yet.

And if McLaws hadn't had an opportunity to reconnoiter the position before his meeting with Lee, then he was seriously remiss in assuring his commanding officer that he could get to his assigned position without being seen. If McLaws really had arrived only moments before being summoned to Lee's headquarters, then he could not have honestly answered Lee the way he said he did.

McLaws was not generally accused of being a liar. As a career soldier, it's hard to imagine he answered Lee the way he did if he hadn't had the opportunity to look around (and harder to imagine Lee asked him in the first place, knowing he'd just arrived). This all suggests that McLaws *didn't* go directly to headquarters when he arrived that morning, but moved his division along Herr's Ridge, where Longstreet met him and helped position his men, as both Fremantle and Black remembered.

He probably performed *some* sort of reconnaissance that morning to get his bearings, but was certainly not the first to discover the Ravine Road. Certainly, the impact of his limited investigation was much less than he had convinced himself. It's more in line with McLaws's character and what we know about the morning of July 2 to believe that McLaws was simply mistaken in his recollections, which were significantly affected by the severe threats to his closely guarded reputation.

MCLAWS ALSO MISUNDERSTOOD JOHNSTON'S RECONNAISsance that morning. In the rough draft of his letter to Longstreet in 1873, he remembered that Lee "remarked that he had ordered a reconnaissance of the [Federal] position."[712] This matched Johnston's own recollection that Lee ordered him to "make a reconnaissance of the enemy's left."[713]

But after thinking on it for a day or two, McLaws scribbled that out and changed it entirely. In his final draft, the copy that was sent to Longstreet and the *New Orleans Republican*, McLaws wrote that Lee ordered the "reconnaissance for the purpose of finding out a way for me to go into position, without me being seen by the enemy."[714] This made sense if Johnston was the one who was to lead the column, but Johnston always disputed that idea. Though McLaws was the first to suggest that it was Johnston who was to scout the route and lead the column, his letter was not widely distributed outside New Orleans. Instead, it was Longstreet's 1877 article that brought Johnston to the forefront of the debate. It was *his* article, not McLaws's, after all, that Fitz Lee sent to Johnston and which prompted Johnston's first words on the matter.

But if Longstreet was relying on McLaws's memory, he was relying on an assumption that even McLaws wasn't entirely sure about. McLaws's accounts all hinged on the facts that Lee was waiting on the results of a reconnaissance and that Longstreet refused to let McLaws reconnoiter for himself. But in his 1873 letter, McLaws wrote that after a long wait, "Major Johnson [sic] of Gen'l Lee's staff appeared to conduct the head of the column, as he, *so I understood,* had made the reconnaissance."[715] In this first account, which provided the baseline memory for all of his later published accounts, McLaws is clear that he simply intuited that Johnston had performed the reconnaissance. Lee never actually told him that.[716] But since it was Johnston who rode up to McLaws before the march started, McLaws assumed it was *his* reconnaissance Lee had been waiting on.

But McLaws didn't have the whole story. Johnston had been back for quite some time before McLaws met with Lee and Longstreet and began his march. Like McLaws, Johnston remembered a long wait before beginning the march. "Soon after" he gave his report, Johnston remembered, he "was ordered to ride with General Longstreet. After no little delay the column got in motion."[717] But Johnston didn't wait with McLaws; he waited with Longstreet. He didn't ride to McLaws's position until much later. Of course, McLaws didn't know that and assumed that Johnston's arrival at the head of his column meant that he had just returned from the route reconnaissance. The assumption was not unreasonable, but neither was it accurate.

This was the assumption that Longstreet picked up on when he published his 1877 article, writing that "General Lee ordered Colonel Johnston, of his engineer corps, to lead and conduct the head of the column."[718] Johnston's role was now indelibly tangled up in the story and so Fitz Lee, who tried to maintain a modicum of objectivity in the matter, reached out directly to Sam Johnston for his side of the story. Though Johnston asked Lee not to publish the letter, it appeared in print as part of Fitz Lee's article only a few months later, in April of 1878.[719]

The response from McLaws, published in February 1879, became one of the primary sources for Johnston's role on July 2 *and* for the countermarch more generally. Here, McLaws was more confident in his recollections than when he jotted down his thoughts to Longstreet five years earlier. McLaws remembered that Lee told him "Major Johnston, of my staff, has been ordered to reconnoitre the ground, and I expect he is about ready." After McLaws waited (and waited…and waited), "Major Johnston, of General Lee's staff, came to me and said he was ordered to conduct me on the march."[720] It was important for McLaws to note that Johnston was on *Lee's* staff, for he announced this twice in the span of two paragraphs.

The pattern was nothing new; the more intense the political and personal controversy became, the more confident the veterans were in their memories. But the assumption was an easy enough one to make even without the extra interference. Johnston *did* accompany Longstreet's column and he *did* reconnoiter that morning. He was also a familiar face, having spent a good deal of time with Longstreet's staff in 1862, so it wasn't unreasonable to assume that he was the one they were waiting on.

Johnston wasn't the only one reconnoitering that morning, though, and his mission only called for a nominal investigation of the roads. As he freely admitted several times, he "examin[ed] the roads over which our troops would have to move in the event of a movement on the enemy's left" during his reconnaissance. But that wasn't his *primary* goal. Rather, making note of the roads was just "part of my duty as a reconnoitering officer and would be attended to without special instructions."[721]

William Pendleton, on the other hand, clearly reported that his reconnaissance on July 2 was specifically to find a route to bring troops to the point of attack.[722] E.P. Alexander, who arrived on the field after Johnston returned, remembered that it had been "Long and Pendleton who had reconnoitered on the right" and delivered their reports to Lee around 10:00 a.m.[723] Alexander arrived between 9:00 and 10:00 a.m., well after Johnston returned, but just as Pendleton's staff was arriving with their messages regarding the route.[724] Alexander probably didn't know at the time that Johnston had made a reconnaissance at all, but he *did* know that Pendleton had made one and reported just before the army started its movement toward the Federal left. And of course, Page remembered that Peterkin had reported to Longstreet that "the way is open" that morning.[725]

McLaws was mistaken, then, in assuming that it was Johnston's report they were waiting on. The reconnaissance "for the purpose of finding out a way for me to go into position, without me being seen by the enemy" was in fact conducted by Pendleton and his staff.

Once again, we see several different views of the same event through various windows. None provides a clear enough view, on its own, to see what happened. But by comparing (like Johnston advised) and sifting (like Kershaw suggested), we get a unique and nearly complete view, a view none of the participants was able to see.

AT LONG LAST, OR SO IT SEEMED TO THOSE WAITING IN THE humid fields, couriers finally arrived with marching orders. Soldiers stood up and quickly stretched out tired joints. The worn-out soles of shoes shuffled back into line in the mud of farm lanes optimistically called "roads." No doubt many said a prayer to themselves, for these were orders with consequences. Men would die. Soon. And they all knew it.

Texan John West, exhausted from the long march the night before, fell asleep as he waited for the fight to begin, dreaming of his wife and young children and dreading the thought of leaving them orphaned. He wrote home to his four-year-old "Little Man," letting him know that as he lay in the field waiting to be sent into battle, "I asked God to take care of you if I am taken away from you."[726]

The sights of the hospitals and wounded men had seriously unsettled A.C. Sims as they passed by in the gloomy light of dawn. The morning passed slowly as they waited in the fields beneath the July sun. "It was indeed hours of great suspense" and they "whiled away there waiting for the time for action." It was Sims's first battle and it weighed on him heavily. Merely the words "Ordnance" stenciled on the wagons "to me…seemed like death," and "I had no appetite for eating."[727]

Sam Johnston, who had been through as many battles as nearly anyone else on the field, spent the remainder of the morning with General Longstreet. "After no little delay the column got in motion," he remembered. Despite later implications, they weren't waiting on Longstreet's mood to brighten, but rather on Lee to issue orders. Though Johnston was politically astute and polite enough to hedge his postwar statements, it was abundantly clear that even he thought Longstreet's delay was unfounded *and* that he wasn't particularly aware of Lee's movements that morning. Having been sent to Longstreet right after giving his report, this is understandable.[728]

McLaws, too, famously complained about the wait. He spent the morning "on my horse and saw in the distance the enemy coming, hour after hour, on to the battle ground."[729] Coupland Page, George Peterkin, and Armistead Long all remembered waiting, too, and as the controversy took hold, almost everyone attributed this to Longstreet's brooding.[730]

Of course, there *was* a wait, but it wasn't an undue one. Lee hadn't issued any orders to march, for Longstreet was ordered to move to the right of Anderson and Anderson hadn't moved yet, either.[731] And since Lee hadn't decided *where* to attack until at least ten o'clock that morning, *when* to attack couldn't have been any earlier than that, nor could it have been particularly soon after. Fourteen thousand troops don't simply move three miles in the blink of an eye.

There's some evidence suggesting that there was, in fact, a particular time that Lee and Longstreet had in mind for the attack. The agreed upon time...four o'clock. A Texan in Hood's Division, James Henry Hendrick, wrote to his mother less than a week after the battle and told her that "it was understood by all that we were going to make the attack at four o'clock."[732]

Likewise, Campbell Brown acknowledged in his memoir that although the attack was initially postponed until 9 a.m., "another [message] put it off till 4:00 p.m."[733] Brown doesn't mention what time the second order postponing the attack arrived, but if he's correct, then at some point during the day Lee and Longstreet were able to coordinate a specific time for the attack.

Campbell Brown wasn't the only one in Ewell's Corps to remember that the attack was postponed until four, either. Jubal Early, of all people, reported in August of 1863 that he had "been subsequently informed that the attack would begin at 4:00 p.m."[734] William Nelson, acting chief artillery officer for Ewell's Corps, remembered that "about 11:00 a.m. I was ordered to bring my battalion to a point immediately in rear of the Gettysburg College, park my batteries, and await events."[735] Not coincidentally, this was just after Lee issued his orders. By the time they trickled down to Nelson, it would have been around 11:00 a.m.

Fremantle, too, thought the attack was supposed to start later in the day. "The whole morning was evidently to be occupied in disposing the troops for the attack," he wrote in his July 2 diary entry, so "I rode to the extreme right with Colonel Manning and Major Walton" and bathed, ate cherries, and got feed for the horses. It was 2:00 p.m., just as McLaws was completing his countermarch, before Longstreet told Fremantle he may want to head back to his tree from the day before in order to see the battle.[liv]

Fitzgerald Ross, the Austrian observer, also remembered that "evidently a long time would elapse before Longstreet's corps, which was to do the chief fighting that day, could be placed in position." Instead of heading south to bathe in the creek and eat cherries, Ross rode into town with the corps' doctors, whom he had befriended.[736]

While Campbell Brown wrote his memoir years after the battle, James Hendrick provides one of the most contemporary accounts that can be expected, well before even the "sly under-currents" began running through the ranks. Both Fremantle and Ross were far away from these undercurrents when their accounts were published. Even Old Jube, who started the conversation about the "fatal delay" at Gettysburg, remembered that the attack was set for 4:00 p.m. Mountains of postwar letters, speeches, articles, and books notwithstanding, four of the most contemporary documents available strongly suggest the Confederate high command intended the fight to begin in the midafternoon all along. Indeed, moving roughly 21,000 troops (including Anderson's Division) into position wasn't a quick endeavor, especially if it was intended to be a hidden maneuver.

---

liv   Fremantle, *Three Months in the Southern States*, 258. A discussion of the timeline and chronology of the countermarch begins at page 309.

July 2

✷ ✷ ✷

WITH ORDERS IN HAND, SO TO SPEAK, ANDERSON AND McLaws stepped off (Hood would wait for his last brigade to arrive and follow Anderson's route). Anderson's route was easy enough. He turned off the Hereter's (Old) Mill Road and followed the Ravine Road to the Pitzer Farm Lane, which led him almost directly to his position on Pender's right.[737] With the exception of a sharp, but quick, firefight with a contingent of Federal troops in Pitzer's Woods as the last brigade swiveled into position, Anderson's deployment was fairly quick and easy.

McLaws had a longer route from Herr's Ridge, sidestepping the towering Bream's Hill in order to take the Black Horse Tavern Road toward the crossroad at the Peach Orchard. His division was looking at a three-to-four-mile march (depending on where one was in the column), but it was necessary to avoid the congestion along the Ravine Road and to keep his column out of sight. What was more, three divisions moving along a narrow farm road would take too much time and clutter the narrow lanes.

Kershaw, who led McLaws's column, was a little over a mile from the Black Horse Tavern Road by way of the concealed route. The head of his column could be on the other side of Bream's Hill in about a half hour. In perhaps an hour and a half, then, (say, 12:30), the vanguard of McLaws's Division could be arriving on Seminary Ridge.[738]

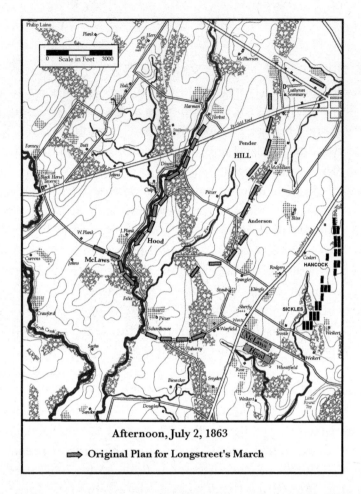

Afternoon, July 2, 1863

 Original Plan for Longstreet's March

The original plan for Longstreet's march into position on July 2, 1863. Map by Philip Laino.

* * *

THE BLACK HORSE TAVERN ROAD IS INEXTRICABLY LINKED to Longstreet's July 2 countermarch. There certainly seemed to be some sort of bad luck associated with the road, for both armies stumbled upon its muddy ruts in those opening days of July. Humphreys's

Federal troops had nearly walked right into Wilcox's Confederate pickets less than twelve hours earlier. They had escaped, but were delayed and exhausted. Going the opposite direction, the road would cause nearly the same problems for the Confederates.

Though McLaws and Longstreet assumed it in their postwar writing, Johnston probably *didn't* scout the road. It's certainly possible Clarke or Smith did, but there's nothing other than conjecture to assume that they did. It's unlikely Pendleton set foot on the road, either.

John Black's troopers, on the other hand, may have scouted it and provided Longstreet intelligence on the road. In his memoir, Black wrote that after placing McLaws's men on Herr's Ridge, Longstreet asked him to "supply...two trusty cavalry subalterns." Black called up the appropriately named Lieutenant Fred Horsey and another lieutenant from his ad hoc command. "Longstreet ordered Horsey to go out 3 or 4 miles in one direction & Marshall in another at full speed with a few men and to come back and report as to whether they could see any enemy or not." North and west were useless to scout, since they were decidedly occupied by the Confederate army. So, Horsey and his colleague must have scouted south and east. South meant the Fairfield Road, which the unnamed troopers galloped down. East, then, could only mean the Black Horse Tavern Road, as it's the only substantial road between the Fairfield and Emmitsburg Roads. It also happened to be the road they ultimately took.

While Horsey was scouting, Black was ordered to place his artillery, a section of Hart's Battery, to "command a road bearing to the right."[lv] Horsey was gone an hour, according to Black, and "had explored the ground Longstreet deployed on," meaning he scouted the Black Horse Tavern Road to Seminary Ridge. If Black's timeline is accurate, this was just before Johnston returned.[739]

It's just as likely, though, that Black's times were off, and Horsey scouted the Black Horse Tavern Road while Lee was having a look at Ewell's line. Either way, if the fundamentals of Black's account are accurate, then *his* men scouted the route McLaws's men took, not

---

lv   This was the Fairfield Road.

Johnston or Pendleton. And Black, remember, was assigned to Longstreet by Lee, who had instructed him at West Point.[740]

Even if Black's recollection is entirely made up and no one scouted the road, it was prominent on all the maps and led right to the position McLaws was supposed to occupy on Seminary Ridge. It's the only route between the Fairfield Road and Seminary Ridge appearing on the 1858 Adams County Wall Map, which is likely the large map Lee had sprawled before him that morning. And with Anderson extending his line farther south on Seminary Ridge, by taking the Black Horse Tavern Road, McLaws would spend most of his trip behind his own lines. At 10:30 that morning, it seemed like a safe route into position.

WHEN THE ORDER WAS GIVEN, KERSHAW'S MEN, TAKING THE lead, "moved by flank from the head of column perpendicularly to the rear." In simpler terms, they faced to the right, formed a column four men across, and the head of the column angled forty-five degrees to the right. This put them in position to turn right down the unnamed farm lane between the Butt Farm and Dr. Hall's house. Marching down the lane onto the west side of the ridge, the column "passed back of the hill, filed under its cover to the left, passed to the right of the building afterwards used as a hospital, and between it and the bridge across a creek at that point."[741]

Kershaw's description, which was written as a letter to John Bachelder in 1876, adds detail to, but doesn't contradict, his report. His report simply stated that his brigade was "directed to move under cover of the hills toward the right, with a view to flanking the enemy in that direction, if cover could be found to conceal the movement."[742] Both his report and letter depict a route from the unnamed farm lane to the west side of the ridge, which quickly took the brigade out of sight of any prying Federal eyes.

As the column moved southwest behind the ridge, Bream's Hill was now on their left. They passed behind it until they reached Marsh Creek, where the column was forced to turn left along another farm lane. That lane finished the loop around Bream's Hill and they emerged at the intersection of the Fairfield Road and the Black Horse Tavern Road, with the namesake tavern on their left. Crossing the Fairfield Road, they continued on until "suddenly, as we rose a hill…the Round Top was plainly visible, with the flags of the signal men in rapid motion."[743]

AS MCLAWS HAD BEEN MARCHING AROUND BREAM'S HILL, Anderson's men tramped behind Seminary Ridge nearly two miles to his east. All had gone smoothly enough so far. Wright, Mahone, Posey, and Perry all managed to get their brigades into position without much excitement.

But since dawn, the Confederate activity on Seminary Ridge had raised eyebrows and pricked ears among the Federal troops on Cemetery Ridge. Around 7:30 that morning, General Birney sent a hundred men from Colonel Hiram Berdan's specialized force of marksmen across the Emmitsburg Road to see what the Confederates were up to.[744]

Their view from the open fields wasn't particularly good. They couldn't see much more than they could from their own lines. So around 11:00 a.m., Birney ordered another hundred sharpshooters, this time supported by the Third Maine infantry, "farther to the left of our lines."[745] Much to his chagrin, Lieutenant Colonel Casper Trepp was assigned command of this second expedition. Trepp wasn't so much annoyed by the assignment as he was disgusted by the way they had to get there. Trepp's assigned route "followed the road in plain view of the enemy," he complained in his official report, even though the "detachment might have been marched from the original position to a point where the engagement took place perfectly concealed from view of the enemy and without loss of time. As we marched, the enemy must have seen every man from the time we reached the road until we entered the woods on the Fairfield road [Eiker's Mill Road, call Millerstown Road today], giving the enemy time to counter-maneuver."[746]

When the patrol reached the woods, they "deployed...in a line running nearly east and west," moving north through the woods toward the Confederate position.[747] It didn't take them long to find Anderson's men moving in "three columns...in rear of the woods." The Confederates, with a line of skirmishers in front, offered irresistible targets and Berdan's men pitched into the southerners "vigorously."[748]

In a rare instance of agreement on both sides, the Confederates remembered the exact same thing. "In taking the new position," Anderson reported, "the Tenth Alabama Regiment, Wilcox's brigade, had a sharp skirmish with a body of the enemy who had occupied a wooded hill on the extreme right of my line."[749] David Lang, who commanded Perry's Brigade that afternoon and was moving into position to Wilcox's left, remembered that the sharpshooters "opened a heavy fire of musketry" on Wilcox's men as the division moved into line.[750]

Lieutenant Colonel Hilary Herbert of the Eighth Alabama watched it all unfold. The Eleventh Alabama, on the brigade's far right, turned into line, "its right flank then exposed to a stone wall some seventy-five yards off. From behind this wall a sudden and severe fire was opened on the flank.... Its gallant commander attempted to swing it around facing the wall, but the fire was too severe, and the eleventh fell back over the eighth."[751] Berdan reported that his men were able to get "close upon" the Confederates and their fire "threw them for a time into confusion."[752]

Meanwhile, Herbert's Eighth Alabama had "occupied a road running parallel with" the stone wall, about two hundred yards off. The Eighth Alabama lay down as the Eleventh fell back behind them, then it pushed up to the stone wall to engage the sharpshooters. (Trepp remembered it was a "rail fence.")[753] "The fire was very brisk for about ten minutes," Trepp reported, and Berdan called for the

Third Maine, which had stayed in reserve.[754] The Maine men rushed across the fields and quickly formed in the woods under a "heavy fire." According to their commander, Colonel Moses Lakeman, they "returned [it] with a good will."

Lakeman was not happy with the situation. While the sharpshooters were free to take cover behind trees, his own men had the "decided disadvantage" of "fill[ing] the intervals" in line of battle. But they held their position nonetheless, taking heavy casualties.[755]

Some of the Federal cavalry patrols Johnston and Pendleton had seen earlier that morning were scouting the area west of Berdan and heard the firing. Sergeant W.T. Bradshaw of the Ninth New York was patrolling with about six or seven other troopers in a patch of woods by a "school house near Willoughby Run. From the high ground just through the woods Bradshaw could see a large force of the enemy's infantry moving rapidly into line in the open fields to the north." Bradshaw and his men fired a few shots into the Confederates and galloped off to find support.[756]

Colonel Thomas Devin, meanwhile, "immediately dismounted and deployed two squadrons in support of Berdan's Sharpshooters," forming a line with a section of artillery in support.[757] Devin didn't say which regiments the squadrons were from, but it was almost certainly the Sixth New York, with an additional twenty men from the Ninth New York.[758]

As the fight heated up, Colonel Forney, of the Tenth Alabama, ordered a charge and the Alabamians rushed over the fence. "This broke the enemy's line," Wilcox reported, and the northerners "fled precipitately from the woods."[759] This is how Moses Lakeman remembered it, too, for he lamented that he "was obliged to leave my dead and seriously wounded on the field."[760] Trepp, on the other hand, remembered he was able to carry off his wounded and retreated in good order, perhaps because they had the advantage of a nimbler formation.

Lakeman's men seem to have gotten mixed up among both the woods and the sharpshooters. Not being trained or accustomed to fighting that way, split between various skirmish formations, Lakeman's command and control suffered, so it isn't surprising he had a harder time directing his retreat. At least a portion of the Third Maine tried to hold off the advancing Confederates, too. Lakeman reported that as Wilcox's counterattack "became quicker," the Federals pulled out of the woods. Out in the open fields, his New Englanders gave "an occasional volley to check [the enemy's] advance" as they fell back.[761]

The sharpshooters and Mainers fell back across the open farm fields between the woods and the Emmitsburg Road. The fences marking the east/west boundaries of the fields contributed to the Third Maine's disorder, along with plenty of Alabama bullets, for when they arrived at the Emmitsburg Road, the regiment "had gotten somewhat confused from loss of men and obstructions in our retreat."[762]

All told, the Maine regiment left almost fifty men in Pitzer's Woods.[763] The sharpshooters, for their part, always maintained they had stopped Longstreet's column and that *they* were the true cause of Longstreet's delay. Like their aim, the sharpshooters' impression was remarkably accurate, though not quite for the reason they thought. Even though Berdan's men didn't exchange shots with anyone in Longstreet's Corps that morning, the twenty-minute fight profoundly affected the battle (and the reputation of more than one southern general).

That Wretched Little Signal Station

"A tradition may grow and flower surprisingly, but it doesn't grow like a kind of historical orchid. It must have its root in something definite."

- Samuel Francis Batchelder, "The Washington Elm Tradition."[764]

"THE REBELS ARE IN FORCE," SHOUTED AARON JEROME, through rapid motions of the large white signal flag, and "our skirmishers give way." A mile to the west of the Federal position, "the woods are full of them."[765] Jerome had watched the skirmish in

Pitzer's Woods unfold and dutifully reported it to headquarters.[766] His messages at 11:45 and 11:55 a.m. count as the first recorded messages from a signal station on Little Round Top. Once Jerome signaled to army headquarters that Confederates were pushing their skirmishers out of the woods, the hill fell silent again. It would be another hour and a half before the next surviving messages.

That begs several questions. Are the messages that exist the *only* messages, or just the ones that survived long enough to make it into the *Official Records*? There's evidence that other messages were sent from the hill that morning and reason certainly allows for messages to have been delivered and lost. They were fighting a battle, after all. Preserving individual dispatches for posterity was not particularly high on the priority list; the point was simply to get the message from one place to another.

But even assuming there were other messages sent at some point, does the gap in the records reflect a gap in the occupation of the hill as a signal station or simply a lack of documentation? The answer is that it probably indicates both. There's a decided lack of preserved signal messages, due to the nature of the communication. Deciphered messages were written down on paper and then relayed to the appropriate officer, much like a written message handed to a courier. Unless someone thought it was a particularly historic dispatch, there was little reason to keep it once the order was delivered. But even accounting for that, there's reason to believe the hill wasn't continuously occupied by Federal signalmen that day.

The Signal Corps divided its officers among the various infantry corps, so that each corps received a pair of signal officers and flagmen.[767] Captain Lemuel Norton, who had just been named acting chief signal officer on June 18 after the prior chief signal officer was captured, reported that "during the whole of [July 1], endeavors were made to open the signal line between general headquarters, Emmitsburg, and Round Top Mountain. But on account of the smokiness of the atmosphere, the desired result was not obtained until 11:00 p.m., when the first message was received."[768] If there were signal flags and torches on Little Round Top on the night of July 1, though, they weren't there the next morning. Norton regrettably informed army chief of staff Daniel Butterfield first thing in the morning on the second that while "communication with Emmitsburg is still open... [there is] no communication yet with Gettysburg."[769]

Keeping in mind the fact that numerous hills were designated "Round Top" throughout the region, there's strong evidence to suggest Norton wasn't referring to *the* Round Top. At least not when he discussed a signal station appearing through the haze at 11:00 p.m. on the night of the first.

Norton reported that the signalmen had been trying to connect with the Round Top Mountain signal station and Emmitsburg *all day* on July 1. But there wasn't any reason for Norton to know about the famous Round Tops in the morning or afternoon of July 1. Other than the reference in Norton's report, there's no evidence that anyone signaled from the hill that day or was even supposed to be there. Instead, the signal officers found perches in cupolas, rooftops, and natural observation points like Cemetery Hill.[770] Little Round Top was two miles south of the Federal position and until late in the day (when the Twelfth and Third Corps arrived) there weren't enough signalmen to even consider setting up a station there. And of course, if Norton wasn't aware of the hill's existence, then he certainly couldn't have been calling it throughout the day on the first. Whatever "Round Top Mountain" Norton was trying to signal all day, it wasn't the one Longstreet's men attacked on July 2.

There was, however, a line of communication between Taneytown, Emmitsburg, and Jacks Mountain, a large round hill near Fairfield.[771] A quick look at the map shows the three points directly connecting Taneytown to Jacks Mountain, with Emmitsburg in between. The observation network allowed the army to keep an eye on the mountain passes and the army's left flank as it moved into Pennsylvania, objects of concern for General Meade and his left wing commander, General John Reynolds. Up until the afternoon of July 1, Federal commanders spent considerable energy worrying about the prospect of a Confederate flanking maneuver through the mountains.[772]

That's also exactly why signal officers Captain Charles Kendall and Lieutenant Louis Fortescue were sent to Jacks Mountain on June

29. Their orders specifically instructed them to keep an eye on the army's left flank and watch for any surprises from Confederates that may be hidden by the mountains. As Fortescue later remembered, "Norton directed Kendall and I to proceed to the mountain range to the rear and north of Emmitsburg...[so] that General Meade... might be kept informed of any movements observed by us from that elevation."[773]

Fortescue and Kendall found a superb vista from the summit of Jacks Mountain. From the "spur of the mountain" and with the aid of a glass, they could see the "Taneytown church steeple [headquarters], and the beautiful valley north and east to Gettysburg."[774] Fortescue and Kendall remained there throughout the battle, but had a difficult time communicating with Taneytown on July 1. "We can see the outlines of the Taneytown steeple," Fortescue wrote, "but the heavy atmosphere precludes the possibility of our reading a message from them, or of their being able to decipher one from us at present."[775]

That was on the *morning* of July 1. Fortescue and Kendall left the mountain during the afternoon to reconnoiter to the southwest, looking for a good vantage point to see if any Confederate troops were approaching from the west. During that time, of course, their signal station was unoccupied and couldn't be reached, which almost certainly accounts for some of Norton's inability to communicate "all day."

Seeing nothing to the west, they returned to Jacks Mountain around 7:00 p.m. and tried to connect with the other stations. It was well after dark, though, by the time they reached anyone. "After swinging our torch for some time," Fortescue recalled, "we succeeded in getting the Taneytown steeple and communicated the result of our observations...the delay in attracting their notice being on account of the thick atmosphere." Norton finally replied and told them to stay put until daylight. After that message, Fortescue retired to Mount Saint Mary's in Emmitsburg to spend the night.[776]

Fortescue and Kendall's station on Jacks Mountain is a much more likely candidate for Norton's inaccessible July 1 "Round Top" station. Fortescue and Kendall had a signal station on the large, broad hill that was directly plugged into the headquarters/Emmitsburg communication line and had been communicating with headquarters for two days prior to the battle. Then, inexplicably from Norton's perspective, the station disappeared on July 1. In the morning, and then again in the evening when they returned, the station had trouble communicating with headquarters due to the atmospheric conditions. Finally, in the pure darkness of the Pennsylvania night, headquarters caught the messages from the torch on the mountain.

Norton's and Fortescue's accounts align perfectly, with the sole exception of Norton's terminology. Since the moniker "round top" was such a ubiquitous name at the time (for Norton wasn't writing with much hindsight), it seems unreasonable to dismiss the mountain of evidence suggesting Jacks Mountain was Norton's July 1 "Round Top" signal station in favor of Norton's generic term. This is especially true in light of the fact that there's no evidence anyone was even expected to be on either of the famous Round Tops on July 1.

Indeed, Norton's first job as acting chief signal officer was to connect the communication lines from headquarters to the regional stations so Meade could stay up to date with the latest intelligence. On the night of June 30, Meade familiarized Norton with the communication network necessary to facilitate the Pipe Creek line, if that contingency panned out. It was in this context that Norton tried reaching the "Round Top Mountain station" on July 1.[777] Once again, the context doesn't support Norton's July 1 "round top" being the famous hill.

Norton's report provides more evidence that the Little Round Top station was a July 2 realization. "I reported at an early hour [on July 2]," he wrote, "at the point selected for headquarters of the army...but found the signal officers, who had been previously assigned to the different army corps, already on the field."[778] By 11:00 a.m., "every desirable point of observation was occupied by a signal officer." As we'll see, Little Round Top was occupied sporadically from around 10:30 until late in the afternoon, when a more permanent station was established.

It's not impossible, though, to imagine a station on the hill early on the morning of the second. Geary's men may have taken a signal officer with them when they spent the night near the hill. Though there's no documentation that they did, it's not an unreasonable logical leap to think they did. But only two brigades from the Twelfth Corps were sent to the left that night. It's not likely the signalmen would be sent away from their established station to accompany two brigades to guard the flank at night.

But even if there *had* been a station established overnight with Geary's men, it left with the infantry at 5:00 a.m. Norton reported that all of the signal officers were with their respective corps when he reported to headquarters that morning. By the time Norton arrived that morning, no infantry occupied the Round Tops.

As surprising as that may seem today, the famous hill wasn't nearly as prominent in the minds of the soldiers and generals as it would be by the end of the day. The hill was two miles south of the main Federal line with no support. Meanwhile, Jacks Mountain could see all the way to Taneytown and had a clear view of Gettysburg and the other signal stations, meaning Little Round Top wasn't vital to the signal line.

The order of messages suggests that the hill remained empty through most of the morning, too. While most of the messages from the Little Round Top signal station are time-stamped, one important dispatch is not. At some point on July 2, Norton and Lieutenant Peter Taylor, one of the signal officers assigned to the Second Corps, sent a message to Captain James Hall, the other Second Corps signalman, from the slopes of Little Round Top. They told Hall they could see a "column of enemy's infantry move into [the] woods on [the] ridge, 3 miles west of the town, near the Millerstown [modern Fairfield] road. Wagon teams parked in [an] open field beyond the ridge, moved to the rear, behind [the] woods." They also saw "wagons moving up and down on the Chambersburg pike, at Spangler's," which led them to believe that "the enemy occupies the range of hills 3 miles west of town in considerable force." In a revealing post-script, they told Hall "this is a good point for observation."[779]

Norton's distances are off, for there aren't large woodlots three miles west of town and none that can be said to be on the Fairfield Road. While there are patches of trees, only the Herr's Ridge Woods and Pitzer's Woods fairly constitute "woods" south of the Chambersburg Pike.[lvi] Norton couldn't have meant the modern Millerstown Road (which confusingly is sometimes referred to in contemporary reports as the Fairfield Road). If he was, the rest of his message doesn't make sense. That road is decidedly south, not west, of town. More likely, he simply misjudged the distances from Little Round Top.[lvii]

The message also suggests Norton and Taylor were on the hill before Jerome. Norton's presence with Taylor suggests the two were looking for a good place for the Second Corps signalmen to establish a station. Hall had found a spot somewhere on the field earlier that morning, for he was signaling by 9:00 a.m.[780] A message from Fortescue suggests Hall's station may have been on the Taneytown Road that morning, for he and Kendall spotted flags waving there around 9:00 a.m. By eleven, though, the station was ordered to pack up and report to headquarters.[781]

If that's the case, then Norton and Taylor may well have been scouting out positions for the Second Corps station before moving Hall up the road around 11:00 a.m. Norton acknowledged earlier that morning that there hadn't been any communication with Gettysburg "yet." That meant Norton's primary responsibility, the signal network between the army and the mountain range, was broken. Reconnecting that was the primary objective. Once Norton arrived, he was able to correct that through the "exertions" of the signal officers. Only then did Norton turn his attention to local observation.

lvi There are many alternate names for various woods, woodlots, hills, etc. on the battlefield and some denote specific areas of the more general designation. There are subsets of the Herr's Ridge and Pitzer Woods, such as Hall's Wood and Wible Woods, but for the sake of space and ease of reading, the general terms are used here.

lvii The Federals often referred to the Fairfield Road as the Millerstown Road, as evidenced by Bachelder's designation on his 1863 isometric map.

With Lieutenant Taylor, Norton went about looking for a good spot to place him. Little Round Top proved to be that place.

What Norton saw suggests they were there before Jerome. He reported seeing wagons arriving along the Chambersburg Road and a considerable force of Confederate infantry on the ridges west of town. This indicates Longstreet's two divisions had already arrived and Anderson's men had moved up from Knoxlyn Ridge. If Norton was on the hill between 10:30 and 11:00 a.m. looking for a vista, then Anderson was already moving into position. The wagons may well have been the rear of Longstreet's column trailing behind Alexander's battalion, which had arrived around 10:00 a.m. The column of Confederate infantry spotted by Norton moving into the woods along the Fairfield Road was probably Anderson's men crossing Pendleton's Hill onto the Ravine Road.

Unfortunately, there's no other surviving message from Norton and Taylor on Little Round Top that day. Did Norton send a courier out for Jerome, knowing he was with the cavalry and not currently stationed anywhere?[782] Or did Jerome see the flag from his (presumed) position near the Peach Orchard and ride to the hill on his own accord? Perhaps he moved forward with a group of sharpshooters that occupied the hill and surrounding area late that morning and into the afternoon. Or perhaps it was just another part of Buford's mission to observe the area between Gettysburg and Fairfield.

There's no available documentation to know for sure, but within a few minutes of the message from Norton to Hall, Jerome began messaging. One probably had something to do with the other.

AS THE NEW CHIEF SIGNAL OFFICER, NORTON HAD REASON to exaggerate the efficiency of the signal operations. By most contemporary accounts, the Signal Corps wasn't particularly well-regulated during the last day of June and the first two days of July. That's not unreasonable. Norton had only been in charge for two weeks and took over in the middle of a campaign. He can be forgiven for not running a tight operation.[lviii]

As of the morning of July 2, the organization of the Signal Corps had left much to be desired. Fortescue's frustration dripped into the ink of his memoir. Signal stations simply disappeared without warning and didn't seem to be where they were supposed to be. In addition to the temporary station on the Taneytown Road, Fortescue remembered the headquarters station in the Taneytown steeple simply packed up and left without telling anyone. "The station in the Taneytown steeple has probably been abandoned," Fortescue guessed, seeming to throw his hands up in exasperation, "as no flag can be seen there, notwithstanding we have called the station, which is distinctly visible, for an hour."[783]

The communication trouble continued the next day. "During the entire morning [of July 3] efforts were made to reach [other stations], notably that on Round Top Mountain," Fortescue wrote, "but each time, after repeatedly calling, the effort was abandoned."[784] The Little Round Top station was under fire on the morning and afternoon of July 3, making communication dangerous and difficult.[785] But Fortescue and Kendall seemed to be having trouble reaching *any* station on the battlefield.

What to make of it all? The most likely timeline puts Norton on Little Round Top around eleven o'clock on the morning of the second, with Jerome following shortly thereafter. Soon after Norton and Taylor signaled Hall, Jerome arrived on the hill. Exactly why remains unknown, but Norton's signaling to Hall probably had something to do with it. Jerome, though, was attached to Buford's cavalry and Buford's troopers left the field between noon and 1:00 p.m. Not coincidentally, Jerome's last recorded message is five minutes before noon.[786] His short stint on Little Round Top was fortuitous, though, for his message helps us place the Pitzer Woods fight into the day's

---

lviii   Unlike Meade, who also took over in the middle of the campaign, Norton was only a captain without a long career and significant experience to guide him.

chronology and probably had something to do with redirecting McLaws's Division.

When Buford and Jerome left, the hill was empty again. James Hall eventually reached Little Round Top, for he saw and reported a portion of McLaws's countermarch at about 1:30 that afternoon. Looking out over the countryside, he reported that "a heavy column of [the] enemy's infantry, about 10,000 strong, is moving from opposite our extreme left toward our right."[787]

Given the Confederate emphasis on the signal station after the war, it's unavoidably ironic that the only part of the march the signal station *did* see was the countermarch taken to avoid it. Though the countermarch kept the Confederates out of sight until Hood formed on the Emmitsburg Road, that doesn't diminish the irony. And though the waving white flags of the signal station loomed large in Confederate memory, there was another, more important, reason McLaws found himself stuck on a hill in the valley of Willoughby Run.

"THAT WRETCHED LITTLE SIGNAL-STATION UPON ROUND Top that day caused one of our divisions to lose over two hours, and probably delayed our assault nearly that long," lamented Porter Alexander more than twenty years after the battle.[788]

The Little Round Top signal station has taken its place as one of the more prominent, perhaps even mythical, parts of the July 2 story. From the mid-1870s until today, the "wig-wagging" flags of the signal men on the famous hill have become a standard part of the narrative.[789] Like most myths, it's rooted in truth, but quickly grew well beyond the bounds of reality. The staying power of a myth is its ability to answer a question that is otherwise unanswerable (or at least uncomfortable to answer). For Confederates, that question was *why* did they lose the battle?

"A tradition may grow and flower surprisingly," wrote one historian near the turn of the century, "but it doesn't grow like a

kind of historical orchid. It must have its root in something definite."[790] For McLaws, the flower was the signal station and it ultimately became the primary reason he stopped his column and was
forced to turn around. "Suddenly, as we rose a hill on the road we
were taking," he told his *Southern Historical Society Papers* readers,
"the Round Top was plainly visible, with the flags of the signal men
in rapid motion."[791]

Almost ten years later, in an article for the *Philadelphia Weekly
Press*, McLaws thought the signal station was even more obvious.
"Suddenly, on rising a hill, as Major J[ohnston] and myself rode
on, we observed the signal flags of the enemy on top of Round Top
signaling rapidly, and it was plain that the command, if it came up
that hill, would be plainly visible to the enemy long before it got
into position."[792] By 1896, the signal flags were the dominant feature,
"waving furiously," while Little Round Top was relegated to "an
abrupt little mountain in our front."[793]

But in his very first account, preempting an anticipated verbal
assault from Longstreet, McLaws didn't mention the signal station
at all. He *did* mention Little Round Top and the presence of "the
enemy," but given the primacy the signal flags received later, their
omission is revealing. The other differences in his first account to
Longstreet in 1873 are significant, if not quite as glaringly evident.

Johnston and McLaws "went on ahead of the command,"
McLaws wrote Longstreet in the summer of 1873, "when suddenly
we arrived on the top of a hill, giving a fair view of the enemy on the
Round Top and to the left, and of course my troops could be seen by
the opposite side, and their numbers estimated if they were allowed
to proceed." McLaws then went to get Longstreet to show him "how
plainly the enemy could watch our movements if we went on."[794] If
it weren't for the "wretched" signal flags, they would have been in
position exactly when they were supposed to (and it was *Lee's* staff
officer, not anyone in the First Corps, who was guiding the column,
by the way).

In his 1873 letter, McLaws noticed more than just "the enemy on
the Round Top." He also noticed Federals "to the left." These troops
couldn't be Sickles's men in the Peach Orchard, for not only was it

hidden from view, it wasn't off to their left. The orchard was directly ahead of them. In any event, Sickles wasn't in the Peach Orchard yet and even if he had been, McLaws couldn't see him.[795]

Instead, McLaws must have seen Berdan's contingent and Buford's cavalry squadrons. Pitzer's Woods was barely a mile in front of him and off to his left. It was also a mere 600 yards or so from where he was supposed to form up on Seminary Ridge. If McLaws's Division reached the hill before the shooting started, they would have seen Berdan's men creeping north through the fields and woods of Seminary Ridge, while Bradshaw's troopers prowled the open fields to the left.

If it was the shooting itself that startled McLaws (and it probably was), then he would be able to see Federal cavalry darting back and forth as Sergeant Bradshaw galloped off for reinforcements and the Sixth New York rushed in with a supporting squadron, with gray smoke wisping above the trees. Unlike the booming bass of cinematic gunshots, the isolated cracks of the carbines and pops of the muskets would echo within the woods and ricochet across the valley to their ears. The volleys would crackle in waves, but there would be more shouting than anything, individual voices barking commands, shouts of adrenaline, and scattered firing. All of this going on directly in McLaws's path would certainly be enough to elicit a *This won't do* from Longstreet.

The fight was noticeable all along the southern portion of the field, too. William Pendleton, who was at the front near the Point of Woods at the time, mentioned the sharp fighting in his report.[796] John Coxe, a private in Kershaw's Brigade, later remembered stopping in the vicinity of the Black Horse Tavern, just after he "heard desultory picket firing in the distance on our left."[797]

McLaws's insistence that the signal flags stopped him in his tracks is inherently suspect, too. From nearly three miles away, a human would appear as barely more than a speck, hardly noticeable with the naked eye even under perfect atmospheric conditions and with excellent eyesight. But the day was humid and atmospheric conditions were *not* great during the battle (as anyone in the Federal signal corps could have attested). McLaws was also riding on horseback. Even an experienced rider walking the horse at a casual gait would be somewhat jostled, interfering with long distance focus.[798]

But of course, McLaws consistently said that the signal flags appeared "suddenly" as they rode up the ridge. That means he wasn't looking through a field glass but rather the waving flags surprised him as he rode up the ridge. That simply couldn't have been the case. More likely, McLaws and his staff were startled by the appearance of Federal troops in front of them and the eruption of fighting in the woods to their front and left. Then, as McLaws took stock of the situation, Jerome's flags became noticeable as they alerted Federal headquarters to the fight in the woods. That is, if Jerome was still there: the last recorded message was 11:55 a.m. There's a real possibility he wasn't there when McLaws looked at the hill under magnification.

Regardless of Jerome's presence, McLaws *would* have seen Major Homer Stoughton's Second U.S. Sharpshooters. At some point during the morning, but after Johnston left the area, Stoughton was sent "to cover a ravine near Sugar Loaf hill, which I did by putting Company H on the brow of the hill, with vedettes overlooking the ravine, and Company D in the ravine near the woods, to watch the enemy's movements in that direction." He put four additional companies of sharpshooters in "a line perpendicular to the cross-road that intersects with the Emmitsburg pike." The sharpshooters stayed there until "about 2:00 p.m."[799]

While Stoughton's men wouldn't have stopped McLaws cold for the same reason Jerome's signal flag couldn't, the sharpshooters *would* cause a considerable problem for him. They were specifically positioned to watch for enemy movements toward the Federal left, which of course is exactly where McLaws was trying to go. And though the bewhiskered Georgian wouldn't have any way of knowing their orders, he was fully capable of realizing that these Federals would be able to monitor his troops as they continued on their way. As McLaws reminded Longstreet in 1873, "of course my troops could be seen by the opposite side, and their numbers estimated if they were allowed to proceed."[800], [lix]Even if McLaws didn't see a signal flag, he had reason enough to be wary about passing in view of the Round Tops.

Not until 1878 would McLaws specifically mention a signal station.[801] Then again, both Longstreet and Alexander had mentioned a signal station in the meantime, too.[802] McLaws may have simply incorporated their memories into his own to subconsciously fill a gap in his own memory. We really can't know. But we *can* conclude that the signal station couldn't have stopped him in his tracks as he rode over the hill. Even more important, though, than a solitary signal flag waving on a hilltop, there was infantry and cavalry in his way!

The view from McLaws Hill, facing east toward the Round Tops. The white building above the first tree line marks the Plank Farm. The fight between Berdan's sharpshooters, the Third Maine, and Wilcox's Alabamians occurred just beyond the Plank Farm. The foreground would have been mostly open during the battle, creating a clearer line of sight. Author photo.

---

lix   If Stoughton's men were among those troops McLaws saw on Little Round Top that afternoon, then they could take credit for foiling the Confederate attack twice, for they also pulled Law's Brigade further to the right, extending the line and essentially isolating the Alabamians. O.R. 27.2: 518–519.

From Joseph Kershaw's perspective, which was quite limited at the base of Bream's Hill, it looked as though Longstreet and McLaws had ridden on to reconnoiter a new route. Kershaw reported that after his brigade stopped "at the hill beyond the hotel [Black Horse Tavern], at the stone bridge on the Fairfield Road...Generals Longstreet and McLaws reconnoitered the route. After some little delay," Kershaw remembered, "the major-general commanding [McLaws] returned, and directed a countermarch."[803]

McLaws, on the other hand, doesn't mention any further reconnaissance with Longstreet. Instead, he remembered that he "rode with Major Johnston rapidly around the neighborhood to see if there was any road by which we could go into position without being seen." Of course, there wasn't, and when they returned to the column, Longstreet was there, checking in to see why the march had abruptly ground to a halt. McLaws pointed out the troops on Little Round Top and "how plainly the enemy could watch our movements if we went on." Realizing this as well, Longstreet muttered, "why this won't do. Is there no way to avoid it?" McLaws then revealed that he had, in fact, performed a reconnaissance that morning and had discovered a hidden route into position. The only problem was that they had to countermarch to get there. Longstreet agreed to let McLaws turn his column around "and the movement commenced."[804]

Longstreet's first article on the subject echoes McLaws's story. In his *Philadelphia Weekly Times* article in 1877, Longstreet wrote that once the column was put in motion, he "rode along with Hood's Division, which was in the rear." The march was generally slow, with the "conductor frequently encountering points that exposed the troops to the view of the signal station on Round Top." But eventually the column stopped completely. "After waiting for some time," Longstreet sent a messenger to the front to see what was going on. The report came back that "the column was awaiting the movements of Colonel Johnston, who was trying to lead it by some route by which it could pursue its march without falling under view of the Federal signal station." That's when he looked up "toward Round Top [and] saw that the signal station was in full view."

Longstreet then made the fanciful claim that he had no control over McLaws's Division, since Lee's order to Johnston to lead the column into position overrode any authority he had as corps commander. Fortunately, Johnston apparently had no authority over Hood's Division, so Longstreet was able to order Hood's men "forward by the most direct route."[805] Of course, the idea that an engineer captain could override the second ranking officer in the army is absurd. At most, Johnston was simply a guide (and as we'll see, he probably wasn't even that). If Longstreet was aware of a better road for his corps, he certainly had the authority to direct it there, *especially* if the guide was proving ineffective, as he claimed.[806]

Johnston, meanwhile, denied all of this. "The corps was not put under my charge to be taken where I saw fit, for certainly I had not received any instructions from either Gen'l Lee or Gen'l Longstreet as to where the latter was to go." While McLaws maintained Johnston had ridden "around the neighborhood" with him while they scouted a new route, Johnston remembered riding with Longstreet nearly the whole time. "I am sure I rode with [Longstreet] during the entire march," Johnston told Fitz Lee, "except the short distance from the bend of the road to the top of the hill" where he halted the column.[807] Johnston never mentioned looking for a new route with McLaws or reconnoitering the area by McLaws Hill.[lx] Instead, his only contribution—according to him—was to tell McLaws he was about to be seen.

In fact, McLaws is the only person who mentioned seeing Johnston at McLaws Hill. Longstreet only ever wrote that he *heard* Johnston was reconnoitering a new route, while Kershaw reported that only McLaws and Longstreet went looking for another road.[808] McLaws's adjutant, Major James Goggin, didn't remember any guide at all! "My division was the leading division," Goggin wrote to Longstreet in 1887. "There were many halts, the question arising as to the proper route to be pursued…as we had no guide."[809] Given McLaws's other inaccuracies, it's fair to question whether Johnston was at McLaws Hill at all.

lx Instead of referring to the hill as "the hill McLaws stopped his column at," we'll call this McLaws Hill.

WHILE KERSHAW MAY HAVE BELIEVED MCLAWS AND LONG-street rode forward to reconnoiter a new route, they probably simply went to ask for directions.

As Kershaw and his men waited along the creek near the Black Horse Tavern, McLaws and Longstreet seem to have ridden toward William Pendleton, who was heading south from the Point of Woods. Pendleton had performed the route reconnaissance that morning and it had been his aide, George Peterkin, who had ridden to Long-street earlier to tell him "the way is open, (or words to that effect)."[810]

Peterkin's diary entry for July 2 notes that "at Gen'l Longstreet's request Gen'l Pendleton sent me to guide Genl McLaws by the road along the creek bottom toward the Peach orchard, Gen'l Kershaw being in front - the road he had started to move on being too much exposed." In an 1875 letter, Peterkin also told Pendleton that Long-street first "endeavored...to march straight across the little valley towards the Peach orchard, and when they found that would not do...you sent me to put into use the knowledge of the other road which we had acquired in our early morning ride."[811] The letter includes the standard anti-Longstreet opinions, but the facts seem to be accurate.

Pendleton's report corroborates this. After meeting with Porter Alexander and investigating Pitzer's Woods after the skirmish there, Pendleton "returned to General Longstreet, for the purpose of conducting his column to this point [the woods], and supervising, as might be necessary, the disposition of his artillery." Longstreet's column "was advancing by the ravine road (as most out of view), time having been already lost in attempting another, which proved objec-tionable, because exposed to observation."[812]

Though written years later, Coupland Page's account is similar. When Page found Pendleton after dropping his prisoners off at headquarters, he "learned that Peterkin had reported that he had met the head of McLaws' Division." Lee had not been at headquar-ters when Page arrived with his captured cavalrymen, having gone off to reconnoiter Cemetery Hill. Page waited for him to get back, then eventually found Pendleton again.[813]

Of course, neither McLaws nor Longstreet could very well acknowledge that they had sought out Pendleton and his staff to guide them into position. That would amount to an admission that the fault lay somewhere in the First Corps. Even more importantly, with Pendleton leading the charge against Longstreet's reputation and McLaws's own reputation precariously tethered to Longstreet's, neither could acknowledge that it was Pendleton and his staff that put the First Corps back on the right track.

Even worse from McLaws's perspective, acknowledging that there was no guide *and* that they needed *Pendleton's* help might validate the July 1863 rumors that he was to blame for the delay. Both Fitzgerald Ross and Francis Lawley heard the suggestions that the attack was delayed because McLaws was "too slow."[814] Since then, McLaws had been on vigilant lookout for any slights that could throw his reputation into the same hole Longstreet's had fallen into. And despite his reputation for being slow on the battlefield, he was undeniably quick in responding to affronts, as we saw with the "sly undercurrents" published in the *Savannah Republican* before the end of July.

McLaws may simply have convinced himself that he reconnoitered with Johnston after halting his column. The mind is alarmingly capable of tricking itself. Of the various reasons for self-deceit, McLaws could boast many. To begin with, he was defending something valuable to him amidst a very combative situation. He also had no notes to refresh his memory or correct any errors in his recollection. And the subject had more than its fair share of opinions, tossing about numerous memories for McLaws's mind to latch onto in order to fill in the gaps.

The battlefield is a less than desirable place to form accurate memories. The anxieties, emotions, and general experience of the day are recalled much more readily than the specific sights, sounds, and orders. McLaws's mind would tuck away these initial perceptions in his memory, while many of the particulars would be lost as the calendar pages turned. As he told his wife on July 7, he thought the battle's loss had much to do with the failure to reconnoiter.

That perception would categorize his memories when he recalled them later. Having had his reputation questioned throughout most of his tenure with the Army of Northern Virginia and then having been unceremoniously tossed into the swamps of Georgia and South Carolina, McLaws simply seems to have succumbed to a very human condition: biased and false memory.

AFTER MEETING WITH PENDLETON AND SECURING PETERKIN as their guide, McLaws rode back to his division and directed the countermarch. Longstreet remained behind, probably staying near Pendleton's Hill to confer with Lee about the new development.[815]

Postwar claims to the contrary notwithstanding, there's abundant evidence Lee was in the area at the time. Pendleton reported that after Pitzer's Woods had been "cleared of the enemy," he headed in that direction to examine the ground for artillery positions. There, he "met the commanding general, *en route* himself for a survey of the ground." Rather than simply sitting back and hoping things played out according to plan, Lee was actively engaged along the line.

Pendleton also remembered that Armistead Long was with Lee at Pitzer's Woods. According to Pendleton's report, he, Long, and General Cadmus Wilcox rode over to "the farm-house at the summit, where the cross-road from Fairfield…emerges."[816] This was precisely where McLaws was headed (both according to the original plan and after the countermarch). It's no coincidence that's where Long said Lee went, too. According to Long's memoir, Lee "proceeded to the point where he expected the arrival of the corps," where he "waited for some time."[817]

While they waited, Long recalled that "a Federal sergeant was captured, who was found, on examination, to belong to a division which had taken position in the peach orchard."[818] Of course, more than one Federal sergeant was captured at the battle, but the timing suggests Coupland Page had just arrived with news of the captured cavalry sergeant, George Barber. Page, remember, had returned to Pendleton after delivering his prisoners to headquarters. When he located the general and reported, he found out Peterkin had gone to help McLaws.

Capturing a Federal cavalry trooper was a highlight of Page's battle experience and there's little doubt he eagerly told his story to the other staff officers.[lxi] And Barber was a member of Buford's division, which *was* stationed in the Peach Orchard that morning, like Long remembered.[lxii] Long is also vague as to *who* questioned the prisoner, and he may well have simply been recalling the news that Page delivered about the captured Federal cavalryman while the headquarters coterie waited on Seminary Ridge.

Porter Alexander, who was also in the general vicinity after surveying the front with Pendleton, remembered that both Pendleton and Long were with Lee that morning.[819] And Lindsay Walker, the Third Corps artillery chief, remembered riding south along Seminary Ridge with the commanding officer toward Longstreet's position.[820]

Despite the later recollections that Lee spent the morning wondering where 14,000 men and their commander went, Lee was right in the middle of things and fully aware of what was going on. In the 1870s, when most of the accounts were written, the standard assumption that all of Lee's movements on July 2 revolved around his frustration with Longstreet was rapidly taking hold, coloring the veterans' memories of the battle. The truth was already irretrievably sinking beneath the developing narrative, its decayed remains ossifying into immovable myth.

---

lxi   Out of eighteen typewritten pages of his battle account, Page spent three and a half (nearly a fifth of his narrative) describing the encounter with the Federal cavalrymen. There's little chance he didn't tell Lee or Long about it.

lxii Long referred to the captured Federal's *division* when he related the story, offering another piece of evidence that it was Barber. No full infantry division occupied the Peach Orchard at the time the meeting between Lee, Long, and Pendleton occurred. At that point in the day, only Buford's division had taken a position there.

PORTER ALEXANDER HAD A LOT TO SAY ABOUT THE BATTLE
of Gettysburg and he said it eloquently. It's no surprise that historians have reached for his memoirs when looking for a descriptive
account of the battle or an astute analysis by someone who was there.

Porter Alexander spent his life synthesizing raw data and turning
it into understandable and useful results. He had engineering and
mathematical training from West Point and after the war, secured a
professorship at the University of South Carolina. He was a railroad
executive, was offered a position in the Egyptian army, and spent
time in Nicaragua arbitrating a border dispute between that country
and Costa Rica. As we saw, he was also tasked with compiling the
history of the First Corps. Though he never formally completed the
First Corps history, his published manuscript incorporated much of
the information he had collected. He also managed to find time to
scribble down a rough draft of a second, more personal manuscript,
discovered and published in the 1980s.[821]

Alexander's pen smoothly and insightfully analyzed the war. His
more personal memoir, though it waited tucked away in archives for
nearly a century, presented a unique, readable, and entertaining
view of Confederate army life. There's a very good reason historian
Gary Gallagher credits Alexander with "easily being the most astute
military analyst among Lee's lieutenants."[822]

There's no question Alexander lived a remarkable life and
provided posterity with equally remarkable insights into subjects that
have proven to be some of the most difficult to reach. The praise is
well-deserved. But Porter Alexander was human, of course, and his
analytical mind was subject to the same heuristic and memory flaws as
anyone else. Indeed, the intense study he gave topics like Gettysburg
worked against him in one important way. His own memories were
flooded by others' and as we saw, once the mind is infiltrated with
others' experiences, it can be difficult for the brain to sort it all out.

So, what did Alexander have to say and how does it compare
with what everyone else remembered?

July 2

* * *

ALEXANDER'S ARTILLERY ROLLED TO A STOP IN THE OPEN fields along Herr's Ridge late on the morning of July 2. "Arriving on the field," he wrote, "I was ordered...to accompany the movements to the right, then being commenced by Hood's and McLaws's divisions."[823] His battalion "halted in a wood," he remembered, though he later thought he parked the battalion in "a grassy open grove." He eventually split the difference, writing in his memoir that his artillery rested that morning "in a very thin wood, with grass under the trees." That's how "I have put it in my notes," anyway.[824]

After parking his artillery, Alexander went to see Lee and Longstreet "in person."[825] Or he may have "fed and watered" the horses first, before being "sent for by General Longstreet."[826] In his personal memoirs, Alexander remembered that Colonel Walton, the First Corps' artillery chief, went to see Longstreet and was gone about a half hour, returning with a message for Alexander to report to headquarters.[827]

However long he remained with the guns before heading to headquarters on Seminary Ridge, Alexander found Lee and Longstreet together when he arrived. "I was told that we were to attack the enemy's left flank, and was directed to take command of my own battalion," along with the other battalions assigned to Hood and McLaws, "and to reconnoitre the ground and co-operate with the infantry in the attack."[828] Alexander "was especially cautioned in moving up the guns to avoid exposing them to the view of a signal station of the enemy's on Round Top mountain."[829] Years later, he remembered looking at the hills and seeing the signal "flags wig-wagging on Little Round Top."[830] But in the 1880s, he thought the signal station was on *Big* Round Top, for he wrote that "the two Round Tops looked over everything, and a signal-flag was visible on the highest."[831]

"In ten minutes after I reported," Alexander wrote, he "was off to examine all the roads leading to the right & front, & to get an understanding of the enemy's position & how & where we could best get at it."[832] Pendleton, as the army's chief artillery officer, "conducted the colonel to the advanced point of observation previously visited." This was probably the Point of Woods, as McMillan's Hill could never have been considered an "advanced point" that day.

While Pendleton was helping Alexander get an understanding of the battlefield from the Point of Woods, "a sharp contest occurred in the woods to the right and rear of this forward point. Anderson's division," Pendleton wrote, "had moved up, and was driving the enemy from these woods."[833]

Then Alexander went off to find artillery positions. He "rode fast—having a courier or two with me, & I don't think it took me much over an hour to get a very fair idea of the ground & roads," find the other two battalions, and "give them what instructions were needed."[834] After delivering the orders to Cabell's and Henry's battalions, he rode off to personally lead his "own battalion to the schoolhouse on Willoughby run."[835]

ALEXANDER WAS VERY DETAILED IN HIS MEMORIES OF WHAT happened along Willoughby Run. He was also contradictory. In his report, submitted in August 1863, he remembered that the artillery's "march into position was performed with [Hood's and McLaws's] divisions." That's how he remembered it in two other published articles, too. In an 1877 letter, published the next year in the *Southern Historical Society Papers*, he wrote that he only accompanied his own battalion into the valley. When he reached his position, he "then went about hunting up the other battalions which were attached to the infantry in order to give them all their positions for opening the attack."[836] He wrote the same thing in his personal memoirs.[837]

But in his *Military Memoirs* and his *Century* article, Alexander remembered that he brought all three battalions with him to the valley at the same time. After waiting a while for the infantry to arrive, he rode back "to learn the cause of their non-arrival."[838] Like his memory of his original position on Herr's Ridge, Alexander's struggle to remember the exact order of things is evident. Most likely, he was conflating two different events when he tried to reconstruct it all later.

According to Alexander, the whole affair took perhaps three hours, including the time it took the artillery to rumble along the farm lanes into the "valley of Willoughby Run."[839] Alexander estimated the time at eleven or twelve, but it was quite a bit later than that. Though his own estimates of his arrival time are scattered, his artillery probably arrived around 9:30 or 10:00 a.m. Osmond Taylor, one of his battery commanders, remembered arriving "about 10:00 a.m." Alexander apparently thought Taylor was right, for he amended his own report accordingly.[840] Alexander also remembered that the infantry was moving when his artillery arrived, supporting Taylor's estimate.[841]

If the first guns in Alexander's Battalion didn't roll onto Herr's Ridge until around 10:00 a.m., it easily could have been 11:00 or 11:30 by the time Alexander reported to Lee and Longstreet. In any event, he was at the Point of Woods just before noon, for Pendleton noted he was with Alexander at the front when they heard the "sharp contest" with Berdan and the Mainers to the right and rear.[842] From there, he would have been able to see Jerome's signal flag waving, as he always said he did. If he reported to headquarters and surveyed the front soon after he arrived, then he couldn't have arrived earlier than ten o'clock.

AFTER HE RODE TO THE POINT OF WOODS WITH PENDLETON and got a feel for the lay of the land and the respective battle lines, Alexander conducted his reconnaissance to find suitable artillery positions. "My instructions were to reconnoitre the flank to be attacked, and choose my own positions and means of reaching them," he wrote in 1877.[843] In his personal memoir, he remembered that he rode "off to examine all the roads leading to the right &

front, & to get an understanding of the enemy's position."[844] This is exactly what Pendleton reported in 1863.[845]

After leaving the Point of Woods, Alexander may have followed Pendleton to the "the farm-house at the summit, where the cross-road from Fairfield...emerges."[846] Though neither Pendleton nor Alexander specifically mentioned that they rode with each other after observing the front, Alexander wrote that his survey of the front also included getting a feel for the roads he would need to get into position and scout artillery positions to support the attack (which at that point, was supposed to step off near the Peach Orchard crossroad). Pendleton had already done that and must have at least told Alexander about the Ravine Road and the local farm paths, if he didn't actually accompany him. In any event, Alexander's artillery ultimately ended up in the same place Pendleton scouted after leaving the Point of Woods, indicating that Alexander was at least nearby.

Whether Alexander accompanied Pendleton into Pitzer's Woods or not is conjecture, but wherever he went, Alexander thought that "this duty occupied me, according to the best of my recollection, one or two hours." Then he "rode back, and in person conducted my own battalion to the school-house on Willoughby run," the area that had been cleared of Federal troops and visited by Pendleton, Long, and Lee.[847] It took another hour and a half to get his artillery into position, according to his estimate in his *Century* article.[848]

Where, exactly, he went, is another question.

ALEXANDER'S MARCH TO THE VALLEY IS ONE OF JULY 2'S enigmas. Most historians have concluded that he took the Herr's Ridge Road behind Bream's Hill and followed the Black Horse Tavern to Willoughby Run, simply rolling around McLaws Hill to avoid being seen by the signal station.[849]

"At one point," Alexander remembered, "the direct road leading to this place [Pitzer's schoolhouse] came in sight of the enemy's signal station, but I turned out of the road before reaching the exposed part, and passing through some meadows a few hundred yards, regained the road without coming in sight."[850] Alexander was silent as to which direction his detour took...until he sat down to write his personal memoir. There (and only there), he specifically remembered that he "avoided that part of the road by turning out to the left, & going through fields and hollows, & getting back on the road again a quarter mile or so beyond."[851]

Alexander's swerve to the left has caused historians agita ever since it was discovered. Gary Gallagher, editor of Alexander's newfound memoir, footnoted the perceived error, noting that "EPA's detour turned right, not left, beyond any reasonable doubt."[852] Harry Pfanz also noted that "it seems more practical for his battalion to have turned out to the right."[853] Assuming he was on the Black Horse Tavern Road trying to avoid McLaws Hill, that's a reasonable conclusion.

But Alexander said he turned *left*, not right. Though memory certainly played its tricks on him and every other veteran of the battle, Alexander *did* have the benefit of reviewing maps before he wrote his memoirs. Confusing a cardinal direction seems an odd oversight for a mathematician, engineer, and railroad executive whose professional life had revolved around just this sort of precision.

If Alexander turned out of the road at McLaws Hill, then his account is irreconcilably wrong. As Pfanz and Gallagher noted, he could not have turned left, for that would have brought him back up the hill. If he turned left beyond the hill, where there is more cover, then he had already brought the artillery into view of the Federal station and the detour was moot. And if the artillery turned out to the right, then his description is entirely inaccurate.

McLaws Hill is not a rounded knoll, but a ridge, running at relatively consistent elevation about a third of a mile to the southwest of where McLaws tried to cross it. To move around the hill to the right, Alexander's detour would have been nearly a mile, four times as long as his estimate. That makes his account just as inaccurate as getting his directions mixed up.

On the other hand, if Alexander followed Herr's Woods Lane, he would have run over the top of Pendleton's Hill, which in 1863 was high and bare, as Alexander remembered. Moving out to his left, his batteries would have cut between Henry Meals's and Sam Dickson's houses, through their fields and orchards along the banks of Willoughby Run, catching up with the Ravine Run Road three to four hundred yards south of the hill.

Alexander himself, when he had an opportunity to retrace his steps, took the Ravine Road route. In 1893, he led a group of prominent veterans, including Longstreet, Dan Sickles and Henry Tremain, David M. Gregg, Oliver Howard, and Billy Mahone, along with politicos, journalists, the guide James Long, and future park commissioner John Nicholson, "over the route pursued by General Alexander in bringing his artillery into position. Colonel Nicholson afterward said it was a path never traveled by tourists."

The route was not for the faint of heart. "The younger members of the expedition showed at many times in their countenances their inward trepidation," but they didn't dare say anything. After all, they were following a bunch of "aged heroes" and their pride "forbade them from deserting the vehicles." The path "might have been fun for artillerymen" but it "seemed threatening to the occupants" in their coaches. "Part of the road was directly in the bed of Willoughby Run," while others traveled along "precipitous heights, where a faulty movement of horses or driver meant a serious tumble into the stream far below."[854]

The path down which Alexander led his tourists was clearly along the Ravine Road, for the Black Horse Tavern route only crosses Willoughby Run once and doesn't follow along "precipitous heights," even accounting for journalistic hyperbole. The Ravine Road, however, *did* parallel the creek, sometimes running right through it, just like the visitors remembered.[855]

April showers seem to have made the creek quite full during the 1893 tour, so the "precipitous heights" traveled by the tourist group were probably where the artillerymen had followed along the nearly dry creek during the battle. And indeed, there are steep slopes following along the modern-day Willoughby Run Road which closely, but not perfectly, traces the old Ravine Road.

The route along the Ravine Road was also more than a mile shorter than the one along the Black Horse Tavern Road, making it "short and direct," as Alexander remembered. By cutting through Herr's Ridge Woods and following the Ravine Road, Alexander's battalion would have marched just short of three miles.[lxiii] At a normal pace, they'd be in position in about an hour, perhaps a shade over. This also happens to be how long Alexander remembered the move to Willoughby Run taking.[856]

So at about 1:30 or 2:00 p.m., a little more than three hours after getting his orders, Alexander reached the Pitzer schoolhouse on Willoughby Run, alone. At least according to his postwar articles. As he told it, he waited along the creek for a little while, but then he began to get restless. Where were the other battalions? Where was the infantry? Leaving his artillery parked behind Seminary Ridge, safely out of view of the signal flags, Alexander mounted up and went to see for himself. Or did he?

Countermarching

"The facts of the matter seemed to lie forever concealed by a lack of correct information engendered by personal conflicts and the failure of participants simply to report what they had done."

- Harry Pfanz, ***Gettysburg: The Second Day***[857]

"At Gen'l Longstreet's request Gen'l Pendleton sent me to guide Gen'l McLaws by the road along the creek bottom toward the Peach orchard. Gen'l Kershaw being in front—The road he had started to move on being too much exposed."

- George Peterkin[858]

From his position near the Black Horse Tavern, Joseph Kershaw finally saw the lone figure of Lafayette McLaws riding back over the hill.

---

lxiii   The Black Horse Tavern route, which wound around Bream's Hill, was not only anything but "direct," it was nearly four miles long.

The elegantly bearded Georgian rode up to Kershaw "and directed a countermarch."[859] The head of the long column lurched itself backward and to the left, dragging the rest of the body along with it.

The mechanics of a countermarch are easy to understand and the maneuver was commonly performed in moving nineteenth century armies. In essence, the first company would wheel to the left and march straight toward the rear. Then, when they passed the next company in line, that company would follow suit, and so on down the line, so that the regiments cascaded to the left, absorbed into the new column.[860]

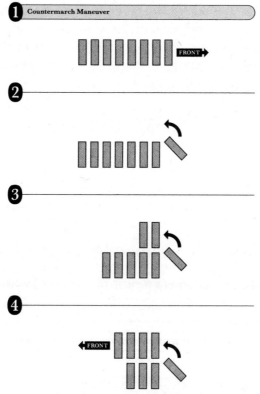

The mechanics of a countermarch.

Where, exactly, the column went has long been the subject of debate, primarily because no one thought it important enough to write about for the first decade after it happened. The silence alone speaks volumes, for the diaries and letters are filled with events the participants *did* find important. Of course, the most important details were who was killed, who was wounded or captured, and making sure loved ones at home knew their soldier was safe. But the reasons for the loss were often noted, too, especially among the officers.

McLaws, of course, blamed Longstreet and the lack of reconnaissance.[861] More than a month later, he added that if they had had enough troops, the battle would have been won.[862] Walter Taylor also thought if they had just had another 10,000 men, they could have pushed the Federal army off the heights.[863] Both Osmun Latrobe, one of Longstreet's staff officers, and Jed Hotchkiss scribbled in their diaries that the loss was due to lack of coordination, rather than the time the attack started.[864]

At the time, it seems that the countermarch was quite literally nothing to write home about. It certainly wouldn't be the first time a column went the wrong direction or had to change course. So the accounts that survive are naturally vague as to the details of the march into position and tell only a brief part of the larger story. And of course, the authors all tell their stories looking through their own windows, often at widely different angles. But put together, they provide a coherent, if incomplete, picture of the countermarch.

THE COLUMN "WAS MARCHED TO THE LEFT, BEYOND THE point at which we had before halted," Kershaw reported, "and thence, under cover of the woods, to the right of our line of battle."[865] One of Kershaw's regimental commanders, Major R.C. Maffett, also reported that "when at Bream's hotel...on the road leading from Gettysburg to Fairfield, we were countermarched nearly to the pike that we had left early in the morning, to gain the cover of a range of hills."[866] As far as contemporary accounts of the countermarch go, that's it.[867]

But even these sparse accounts offer clues, especially when sifted and compared to later accounts. If Kershaw marched *beyond* the point his brigade rested earlier that morning, then he marched farther north than the unnamed road.[lxiv] Kershaw expounded on this in a slightly more detailed letter to John Bachelder in 1876. After being ordered to countermarch, he wrote, his brigade "filed to the rear passing nearly the same ground as before, crossed our line of march near the end of the lane, [and] moved straight towards Round Top."[868]

If Kershaw is accurate, then his brigade retraced its steps ("passing nearly the same ground"), marched back up Herr's Ridge along the unnamed lane to Herr's Ridge Road ("crossed our line of march near the end of the lane") and then took either Hall's Lane or Hereter's Mill Road to Herr's Woods Lane, which ran southeast ("straight towards Round Top").

In a final recollection, Kershaw remembered taking "a country road to Willoughby Run" *after* they had "moved back to the place where we had rested during the morning," which was at the unnamed lane. In the process, Kershaw noted, the brigade "passed Hood's division."[869]

Confederates weren't the only ones to comment on the countermarch, either. Captain James Hall, who had eventually made it to Little Round Top, spotted much of McLaws's Division backtracking up the Herr's Ridge Road to Hereter's Mill Road. At 1:30, he alerted headquarters that "a heavy column of enemy's infantry, about 10,000 strong, is moving from opposite our extreme left toward our right." In a follow-up message forty minutes later, he pointed out that "those troops were passing on a by-road from Dr. Hall's house to Herr's tavern, on the Chambersburg Pike. A train of ambulances is following them."[870, lxv]

---

lxiv   Kershaw's report, taken on its own, could be interpreted as moving back beyond the hotel, where it had halted "before." It would be an odd way to interpret what Kershaw meant by "before," but it's possible. However, when read in conjunction with other accounts, like Maffett's and signalman James Hall's, and then compared to Kershaw's later recollections, this interpretation doesn't hold up.

lxv   The identification of particular houses suggests the presence of a local citizen, though the 1858 Adams County Wall Map does show Dr. Hall's house. Daniel Klingel may have been on Little Round Top

If *Captain* Hall could see *Doctor* Hall's house, then he could also see the lane across the street, which led into Herr's Ridge Woods. South of Doctor Hall's house, the Herr's Ridge Road runs along the spine of the ridge, easily visible from Little Round Top with the aid of a glass and probably noticeable even without one.

Hall's message also doesn't precisely indicate whether he saw the column turn off the road or not, though it implies he did. A Confederate column marching due north onto the Chambersburg Pike could not very well be said to be marching toward the Federal right. The Federal line ran at roughly a forty-five-degree angle to the Emmitsburg Road and the Confederate line. To be fairly considered moving *toward* the Federal right, McLaws's column would have to have been heading east (or at least northeast). If Hall spotted McLaws's column turning right off the Herr's Ridge Road, say at Hall's Lane or Hereter's Mill Road, then he could accurately report they were marching east, toward his army's right.

While Hall's Lane, toward the top of one of the high points of Herr's Ridge, was visible to the Round Top signal station, Hereter's Mill Road intersected Herr's Ridge Road twenty to forty feet lower. Hall may have seen them either way, but from a Confederate perspective, the lower road made more sense. Whichever lane they took off of Herr's Ridge, though, they came upon Herr's Woods Road fairly quickly. A right turn took them south and directly to the Ravine Road, "straight towards Round Top."[lxvi]

---

with the signal corps that day, though his account is third hand and recounted in 1892. Klingel related his story to a friend, who then told the newspaper the story. The details should be read with caution as to their absolute accuracy, to say the least. But the account does lend credence to the idea that the signal station had the help of locals. Klingel's account notes that he "told the places the rebels were putting their wounded of the first day in, names of roads, distances, and where they led to." He also mentioned that this was *before* the first Confederate guns fired "at Warfield's blacksmith shop." Durborow, I.N., "The Big Battle: A Comrade Sends Reminiscences of Citizen at Gettysburg," *National Tribune*, Dec. 8, 1892 (4).

lxvi   Another route, shorter than the one along Herr's Ridge Road, was available, too. A lane cuts through the woods on the northeastern slope of Bream's Hill, leading straight to Adam Butt's farmhouse. The Fairfield Road is only 500 yards from the Butt farmhouse, sav-

MCLAWS TURNED HIS COLUMN AROUND AT ABOUT 12:30, a little more than a half hour after he stopped it by the Black Horse Tavern. That meant he couldn't have left his position on Herr's Ridge Road much past eleven o'clock that morning. The march from the unnamed lane to McLaws Hill was about a mile and a quarter. Under normal marching conditions, it would take about twenty-five or thirty minutes to get there, and no one ever described the pace as break-neck.[871] If McLaws left Herr's Ridge Road between 11:00 and 11:15 a.m., then the head of the column was passing the Black Horse Tavern just as Berdan's men were opening fire on Wilcox's Alabamians.

After stopping the column, McLaws spent at least a few minutes evaluating the situation and waiting for Longstreet to arrive. It was here that he probably saw, through his field glass, Jerome's signal flag waving. Eventually both McLaws and Longstreet rode off toward Seminary Ridge to get directions from Pendleton.[872] If they moved with any sort of urgency, it took them a little over five minutes to get there. In the meantime, Alexander and Pendleton had just concluded their survey from the Point of Woods.

---

ing the column a lot of walking and even more time. But the farm lanes all cross one of the highest points on the ridge. The eastern extension of the Butt farm lane is called Paddock Drive today. The road is wooded and about six feet lower than it would have been in 1863 due to grading for the modern road, but a general feel for the elevation can be gained. If they were going to cross this lane, they may as well have crossed McLaws Hill. Based on the 1868 survey, the elevation of McLaws Hill is 420 feet (these elevations were proven slightly inaccurate as technology advanced, but they serve to compare the differences in height between hills, if not actual elevation). By comparison, what is today Paddock Drive was 460–420 feet above sea level, from the top of the hill to the bottom. (For comparison, Hall's Lane begins at 380 feet and Hereter's Mill Road at 360 or so— it begins on the slope between topographic contour lines). Though shorter, the Butt farm lane route was impractical for their purposes.

In any event, even if it made more sense to go that way, they didn't. All the contemporary accounts put the column on the Herr's Ridge Road at least as far north as the unnamed lane.

July 2

It shouldn't have taken long for Longstreet and McLaws to spot Pendleton somewhere between the Point of Woods and the Fairfield Road. When Longstreet and McLaws found him, they provided a brief explanation of what had happened. According to George Peterkin, the First Corps commanders explained that McLaws's route was "too exposed," and they needed a guide. Peterkin was tapped to lead the column, though he doesn't seem to have personally gone back with McLaws. More likely, McLaws was to get back to the Ravine Road and Peterkin would take him to his position along Warfield Ridge.[873]

After conferring with Pendleton and Peterkin, McLaws had another five- or ten-minute ride back to the halted column, depending on how fast he spurred his horse.[874] Within a few minutes, McLaws's men would have pulled themselves up from the ground and taken their place back in the column. The first steps of the countermarch pressed into the soft dirt alongside the Black Horse Tavern Road at just around 12:30. The head of the column had a nearly two-mile march back to Hereter's Mill Road, taking Kershaw's men perhaps forty-five minutes to complete. Due to the mechanics of the countermarch, the rest of the column didn't have to backtrack quite as far.

If Kershaw started countermarching around 12:30, the head of the column would be turning into the woods on Hereter's Mill Road around 1:15. Fifteen minutes later, when Captain Hall noticed large numbers of troops passing that way, the tail end of McLaws's column would be marching north along the spine of Herr's Ridge, the division's ambulances trailing behind. In order to accurately estimate the troops marching toward the Federal right, Hall would have to have seen the whole column. Without seeing the end of the column, he couldn't know whether the whole column had passed or not, meaning he wouldn't know if the column was 5,000 men long, 10,000, or even 20,000.[lxvii]

---

lxvii   The ambulances would have indicated the infantry column had end-
        ed. Hall's estimate shouldn't be read precisely, either. He probably
        didn't see the entire column and even if he did, he wasn't counting
        individual heads. He was offering an estimate to headquarters, which
        was based on the column's length, number of flags, rough estimates
        of unit strengths, etc.

The Black Horse Tavern and the stone bridge on the Fairfield Road, as it appeared circa 1890. Bream's Hill is visible beyond the bridge. Kershaw's column was halted along the road marked by the rail fence just beyond Marsh Creek. Photo courtesy of National Park Service, Gettysburg National Military Park, Museum Collection, GETT 041136-T2225, William H. Tipton Photographic Prints.

WHILE MCLAWS'S DIVISION WAS WAITING BY THE TAVERN on the banks of Marsh Creek, Hood's men were preparing to move. Evander Law and his brigade had just arrived and the whole division began to form up, ready to move along Herr's Woods Road toward the Ravine Road.

Law remembered that he arrived "shortly before noon" on July 2, after a twenty-four-mile march from New Guilford, Pennsylvania. Law's march was impressive. Leaving at 3:00 a.m., his brigade covered those twenty-four miles in just under nine hours.[875]

316

Longstreet reported that he had decided to wait for Law to arrive before moving Hood's Division into place.[876] Once the timing of the attack became an overriding concern after the war, Longstreet fielded a fair amount of criticism for his decision, particularly for taking it upon himself to wait. But Lee probably acquiesced or at least knew about it. Over time, though, that acquiescence transformed into explicit approval as Longstreet retold the story amidst increasing criticism of his performance on July 2.[877]

At the time, though, it made sense. McLaws was to get into position through a march around the right, with Hood forming behind him in support. If they both took the same road, that would extend the time it took to get into position. Hood, resting in the fields east of McPherson's Ridge, would be adding unnecessary miles and time to his march. So, Hood was slated to march due south down the Ravine Road, after Anderson. Anderson and McLaws both started around 11:00 that morning. By the time Law was due to arrive, Hood would be just about ready to move.[lxviii]

When Law arrived, the other brigades in the division were resting, lying in the grass like Texan John West.[878] Law remembered that the "rest of the division [was] resting" along the road. "They had arrived some time before, but were not in line."[879] If Hood's Division was supposed to be moving in conjunction with McLaws's, there's no indication *they* knew that. And with Lee only a few hundred yards away along Seminary Ridge, the reasonable conclusion is that Hood wasn't supposed to be moving at noon when Law arrived.

In fact, everything seemed to be going according to (the revised) plan when Law arrived. But within minutes, Berdan's skirmishers pitched into Anderson's flank and changed all that. McLaws was forced to turn around and Longstreet gave Law's men a much-

---

lxviii   The exact time of Law's expected arrival probably wasn't known to Longstreet, but he could do the math. Law had orders to march quickly to the field and Longstreet knew as well as anyone how fast a brigade of infantry could move. As Law approached, he no doubt sent a courier ahead to report, get orders for his position, and perhaps obtain a guide to lead him to his assigned position. Unfortunately there's no direct documentation for this, but it was standard practice to alert superior officers of the arrival.

needed breather. By the time Hood's men were ready to march, around 1:00 p.m., McLaws was approaching along the Hereter's Mill Road. As we'll see, Hood waited a few more minutes, letting at least Kershaw's lead brigade pass, and then began his march.[880]

THE COUNTERMARCH WAS NOT HURRIED BY ANYONE'S recollection. Longstreet remembered the "march was necessarily slow," but thought it was because Johnston "frequently encounter[ed] points that exposed the troops" to the signal station.[881] Johnston, in turn, didn't think it was "at all rapid," commenting to Fitz Lee on the "slowness of the march."[882] Of course, this all came back to McLaws, which he well knew. And so his accounts made sure to address the reasons for his division's want of alacrity.

The countermarch, according to McLaws, experienced "considerable difficulty, owing to the rough character of the country in places and the fences and ditches we had to cross." But eventually the march was "effected, and my troops were moving easily forward" along a much better road. But even that road wasn't perfect.

McLaws maintained that, at least at some point, his division marched along in columns of companies. As a body of infantry began to get close to the front, this was a common formation. It meant that each company (twenty to forty men) formed a battle line, one behind the other. That widened the front of the column from four men to around fifteen or so, depending on the size of the company. When this stack of battle lines reached its position or met the enemy, each company could simply wheel to its left or right to rapidly deploy into a full regimental battle line.[883]

But the road wasn't wide enough to hold the individual company battle lines, according to McLaws, so they had to peel men from the side of the column and put them behind each company. This, in turn, slowed down the march.[884]

McLaws's Division, whether in columns of companies yet or not, snaked back around Bream's Hill, climbed Herr's Ridge at the unnamed lane, and headed north. Veering off the road either by Doctor Hall's house or Hereter's Mill Road, they crossed Herr's Ridge and headed due south. Passing Hood's Division, which had formed up and was prepared to march near Heretor's Mill Road and Willoughby Run, the column approached Pendleton's Hill from the north. Then, for the second time in an hour, it stopped.

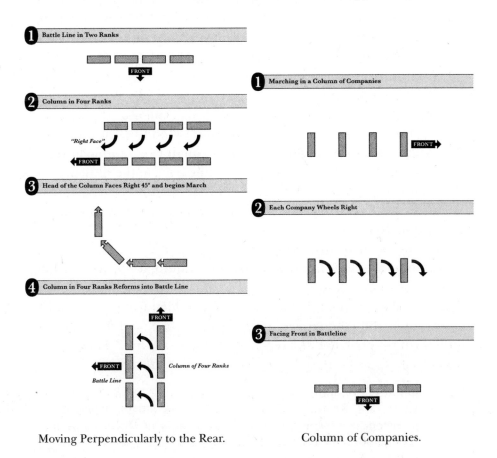

Moving Perpendicularly to the Rear.

Column of Companies.

SAM JOHNSTON, WHO WAS WITH LONGSTREET SOMEWHERE near Hereter's Mill Road and Willoughby Run (for that's where Hood's Division was), saw McLaws's column approaching through the woods. He told Longstreet that if they came down the Herr's Woods Road, they'd march right over the top of Pendleton's Hill, exposing them to view. Either on his own accord or at Longstreet's request, Johnston rode out to McLaws to let him know.[lxix]

Johnston was relatively consistent on this. McLaws's column "moved under the cover of the ridge and woods," he remembered, "until it came to within about one and a half miles of the right of the position that was finally taken by Gen'l Hood's Division; here, the road turned to the right," he told Fitzhugh Lee, "and led over a high hill where it intersected a road leading back in the direction of the Round Top." And it wasn't just *any* road that intersected Herr's Woods Road. It was "the one that Gen'l Longstreet had to follow": the Ravine Road.[lxx]

At the bend in the road, Johnston "called Gen'l Longstreet's attention to the high hill over which he would have to pass in full view of the enemy, and pointed out a route across the field shorter than the one over the hill and completely hidden from the enemy's observation." But "Longstreet preferred the road, and did follow it until the head of his column reached the top of the hill." Then Longstreet "halted, and ordered Gen'l Hood to take the advance."[885], [lxxi]

---

lxix   Johnston's position is based on Longstreet's, which in turn is based on Hood's. All three officers' positions are discussed below. For Johnston being with Longstreet and in sight of McLaws's column turning down the road, see Johnston to F. Lee, Feb. 11, 1878, in S.R. Johnston Papers, VHS.

lxx   There is another candidate for this hill at the Plank Farm along Willoughby Run. While there is a modern road that bends to the right, this road wasn't there at the time, meaning Plank's Hill can't be the one Johnston referred to.

lxxi   Johnston either thought Hood's position was closer than it really was or he estimated wrong, for Hood's *actual* position wasn't a mile and a half from the point *any* road crosses a high hill.

Johnston said substantially the same thing in his letter to McLaws in 1892. "We marched under cover of the ridge and woods until we got to the Fairfield Road," he told the aging general. "Your column turned to the right to follow this road, and without being asked I told General Longstreet that you would disclose your movements to the enemy." Despite that, "we moved on until the head of your column got in full view of the enemy, then you halted. General Hood was ordered to take the advance, you followed, [and] the march was continued without interruption."[886]

The details are slightly different in the accounts given to Fitzhugh Lee and Lafayette McLaws, which is to be expected with honest retellings fourteen years apart. But the substance is the same. In both accounts, the column marched through the woods and "under cover of the ridge," made a right turn, came upon the Fairfield Road and the Ravine Road ("the one that Gen'l Longstreet had to follow and which led back in the direction of the Round Top"), and then Hood moved forward.

Longstreet remembered essentially the same thing Johnston did, though of course from his own perspective. "Again I found there was some delay," Longstreet sighed to his *Century* readers, echoing Johnston's recollection of a second halt. "Ordering Hood's division, then in the rear, to move on and double with the division in front, so as to save as much time as possible," Longstreet rode to the front of the column "*again* to see the cause of the delay."

When the Old War Horse reached the head of McLaws's column, "it seemed there was doubt...about the men being concealed." Longstreet looked around again. "I could see the signal station," he remembered, not knowing or caring that it was Hall's flag now and not Jerome's, "and there was no reason why they could not see us. It seemed to me useless," Longstreet thought, "to delay the troops any longer with the idea of concealing the movement." Conceding this issue to the inevitable, Longstreet pushed Hood forward alongside McLaws.[887]

Just like Johnston's recollection, Longstreet remembered sending both Hood and McLaws forward over the hill, signal flags be damned. But Longstreet's recollection fills in a very important gap in Johnston's account: this all happened at the *second* stop, not the first one at McLaws Hill. Longstreet's staff officer, Moxley Sorrel, also remembered "much unnecessary delay in the movement of the division, as from time to time it was about to come under the observation of the signal station." *From time to time* is just another way of saying "at least twice."[888]

John Coxe, the South Carolina private, also remembered Hood's Division rushing to the front alongside McLaws's. As he marched along the Ravine Road, Coxe "saw General Hood at the head of his splendid division riding forward parallel to us about fifty yards to the left." It was Coxe's opinion that "this explained our last halt."[889] If Coxe remembered correctly, then he observed Hood doubling his column on McLaws's, like Longstreet ordered. (Johnston, who stayed with Longstreet, probably only saw Hood move toward the front, so he must have assumed Hood took the lead).

McLaws's adjutant, Major James Goggin, saw this, too. Goggin had ridden out to keep in touch with Wofford's battalion of sharpshooters that had been deployed ahead of the column during the march (perhaps to inform them of the countermarch?) On his way back, he found the column "again at a halt." Clearly, this wasn't the first time the column had stopped. "On inquiry I was informed that the halt had been ordered that Hood's command might be moved to the front and [Longstreet] and Gen'l McLaws were pointed out to me engaged, it appeared, in *very earnest* conversation. The change was made, and many of our command felt aggrieved."[890]

NONE OF THE ACCOUNTS MATCH ANY FAIR DESCRIPTION of the events on McLaws Hill. Aside from the non-specific references to a halt on a hill to keep out of view of a signal station, there's not much to suggest Longstreet or Johnston were describing the particular halt at McLaws Hill. Neither so much as mention McLaws turning around or countermarching, an awfully strange omission given the primacy of the countermarch in the postwar debate. On the contrary, Longstreet and Johnston remembered both divisions simply being pushed *forward,* over the crest of the hill.

McLaws's account conflates the two halts, for he mentions both an entanglement with Hood's column and Longstreet's "request" that Hood take the lead. In McLaws's version, this seems to take place on McLaws Hill, though he doesn't actually explicitly say so. McLaws always said that Longstreet acquiesced and allowed his division to continue at the head of the column, which isn't wrong, per se. While Hood was moved forward to double on McLaws's column, McLaws's Division still maintained the lead, for Kershaw reported that Hood passed *behind* his brigade after it was formed. Thus, it wasn't until McLaws had begun to form up along the ridge that Hood actually moved past him.[891] This is consistent with Johnston's, Longstreet's, Coxe's, and Goggin's recollections.

Johnston's description of the road, too, is consistent with an approach to Pendleton's Hill. In the traditional story, the Black Horse Tavern Road played havoc with cardinal directions. Alexander wrote that he turned off to the left—where there is no left turn. Johnston remembered a bend in the road to the right, but the Black Horse Tavern Road only bends slightly to the left. The turn is hardly noticeable and doesn't radically change the direction of the march. It's odd that Johnston would distinctly remember this inconspicuous bend while confusing his left and right. Rather than imagine that two trained engineers both confused their left and right at the same place on the same day, it's more reasonable to assume they weren't talking about the Black Horse Tavern Road in the first place. Especially when there's another location that *does* match the memories of both officers.

According to Johnston, not only did the road turn to the right, it intersected another road, which Longstreet was assigned to take, taking them "back in the direction of the Round Top."[892] Not only does the Black Horse Tavern Road not turn to the right between the

Fairfield Road and McLaws Hill, there's no intersection leading back toward Round Top between the tavern and McLaws Hill. The only intersection is with the Ravine Road three quarters of a mile *past* McLaws Hill. And of course, it wasn't at McLaws Hill that Hood was pushed forward to double on McLaws's Division. Rather, McLaws's whole column turned around at that hill. *No one* was pushed forward there.

So how did Johnston come to believe that a right turn near the Fairfield Road put them on a road headed toward the Round Tops, just as Hood was pushed to the front alongside McLaws? Simply put, because Johnston was referring to the march from Hereter's Mill Road to Pendleton's Hill, *not* the march from Herr's Ridge to McLaws Hill.

Both Hereter's Mill Road and Hall's Lane intersect Herr's Woods Lane in the woods "under the cover of the ridge." A right turn at Herr's Woods Lane would put the column on the Ravine Road headed "back in the direction of the Round Top" and was, indeed, the road "that Gen'l Longstreet had to follow."[893] *That* road *does* lead over a high hill: Pendleton's Hill. The road also passed right by Hood's column, which was waiting to funnel into the Ravine Road, as Kershaw remembered.[894]

Having scouted the area with Pendleton the day before, Johnston would be well aware of the Ravine Road, Herr's Woods Road, and Hereter's Mill Road. Indeed, he may have followed the exact path as he rode with Pendleton down Herr's Ridge looking for artillery positions the afternoon before. He was certainly more familiar with *that* area than he was with the Black Horse Tavern Road. Indeed, Johnston may never have set foot on the Black Horse Tavern Road at all!

Johnston's recollection that he only rode with McLaws the "short distance from the bend of the road to the top of the hill where the head of his column was first observed by the enemy" also makes sense if he's referring to the slight right turn from Hereter's Mill Road onto Herr's Woods Road.

Like his references to a 4:00 a.m. departure from headquarters, Johnston's description of McLaws's march muddies the water,

for he refers to the hill at which McLaws was first seen. That naturally takes the mind back to McLaws Hill. But the column only
stopped at McLaws Hill. No one ever claimed they were actually
seen. Johnston wasn't there anyway, so for him, this was the first
stop that he personally observed *and* the first place Confederate
leadership believed the column had actually been seen (they didn't
seem to realize Hall had seen the column heading north on Herr's
Ridge Road.)

Johnston also never mentioned a countermarch (not once!),
but rather only ever remembered Longstreet stubbornly moving
forward, despite the column clearly being seen by the Federal troops.
Johnston never referenced a signal station, either, which is curious if
he was at McLaws Hill and the traditional interpretation is accurate.
After all, the whole reason for countermarching was to avoid a signal
station. After the war, the signal flags dominated the discussion of the
subject.[895] If McLaws and Johnston were riding together as McLaws
remembered, then why didn't Johnston mention the signal flags that
so startled McLaws?

Johnston didn't seem to pay much attention to the postwar
debate. He claimed he only heard about Longstreet's article from
Fitzhugh Lee, so there's a good chance he didn't realize the importance the signal flags played in the narrative.[896] If he was, indeed,
relating his true recollections without much interference from third
parties, and if the signal station per se wasn't the primary concern,
then his omission makes sense.

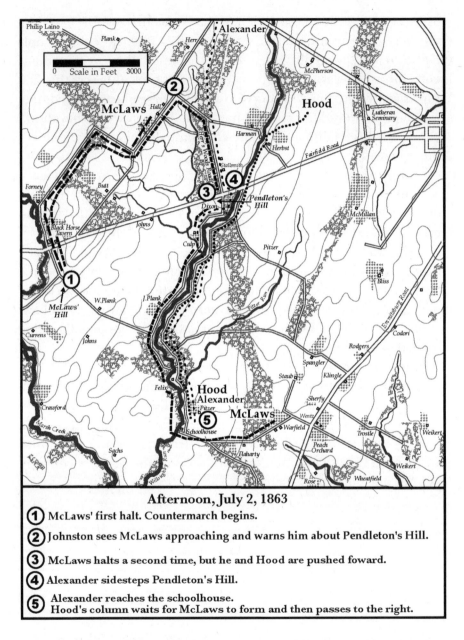

Afternoon, July 2, 1863

(1) McLaws' first halt. Countermarch begins.

(2) Johnston sees McLaws approaching and warns him about Pendleton's Hill.

(3) McLaws halts a second time, but he and Hood are pushed foward.

(4) Alexander sidesteps Pendleton's Hill.

(5) Alexander reaches the schoolhouse.
Hood's column waits for McLaws to form and then passes to the right.

The march of the First Corps into position on July 2, 1863. Map by Philip Laino.

July 2

✳ ✳ ✳

PENDLETON'S HILL IS ABOUT 550 FEET HIGH, TWENTY-FIVE feet higher than McLaws Hill.[lxxii] That's what had attracted Pendleton to it in the first place. From the broad summit of the knoll, he had been able to see all the way to the Emmitsburg Road, observing the approaching Federal infantry and prowling cavalry earlier that morning.

It was also the hill Alexander had sidestepped through the meadows and fields of Sam Dickson and Henry Meals. Alexander remembered that after placing his artillery, he rode back the way he came and found "the head of the infantry column…halted, where its road became exposed to the Federal view…. The exposed point had been easily avoided by our artillery," he pointed out, "by turning out through a meadow."

By his own account, though, Alexander rolled along the Ravine Road to Pitzer's schoolhouse on July 2, *not* the Black Horse Tavern Road. If Alexander rode back the way he came, then he rode north along the Ravine Road toward the Fairfield Road. And if he had followed the Ravine Road route back to the hill he had skirted earlier and there encountered Longstreet's men, then he found the column halted on Pendleton's Hill, not McLaws Hill. (As we'll see, Alexander probably didn't ride back after he placed his artillery, but rather after he finished his reconnaissance. But either way, he didn't ride to McLaws Hill.)

Alexander, confusing his chronology through secondhand accounts, thought *this* was where the countermarch was ordered. Perhaps this is where he first *heard about* the countermarch. But it wasn't the hill that caused the countermarch. Instead, this was where Hood was ordered forward alongside McLaws. The countermarch had already been completed. It was an easy enough mistake for Alex-

---

lxxii   Elevations are approximate per Google Earth. For comparison, Bream's Hill stands about 580 feet and McLaws Hill is about 530 feet high. The rise of ground on either side of Willoughby Run at the Fairfield Road, what we've called Pendleton's Hill, is the highest place devoid of trees in the area.

ander to make, given the literature to which he was privy. Indeed, even with archives, libraries, historical societies, online repositories, and the benefit of 160 years' worth of hindsight, what happened west of Seminary Ridge on July 2 has remained murky, to say the least. Alexander's confusion simply traveled along the pages of history where it's joined McLaws's account to become part of the standard story.

Given the extensive involvement Alexander had in collecting memories, it's not surprising that his own memories were jumbled with others'. Most of his information on the countermarch, after all, was secondhand. And when it came to his own memories, he clearly had chronology trouble, as he admitted himself.[897]

Alexander also had a difficult time understanding why the infantry wouldn't follow his detour. Johnston, too, remembered that Longstreet "preferred the road," which made the engineer scratch his head. He remembered pointing out a shortcut across the field, perhaps the one Alexander had taken or maybe one that cut across the Ravine Road and through the fields behind Seminary Ridge. He had ridden cross country on his way back from his reconnaissance and could personally attest to the shortcut's utility. But the infantry remained adamant about keeping to the roads and didn't listen to Johnston's suggestion, either.

But Longstreet was resigned to the fact that they had already been spotted and decided that it was better to push forward quickly rather than waste more time.[898] As his aide, Moxley Sorrel, fatalistically remembered, "we were seen from the start and signaled constantly."[899] And it was from this hill—Pendleton's—during the *second* long halt, that Longstreet rode forward, figuratively threw his hands in the air, and pressed on.

It was also here that Longstreet seems to have discovered that the Federal line wasn't where he thought it was. Sickles made his initial move to the Emmitsburg Road around 1:30 or so, just as McLaws was crossing Pendleton's Hill.[900] If they couldn't actually see the move from the hill, surely Anderson's skirmishers, who had been exchanging shots with the opposing Federal skirmish line and had a closeup view, reported it to someone.

Goggin had also discovered the Federal shift while he was checking in on Wofford's sharpshooters. Riding out to look for them, he "saw several footmen approaching at a very brisk pace. I soon discovered they were our own men and of the sharpshooters." He couldn't remember the name of the officer that ran up to him, but the "information was to the effect that General Sickles was approaching very rapidly and could be cut off if we moved promptly." Goggin remembered that when he arrived back at Longstreet's column, he found McLaws and Longstreet arguing. In Goggin's mind, the halt had been ordered specifically to allow Hood to cut in front of McLaws.[901] And if Goggin was right, if the argument was that Hood was to lead the attack, then Longstreet already knew Sickles was moving up to the Emmitsburg Road, for it was the change in the Federal position that caused Longstreet to send Hood farther to the right.

Even Kershaw's report obliquely references that they knew Sickles occupied the Peach Orchard during the march down the Ravine Road. "Arriving at the school-house, on the road leading across the Emmitsburg road by the peach orchard, *then in possession of the enemy*," Kershaw wrote, "the lieutenant-general commanding [Longstreet] directed me to advance my brigade and attack the enemy at that point, turn his flank, and extend along the cross-road."[902] Kershaw's report reveals that Longstreet was aware of Sickles's occupation of the Peach Orchard well before any of McLaws's men reached their position.

Initially, Hood was supposed to be *behind* McLaws, but the situation had changed. The Federal line had shifted. Rather than hit the unprotected flank that had dangled in the air earlier that morning with one powerful punch, Longstreet would have to extend the line. The intended uppercut would now be a one-two punch, Hood on the right and McLaws on the left, with Anderson following up to exploit any successes.[903]

The view from Pendleton's Hill may have revealed Sickles's men in the Peach Orchard and along the Emmitsburg Road Ridge (even though the Federals in the Rose farm and Devil's Den would still be hidden). The plan would have to change and Hood would be shifted to the right, rather than behind McLaws. It would be *Hood's* Division that led the attack now, rather than McLaws's. That would be enough to trigger a "very earnest" conversation between Longstreet and McLaws who, as Goggin pointed out, felt slighted.[904]

IF ALL OF THIS TOOK PLACE ON PENDLETON'S HILL, THEN Johnston's claim that he wasn't leading the column has merit. None of his accounts mention the halt at McLaws Hill, even though they've often been interpreted that way. Instead, Johnston seems to have met the column on Herr's Ridge *on its way back* from McLaws Hill. If that was the first involvement he had with McLaws's column, then he certainly couldn't have been leading it anywhere.

It also supports Goggin's recollection that McLaws's Division had no guide.[905] Goggin left the column to look for the sharpshooters after the march began. If Johnston was there to lead the column, he would have known. Yet not only did he fail to mention Johnston, he specifically mentioned that the column had no guide at all. Kershaw, who was as close to the situation as anyone, failed to even hint at Johnston's presence.

Though it's not surprising that Kershaw wouldn't mention Johnston in the brigade's official report, the failure to mention the engineer in any other account is revealing. Kershaw wrote a detailed account of his brigade's actions during the battle in 1876, a year before Longstreet's article indicting Johnston. Kershaw's failure to mention either Johnston or a signal station is curious.[906] Not until his *Century* article in the 1880s, well after the articles by Longstreet and McLaws established the narrative, did Kershaw mention a signal station.[907] In *neither* account, though, does Kershaw bring up Johnston. Though not definitive, the failure of the lead brigade commander to mention him supports Johnston's recollection that he wasn't leading the column.

July 2

In his *Southern Historical Society Papers* article, McLaws remembered that "at length—my recollection is that it was about 1:00 p.m.—Major [sic] Johnston, of General Lee's staff, came to me and said he was ordered to conduct me on the march." But this was far too late in the day for McLaws's march to begin. If Johnston rode up to McLaws and his column around one o'clock, then it was here, at the intersection of Hereter's Mill Road and Herr's Woods Road. And it wasn't at the *beginning* of McLaws's march, but in the middle of it. In fact, it was just as McLaws was turning off of Herr's Ridge Road around 1:15 p.m.

Though Johnston couldn't have been the guide for the entire march if he was just joining the column at the Hereter's Mill Road, he *may* have briefly acted as a guide for the division from there to the Ravine Road. He told Fitz Lee that he rode along a road from the slight right turn until the high hill; in other words, from Hereter's Mill Road to the Ravine Road.[908]

It would have been entirely appropriate for Johnston to have been positioned near the intersection to meet McLaws and point him down the correct road. Staff officers were commonly used as waymarkers, as Coupland Page recalled while he and Pendleton placed artillery that morning.[909] Johnston may have been acting in this capacity, marking the intersection and taking McLaws to George Peterkin on the other side of Pendleton's Hill, who was waiting to guide McLaws into position "by the road along the creek bottom toward the Peach orchard."[910]

Either way, it's not hard to see why McLaws misunderstood Johnston's role. With Johnston meeting the column as the division headed along the new road and then riding with the head of the column for another half mile or so, it may well have appeared to McLaws that Johnston was there to lead them in the right direction. That Johnston ultimately met McLaws very close to the division's morning position couldn't have helped McLaws's confusion years later.

Though he conflated the events on the McLaws and Pendleton's Hills, McLaw's memory did come *close* to the real order of events.... After Johnston rode out to meet McLaws, "Major

Johnston and myself [rode] some distance ahead. Suddenly, as we rose a hill on the road we were taking, the Round Top was plainly visible, with the flags of the signal men in rapid motion."[911] McLaws may have *thought* this all happened near Bream's Hill and the Black Horse Tavern. But Sam Johnston was only present for the second stop, the halt at Pendleton's Hill, more than a mile east of McLaws Hill.

As we've seen again and again, McLaws simply conflated several events into an easy to recall narrative, one that also had the benefit of absolving him of any blame. McLaws may have selectively remembered Johnston leading them to the Ravine Road, while blocking out Peterkin's role entirely.

McLaws couldn't say *Pendleton's* men had anything to do with guiding his column. *That* would ignite Longstreet and summon a wrath of culpability that he had been working so diligently to avoid. So, whether consciously or not, McLaws remembered Johnston, not Peterkin, as the guide and thought he had been there the whole time. Indeed, it had been "Lee's staff and engineer officers [who] were directed to lead the two infantry divisions into position," Alexander testified in a supporting letter for one of McLaws's articles. "Every halt they made and every step that they took were under the direction of these officers."[912] With Alexander's endorsement, who could challenge McLaws?

Johnston may have been lumped in with Alexander's indictment, but it had also been Alexander who remembered that Pendleton and Long had performed the route reconnaissance that morning, *not* Sam Johnston.[913] And of course, Alexander wasn't in any position to actually know what Lee's staff officers and engineers were up to, for he was reconnoitering and marching with his artillery all morning. Once again, Alexander's role as unofficial First Corps historian seems to have imported memories of things he didn't personally experience.

JOHNSTON ALWAYS INSISTED HE RODE WITH LONGSTREET that day, except for his brief jaunt with McLaws from Hereter's Mill Road to Pendleton's Hill. Longstreet, for his part, always maintained he rode with Hood. If Longstreet was with Hood and Johnston was with Longstreet, then Johnston was also with Hood. At the time McLaws approached Herr's Woods Road, Hood was formed up and ready to move nearby, probably near the ford where Hereter's Mill Road splashed across Willoughby Run.

Longstreet insisted that because he "was relieved for the time from the march" while Johnston was in charge of the column, "I rode near the middle of the line."[914] In his 1877 article, he wrote that "I...rode along with Hood's Division, which was in the rear."[915] Hood's Division may have been the rear division, but that doesn't mean Longstreet rode at the rear of the entire column. Instead, he was *trying* to say he rode with the rear *division*. Longstreet wasn't known for his precision with words.

At about 1:00 p.m., as McLaws's column was nearing the Hereter's Mill Road, Hood's men were just forming up for their anticipated march down the Ravine Road.[lxxiii] They may not have been precisely at the Willoughby Run ford, but they must have been close, for Johnston was able to see McLaws coming down the road from their position only six hundred yards away.

"Gen'l Longstreet says that he rode at the rear of his column and intimates that I rode at the head of the column and conducted the movement of McLaws' Division," Johnston wrote to Fitz Lee in 1878, misinterpreting Longstreet's first article.[916]

---

lxxiii   Captain Hall saw the end of McLaws's column on Herr's Ridge at 1:30, meaning the head of the column had already turned off into Herr's Woods Road. Lieutenant Colonel William Shepherd, in Hood's Division, remembered taking up the line of march around 1 p.m. O.R. 27.2: 420. McLaws's Division would be appearing at about the same time, at roughly 1:15 p.m. Given the problems with time in the mid-nineteenth century, a fifteen-minute difference in the records is well within the margin of error.

But "Gen'l Longstreet is certainly mistaken. I am sure I rode with him during the entire march, except the short distance from the bend of the road to the top of the hill where the head of his column was first *observed* by the enemy; this short distance I rode with Gen'l McLaws at the head of his Division."[917] This was the short trip from the "bend of the road" where Hereter's Mill Road turns onto Herr's Woods Road. The hill Johnston referred to was Pendleton's Hill.

As we've seen, this is often interpreted as the halt at McLaws Hill. But it was crossing Pendleton's Hill that the Confederates first believed they had been spotted. And since Johnston was with Longstreet near McPherson's Ridge, he was a mile away from McLaws Hill when the column stopped there.

On the other hand, if Johnston was describing the halt at Pendleton's Hill, his account makes sense. Though Hood was preparing to march down the Ravine Road at 1:00 p.m., McLaws's approaching division would need the road, forcing Hood's column to wait for the troops to pass. Sitting astride their horses by the creek, Johnston and Longstreet could see McLaws's column arriving along the Hereter's Mill Road and then make the right turn onto Herr's Woods Road.

"Without being asked" Johnston said, "I told General Longstreet that [McLaws] would disclose [his] movements to the enemy" as the column "turned to the right to follow this road." Johnston rode up to McLaws to let him know, but nevertheless, "we moved on until the head of [McLaws's] column got in full view of the enemy."[918] That's because Longstreet decided to press on over the top of Pendleton's Hill.

This all means that Johnston was not, in fact, leading the column. His accounts exclusively describe the march on Herr's Woods Road and atop Pendleton's Hill. Unlike Alexander, who was inundated with other accounts as the de facto First Corps historian, Johnston seems to have avoided Confederate literature after the war (except when it was brought to his attention and affected his own reputation).[lxxiv] His memories, then, would be less affected by those of others, so he wasn't incorporating secondhand information into his own recollections.[919] He would be more likely to recognize them as his own memories, but they would be necessarily fuzzier (whereas Alexander's memory interpreted others' experiences as his own, presenting them much clearer and more definitive on recall).

And of course, Peterkin said *he* was the one to lead the division into position along the Ravine Road.[920] Pendleton remembered in his report that after riding to Pitzer's schoolhouse and investigating the woods there, he "returned to General Longstreet, for the purpose of conducting his column to this point, and supervising, as might be necessary, the disposition of his artillery." When Pendleton found Longstreet, "he was advancing by the ravine road (as most out of view), time having been already lost in attempting another, which proved objectionable, because exposed to observation."[921] This also suggests Peterkin arrived as McLaws was moving toward the Ravine Road, rather than at McLaws Hill.

If Pendleton's staff was in charge of leading the column into position, then Johnston wasn't. Instead, Johnston "suppose[d] that Gen'l Lee's object in sending me with Gen'l Longstreet was that I should give him the benefit of the information that I had obtained by [the] reconnaissance I had made of the country and the position of the enemy."[922] That seems reasonable enough, since Johnston was the one that reported the results of the reconnaissance to Lee.[923] But if Johnston wasn't with McLaws's Division until it approached Pendleton's Hill, he couldn't have been the division's guide.

---

lxxiv   Though his son was named after Robert E. Lee, he was born in 1865 before the surrender. The legacy of Johnston's Confederate service was not kind to him in the decade after the war, which must have had an effect on his involvement in postwar veterans' activities. His work on northern railroads certainly played a role in that, too.

THAT IT WAS HOOD'S DIVISION DEPRIVING MCLAWS OF THE lead position in the assault undoubtedly caused much of the "earnest" conversation Goggin remembered. It's not conjecture to say that Hood irked McLaws for the rest of his life. In 1896, just a year and a half before his death, McLaws was still incensed at Hood's perceived slights.[924] Hood, remember, had publicly insulted McLaws after the Battle of Sharpsburg, issued what McLaws took to be an insincere apology, and had then promptly jumped in front of McLaws to make it to the battlefield first, literally leaving McLaws and his division to eat his dust on the road behind him. Finally, on July 2, it seemed as though McLaws and his men would be redeemed in the eyes of the army by leading the attack. And now that, too, was being taken away, in favor of Hood. At least, this is how McLaws saw it.

McLaws, to his credit, remained publicly diplomatic about the whole thing, though in doing so he painted a much more cordial picture of the scene on Pendleton's Hill than what actually happened. "General Hood, in his eagerness for the fray (and he bears the character of always being so), had pressed on his division behind mine so that it lapped considerably, creating confusion in the countermarch." That read well to the public, even if those in the know could read between the lines.

According to McLaws, Longstreet approached him and politely asked him to give way to Hood, since it seemed he was already taking the lead.

"There is so much confusion," Longstreet explained, "owing to Hood's division being mixed up with yours, suppose you let him countermarch first and lead in the attack."

McLaws would have none of it. "As I started in the lead," he protested, "let me continue so." Longstreet assented and McLaws continued on his way.[925]

It strains credulity to think that the same Longstreet who McLaws claimed repeatedly refused to let him reconnoiter, was aggravated about Lee's correction of his troop dispositions, and who McLaws considered generally obstinate, "overbearing," and a "humbug" all day, politely asked McLaws to let Hood go first. Then when McLaws insisted on maintaining the position of honor at the front of the column, the same bull-headed Longstreet timidly assented, despite the logistical nightmare and delay it produced. It also doesn't help McLaws's credibility that absolutely no one else, including his own adjutant, remembered it that way.

None of Longstreet's articles or his memoir references any overlap between his columns. Major Goggin didn't remember it, either. Nor did Johnston. While Goggin and Longstreet had at least some incentive to selectively remember events, Johnston had none. In fact, Johnston would have been vindicated had he mentioned the mix up, for that would have been an additional factor to the delay, which would in turn diminish his own liability. But aside from the holdup at the hill, Johnston remembered the march went relatively smooth. Hood simply pushed past McLaws and the two divisions went over the hill and into position without any entanglement.

As a general matter, Johnston was right. Hood *did* move forward at Pendleton's Hill, and he eventually moved past McLaws. But those were two separate events in two different places. Johnston witnessed Hood begin his march alongside McLaws while the two divisions crossed to the southern side of the Fairfield Road. Because Hood ultimately passed McLaws's position, Johnston either assumed that happened at Pendleton's Hill or he witnessed the two movements and simply conflated them later.

To hurry alongside McLaws, Hood took the Ravine Road on the east side of Willoughby Run, putting him on McLaws's left. This is what Private John Coxe remembered many years later. McLaws recalled the confusion of Hood's men bumping into his own men, but rather than a problem with the countermarch, per se, the "lapping" was caused by Hood being on the east side of the run and McLaws being on the west.[926] Perhaps there was *some* mix up as Hood began to get into position, but only McLaws seems to have written about it. Certainly, it was a bigger deal to him than anyone else.

If Hood doubled on McLaws's column on the east side of the run, and Kershaw maintained the lead ahead of Hood's column, as it appears he did, then at some point along the way, Hood had to leapfrog west of McLaws or vice versa.[927] The process of crossing divisions had the potential to cause some logistical confusion, perhaps leaving the impression of entanglement in McLaws's mind. But not only were there orderly ways to cross the columns, Hood most likely stopped near Pitzer's schoolhouse and waited for McLaws to pass before continuing on his way.

That would be the quickest and easiest way. Private Sims, who had been distraught by the sights of the battlefield earlier in the day, remembered that after resting all morning, "we then made a right flank movement into a thick wood." There, "we were ordered to load our guns and went a little farther…. We then moved out into a field," where the artillery was already in position.[928] Law recalled "frequent halts and deflections" on the march into position, while Texan John Stevens remembered being "moved from place to place."[929]

This begs an important question. *Why form Hood on the right and McLaws on the left?* Why not send McLaws beyond the Emmitsburg Road and keep Hood on Seminary Ridge instead of trying to cross two parallel lines of march?

Frankly, Longstreet needed to keep McLaws close. Lee, remember, had admonished Longstreet that any errors by McLaws would be borne by Longstreet. Despite the preparations that morning, it had been McLaws's column that was stuck getting into position. Though purely bad luck, it seemed that McLaws *had* no other sort of luck. Indeed, both times he stopped and noticed wagging signal flags, those flags had been relaying *other* information to Federal headquarters. During McLaws's first stop, Jerome had been messaging headquarters about the skirmish, not McLaws's column. And when McLaws stopped on Pendleton's Hill, Captain Hall's messages were informing headquarters of the march north on Herr's Ridge, *not* McLaws's column on the hill.

Longstreet never explicitly said that it was a lack of faith in McLaws that determined his corps' dispositions. But he had been clear enough in the letter exchange with McLaws in the summer of 1873, almost exactly ten years after the battle. "It was not until I promised my personal aid and attention to your command" that

McLaws was even allowed to join the army for the campaign, Longstreet reminded him. "I thus became responsible for *everything* that was not entirely satisfactory in your command from that day, and was repeatedly told of that fact."[930] Longstreet may have reminded McLaws of that as they exchanged unpleasantries on Pendleton's Hill in the thick summer humidity of 1863. But even if he didn't, he got his point across in the mail ten summers later.

McLaws's reputation being what it was, it's understandable that Longstreet preferred to send Hood out for the more independent assignment. That allowed Longstreet to retain much tighter command and control of his division. Remember, McLaws complained that Longstreet was "exceedingly overbearing" during the battle.[931]

McLaws was right. Longstreet *did* hover over him at Gettysburg. He led both Kershaw's and Wofford's Brigades out to the Emmitsburg Road during the advance. And he personally gave orders to Kershaw, rather than funneling them through the chain of command. According to McLaws, Longstreet personally directed some artillery placements, ordering a battery into position alongside McLaws's Division (where, exactly, isn't clear, for there was artillery all along the ridge at that point). McLaws objected, arguing that placing the battery where Longstreet wanted it would draw unnecessary artillery fire. Longstreet insisted anyway, the battery was placed, and the Federal artillery began hurling shells into the line.[932]

McLaws, in turn, made sure to point out that any delay in beginning the attack once the line was formed was directly Longstreet's fault. The early criticism of McLaws had been that he was too slow, not just on the march into position, but in beginning his division's attack in support of Hood. The field officers in Hood's Division especially took notice. Captain George Hillyer of the Ninth Georgia complained that "for nearly an hour and a half [there was] no support on its left, the advance of McLaws' division being for some reason thus long delayed, which left the flank...very much exposed to an enfilading fire of the enemy's batteries" and "a flanking party" of Federal infantry.[933] Even Johnston had picked up on this, for he noted one of the causes for the delay was the "time lost in beginning the fight after the line was formed."[934] And years later, Kershaw requested accounts of the fighting at the Rose Farm "in order that McLaws's [Division] may be vindicated."[935]

McLaws, much closer to the ground and able to detect the rumbling vibrations of insinuation and rumor better than any historian, made a point to rebut this, too. Less than a week after the battle, he wrote his wife that "I was directed not to assault until General Hood was in position." In a more famous anecdote, McLaws remembered that Barksdale "had been exceedingly impatient for the order to advance." He had approached McLaws "two or three times" while they waited in line, practically begging to attack. "'General, let me go,' the Mississippi fire-eater pleaded. "General, let me charge!' But, as I was [a]waiting General Longstreet's will," McLaws explained, "I told General Barksdale to wait."[936]

His hands were tied—the delay belonged to Longstreet.

HOOD'S SUBORDINATES, UNLIKE MCLAWS'S, DIDN'T REPORT any countermarching at all. Instead, the regimental and brigade reports almost uniformly tell of a march from their morning position directly into battle line.[lxxv] Major H.D. McDaniel of the Eleventh Georgia, part of George "Tige" Anderson's Brigade (not to be confused with General *Richard* Anderson's Third Corps Division) reported that "the scene of action was reached by a march of several miles, under a burning sun, and for the distance of one mile under a terrific fire of the enemy's batteries."[937] Most of the other reports simply begin with the order to attack the Federal left once they reached the "scene of action."[938]

One Texan remembered that after the men "whiled away" the morning "waiting for the time for action...Colonel P.A. Work... ordered us to fall in line. We then made a right flank movement into a thick wood."[939] Another Texan also remembered "moving by

---

lxxv   There are no known reports currently in existence from any of Long-
        street's division commanders.

the right flank along the edge and through the woods about four miles, until we crossed a creek into an open field."[940] At least from the Texans' standpoint, they simply formed up, right faced, and marched south, a description that suggests a starting point near McPhersons' Ridge and a route along Willoughby Run directly into position about three and a half miles away.[941]

A soldier correspondent, probably from the Seventeenth Georgia, also failed to note any countermarch. "The morning was occupied in maneuvering and waiting for the enemy to advance," wrote the *Savannah Republican*'s correspondent "Tout le Monde." But Lee intended to attack first, so "as soon as everything was adjusted the advance was ordered" and "Hood formed his line on the extreme right of the line of battle."[942] As far as anyone in Hood's command was concerned, the morning was occupied by the usual mechanics of moving an army with nothing particularly abnormal to report.

The closest anyone in Hood's Division came to mentioning a countermarch were the commanders in Henry Benning's Brigade. "At 1:00 p.m., [the brigade] again took up the line of march, moving by a circuitous route to the right," wrote Lieutenant Colonel William Shepherd.[943] Colonel Wesley Hodges also used the word "circuitous" to describe the march.[944] Benning used his subordinates' descriptions in his own report, but then explained that once he was in position, he had to move another "500 or 600 yards to the right," in order to let Law's Brigade in front of him.[945]

It is tempting to interpret the references to a "circuitous" march as the infamous countermarch. But the word *circuitous* simply means "not direct."[946] The winding road, crossing the creek, moving through McLaws's column, the stop and start, and then shuffling positions to make room for Law would certainly qualify as "circuitous."

It's also curious that only Benning's men, who had to move out Law's way, used the term in their reports. Even then, not *all* of Benning's commanders thought the route was indirect. Colonel J.D. Waddell, commanding the Twentieth Georgia in Benning's Brigade, simply wrote that the march into position was about three miles.[947] From Hood's bivouac between McPherson's Ridge and Seminary Ridge to the "scene of action" is about three and a half miles, meaning any circuitousness must have been relatively brief. To the exhausted men of Benning's Brigade, whose weary legs felt every step of the "tiresome march" through the mountains overnight, a march through the "excessive heat," with only a brief rest, undoubtedly felt "circuitous."[948]

Contrast the experience of Hood's Division with the two existing reports from McLaws's Division. Both of McLaws's subordinates' reports specifically mention a long halt after the march began, followed by a countermarch. And of course, the countermarch had been a keystone of McLaws's account since he first told it to Longstreet in 1873 (though it's not a feature of his complaint to his wife on July 7, 1863). McLaws was in the lead, so a countermarch would of course be more noticeable and perhaps more aggravating to his men, especially those in the front of the column, like Kershaw and Major Maffett, who would have further to countermarch. That *could* account for a part of the silence in Hood's Division. But then, except for two of Benning's commanders, Hood's men all described a fairly direct three-mile march. If they had followed McLaws to Herr's Ridge, then retraced their steps back to the Ravine Road, not only would it be decidedly circuitous for *everyone*, it would have been significantly longer than three or four miles.

Rather, the more likely scenario is that Hood's men formed up shortly after Law's Brigade arrived, ready to embark down the Ravine Road. But once in column and on the road, they had to stop, wait for McLaws to restart his march, and then march alongside his column until passing McLaws's Division and forming on Warfield Ridge.

WHILE MCLAWS WAS STOPPED, PORTER ALEXANDER WAS A bustle of activity. His recollection that it took three hours from the time he was ordered to survey the field to the time he got his "battalions parked near where our infantry lines were to be formed" was essentially true, though it simplified his activities that day.[949] Alexander actually performed two separate reconnaissances, one in the late morning and one in the afternoon.

His first reconnaissance was the one with Pendleton near the Point of Woods, which started around noon. That one took about an hour and a half, and when he was done, he headed back toward his battalion intending to accompany it on the march into position. But he arrived at Pendleton's Hill just as the infantry was crossing over the top of it. It was *then and there* that all three battalions were ordered forward, so he rounded them up and took them toward Pitzer's schoolhouse.

When the guns reached the schoolhouse, Alexander was again ordered to scout artillery positions, this time across the Emmitsburg Road. "Colonel Alexander, by General Longstreet's direction, proceeded to explore the ground still farther to the right," Pendleton reported, "and Henry's battalion, accompanying Hood's division, was thrown in that direction."[950] By this point, reports of Sickles's move toward the Emmitsburg Road were trickling in. That resulted in the decision to move Hood further to the right than anticipated, meaning Alexander had to head across the Emmitsburg Road to scout more artillery positions. Meanwhile, the artillery rolled alongside McLaws's Division. As Kershaw reported, "a battery of artillery was moved along the road parallel with my line of march" as it approached the schoolhouse.[951]

Alexander probably took John Cheves Haskell, who was second in command of Mathis Henry's battalion, with him across the Emmitsburg Road. This is likely the reconnaissance Haskell remembered on the afternoon of July 2. He wrote in his memoir, which has been used to support his involvement in Johnston's morning reconnaissance, that his ride to the famous hill occurred around 3:00 p.m., "with several couriers and one of our officers."[952] While he couldn't have meant that he rode over the top of Little Round Top, as second in command of Henry's Battalion it was entirely appropriate for him to accompany Alexander and Henry on a reconnaissance of Warfield Ridge that afternoon.

Once Henry's gun placements were selected east of the Emmitsburg Road, Alexander rode back to the schoolhouse to place Cabell's

Battalion. Henry, meanwhile, was to take his guns across the road. By the time Alexander got back to the schoolhouse, the vanguard of Hood's column was most likely already there, waiting for McLaws to pass onto the ridge. Thus, at the end of *both* reconnaissances, Alexander encountered infantry at a halt. It's not difficult to see how he conflated the two reconnaissances and how he seemingly contradicted himself. He really *did* head back to bring up his own battalion (and only his) after his first reconnaissance. But before he could do so, he was ordered to bring *all three* battalions to the front.

According to his *Century* article, Alexander spent three hours reconnoitering and moving his artillery to the schoolhouse. He left for his survey with Pendleton a little before noon and seems to have finished up his reconnaissance of Henry's position around 3:00 p.m. In the meantime, he had scouted the position by the crossroads where McLaws ultimately formed up and brought three battalions of artillery to Pitzer's schoolhouse. All of the pieces of Alexander's story check out, but the chronology—his biggest weakness—is slightly out of order. Given the fluid situation along Willoughby Run and Seminary Ridge that afternoon, it's hard to fault him for that.

ALEXANDER REMEMBERED THAT WHEN HE FINISHED reconnoitering, he went back to the marching column. He didn't remember *why* he went back, though in various accounts he assumed it was either to bring up his battalion, *all three* battalions, or to look for the infantry. In his personal memoir, though, he acknowledged he didn't quite remember the reason.

The confusion was understandable, but he actually went back for the artillery. Initially, he rode back to accompany his own battalion. But when he got to the hill he bumped into "the head of an infantry column, which I think was Hood's division, standing in the road where it was in sight of Round Top." It was at that point that Pendleton ordered *all* of the artillery to the front, so Alexander brought the three battalions to the head of the column and led them toward the schoolhouse. Since the trip was *initially* to bring up his own battalion, but he ended up bringing up all three, his later confusion is entirely understandable.

"For some reason, which I cannot now recall," Alexander remembered, the infantry "would not turn back and follow the tracks of my guns."[953] Perhaps this was because the artillery was still *making* the tracks. As we saw, the traditional story assumed that the artillery and infantry marched separately. But Alexander's guns were rolling alongside the infantry throughout the march. Not until Hood began to double on McLaws was the artillery rushed to the front. Kershaw had noticed this, as some of the lead guns began to rumble alongside his column on a parallel road, perhaps the eastern ravine road ahead of Hood's infantry. If the infantry clogged the top of the hill, then sidestepping it "through some meadows" may have been the only way for Alexander to get his guns to the front.

Though traditionally Alexander took the same path as McLaws, around Bream's Hill to the Black Horse Tavern Road, there's little contemporary evidence for that. As we saw, Alexander rumbled along the Ravine Road with the infantry. Longstreet and McLaws both remembered "that Alexander was with Hood," a pretty clear indication that at least the reserve artillery and Henry's Battalion never saw McLaws Hill.[954] Henry, being assigned to Hood's Division, traveled with them.

What about Cabell's Battalion, then, which was assigned to McLaws? His guns, too, probably rolled along with Hood and the rest of the artillery, for there's no indication that they had any problems marching into position.[955] Cabell's report is short and matter-of-fact, completely devoid of any references to backtracking or countermarching. That's an odd omission if he accompanied McLaws, for the only other reports from the division, Kershaw's and Maffett's, bring it up.

Instead, Alexander's recollection that he returned to the main column to bring up the artillery matches both his own and Pendleton's official reports, as we saw. That is to say, the artillery marched *with* the infantry, not ahead of it, and was rushed to the front as the infantry worked its way along the Ravine Road.[956]

So why did Alexander remember a long wait in the Willoughby Run valley? Once the three battalions rolled up behind Seminary Ridge, Henry's guns thundered up the ridge to the right while Alexander's and Cabell's Battalions trudged along with McLaws's men.[957] As Henry's eighteen guns and Hood's 7,000 infantrymen emerged from behind the ridge and crossed the Emmitsburg Road, both the signal station and Federal artillery immediately took notice.[958] As the division moved into position, "the enemy opened a furious cannonade," which forced the artillery to change course to get into position. Cabell's Battalion "deflected to the right," reported Pendleton, while "Alexander's was mainly parked for a season, somewhat under cover, until it could advance to better purpose."[959]

While Alexander waited in reserve, a massive artillery bombardment erupted. The fire was so "incessant," Cabell reported, he had to pause to let the smoke clear to see what he was shooting at.[960] The guns blasted away at each other for an hour before the infantry stepped off, wreaking havoc on both sides of the Emmitsburg Road.[961] As shells crashed into Cabell's batteries with horrifyingly grim accuracy, it was decided that Alexander's guns could now "advance to better purpose" and his battalion, under the command of Frank Huger, moved up to assist Cabell.[962]

So, Alexander *did* wait by the schoolhouse for "a season" while the infantry arrived and formed up. But not quite in the manner he remembered. Sleep deprived, given a de facto if not official promotion by taking over the First Corps artillery, and engaged in a heavy gunfight with the Federal artillery, the day's events easily rolled into one easy-to-remember narrative.[lxxvi] Rather than waiting in the valley, alone and isolated, wondering where the rest of the army could be, his battalion was simply in reserve. Standing in the valley, Alexander was hardly secluded. He was, quite literally, in the middle of the Confederate movement.

---

lxxvi   Gettysburg Licensed Battlefield Guide Ralph Siegel conducts an excellent program on Alexander's artillery at the Peach Orchard. He aptly refers to the barrage as a "gunfight," and the description deserves wider usage.

July 2

* * *

JOHN WEST, THE TEXAN WHO DREAMED OF HIS HOME AND young family in McPherson's fields after the long march to Gettysburg, described the moments just before the battle began. "We were standing in an open field," he wrote to his "little man," "under the shot and shell of these batteries, for half an hour, before we moved forward, and a good many soldiers were killed all around me. One poor fellow had his head knocked off in a few feet of me," he wrote. The deadly cannonball brought a wave of sadness over the Texan, for "I felt all the time as if I would never see you and little sister again."

But the time for sentimentality quickly passed. The waiting, the reconnoitering, the planning, the marching, the countermarching… all that was over. The troops were in position, the dogs of war were barking, and anxiety and dread rolled over into adrenaline. "The command was given to charge," West told his family, and "we moved forward as fast as we could."[963]

At long last, the attack on the Federal left had begun. The rest, as they say, is history.

EPILOGUE

"Here, however, occurred the great, the fatal failure of the entire occasion."

- William Pendleton[964]

"General Longstreet was not to blame for not attacking sooner than he did on the second of July."

- Lafayette McLaws[965]

"THERE HAS BEEN SO MUCH WRITTEN ON THE SUBJECT THAT it is getting to be *very* difficult to reconcile the versions of undoubtedly honest and well-meaning men."[966] Henry Hunt, Federal chief of artillery, was referring to the battle in general, but he just as easily could have been summarizing the postwar debate about Longstreet's actions on July 2.

The story of the countermarch, Johnston's reconnaissance, Longstreet's attitude, and the movements of the Confederate army in general on July 2 have been shrouded in myth, tradition, poor memory, stubbornness, and posturing. As we've seen, everyone saw the same event from different angles, often widely different angles. They recalled these events with different biases, levels of understanding, and ability to remember. The memories were often recalled with fierce passion and confidence. Phrases like "I remember distinctly" and "it's as fresh in my mind as if it were yesterday" are common in the correspondence. But then, so are "I don't recall exactly" or "my impression is...."

There's a tendency to accept or dismiss particular accounts completely. The same tendency exists toward individuals. Pendleton and Longstreet, for example, are often dismissed or taken with large doses of skepticism, while McLaws and Porter Alexander are rarely questioned.

But the people and their accounts are, for the most part, neither completely false nor completely true. The veterans knew this, for their letters are replete with references to sorting, sifting, and confusion as to which memories were right and which were hazy. Even those who appear most adamant and confident in their positions had moments of self-doubt and reflection. Jubal Early, who honestly believed he was engaged in a quasi-religious literary crusade to create value out of a devastating loss, questioned whether he had gone too far in crucifying Longstreet (who, it turns out, also had the ubiquitously human trait of earnestly believing what *he* said, too). Even William Pendleton questioned whether his memory served him well. This introspection occurred in private, of course. One's public voice is often quite different from the private one.

The veterans, of course, could only write what they remembered. And memory, as we saw, is a devilishly tricky thing. Our brains often actively work against our efforts to produce honest memories, and they do so subversively. We *think* we're telling the truth, even if we're not. That's on top of the other obstacles to accurate memory. Our perception of our experiences is glued together with assumptions based on our personal experience, with the remaining blank spaces painted over with other people's memories. Often, the painting is not done within the lines, and third-person memories bleed into our own, so it can be impossible to sort our personal memories from things we've heard.

We all inherently know this. It's part of being human. But we sometimes expect too much out of our forebears and hold them to the standards of statues and legends. They saw this happening and warned us against it. The letters from veterans to John Bachelder are full of waivers that the memory is "to my best recollection" or "I don't recall completely, but this is what comes to mind...."

Even though the story of the countermarch is rife with contradictions, it's important that we remember that *people* wrote the documents. We do a disservice both to history and to their memories if we accord a level of deference to their motives beyond that of eternal human nature. The men who fought the Battle of Gettysburg were not wired differently than anyone today.

They grew up in a different culture, of course, with different amenities and a drastically different concept of what everyday life was like. But their minds, their memory...they were the same as ours. And though today the books and magazines that carried their now faded words are fragile and musty, they were once brand new, ready to preserve their thoughts and memories. They wrote their accounts in their own present, primarily for a contemporary audience, to be read amidst their own culture, traditions, norms, mores, and sensibilities. Their present just happened to be 160 years ago.

ACCORDING TO WILLIAM PENDLETON AND JUBAL EARLY, the delay in Longstreet's attack was "fatal." Not only did it cost the Confederates the battle, but the loss of the battle directly led to the loss of the war. Of course, Pendleton and Early have been challenged on that accusation since they first made it. Longstreet and McLaws attributed the delay to the countermarch, and insisted that it was Sam Johnston, Lee's engineer, that led them astray. If they were simply following Lee's staff officer, then the fault lay there.

So, what effect *did* the countermarch have on the battle? The short answer is: very little.

As we saw, all of the contemporary evidence, from diary entries scribbled during the battle and letters or reports written shortly after, suggests that once Allegheny Johnson's Division failed to occupy Culp's Hill on the night of July 1, any thought or possibility of a morning attack was dismissed. Every participant who wrote about the morning hours, from Fremantle to private soldiers to Ewell's artillery chief, mentioned that the attack would start in the late afternoon. And by all accounts, Longstreet was in position around three, and the attack started at four after a substantial pre-assault bombardment.

The only rumblings of blame, in the army at least, fell back on McLaws. Much of that, in turn, related to the delay in his division launching its attack, as opposed to his getting into position in a timely fashion. Many of Hood's men, for example, felt that McLaws hadn't adequately supported their left flank. While the feeling was reasonable, given their view of events, it wasn't accurate. McLaws attacked when he was ordered and by all accounts, the assault was ferocious.

McLaws responded obliquely to those attacks, or at least his sympathizers did. The *Savannah Republican* made sure to publish columns by a regular correspondent blaming Lee and Longstreet for failing to reconnoiter, a refrain found in all of McLaws's writings on the battle. It was the *Savannah Republican* that first publicly wondered if perhaps the attack wasn't started as early as it could have been.

As for the battle itself, those with the most information tended to blame a lack of numbers and coordination. Lee maintained that the lack of a simultaneous assault on the entire Federal line was a primary reason the Confederates lost. Lack of troops was simply a corollary to that. Because the Confederate attack was piecemeal, the Federal army was able to pull troops from other portions of their line and plug holes in the right places at the right time. That left the impression that "just another regiment/brigade/division…" would have broken the Federal line, winning the battle.

Not until Lee's death and apotheosis did the timing of Longstreet's July 2 attack become of paramount importance. As we saw, Longstreet's abdication of Southern culture as a northern spoil of war had much more to do with that than any battlefield activity. Longstreet's awkward defenses and ultimate animosity toward his former comrades (who had flatly accused him of treason) only exacerbated an already inflammatory debate.

Epilogue

But a look at the battle, pushing all of the postwar distractions aside, shows that the delay, if there really was much of a delay, had little effect on the outcome of the battle. One doesn't have to engage in "what-ifs" to find the answer, either. For the timing of the attack to have caused the Confederacy's defeat at Gettysburg, Longstreet's attack must have either ended because of darkness, as it did after Jackson's renowned flank attack at Chancellorsville, or the situation must have been materially different at 3:00 p.m. than whatever time the attack *should* have stepped off.

We know darkness didn't cause the battle to end. Hood and McLaws ran out of steam well before the sun set. Anderson, Johnson, and Early all squeezed in attacks between the end of Longstreet's assault and nightfall. There were plenty of reasons the Confederate attacks weren't as successful as they had hoped, but sunset wasn't one of them.[lxxvii] So the questions remaining are simply whether the Federal position affected the battle's outcome and if so, should or could Longstreet have attacked *before* the Federal position changed. The answers to those questions are *yes* and *no*, respectively.

The accusation against the First Corps regarding an early attack has always been full of straw men. *If Longstreet attacked several hours earlier, Sickles wouldn't have been in his salient and the attack would have succeeded* is a common refrain. The argument sounds like it has merit because as an isolated statement, it's generally true. *If* Longstreet had attacked several hours earlier, then Sickles would not have been in his salient.

---

lxxvii   Darkness had a role to play in the evening attacks on Cemetery Hill, but by that point, the chances of a Confederate breakthrough were minimal. Lee's design had been to simultaneously attack, holding the bulk of the Federal army in place during the primary assault, so that either (1) reinforcements couldn't be peeled off or (2) if they were, the demonstrations would be converted into an attack. Though darkness probably contributed to Pender's and Rodes's absence in the Cemetery Hill attack, by that point, the result had been decided. There weren't enough troops to follow up any victory on the hill whether the sun was shining or not. It should also be noted that darkness didn't prevent Pender's Division from attacking alongside Wright that evening. Federal artillery, which wounded Pender and took him out of action, would be a better culprit than darkness.

But the premise is wrong. The attack was never supposed to start in the morning, much less at sunrise. Nor was it supposed to begin in the early afternoon. *No one* in the Confederate army began to move towards an attack until about 11:00 a.m., when McLaws and Anderson began their respective marches. Everyone launching blame at the First Corps in the 1870s understood enough about the movement of armies to know that moving three divisions, over 20,000 men, would not happen quickly. This is why Arthur Fremantle was able to eat cherries and bathe in the creek without worrying about missing the beginning of the attack, why Fitzgerald Ross could go sightseeing in the town, and why John West could fall asleep to dream of his family at least one last time.

The argument that Longstreet *could* have attacked earlier, even if true, is irrelevant, for he wasn't ever *supposed* to. One may as well argue that if Longstreet's Corps was on the field on July 1 the Confederate army could have taken Cemetery Hill. In isolation, the statement is probably true, but it's irrelevant because that was never one of the options. Likewise, Longstreet couldn't have attacked in the morning or early afternoon because Lee hadn't decided when and where the attack would be made until it was too late to launch a morning assault.

So, what time *could* Longstreet have attacked? If McLaws was at the Black Horse Tavern at noon, then he could have reached his position by 12:30. But he still had to form his division on the ridge and Hood had to get into position behind him. It's unreasonable to assume the attack could have started much earlier than 1:30 that afternoon. Indeed, that's a conservative estimate.

This also ignores the fact that the countermarch was more likely caused by the actions of Federal troops, rather than any oversight or error on the part of Johnston, McLaws, or Longstreet. No matter what McLaws, Longstreet, Lee, or Johnston were doing behind Seminary Ridge, Berdan's men were moving into the woods. Berdan was attracted to Anderson's movements, not anything McLaws, Johnston, or Longstreet were doing. To assume McLaws could have reached his position by 12:30, we also have to assume Berdan (or any other Federal unit) wouldn't have reacted to Anderson's march onto Seminary Ridge. But then, we have an entirely new scenario, one that didn't exist. And we certainly can't judge McLaws or Longstreet for failing to react to a situation that never existed.

Knowing that the attack couldn't have started any earlier than 1:30, the only question is whether the outcome would have been different if it started between 1:30 and 4:00 that afternoon. The answer is *probably not*. Sickles began his move to the front around 1:30 p.m. Even if Longstreet attacked at exactly the same time Sickles was moving forward, the Confederate attack would have had to adjust.

Since the attack couldn't have started until the time Sickles adjusted his line, it's irrelevant whether Longstreet attacked an hour later or three hours later. Sickles's position still would have changed, the Confederate dispositions would have been forced to do so in response, and Federal reinforcements would still have been available to plug the holes.

Where the holes in the Federal line opened may have changed. If the attack started earlier, the fighting probably would have occurred in different fields, changing the location of monuments, park roads, and tour stops. But the result likely would have been the same.

All else being equal, an attack at 1:30 p.m., rather than 4:00, meant that Little Round Top would have been empty. But all else was *not* equal. Little Round Top hadn't ever been part of the original plan, so it's possible Hood would have swept right past it. Perhaps more importantly, it was Sickles's move to the Emmitsburg Road and the sight of Confederates moving into position that pulled the Federal Second and Fifth Corps south in support of Sickles, not the hands of the clock. Once the Confederates revealed themselves along the Emmitsburg Road, reinforcements would be on the way no matter the time. Even if Hood stepped off Warfield Ridge at 1:30 that afternoon, the likelihood of Federal troops making it to Little Round Top before he did is high. And if the Federal reinforcements didn't meet Hood *there*, they would have met him *somewhere*. The result, again, would be the same.

There's also the question as to *who* would have attacked Little Round Top had the hill been empty and the attack been earlier. Evander Law's 1,900 men didn't arrive until around noon. The absolute earliest they could have been in position would have been 1:00 p.m. (they arrived around noon and had a three-mile march to the Confederate right: at three miles per hour, it would take another hour to get into position), and that's without giving them a rest after their twenty-four-mile march. The brigade was composed of men, not machines, and their combat effectiveness would be extremely low had they marched an additional three miles along farm paths and creek beds, then double-quicked into battle and up the slopes of *two* Round Tops (assuming Stoughton's sharpshooters still pulled Law's Brigade to the right.) And that's all dependent on the Federal army completely failing to respond to any of this.

The problem with "what-ifs," which at bottom is what the "fatal delay" argument was, is that they tend to rely on everything remaining the same, except for the one altered fact. But that's not how real life works. If Longstreet had been in position earlier, then the Federal army would have reacted. How, we don't know. But that reaction would have caused a new situation, which would have given Longstreet and his men new choices. And that action would have created a new set of reactions for the Federals, and so on and so forth. So while "what-if" scenarios can be wonderful academic and training tools, they are awful at determining what would have actually happened in a given scenario.

All that being said, the most we can hope to say is whether a particular action changed the Confederates' intended plan. We know Sickles's actions forced Longstreet to modify his planned attack. But often overlooked is Edward Johnson's inability to form his troops on Culp's Hill on the night of July 1. While no one can say that the plan Lee envisioned on July 1 would have been successful, we *can* say definitively that Johnson's actions on July 1 (coupled with the intelligence of upcoming Federal forces) forced Lee to change his plans. That pushed back the time of *any* attack on July 2, for Lee had to reconnoiter and contemplate his options. It was the delay in having to develop a new plan and gather the intelligence to do so that caused the "fatal delay," not anything Lee or his War Horse did.

Epilogue

AS THE VETERANS PASSED FROM VIBRANT YOUNG MEN TO elderly icons, and then to statues, photographs, and antiquated woodcuts, so too did their memories ossify into the faded ink and musty paper. Their experiences became revered as history, their words etched into the American narrative. The collections of individual experiences, the views of the events through each particular window, became part of a national story, not quite an origin story, but a transformational one.

The Civil War has often been referred to in terms of an epic. References to the war as America's Odyssey can be found simply by scanning the spines of the books lined up on library shelves and visitor centers. The literature is replete with Biblical references, too. The desire to make sense of it all is natural, and the veterans were no different. Having lived through such an ordeal, they wanted a deeper meaning and a way to understand it all. The natural human tendency is to create a narrative, a story that makes sense and has chronological patterns. A narrative also has heroes and villains.

The human mind is quick to create these narratives, for it allows us to process incredibly complex experiences without overloading our system. The time and energy needed to conduct this sort of analysis on every encounter would make the necessities of daily life impossible.

The veterans instinctively knew this and cautioned us not to take their words as gospel. For even though most of them tried to remember their experiences honestly, they all realized they could only remember bits and pieces, especially as time marched ruthlessly on. "You can't have true history," Joseph Kershaw reminded historian John Bachelder, "but by comparing [and] *sifting—especially sifting*."[967]

History, then, is a collective effort, not just between historians, but between those who created and observed it firsthand. No one individual knew everything that happened behind Confederate lines on the morning and early afternoon of July 2, 1863. They only knew what they saw and no one saw everything. The full story remained tattered and elusive, tucked away in individual memories like pieces of a flag torn from the staff to save it from capture. But by sifting and comparing the scraps of memories they left behind, we can piece together much of the story. Taking a step back to look at the whole picture, we can see what happened on July 2, 1863, in the shadow of the Round Tops.

ENDNOTES

1   Marshall to Long, June 3, 1886, in Long Papers, UNC Wilson Library.
2   Batchelder, "The Washington Elm Tradition," in *Bits of Cambridge History*, 247.

INTRODUCTION

3   Pfanz, *Gettysburg: The Second Day*, 118.
4   Douglas Southall Freeman concluded that "as this account by McLaws is confirmed by the only contemporary report, it must be adjudged as true." Freeman, *Lee's Lieutenants*, vol. 3, 116.
5   Freeman, *Lee's Lieutenants*, vol. 3, 116; Edwin Coddington used McLaws's account almost exclusively in his magisterial work on the Gettysburg Campaign in the 1960s. *Gettysburg: A Study in Command*, 379, 736–737. Pfanz also used Alexander and McLaws as the basis for the countermarch analysis in his phenomenal study of July 2. *Gettysburg: The Second Day*, 118–123, 489–490. Stephen Sears's 2003 study uses primarily Alexander's and McLaws's accounts for his narrative. *Gettysburg*, 258–260, 568–569. One of the most recent works is Cory Pfarr's *Longstreet at Gettysburg*, which uses McLaws and Alexander as the primary first-hand accounts. 75–83, 192.
6   Pfanz, *Gettysburg: The Second Day*, 118–123; Smith, "To Consider Every Contingency," in *Papers of the 2006 Gettysburg National Military Park Seminar*, 98–115.
7   Pfanz, *Gettysburg: The Second Day*, 118–123; Smith, "To Consider Every Contingency," in *Papers of the 2006 Gettysburg National Military Park Seminar*, 98–115; Cooksey, "Around the Flank: Longstreet's July 2 Attack

at Gettysburg," in *Gettysburg Magazine* no. 29 (July 2003), 94. Most accounts of the battle touch on the countermarch and reconnaissance, but these clearly lay out the majority of the tenets of the traditional version of events and do so clearly and concisely.

8   Johnston to McLaws, June 27, 1892, in S.R. Johnston Papers, VHS.

PERCEIVING HISTORY

9   Kershaw to Bachelder, Aug. 7, 1882, in Ladd, *The Bachelder Papers,* 2: 901.

10   Humphreys to McLaws, Jan. 6, 1878. McLaws Papers. Typescript available in GNMP Library, V7-MS-Brigades B11 Barksdale's Brigade.

11   Hunt to Long, Sept. 4, 1884, in Long Papers, UNC Wilson Library.

12   Scott and Fox, *Archaeological Insights into the Custer Battle.*

13   Southwick, et al. "Consistency of Memory for Combat-Related Traumatic Events in Veterans of Operation Desert Storm," 173–177. One of the deficiencies of the study was that all responses were self-reported, so there was no way to verify if the individuals actually experienced what they said they did. This actually helps in a study of memory in the Civil War, since there is similarly no real way to determine the initial veracity of the descriptions. What we can glean from this study is that memories change, whether for the better or worse, although additional evidence suggests the change *distorts* the memory, rather than sharpens it.

14   Chlebowski, MD, et al., "Confabulation."

15   Loftus, *Memory,* 37.

16   Loftus, *Memory,* 64–65.

17   Trivers, *The Folly of Fools,* 4.

18   Trivers, *The Folly of Fools,* 9.

19   Trivers, *The Folly of Fools,* 18.

20   Ross and Sicoly, "Egocentric Biases in Availability and Attrition," 335.

21   Ross and Sicoly, "Egocentric Biases in Availability and Attrition," 329–330.

22   Pickett's quote is widely available, but actual sources are hard to come by. James McPherson references the quote in his contribution to *Why the Confederacy Lost* but does not cite to a primary source. McPherson, "American Victory, American Defeat," in *Why the Confederacy Lost,* 19.

23   Southwick, "Consistency of Memory for Combat-Related Traumatic Events in Veterans of Operation Desert Storm," 175–176.

24   Loftus, "The Reality of Repressed Memories," 530.

Endnotes

25 Humphreys to McLaws, Jan. 6, 1878. McLaws Papers. Typescript available in GNMP Library, V7-MS-Brigades B11 Barksdale's Brigade.

26 Laney and Loftus, "Eyewitness testimony and memory biases," in *Noba Textbook Series: Psychology.*

27 Small, *The Sixteenth Maine Regiment in the War of the Rebellion,* 6–7.

28 Charles Pickett to James Longstreet, Oct. 12, 1892. Longstreet Papers, UNC Wilson Library.

29 Southwick, "Consistency of Memory for Combat-Related Traumatic Events in Veterans of Operation Desert Storm," 173–174. Loftus expands on this, concluding that this process snowballs. "A fringe of untruth probably happens to nearly all of our everyday reports of events," she writes. This "fringe" then becomes a part of the recollection, which is retold again and again. More untruths get added to the memory as time goes on and ultimately the memory becomes less and less accurate. Loftus, *Memory,* 125.

30 Laney and Loftus, "Eyewitness testimony and memory biases."

31 Loftus, *Memory,* 66–69, 77–82.

32 Campbell Brown Notes, July 2 + 3, 1878, in Polk, Ewell, Brown Papers, UNC Wilson Library.

33 Kershaw to Bachelder, Aug. 7, 1882, in Ladd, *The Bachelder Papers,* 2: 901.

34 John Bassler (149th NY) to John Bachelder, in Ladd, *The Bachelder Papers,* 2: 831.

35 Charles Pickett to James Longstreet, Oct. 12, 1892, SHC, UNC Wilson Library.

36 Charles Pickett to James Longstreet, Oct. 12, 1892, SHC, UNC Wilson Library.

37 Kershaw to Bachelder, Aug. 7, 1882, in Ladd, *The Bachelder Papers,* 2: 901. Emphasis in original.

38 Kershaw to Bachelder, August 7, 1882, in *Ladd, The Bachelder Papers,* 2: 900.

39 "Historiography," Merriam-Webster, https://www.merriam-webster.com/dictionary/historiography.

40 *Burlington (VT) Daily Free Press,* April 12, 1853. All emphasis in original.

41 "Time" *Leavenworth (KS) Weekly Times,* March 9, 1876. This was not simply a problem of a fledgling nation considered a backwater on the international scene. A British paper complained of the same sort of thing the *Leavenworth Weekly Times* had, albeit twenty years earlier. Hull, a town in East Yorkshire, England, demanded that Christ Church follow

Greenwich time, sternly admonishing that the time "be strictly adhered to." Only a few days before, the paper noted, "the difference between this clock and the new one at the parish church amounted to not less than eight minutes." "The Standard Time," *Hull* (East Yorkshire) *Packet; and East Riding Times* Nov. 27, 1857.

42   Dominic Ford, "Equation of Time."

43   Bartky, "The Adoption of Standard Time" *Technology and Culture* 30, no. 1, 27; Macrobert, "Time in the Sky and the Amateur Astronomer."

44   Macrobert, "Time in the Sky and the Amateur Astronomer."

45   Kershaw, for example, wrote that the brigade left camp "about sunrise" on the morning of July 2. After arriving on the battlefield, they were "halted until about noon." O.R. 27.2: 366. Major Robert Maffett of the 3rd South Carolina, in Kershaw's Brigade, remembered moving "at an early hour" on July 2. O.R. 27.2: 372. Major General Richard Anderson, commanding a Confederate Third Corps division, remembered staying in the position he occupied on the night of July 1 "until the morning of the 2nd." O.R. 27.2: 613. This is not to say that exact times were not used, but all three of these accounts use rounded times, such as "about 3 p.m." (Kershaw) or times rounded to the hour or half hour.

46   Even a coordinated attack relied more upon contingent movements than precise times, for these very reasons. On July 2, for example, the coordinated attacks of Ewell and Hill were contingent upon Longstreet's movements, not any particular time. Ewell, for example, reported that his attack was to be delayed "until I heard General Longstreet's guns open on the right." O.R. 27.2: 446.

47   O.R. 27.2: 617.

48   O.R. 27.1: 515, 507.

49   O.R. 27.2: 350. Pendleton notes Longstreet arrived "about midday" and directed Alexander to get a feel for the lay of the land.

50   Early address, *Survivors' Association of the State of South Carolina*, 37.

51   Early, *The Campaigns of Robert E. Lee*, 53.

PART ONE THE FATAL DELAY: LONGSTREET LOSES THE CAUSE

52   Early, *Address to the Survivors' Association of the State of South Carolina*, 19.

53   Early, *The Campaigns of Robert E. Lee*, 53.

54   Longstreet, *From Manassas to Appomattox*, 377.

Endnotes

55   "General R.E. Lee's Birthday – Address of General Jubal Early," *Charleston (SC) Daily Courier*, Jan. 26, 1872. The name of the institution was changed from Washington College to Washington and Lee University by the Board of Professors and Students of the College in November 1870. "The 'Washington and Lee University,'" *Staunton (VA) Spectator and General Advertiser*, Nov. 8, 1870. For a brief but thorough overview of Early's post-war construction of the Lost Cause, see Gallagher, "Jubal A. Early, the Lost Cause, and Civil War History: A Persistent Legacy," in Gallagher and Nolan, ed., *The Myth of the Lost Cause and Civil War History*, 35–59.

56   Welsh, M.D., *Medical Histories of Confederate Generals*, 136. Welsh concludes Lee probably died of a combination of pneumonia, heart disease, and a stroke.

57   "Oration by Hon. Thomas J. Semmes," *New Orleans Times-Picayune*, Oct. 23, 1870.

58   "The Death of Gen'l Lee – A Day of Mourning in Richmond," *Richmond (VA) Dispatch*, Oct. 14, 1870.

59   "Meeting at Williamsburg – Respect to the Memory of Lee," *Norfolk Virginian*, Oct. 19, 1870; "Oration by Hon. Thomas J. Semmes," *New Orleans Times-Picayune*, Oct. 23, 1870; "Death of Gen. Robert E. Lee," *Vicksburg Times and Republican*, Oct. 14, 1870; "Gen. Robt. E. Lee is Dead," Shreveport *South-Western*, Oct. 19, 1870.

60   "The Death of Gen'l Lee – A Day of Mourning in Richmond," *Richmond (VA) Dispatch*, Oct. 14, 1870.

61   "Monument to Gen. Lee," *Baltimore Sun*, Oct. 31, 1870.

62   "Monument to Gen. Lee" *Baltimore Sun*, Oct. 31, 1870; Bernard C. Steiner, *Life of Reverdy Johnson*, 37, 55, 115. The quote from Johnson is a summary of his remarks by the paper.

63   *Ceremonies Connected with the Inauguration of the Mausoleum and the Unveiling of the Recumbent Figure of General Robert Edward Lee.*

64   D.H. Maury to Campbell Brown, May 16, 1874, Polk-Brown-Ewell Papers, UNC Wilson Library.

65   Early, *The Campaigns of Robert E. Lee*, 51.

66   Early, *Address to the Survivors' Association of the State of South Carolina*, 17–18. Jubal Early, in his speech to South Carolina veterans, pointed out that the opponents to southern culture had proven Southern fears to be accurate by their behavior since the end of the war—"if it indeed be closed."

67 Early, *Address to the Survivors' Association of the State of South Carolina*), 19.

68 Early, *The Campaigns of Robert E. Lee*, 51–52.

69 Early, *Address to the Survivors' Association of the State of South Carolina*), 38.

70 Early, *The Campaigns of Robert E. Lee*, 52–53.

71 Early, *Address to the Survivors' Association of the State of South Carolina*, 37.

72 Early, *The Campaigns of Robert E. Lee*, 51–52.

73 "General Longstreet and His Position," *Charleston Mercury*, June 24, 1867, quoting the *Philadelphia Press*.

74 Early, *Address to the Survivors' Association of the State of South Carolina*, 20.

75 Early, *Address to the Survivors' Association of the State of South Carolina*, 19.

76 Early, *The Campaigns of Robert E. Lee*, 53.

77 Early, *Address to the Survivors' Association of the State of South Carolina*, 19.

78 De Peyster, "Military Memoir of William Mahone," 397.

79 Early to Walter H. Taylor, April 9, 1871, in The Archives of the Robert E. Lee Memorial Foundation, Papers of the Lee Family: Walter Herron Taylor Papers. Early tells Taylor that he lent Mahone a copy of the magazine article and that he had not yet heard back "though I believe he has been here all the time."

80 Mahone to Early, May 24, 1871. Transcript in *A Correspondence Between Generals Early and Mahone,* 8. Original manuscript in LOC, Jubal Early Papers.

81 Pendleton, "Personal Recollections of Lee," in *Southern Magazine* 15, 604, 635.

82 Pendleton, "Personal Recollections of Lee," in *Southern Magazine* 15, 630. Pendleton is specifically referencing the fighting in the Overland Campaign here.

83 Pendleton, "Personal Recollections of Lee," in *Southern Magazine* 15, 617.

84 Pendleton, "Personal Recollections of Lee," in *Southern Magazine* 15, 629.

85 Pendleton, "Personal Recollections of Lee," in *Southern Magazine* 15, 628–629.

86 Early, *The Campaigns of Robert E. Lee*, 44–45. Early told his audience "General Lee had not been conquered in battle, but surrendered because he had no longer an army with which to give battle."

87 Early, *The Campaigns of Robert E. Lee*, 44–45.

88 Early, *The Campaigns of Robert E. Lee*, 47–51. Though the war raged for four years, Lee was at the helm of the Army of Northern Virginia from June 1862 until the surrender in April 1865. Early wondered, "Where shall we turn to find the peer of our great and pure soldier and hero?

Certainly, we shall not find one among the mythic heroes of Homer....
Nor shall we find one among the Grecian commanders of a later period,
though in the devotion of the hero of Thermopylae, and the daring of
the victor of Marathon, may be found similes for the like qualities in our
hero." Alexander "could not control himself, but fell a victim to his own
excesses." Hannibal was close, but his army was nearly equal in numbers
to the Romans and he didn't have to worry about a supply line, as they
"foraged on the country in which they operated." Caesar was a great military leader, but "turned his sword against the liberties of his country."
He went to "search in vain for [an equal] among the Generals of the
[Roman] Empire...nor shall we find one among the leaders of the barbaric
hordes...nor in the dark ages; nor among the Crusaders...nor among the
chieftains of the middle ages." While militarily adept, the examples all
had serious moral flaws. "Shall we compare Lee to the great Napoleon,
or his successful antagonist, Wellington? Napoleon was a captain of most
extraordinary genius, but success was always necessary to him...but he
could never stand reverses.... He would have been unable to conduct the
campaigns of General Lee against the constantly accumulating and ever
renewing armies of the enemy." The Iron Duke—Wellington—while "a
prudent, good soldier," he "was emphatically a favorite child of fortune,"
winning his most notable battle "against the desperate gambler whose last
stake was up, when he had all the odds on his side." Certainly not something Lee could say. Perhaps Washington came closest, as they were similar
in "their great self-command, in their patriotism, and in their purity and
unselfishness of character," but Lee operated "on so much grander a scale
than" Washington and the country had changed so much more: steam
power, railroads, telegraphs, etc. made the two contests incomparable.

89   Early, *The Campaigns of Robert E. Lee*, 24, 46. Specifically, Early is referring to the Antietam Campaign, but he notes that had those men and
supplies been given, Lee "would...have dictated the terms of the peace in
the Capital of the enemy.

90   Early, *The Campaigns of Robert E. Lee*, 31.

91   Early, *The Campaigns of Robert E. Lee*, 10.

92   Early, *The Campaigns of Robert E. Lee*, 13. Early wrote that "all the
fighting on our side was done by Jackson's corps, except an affair about
dusk between a part of McDowell's corps and the advance of Longstreet's
command, which began to arrive between eleven and twelve in the day,
but did not become engaged until at the close." Likewise, the following

day, "Longstreet did not become engaged until late in the afternoon" when he attacked. In truth, Longstreet's flank attack at Second Manassas is generally considered one of the most devastating attacks of the war.

93 Early, *The Campaigns of Robert E. Lee*, 34.

94 Pendleton, "Personal Recollections of General Lee," in *Southern Magazine* 15, 625.

95 Pendleton, "Personal Recollections of General Lee," in *Southern Magazine* 15, 625.

96 Pendleton, "Personal Recollections of General Lee," in *Southern Magazine* 15, 625–626; "General Lee's Final and Full Report of the Pennsylvania Campaign and Battle of Gettysburg," in *SHSP* vol. 2, 41–43. In describing the attack on July 2, Lee simply describes the plan and then states "About four P.M. Longstreet's batteries opened, and soon afterwards Hood's division...moved to the attack." Describing July 3, Lee reported that "General Longstreet's dispositions were not completed as early as was expected." In a letter to Longstreet on May 7, 1875, Marshall confirms this. "I have no personal recollection of the order to which you refer [sunrise attack order]. It certainly was not conveyed by me. Nor is there anything in Genl Lee's report to show that the attack on the 2nd was expected by him to begin earlier.... He does comment in his report on the fact that the attack on the right was expected to begin much earlier on the 3rd than it did...." Longstreet Papers, UNC Wilson Library.

97 Pendleton, "Personal Recollections of General Lee," in *Southern Magazine* 15, 626–627.

98 Pendleton, "Personal Recollections of General Lee," in *Southern Magazine* 15, 627.

99 Pendleton, "Personal Recollections of General Lee," in *Southern Magazine* 15, 622.

100 Pendleton, "Personal Recollections of General Lee," in *Southern Magazine* 15, 622–623.

101 Pendleton, "Personal Recollections of General Lee," in *Southern Magazine* 15, 626.

102 Early, *The Campaigns of Robert E. Lee*, 35–36.

103 Goree to Longstreet, May 17, 1875, in Cutrer, *Longstreet's Aide*, 158–159. Longstreet aide Thomas Goree told his old commander how he learned of the charge: "When Pendleton delivered his lecture in Galveston in 1873 in which he made his charges against you, a report was made of his lecture in the city papers..." Reviews were mixed.

104   Lee to Early, March 30, 1865. Early Papers, LOC. Lee wrote "While my own confidence in your ability, zeal and devotion to the cause is unimpaired, I have nevertheless felt that I could not oppose what seems to be the current of opinion, without injustice to your reputation and injury to the service. I therefore felt constrained to endeavor to find a commander who would be more likely to develop the strength and resources of the country and inspire the soldiers with confidence…"

105   Pendleton, "Personal Recollections of General Lee," in *Southern Magazine* 15, 625.

106   For example, see *Brooklyn Daily Eagle*, January 22, 1864: "As a war correspondent William [Swinton] has no superior if an equal, his letters while to the point are scholarly and elegant, as a magazinist and reviewer he ranks with the first writers in the country." *Portsmouth (OH) Daily Times* called him "the accomplished army correspondent" in its July 23, 1864 edition. Not everyone was a fan, however. The *Rutland (VT) Herald* found Swinton "pompous and windy." *Rutland (VT) Weekly Herald*, Dec. 1, 1864. Rutland's aspersions aside, the *Memphis (TN) Daily Commercial* reprinted the *New York Times*'s review of Swinton's tome in its May 5, 1866 issue. The *Richmond Dispatch* printed a semi-review in the May 2, 1866 issue; having not read the book, they critiqued what they could see from the *New York Times*'s review. The *New Orleans Crescent* (June 13, 1866) and *Brooklyn Daily Eagle* (June 18, 1866) also featured reviews.

107   *New Orleans Crescent*, June 13, 1866.

108   The editors, publishing and commenting on a reprint of the *New York Times*'s review, wrote "As to General Lee, we are furnished with meagre quotations, yet enough is reproduced to allow us to see that Mr. Swinton recognizes him as a great chieftain."

109   Swinton, *Campaigns of the Army of the Potomac*, 340.

110   Swinton, *Campaigns of the Army of the Potomac*, 340–341. Such a promise would have been so far out of Lee's character that it most certainly did not occur. To be generous, it is possible a simple conversation about preferences before or during the campaign yielded a comment about the benefits of fighting on the defensive, which then warped over time and politics into a "promise." In any event, there is little contemporary evidence to suggest Longstreet wanted to swing around to the right on the evening of July 1. Most, if not all, of the written accounts indicating Longstreet wanted to move to the right on July 1 come after the war. There is ample contem-

porary evidence that Longstreet wanted to do so on the night of July 2, however, so perhaps Longstreet is granting himself foresight. Indeed, in discussing the loss with Fremantle on July 4, Fremantle recalled Longstreet assessing the reasons for the loss as twofold: 1) failing to concentrate the army and 2) making "Pickett's Charge" with less than thirty thousand men. Fremantle, *Three Months in the Confederate States*, 274. Failing to move to the right wasn't a reason Longstreet gave Fremantle for the loss.

111   Swinton, *Campaigns of the Army of the Potomac*, 340, footnote. In a footnote on page 341, Swinton again credits Longstreet as the source of the information regarding the flank maneuver and promise to fight on the defensive.

112   "A Northern History of the War," *Richmond Dispatch*, May 2, 1866.

113   Early, *The Campaigns of Robert E. Lee*, 36.

114   "A Northern History of the War," *Richmond Dispatch*, May 2, 1866.

115   "The Longstreet Picnic in Texas (From the Galveston News)," *Opelousas (LA) Courier*, May 12, 1866.

116   Francis Lawley to Early, May 14, 1872, Early Papers, LOC. Francis Lawley, "The Confederacy. The Dying Hours and Struggles - The Nobility of Lee - The Hopelessness of the Struggle - A Thrilling Account by an Impartial Observer." *Yorkville (SC) Enquirer*, Nov. 30, 1865.

117   "General Longstreet with a New Vocation," *Edgefield (SC) Advertiser*, Jan. 31, 1866. Lee references Early's departure to Mexico in a March 16, 1866 letter to Early. Lee to Early, March 1866, Early Papers, LOC. Also reprinted in Lee, *Recollections and Letters of General Robert E. Lee*, 220.

118   U.S. Congress. *An Act to Provide for the More Efficient Government of the Rebel States.* Statutes at Large, 39th Congress, 2nd Session. LOC. http://memory.loc.gov/cgi-bin/ampage?collId=llsl&fileName=014/ llsl014.db&recNum=459ebates, 1774 - 1875 (loc.gov); U.S. Const. Amend. XIV; Wert, *General James Longstreet: The Confederacy's Most Controversial Soldier,* 410; *Dred Scott v. Sandford,* 60 U.S. 393 (1857).

119   *New Orleans Times*, March 17, 1867.

120   *New Orleans Times,* March 19, 1867.

121   "Gen. James Longstreet on the Situation," in *New Orleans Times*, March 19, 1867.

122   Lee to Hon. John Letcher, Aug. 28, 1865, in Jones, *Life and Letters of Robert E. Lee*, 387.

123 Lee to Capt. Josiah Tatnall, Sept. 7, 1865, in Jones, *Life and Letters of Robert E. Lee*, 387–388.

124 Proclamation of Amnesty and Reconstruction, May 29, 1865, in Richardson, *A Compilation of the Messages and Papers of the Presidents*, 310–312.

125 "Gen. Longstreet Speaks," *Columbia (SC) Daily Phoenix*, March 28, 1867.

126 "Gen. Beauregard on the Situation - He Counsels Submission," *Nashville Union and American*, March 30, 1867. Reprinted article from *New Orleans Times*, March 26, 1867.

127 "Meeting of the Colored People at Columbia - Addresses by General Wade Hampton, Hon. E.J. Arthur and Others," *Charleston Mercury*, March 20, 1867.

128 "Southern Reconstruction - The Power and the Programme of Secretary of Stanton," *New York Daily Herald*, March 20, 1867.

129 Longstreet to R.H. Taliaferro, July 4, 1867, quoted in Piston, *Lee's Tarnished Lieutenant*, 106. Original in Collection of Edward M. Boagni, M.D., Baton Rouge, La.

130 "The Situation. The Views of Eminent Men. Letters from Gen. Longstreet, Judge Campbell, and Hon. Christian Roselius." *New Orleans Times*, April 7, 1867.

131 "Letter of Gen. Longstreet," *New Orleans Times*, June 8, 1867.

132 "The World Upside Down," *New Orleans Times*, June 6, 1867.

133 *New Orleans Times*, June 8, 1867. Parker's letter to Longstreet was published in the *Shreveport South-Western* on June 19, 1867.

134 Wade, *Augustus Baldwin Longstreet*, 355. The story was related to Mr. Wade, Augustus's biographer, by a Ms. L.B. West, who remembered James Longstreet visiting during the summer of 1867. It was then that Augustus counseled him against publishing the letter. William Garrett Piston placed the visit during the spring of 1867. The spring visit makes more sense, but still does not explain the chronology of Longstreet's *New Orleans Times* publications. Thomas Hay suggests the letter Augustus warned his nephew about was the private June 3rd letter to Parker, not the response he later published. Sanger and Hay, *James Longstreet: Soldier, Politician, Officeholder & Writer*, 334. It seems Longstreet intended to publish the letter originally, but held off until pressed. The *Times'* criticism appeared on June 6th, with Longstreet's reply drafted June 7th and published June 8th. There was simply no time for him to have traveled to Mississippi, consulted with Augustus, and sent the letter for publication. Rather, the

publication of the letter to Parker and his reply seem to have been a knee jerk reaction.

135 Longstreet to "My Dear General," June 8, 1867, James Longstreet Papers, UNC Wilson Library (a review of the letter authenticates it as a letter to Lee, when compared to Lee's reply); Lee to Longstreet, Oct. 29, 1867, Helen M. Taylor Collection, VHS. A more accessible copy of the letter is available in Jones, *Personal Reminiscences of General Robert E. Lee*, 227–228.

136 Longstreet to J.M.G. Parker, Esq., June 3, 1867, in *New Orleans Times*, June 8, 1867.

137 Longstreet to the Editor of the N.O. Times, June 7, 1867, in *New Orleans Times*, June 8, 1867.

138 Longstreet to Parker, June 3, 1867, in *New Orleans Times*, June 8, 1867.

139 Piston, *Lee's Tarnished Lieutenant*, 105; Wert, *General James Longstreet*, 412. Even Longstreet seemed to believe that was the case.

140 Longstreet to the Editor of the N.O. Times, June 7, 1867, *New Orleans Times*, June 8, 1867; Piston, *Lee's Tarnished Lieutenant*, 105.

141 Longstreet to J.M.G. Parker, Esq., June 3, 1867, in *New Orleans Times*, June 8, 1867.

142 Early, *Address to the Survivors' Association of the State of South Carolina*, 37.

143 Pendleton, "Personal Recollections of General Lee," in *Southern Magazine* 15, 612.

144 "General Longstreet," *New Orleans Times*, June 8, 1867.

145 "General Longstreet," *Shreveport South-Western*, June 19, 1867.

146 "General Longstreet," *New Orleans Times*, June 8, 1867.

147 "General Longstreet," *Shreveport South-Western*, June 19, 1867.

148 "General Longstreet and His Position," *Raleigh Weekly Sentinel*, July 9, 1867.

149 "General Longstreet," *Shreveport South-Western*, June 19, 1867.

150 "General Longstreet and the Doctrine of Force," *Knoxville (TN) Daily Free Press*, July 2, 1867, reprinted in *Charleston (SC) Mercury*.

151 "General Longstreet and His Position," *The Charleston (SC) Mercury*, June 24, 1867.

152 "General Longstreet and His Position," *The Charleston (SC) Mercury*, June 24, 1867, quoting *The Philadelphia Press*.

153 Reprinted in the Knoxville *Daily Free Press* in part, under the title "General Longstreet and the Doctrine of Force," July 2, 1867; "General Longstreet's Position," *Memphis Public Ledger*, July 8, 1867.

154 Early to brother, July 15, 1867, Early Papers, LOC.

155 Bragg to Early, June 27, 1872. Early Papers, LOC.

156 Francis Lawley to Early, May 14, 1872, Early Papers, LOC.

157 Lawley, in *Times* (London), Aug. 18, 1863.

158 Pendleton to Capt. Charles A. Davidson, May 29, 1873. Pendleton Papers, UNC Wilson Library. Captain Davidson was the Secretary of the Lee Memorial Association.

159 For Pendleton, the war had always had a religious aura about it. In a letter home, Pendleton wrote "God we may rest assured is not wicked. He will not be deceived. If our cause be right, as we so fully believe, and if we as a people faithfully do our part, we may trust He will still deliver us from our enemies so unprincipled. There seems much suffering in store for us.... But we can, I trust, by God's blessing endure to the end." Pendleton to My Darling Love, Nov. 13, 1863, in Pendleton Papers, UNC Wilson Library.

160 McLaws to Longstreet, June 12, 1873, McLaws Papers, UNC Wilson Library.

161 Kershaw to Bachelder, August 7, 1882, in *Ladd, The Bachelder Papers*, 2: 900.

162 McLaws to General, April 22, 1864, McLaws Papers, UNC Wilson Library; McLaws to wife, July 7, 1863. McLaws Papers, UNC Wilson Library. The unspecified "General" in McLaws's 1864 letter is probably Bragg, given the context and date.

163 Lafayette McLaws, "Gettysburg" in *SHSP* v. 7, 87–88. Major Sorrel had been promoted to Colonel, but the commission arrived on July 3, just after Pickett's Charge. During the campaign, he was Major Sorrel. Sorrel, *Recollections of a Staff Officer*, 170.

164 McLaws to General, April 22, 1864, McLaws Papers, UNC Wilson Library. In 1886, McLaws wrote a brief, apparently unsolicited letter to a newspaper editor, probably the *Philadelphia Weekly Press*, refuting the idea that Federal General Samuel Crawford's men pushed his division back. According to McLaws in this version of the story, "Gen. Wofford, the only brigade commander who had brought his brigade from the front, had been ordered back by Gen. Longstreet." Indeed, "there was no pursuit, not a gun being fired" and McLaws "had every reason to believe that Gen. Wofford had really been ordered back, and was not followed by any one when he retired."

After the war, General Crawford had come to McLaws's office in Georgia and requested an acknowledgement that his division had run

McLaws out of their position. Crawford had been so adamant that McLaws began to doubt his own memory and wrote to everyone still alive about the event. When he received their replies, he was confident that his memory was accurate and he had not been driven back. McLaws's letter to the editor of the *Weekly Press*, reprinted in *Army and Navy Journal*. "McLaws's Division at Gettysburg," in McLaws Papers, UNC. McLaws wrote Longstreet, as well, who promised that his next article would "put the Crawford matter in its true light, so far as it can be done by me." Longstreet to McLaws, Sept. 24, 1886, in McLaws Papers, UNC Wilson Library.

165   McLaws to Longstreet, June 12, 1873, McLaws Papers, UNC Wilson Library.

166   McLaws to Longstreet, June 12, 1873, McLaws Papers, UNC Wilson Library. Throughout his writings, McLaws spells "reconnaissance" as "reconnoissance." For readability, it is spelled "reconnaissance" here, as are other consistent antiquated or inaccurate spellings in McLaws's writing.

167   McLaws to Longstreet, June 12, 1873, McLaws Papers, UNC Wilson Library.

168   McLaws spells Moncure's name wrong. There is no "t." Moncure, Thomas J. file, NARA, RG 109 M258. McLaws abbreviated the word "Virginia" in the original letter.

169   McLaws to Longstreet, June 12, 1873, McLaws Papers, UNC Wilson Library.

170   The time, as all times at Gettysburg, are estimates. Four o'clock seems as reasonable as any and serves as a round estimate for the late afternoon start time. Pfanz, *Gettysburg: The Second Day*, 123.

171   McLaws to Longstreet, June 12, 1873, McLaws Papers, UNC Wilson Library.

172   A transcript of the letter dated July 25, 1873 is available in GNMP, V5-Longstreet, James. The original is found int the McLaws Papers, UNC. Longstreet's letter refers to McLaws's letter "of the 16th inst." However, given the contents, Longstreet is clearly referring to McLaws's letter of June 12, 1873. McLaws may have sat on the letter for a few days—only a copy of the letter he sent Longstreet exists in his own files. He may have made two copies and waited to send it until June 16, 1873. Though it is also possible McLaws followed up with another letter, Longstreet only references the one and clearly responds to the June 12 letter. Perhaps

Longstreet simply read the date wrong or the reference to the "16th" is simply an error on Longstreet's part.

173   Longstreet to McLaws, July 25, 1873, GNMP V5-Longstreet, James.

174   William Garrett Piston wrote that "Chickamauga was the greatest achievement of his [Longstreet's] career." *Lee's Tarnished Lieutenant*, 71–72. Jeffry Wert outlines the various praise for Longstreet, both contemporary and modern, in Wert, *General James Longstreet*, 320–321.

175   Piston also offers a succinct description of the political and personality tensions between the commanders in Tennessee, which led to Longstreet's Knoxville campaign. *Lee's Tarnished Lieutenant*, 73–76. Sanger gives an overview of the situation, as well, but is much more sympathetic to Longstreet. *James Longstreet: Soldier, Politician, Officeholder & Writer*, 218–221.

176   Donald Sanger wrote that "the Longstreet of this period is not one to whom great deeds can be credited." Sanger and Hay, *James Longstreet: Soldier, Politician, Officeholder & Writer*, 219.

177   Longstreet reported that the objective was "to make a rapid movement by the most retired route into East Tennessee with a force of 20,000, and to strike the enemy so suddenly and so severely that his force should be crushed before he could know anything of our purposes." O.R. 31.1: 455.

178   When the Confederates began building the works, they named it Fort Loudon and called it that throughout the war. When Federal troops captured the partially built fortifications, they named the completed fortification Fort Sanders. Alexander, "Longstreet at Knoxville," in *Battles & Leaders*, 3:747–748. Benjamin Humphreys remembered the attack being postponed at least once due to weather. Humphreys to General, Feb. 16, 1864. McLaws Papers, UNC Wilson Library.

179   Longstreet reported the examination of the works with Alexander, Micah Jenkins, and General Denville Leadbetter, calling it a "more careful reconnaissance" than the one done the day before. O.R. 31.1: 460. E.P. Alexander later wrote that the berm had been removed, as the Federal engineer officer, Orlando Poe, anticipated an attack and ordered its removal. Alexander also describes the slippery conditions. "Longstreet at Knoxville," in *Battles & Leaders*, 3:749.

180   Sorrel to McLaws, Dec. 17, 1863, in McLaws Papers, UNC Wilson Library.

181   Specifications for Neglect of Duty Charge, O.R. 31.1: 503–504.

182   O.R. 31.1: 506; Wert, *Longstreet*, 363. Wert has a concise and fair discussion of the trial at 359–365.

183   Finding and Sentence of the Court, O.R. 31.1: 505–506.

184   O.R. 31.1:488, 506.

185   O.R. 31.1:489. Of the numerous opinions solicited, McLaws received confirmation that "during this period we were without…carpenters, tools, blacksmiths +c, had no appliances for the manufacture of ladders + had no lumber out of which they could have been made properly. Had an order for such articles been issued, it would have been necessary to call for large details + for said details to have found their own tools." Statement of J.J. Middleton, McLaws Papers, UNC Wilson Library.

186   O.R. 31.1: 506.

187   Longstreet initially worked to prevent McLaws's return to the Army of Northern Virginia, but Lee was supportive of this. Lee told President Jefferson Davis that "it would be better if [McLaws] was put on duty elsewhere," though McLaws did, of course, have "a right to go back" if he wanted. Another offer was made to McLaws, which he declined. It was then that Davis ordered him to Savannah. Oeffinger, ed., *A Soldier's General: The Civil War Letters of Major General Lafayette McLaws*, 44–47.

188   O.R. 31.1: 471. "Brig. Gen. E.M. Law…did tender the resignation of his office as brigadier-general in the service…and did obtain a leave of absence" under "false pretenses. Specifically, Longstreet charged that Law told him that he wanted to petition for a cavalry commission. In reality, according to Longstreet's specification, Law intended to petition the Confederate government to move his whole brigade to a different command.

189   Oeffinger, ed. *A Soldier's General*, 215 n. 6; Polley, *Hood's Texas Brigade*, 225; Wert, *Longstreet*, 360–361.

190   McLaws ultimately ended up along the Salkehatchie River. Bachelder to McLaws, Feb. 2, 1865, in *Ladd, The Bachelder Papers*, 1: 184–185. Oeffinger, ed., *A Soldier's General*, 46–47.

191   Longstreet to McLaws, July 25, 1873. GNMP, V5 - Longstreet, James.

192   Longstreet to McLaws, June 3, 1863, McLaws Papers, UNC Wilson Library.

193   McLaws to wife, Nov. 10, 1862, in Oeffinger, ed., *A Soldier's General*, 158. Larry Tagg suggests that McLaws was unhappy with his position in the Army of Northern Virginia. Not only had he been passed over for corps command, Tagg also points to McLaws's view of the army's favoritism toward Virginians. Tagg, *The Generals of Gettysburg*, 211.

194   Sorrel, *Recollections of a Staff Officer*, 133.

195   Dickert, *History of Kershaw's Brigade*, 338.

196   McLaws is rarely mentioned in the personal stories or anecdotes told by his fellow officers. Fremantle, for example, peppers his narrative with lively anecdotes of Longstreet's staff officers and division commanders. He relates his introductions to all Longstreet's staff and division commanders, with the notable exception of McLaws. And though he mentions riding with McLaws's Division for the first few days of his visit, the only personal anecdote comes from the retreat to Virginia, when McLaws and his staff ate Longstreet's dinner. "Our bivouac being near a large tavern, General Longstreet had ordered some supper there for himself and his Staff; but when we went to devour it, we discovered General M'Laws and his officers rapidly finishing it." Fremantle, *Three Months in the Southern States*, 279.

197   Sorrel, *Recollections of a Staff Officer*, 133.

198   For one example, see the notes of Benjamin G. Humphreys in response to Walter Taylor's book *Four Years with General Lee*. Humphreys takes issue at the short shrift he claims Taylor gave Hood's and McLaws's men for their fighting on July 2. "They 'advanced,' forced back, 'and captured some trophies and prisoners.' Wonderful achievement but then they were only Carolinians, Georgians, Floridians, Alabamians, Mississippians, Louisianians, and Texans. Not a Virginian, there - is the wherefore." He then critiqued Taylor's focus on Early's July 2 attack on Cemetery Hill. "He knew more about Cemetery Hill and the operations of Early, - the Virginian." As to the criticism of Longstreet, which Taylor assumed was "generally conceded," Humphreys thought it was "conceded by Virginians, authors, orators and divines." "Was Longstreet stupid?" Humphreys jotted rhetorically. "Or have Taylor and Venable together with Virginia authors, orators and divines simply muddled history in their laudable efforts to make Longstreet a 'scapegoat' - and establish the 'infalibility' [sic] of Lee?" Everett, "Delayed Report of an Important Eyewitness to Gettysburg - Benjamin G. Humphreys," *The Journal of Mississippi History*, 311, 314, GNMP V7-MS21. In a letter to McLaws in 1887, Longstreet expressed similar sentiments: "As for Fredericksburg, your division did more and better work than all the balance of the army together, but you were not of Virginia, and I doubt if there was a Virginian in all your infantry command. It is simply shameful how they have treated the army not of Virginia." Longstreet to McLaws, June 17, 1887, McLaws Papers, UNC Wilson Library.

199 Larry Tagg suggested McLaws believed he was passed over in favor of Virginians. *The Generals of Gettysburg*, 211. Lee had long thought highly of Hill, dating back to at least October of 1862. "Next to [Longstreet and Jackson] I consider General A.P. Hill the best commander with me. He fights his troops well, and takes good care of them." O.R. 19.2: 643. Then in 1863, when it came time to reorganize the army after Jackson's death, Lee wrote to President Jefferson Davis that A.P. Hill "I think upon the whole, is the best soldier of his grade with me." O.R. 25.2: 810.

200 Though Hill entered a questionable performance at Gettysburg and history has not remembered Ewell favorably, the decision was sound. Both commanders had performed ably and as Lee noted, he had to pick from the selection he had before him. "I do not know where to get better men than those I have named," he told President Davis in recommending Ewell and Hill. O.R. 25.2: 811. Douglas Southall Freeman concluded that "McLaws had ruled himself out of promotion by what he had not done at Maryland Heights and at Salem Church." Freeman, *Lee's Lieutenants*, vol. 2, 694.

201 O.R. 19.2: 606–608.

202 O.R. 19.1: 148. In McLaws's official report, he spent several paragraphs describing the cause of the delay in detail, noting that Lee had been trying to find out where he was throughout the sixteenth ("I received several communications from your headquarters in relation to my position, which were obeyed so far as circumstances permitted, and I acted, in departing from them, as I believed the commanding general would have ordered had he known the circumstances." In a supplement to his report two days later, McLaws added that the troops were tired and worn out from their experience at Harper's Ferry and Crampton's Gap. O.R. 19.1: 856, 857. After the war, he wrote articles on his actions in the Maryland Campaign and Harper's Ferry, attempting to justify himself. See "The Capture of Harper's Ferry: An Interesting Narrative of the Maryland Campaign of 1862 – A Confederate Success Not Due to Stonewall Jackson," *Philadelphia Weekly Press*, Sept. 19, 1888 and Lafayette McLaws, *The Maryland Campaign*, Speech Given Before the Georgia Historical Society, 1888, in McLaws Papers, UNC Wilson Library. Glenn Tucker also discusses McLaws's reputation in *Lee and Longstreet at Gettysburg*, 14–16.

203 Tagg, *The Generals of Gettysburg*, 303.

204 O.R. 19.1: 818.

205 O.R. 19.1: 923.

206   Rev. Nicholas A. Davis, *The Campaign from Texas to Maryland*, 92.

207   Tucker, *Lee and Longstreet at Gettysburg*, 22–26. Hood to McLaws, June
       3, 1863, McLaws Papers, UNC Wilson Library. Eventually, Nicholas
       Davis apologized and promised to correct the "injustice" he had done,
       telling McLaws he had simply been relying on the "the facts in the case
       as reported to me by gentlemen from the field." He had since realized he
       had wronged McLaws and vowed "to make an honorable amend for that
       injury" by "correcting the matter" in the next edition. Davis to McLaws,
       July 30, 1863, McLaws Papers, UNC Wilson Library.

208   William Proctor Smith, "Report of the Battle of Gettysburg, Letter Book
       1863-1864," Martin F. Schmidt Research Library, KHS . "I ordered
       Captain Boswell on the 'Plank Road' Capt. Johnston on the Turnpike
       and going myself with Capt. Hinrichs on the Mine Road."

209   OR 25.1: 797–802.

210   Lawley, in *The Times* (London), Aug. 18, 1863. There were other factors at
       play beyond Lawley's observation, but he wasn't the only one to complain
       that McLaws's attack didn't step off alongside Hood.

211   Ross, *A Visit to the Cities and Camps of the Confederate States*, 59.

212   Kershaw, "Official Report of General J.B. Kershaw," in *SHSP* vol. 4, 178;
       O.R. 27.2: 366. Technically, Kershaw was reporting to Major Goggin,
       McLaws's adjutant.

213   Oeffinger, ed., *A Soldier's General*, 44–47. Longstreet initially worked to
       prevent McLaws's return to the Army of Northern Virginia, but Lee was
       supportive of this. Lee told President Jefferson Davis that "it would be
       better if [McLaws] was put on duty elsewhere," though McLaws did, of
       course, have "a right to go back" if he wanted. Another offer was made to
       McLaws, which he declined. He was eventually assigned to the defenses
       of Savannah.

214   OR 27.2: 366.

215   McLaws to Longstreet, June 12, 1873, McLaws Papers, UNC Wilson
       Library.

216   "Longstreet At Gettysburg – Letter from General McLaws – Pendleton's
       Statement Reviewed," *New Orleans Republican*, August 10, 1873.

217   McLaws to Longstreet, draft, June 10, 1873, McLaws Papers, UNC
       Wilson Library. Emphasis added.

218   Johnston to McLaws, June 27, 1892. S.R. Johnston Papers, VHS. John-
       ston wrote that Lee "said nothing about finding a route over which troops
       could be moved unobserved by the enemy, but it was not necessary as that

was a part of my duty as a reconnoitering officer, and would be attended to without special instructions. Indeed he said nothing about the movement of troops at all, and left me with only that knowledge of what he wanted which I had obtained after long service with him, and that was that he wanted me to consider every contingency which might arise."

219　Johnston said he "did not hear the orders given to General Longstreet by General Lee" and that "I had no idea where [Longstreet] was going, except what I could infer from the movement having been ordered soon after I made my report." Johnston to F. Lee, Feb. 11, 1878, S.R. Johnston Papers, VHS.

220　McLaws to Longstreet, June 12, 1873, McLaws Papers, UNC Wilson Library. Fitz Lee saw through the argument as well, responding to Longstreet's article: "General Longstreet, in his narrative, contends that the delay of several hours in the march of his column to the right was General Lee's fault, since the column was moved under the special directions of Colonel Johnston, an engineer officer of the Commanding General." Lee, "A Review of the First Two Days' Operations at Gettysburg and a Reply to General Longstreet," in *SHSP*, vol. 5, 182.

221　Glenn Tucker, *Lee and Longstreet at Gettysburg*, 14.

222　Pfarr, *Longstreet at Gettysburg*, 75–83.

223　Sears, *Gettysburg*, 252–262; Trudeau, *Gettysburg: A Testing of Courage* , 289–290; Coddington, *The Gettysburg Campaign*, 374-380; Pfanz, *Gettysburg; The Second Day*, 109–113. Pfanz is the most diverse, citing to a variety of sources, though he does take McLaws at face value. Most of the historians here also refer to the letter exchange between McLaws and Johnston in 1892.

224　In a letter to Thomas Goree, one of his aides during the war, Longstreet wrote that although friends had asked him to counter Pendleton's charges, it was not necessary. "About that time General McLaws and General Humphreys published accounts completely vindicating the First Corps and myself which I thought sufficient and preferred to let the matter rest there." May 12, 1875, in Cutrer, *Longstreet's Aide*, 157.

225　"Gen. James Longstreet on the Situation" March 18, 1867, in *New Orleans Times*, March 19, 1867.

226　McLaws, "Gettysburg," in *SHSP*, vol. 7, 68.

227　Lt. Col. William S. Shepherd's report is at O.R. 27.2: 420. Colonel Wesley C. Hodges of the 7th Georgia reported an initial halt at midnight. He wrote that the regiment then moved at 3 p.m., which is probably a transcript error by the compilers of the *Official Records*. The context of the rest of the report indicates the regiment halted until 3 a.m. O.R. 27.2: 424. Hodges wrote: "Arriving with my command near the battle-field of Wednesday, July 1, at 12 p.m., the men, after a fatiguing march through the mountain pass, by way of Cashtown, were permitted to rest upon their arms until 3 p.m., at which time the march was resumed. After one other temporary halt, my regiment, in its place in Benning's brigade, was pushed forward to our right to assume position in lines assigned it." It seems the 12 p.m. time refers to midnight, with the march resuming at 3 a.m., followed by a temporary halt at Gettysburg and then the move to the right. Shepherd's account also refers to midnight as "12 p.m." with a brief halt until 3 a.m. A letter from J.S.D. Cullen, First Corps medical director, to Longstreet in 1875, which Longstreet published in his memoir, supports this. "Orders were issued to be ready to march at 'daybreak,' or some earlier hour, next morning." Cullen to Longstreet, May 18, 1875, in Longstreet, *From Manassas to Appomattox*, 384.

228   McLaws to Longstreet, June 12, 1873, McLaws Papers, UNC Wilson Library. "My Division was leading Longstreet's Corps and of course the other divisions came up later. I saw Hood's Division next morning and understood that Pickett had been detached to guard the rear and then to take charge of the provisions captured on the 1st." If McLaws was in front of Hood to end the night, but then noted Hood the next morning, it is a fair inference, among the other evidence, that Hood passed him that morning.

229   O.R. 27.2: 366. In a later article, Kershaw would state that the cause of the delay was due to Ewell's trains. "Kershaw's Brigade at Gettysburg," in *Battles & Leaders*, 3:331. His report does not specify whose trains were ahead of him. In the context of the report, Kershaw appears to mean that there was very little interference from the trains on July 2, as opposed to July 1. On July 1st, "Ewell's wagon train occupied the road until 4 p.m.," meaning McLaws couldn't use the road. Conversely, on July 2, McLaws's Division reached Gettysburg "with only a slight detention from trains in the way." Whether these trains were Ewell's or Hood's is not stated.

230   McLaws, "Longstreet at Gettysburg" *Philadelphia Weekly Press*, Feb. 15, 1888. In GMNP V5-McLaws, Lafayette. Emphasis added.

231   McLaws, "Gettysburg," in *SHSP* vol. 7, 78. Though McLaws eventually came around to believing Johnston timely conducted the reconnaissance, he always maintained Johnston led the march. McLaws, "The Battle of

Gettysburg,", 73–74, in GNMP, V5-McLaws, Lafayette. McLaws wrote Johnston a series of questions on June 8, 1892. Johnston replied June 27, 1892. S.R. Johnston Papers, VHS.

In his July 7, 1863 letter to his wife, McLaws thought "Longstreet is to blame for not reconnoitering the grounds." McLaws to wife, July 7, 1863, in McLaws Papers, UNC Wilson Library. In his *Southern Historical Society Papers* piece, he also brings up his perception that there was very little reconnaissance. Besides insisting he wasn't allowed to reconnoiter, he wrote that "General Longstreet had not done it, and General Lee had not." McLaws, "Gettysburg," in *SHSP* vol. 7, 69, 78. It's also a staple of McLaws's account that he was supposed to be on the flank, but ended up facing the Federal line directly. See McLaws, "Gettysburg," in *SHSP* vol. 7, 71; McLaws "The Battle of Gettysburg," in GNMP V5-McLaws, Lafayette.

232 In his final report of the battle in 1864, Lee wrote that "Longstreet was directed to place the divisions of McLaws and Hood on the right of Hill, partially enveloping the enemy's left, which he was to drive in." O.R. 27.2: 318. Longstreet interpreted his orders to "gain the Emmitsburg road," and later clarified that to mean the attack was to "follow. . . up the direction of the Emmitsburg road toward the Cemetery Ridge, holding Hood's left as well as could be *toward* the Emmitsburg road." (Emphasis added) O.R. 27.2:358; Longstreet, "Lee's Right Wing at Gettysburg," in *Battles & Leaders*, 3:340–341. Kershaw mentions wheeling left when across the road to hit the flank. Longstreet "directed me to advance my brigade and attack the enemy at that point, turn his flank, and extend along the cross-road [Wheatfield Road], with my left resting toward the Emmitsburg road." O.R. 27.2: 367. For a discussion of the Federal left during the Confederate planning stages and the order to "partially enve-lope" the left, see Thompson, "In Defense of Captain Samuel Johnston," *Gettysburg Magazine*, no. 61, 20–48.

233 O.R. 27.2: 358. Emphasis added.

234 James Longstreet, "Battle of Gettysburg: Gen. Longstreet's Part In It," partially reprinted in *The New York Times*, Nov. 5, 1877. A more accessible version is available as "Lee in Pennsylvania," in *Annals of the War*, 423.

235 J. William Jones to Early, May 2, 1878. Jubal A. Early Papers, LOC.

236 Johnston to F. Lee, February 11, 1878, S.R. Johnston Papers, VHS.

237 Lee, "A Review of the First Two Days' Operations at Gettysburg and a Reply to General Longstreet," in *SHSP*, vol. 5, 182–184.

Endnotes

238   In addition to the February 11, 1878 letter to Fitz Lee, Johnston answered a follow-up letter from Lee on February 14, 1878. The next letter was a reply to McLaws in 1892 and the last letter Johnston wrote on the subject was in 1895, in response to an article mentioning the reconnaissance. Johnston wrote the letter to George Peterkin, apparently unsolicited. S.R. Johnston Papers, VHS.

239   *(Frederick) News*, Dec. 14, 1885; *(New York) Daily News*, Dec. 14, 1885. In fairness to McLaws, Johnston bounced around the country in his postwar career as a master of roads for various railroads, primarily in the north. He doesn't seem to have had much involvement in Confederate veterans circles after the war, though his job would have made it difficult. Finding an address to reach Johnston couldn't have been easy.

240   Baylor to Johnston, June 9, 1892, in S.R. Johnston Papers, VHS; McLaws to Baylor, undated, S.R. Johnston Papers, VHS. Though undated, the letter from McLaws to Baylor asks him to review a letter to Johnston and appears with Baylor's letter in the Virginia Historical Society's collection. Since this is the only correspondence known between McLaws and Johnston, and Baylor forwarded the letter from McLaws to Johnston the day after McLaws's letter is dated, it is safe to assume the letter was written to Baylor for the purpose of reviewing and forwarding the June 8, 1892 letter.

241   Baylor to Johnston, June 9, 1892, in S.R. Johnston Papers, VHS; Johnston to McLaws, June 27, 1892, in S.R. Johnston Papers, VHS.

242   Johnston to F. Lee, February 11, 1878, S.R. Johnston Papers, VHS

243   Johnston to McLaws, June 27, 1892, S.R. Johnston Papers, VHS.

244   O.R. 1.11.2, 519.

245   Walter H. Stevens recommendation, September 15, 1864. Johnston, Samuel R. file, NARA M258, RG 109.

246   O.R. 1.25.1, 825.

247   McLaws to Hood, May 31, 1863, in Oeffinger, ed., *A Soldier's General*, 182.

248   McLaws to Longstreet, June 12, 1873, McLaws Papers, UNC Wilson Library.

249   Kershaw to Bachelder, Aug. 7, 1882, in Ladd, *The Bachelder Papers*, 2: 900.

250   O.R. 27.2: 362–363. This also suggests Longstreet at least agreed with the rumors that McLaws shared some blame in the results of July 2, even if he didn't outright blame him publicly.

251 Glenn Tucker describes McLaws's tone well: "McLaws was courteous, helpful, but not markedly affectionate in his responses to his old chief." *Lee and Longstreet at Gettysburg,* 16.

252 Alexander to Goree, April 24, 1868, in Cutrer, *Longstreet's Aide,* 156.

253 Desjardin, *These Honored Dead,* 84.

254 Bachelder, *Descriptive Key,* 49; Ladd, *The Bachelder Papers,* 1: 9–10; Sauers, "John B. Bachelder," *Gettysburg Magazine* no. 3, 115–116; Desjardin, *These Honored Dead,* 84.

255 Bachelder, *Descriptive Key,* 50.

256 Bachelder, *Descriptive Key,* 31–33, 49–51; Bachelder to McLaws, Dec. 23, 1874, in McLaws Papers, UNC Wilson Library.

257 Bachelder, *Descriptive Key,* 51–52. Emphasis in original.

258 Ladd, *The Bachelder Papers,* 1: 9–10; Sauers, "John B. Bachelder," *Gettysburg Magazine* no. 3, 115–116; Bachelder, *Gettysburg Battlefield* map.

259 The first letter appearing in Bachelder's published papers is from George B. McClellan, former commander of the army (and the commander during the time Bachelder had accompanied it on the Virginia Peninsula) from October 1, 1863. The first letter pertaining to Gettysburg specifically addressed to Bachelder is from Third Corps commander Charles Graham, dated November 20, 1863. Ladd, *The Bachelder Papers,* 1: 42, 45.

260 Bachelder to McLaws, Feb. 2, 1865, in Ladd, *The Bachelder Papers,* 1: 184–185.

261 For information on the Battle of River's Bridge, see "These Honored Dead: The Battle of Rivers Bridge and Civil War Combat Casualties," https:// www.nps.gov/articles/these-honored-dead-the-battle-of-rivers-bridge-and-civil-war-combat-casualties-teaching-with-historic-places.htm#:~:-text=Rivers%20Bridge%20was%20one%20of%20the%20first%20 historic,open%20daily%20from%209%20a.m.%20to%206%20p.m.; McAden, *Battle of Rivers Bridge State Historic Site Preserves Civil War Battlefield,* https://discoversouthcarolina.com/articles/rivers-bridge-state-historic-site-preserves-civil-war-battlefield; "Battle of River's Bridge," in South Carolina Encyclopedia, https://www.scencyclopedia.org/sce/entries/rivers-bridge-battle-of/

262 Evander Law, for example, wrote Bachelder in March, 1876 that "I had a copy of *my* report of the battle…" (Emphasis added). Law to Bachelder, March 16, 1876, Ladd, *The Bachelder Papers,* 1: 451. Likewise, Kershaw told Bachelder a few days later that "I preserved…an original Ms. [manuscript] draft of *my* report of the operations of my brigade at Gettysburg."

(Emphasis added). Kershaw to Bachelder, March 20, 1876, Ladd, *The Bachelder Papers*, 1: 453.

Kershaw does give another possibility in a letter to John Bachelder in 1876. He acknowledges that "the desk of papers containing our division records was sent by Maj. Goggin to Lynchburg, Va. To his friends there for preservation a short time before the fall of Richmond." Kershaw to Bachelder, April 1, 1876, in Ladd, *The Bachelder Papers*, 1: 470. Kershaw implies the records were saved, but they may never have made it out of Richmond. Either way, McLaws never actually referenced making his own report.

263   McLaws to Bachelder, Feb. 2, 1865, in Ladd, *The Bachelder Papers*, 1:184–185. For comparison, Kershaw wrote Bachelder that he had lent out "an original [manuscript] draft of *my* report." (Emphasis added). Kershaw to Bachelder, March 20, 1876, in Ladd, *The Bachelder Papers*, 1: 453.

264   Bachelder to McLaws, Dec. 23, 1874. McLaws Papers, UNC Wilson Library. For Kershaw's limited correspondence, see Ladd, *The Bachelder Papers*, 1: 453–458, 462–463, and vol. 2, 900–902.

265   Curt Musselman, "In the Footsteps of the Topographical Engineers;" Sauers, "John B. Bachelder," 115–116; Bachelder, *Gettysburg Battlefield* map.

266   Bachelder to McLaws, Dec. 23, 1874. McLaws Papers, UNC Wilson Library.

267   Kemper to L. Stevenson, Nov. 12, 1865, in Ladd, *The Bachelder Papers*, 1: 224.

268   Pendleton to Editor-in-Chief of *Johnson's Universal Cyclopedia*, Dec. 21, 1875. Pendleton Papers, UNC Wilson Library.

269   Venable to Taylor, Aug. 21, 1869, in Papers of the Lee Family, Archives of the Robert E. Lee Memorial Foundation. Despite Venable's objections to Lee attending, he thought it prudent for one of his staff officers to attend "as his representative. You know well that you & and I know more of that field than the old man & could tell more to keep those Yankees straight."

270   Bachelder to McLaws, Dec. 23, 1874, McLaws Papers, UNC Wilson Library. In his letter, he asked for the names and addresses of Generals Evander Law, Henry Benning, George "Tige" Anderson, Joseph Kershaw, William Wofford and "as many others as possible."

271   Anderson to Bachelder, Ladd, *The Bachelder Papers*, 1: 449–450.

272   Law to Bachelder, March 16, 1876, Ladd, *The Bachelder Papers*, 1: 451.

273   Law to Bachelder, May 23, 1876, Ladd, *The Bachelder Papers*, 1: 491; Law to Bachelder, June 11, 1876, Ladd, *The Bachelder Papers*, 1: 493; Law to Bachelder, June 13, 1876, Ladd, *The Bachelder Papers*, 1: 494–499.

274   Kershaw to Bachelder, March 20, 1876, in Ladd, *The Bachelder Papers*, 1: 452–453.

275   Kershaw to McLaws, May 25, 1888, McLaws Papers, UNC Wilson Library.

276   Kershaw to Bachelder, Aug. 7, 1882, in Ladd, *The Bachelder Papers*, 2: 901.

277   Kershaw to Bachelder, March 20, 1876, Ladd, *The Bachelder Papers*, 1: 452.

278   Longstreet to Bachelder, April 10, 1876, *The Bachelder Papers*, 1: 475–476.

279   Ladd, *The Bachelder Papers*, 1: 476–502; Taylor to Bachelder, August 16, 1876, in Ladd, *The Bachelder Papers*, 1: 500–502.

280   In 1878, Kershaw wrote Bachelder that he would reach out to several "friends of influence" to try to persuade them to provide information, as he believed Bachelder's project was worthwhile. Ladd, *The Bachelder Papers*, 3. Two years earlier, Kershaw had declined a request to visit Gettysburg, but he did provide several additional leads. Kershaw to Bachelder, May 5, 1881, Ladd, *The Bachelder Papers*, 2: 753.

281   Gallagher, ed., *Fighting for the Confederacy*, xv.

282   Certification of John Leconte, July 13, 1868, in Edward Porter Alexander Papers, UNC Wilson Library; Golay, *To Gettysburg and Beyond*, 277–278. In 1885, McLaws wrote Longstreet that "I have been out of employment and out of business entirely and partly made out of means." Seeking to leave Georgia due to the political climate, "I ask your influence to get me something to do," Nov. 30, 1885, McLaws Papers, UNC Wilson Library. Bachelder had invited W.S. Shumate of the 2nd South Carolina in Kershaw's Brigade to a reunion on the battlefield in 1882. "I should like very much to attend the re-union on 7th prox.," Shumate replied, "and would do so, were it not that my financial condition is at present very much straightened, and I feel that I could not spare the money for the trip." Shumate to Bachelder, May 24, 1882, in Ladd, *The Bachelder Papers*,2: 880–881.

283   Jorgensen, "Edward Porter Alexander," *Gettysburg Magazine*, no. 17, 42–44; Gallagher, ed., *Fighting for the Confederacy*, 21, 115. Alexander thought the balloons offered great reconnaissance tools and also demoralized the opposing side, forcing them to try to stay out of sight of the

balloons and take "roundabout roads & night marches." Alexander, "Artillery Fighting at Gettysburg," *Battles & Leaders* 3:358, footnote. "I have never understood why the enemy abandoned the use of military balloons early in 1863.… Even if the observers never saw anything, they would have been worth all they cost for the annoyance and delays they caused us in trying to keep our movements out of their sight." Gallagher, ed., *Fighting for the Confederacy*, 21.

284   Abstract Report Questionnaire, in Alexander Papers, UNC Wilson Library.

285   Alexander to Goree, April 24, 1868, in Cutrer, *Longstreet's Aide*, 156. A perusal of Alexander's papers held at the University of North Carolina justifies his complaints, though he did manage to get quite a bit of information from commanders regarding the Seven Days Battles. The Seven Days were a shining example of Lee's prowess, in which the Yankee invaders were driven from the gates of Richmond in humiliating fashion back where they came from. Lee had ridden from his desk job to the front and almost instantly transformed defeat into astounding victory. There were plenty of missteps along the way, which historians can readily point to (Malvern Hill being a major one), but in retrospect, the story was grand and a shining light after the surrender.

286   Featherston to E.P. Alexander, Nov. 10, 1867, Alexander Papers, UNC Wilson Library.

287   For example, see Law to Bachelder, May 28, 1882, declining attendance due to financial difficulties (his crop had failed the year before), in Ladd, *The Bachelder Papers*, 2: 884–885. The fact that the reunion seemed to be that of the 140th Pennsylvania may have had something to do with it, as well.

288   Aiken to Kershaw, June 16, 1882, in *Charleston (SC) News and Courier*, June 21, 1882, in GNMP, V7-SC-7A.

289   For example, see *New Orleans Times-Democrat*, June 28, 1882. The paper wrote that "Col. Aiken is very desirous of stimulating an interest among Confederate officers who were engaged at Gettysburg in the record of the battle now being prepared at national expense by Mr. John B. Bachelder. Mr. Bachelder has complained that Southern commanders have left him almost in the dark as to the disposition of their troops."

290   Aiken to Kershaw, June 16, 1882, in *Charleston (SC) News and Courier*, June 21, 1882, in GNMP, V7-SC-7A.

291   Aiken to Kershaw, June 16, 1882, in *Charleston (SC) News and Courier*, June 21, 1882, in GNMP, V7-SC-7A.

292   Kershaw to Bachelder, Aug. 7, 1882 in Ladd, *The Bachelder Papers*, 2: 900–901; Kershaw to Bachelder, May 5, 1881, in Ladd, *The Bachelder Papers*, 2: 753.

293   Sauers, "John B. Bachelder," *Gettysburg Magazine*, no. 3, 119.

294   "Making War History,: Second Day of the Remarkable Reunion at Gettysburg," *The Philadelphia Times*, May 1, 1893.

295   "Again at Gettysburg: Confederate Generals Visit the Scene of the Historic Conflict," *The Philadelphia Times*, April 29, 1893.

296   "Again at Gettysburg: Confederate Generals Visit the Scene of the Historic Conflict," *The Philadelphia Times*, April 29, 1893.

297   On May 25th, 1893, Nicholson went to Philadelphia, then returned on May 29th with the Union League group. According to his diary, "the afternoon was spent in going over the First day's field." He then returned to the office at 6 p.m. and "at 7:30 P.M. General Alexander came and went over the Maps in the office having in view the location of his Battalion of Artillery upon the field. Remaining until 10 o'clock." GETT 41143 GNPC Office of the Commissioners, Commissioners' Correspondence, 1893–1921, May 29, 1894.

298   "A Visit to Gettysburg: Brooklynites, New Yorkers and Philadelphians Invited Guests of Mr. John Russell Young," *Brooklyn Daily Eagle*, May 31, 1894.

299   Murray, *On a Great Battlefield*, 11–13.

300   GETT 41143 GNPC Office of the Commissioners, Commissioners' Correspondence, 1893–1921; Murray, *On a Great Battlefield*, 13.

301   "Annual Report of the Gettysburg National Military Park Commission to the Secretary of War, 1898, in GNMP, *Annual Reports of the War Department*, 31–33.

302   Early, *Address to the Survivors' Association of the State of South Carolina*, 19–20; Early, *The Campaigns of Robert E. Lee*, 53.

303   O.R. 27.2: 308, 318–320, 350–351, 358, 366–367, 372. Regarding the timing of the attack, Lee simply reported that "the preparations for attack were not completed until the afternoon of the 2d." Contrast that with his description of the third day: "General Longstreet's dispositions were not completed as early as was expected." Pendleton noted the state of affairs at the end the second day in his report: "Thus stood affairs at nightfall, the 2d: On the [Confederate] left and in the center,

nothing gained; on the right, batteries and lines well advanced." O.R. 27.2: 351. According to Pendleton himself, the only Confederate successes on July 2nd were on Longstreet's front.

304   In a conversation with William Allan on April 15, 1868, Lee is recorded as saying "Stuart's failure to carry out his instructions *forced the battle of Gettysburg, & the imperfect, halting way in which his corps commanders* (especially Ewell) *fought the battle gave victory...finally to the foe."* Ewell's specific error was that he convinced Lee to leave him by Culp's Hill, rather than move south of the town. Allan, "Conversations with General Lee," in William Allan Papers, UNC Wilson Library. Gary Gallagher has published the conversations in a compilation of documents pertaining to Robert E. Lee. "Memoranda of Conversations with General Robert E. Lee," in Gallagher, *Lee the Soldier*, 14–15. Then again on February 19, 1870, Lee told Allan that "Stuart failed to give him information, and this deceived him into a general battle" and he "never could get a simultaneous attack on the enemy's position." Allan, *Memoranda of Conversations with General Robert E. Lee*, 17–18.

305   Many psychologists believe "that human cognition and narrative are tightly related," with some "arguing that experience and memory happen 'in the form of narrative.'" The narrative has a sequence of causally-related events which include particular "characters" in an organized fashion. Leon, "Architecture of Narrative Memory," *Biologically Inspired Cognitive Architectures*, 19–20. Thus, we end up with one-sided stereotypes of heroes and villains, liars and honest men, rather than real people who sometimes act as we hope, and sometimes do not.

     For an overview of narrative and memory, see Linde, "Memory in Narrative." Linde focuses on personal narratives of "milestone events." Notably, the narrative can change: "The particular narratives included in the life story change throughout the life course. Some stories about past events are no longer retold if they become contradictory to a person's current understanding of who they are. Other past events come to be seen as relevant and even predictive of the speaker's current situation." The constant retelling, as we see in the post-war narratives, runs into a familiar problem, though. "Does the teller remember experientially the events that are retold, or is it the previous tellings that are remembered?" For a more technical study, see Bower, Black, and Turner, "Scripts in Memory," in *Cognitive Psychology*, 177–220.

William Bernstein has an informative analysis in *The Delusion of Crowds*, ultimately pointing out that the narrative speaks to the portion of the brain relying on instinct, or immediate emotion, rather than the rational part of the brain, which analyzes hard facts and data. A good story always trumps rational analysis. Bernstein, *The Delusion of Crowds*, 28–37.

306   In his article for *Century* that became part of the *Battles & Leaders* collection, Law stated that he had not written a report. "Owing to the active and constant movements of our army for some weeks after the battle, I was only able to obtain the reports of brigade commanders a very short time previous to being ordered to the army of General Bragg at Chickamauga. This prevented me from making a report at the time, and it was afterward neglected." Law, "The Struggle for 'Round Top,'" in *Battles & Leaders* 3:319. However, in a letter to Bachelder, he claimed he had given his report to a historian and hadn't received it back. Law to Bachelder, March 16, 1876, in Ladd, *The Bachelder Papers*, 1: 451.

307   The Third South Carolina's Colonel, James Nance, filed a supplemental report in August 1863, but relied on Maffett's report for the battle. O.R. 27.2: 373.

308   Longstreet's report is dated July 27, 1863, O.R. 27.2: 357. Kershaw's report was dated October 1, 1863, O.R. 27.1: 366. Major Robert Maffett, Third South Carolina Infantry, Kershaw's Brigade, submitted his report July 31, 1863, while the only other surviving report from McLaws' infantry is dated August 1, 1863. O.R. 27.1: 371, 373. Hood, of course, was horribly wounded on July 2. He did, however, explain his failure to submit a report in a letter to Longstreet in 1875. "Hood to Jones," in *SHSP* vol. 4, 145–146. McLaws does not mention ever writing one (most commanders, when asked for a report they no longer had in their possession, would say that they cannot find the copy—McLaws never references a lost report, strongly suggesting he didn't write one).

PART TWO 1863

309   O.R. 27.2: 308.

310   Long, *Memoirs of Robert E. Lee*, 275.

311   Coddington, *Gettysburg: A Study in Command*, 166; Hoke, *The Great Invasion*, 170–171, 171 fn. Hoke includes a transcript of a letter from

Jubal Early to Professor J. Fraise Richard in which Early defends and explains the burning of the works. "They were burned by my order," Early acknowledged. "My reasons for giving the order were founded on the fact that the Federal troops had invariably burned such works in the South, wherever they had penetrated," including John Bell (one of the southern candidates who lost in the election of 1860). "Moreover, in some speeches in congress, Mr. Stevens had exhibited a most vindictive spirit toward the people of the South, as he continued to do to the day of his death." Burning his iron furnace, which employed around 200 workers, "was simply in retaliation for various deeds of barbarity perpetrated by Federal troops in some of the Southern States." Early would also consider the burning of Chambersburg the following year similarly justified. Early to J. Fraise Richard, May 7, 1886, in Hoke, *The Great Invasion*, 171 fn. The remains of the furnace can be visited at Caledonia State Park today.

312   O.R. 27.2: 348. While no one depicts the precise gait Lee rode with, Pendleton reported that the "commanding general, finding the cannonade to continue and increase, moved rapidly forward." Pendleton's account is taken from his report, submitted September 12, 1863. His postwar writings, as we saw, are quite colored by politics and poor memory, but he was one of the few to leave a detailed contemporary account pertinent to this study.

313   O.R. 27.2: 348. In his diary, Pendleton's aide George Peterkin noted they "Got up to the fight about 12 m[eridiem]," or noon. Peterkin to Pendleton, Dec. 6, 1875, Pendleton Papers, UNC Wilson Library. Jedediah Hotchkiss, Ewell's engineer officer, wrote in his diary: "12.30 [pm] Hill artillery brisk on the right." Hotchkiss Papers, LOC. Pendleton described Ewell's guns on Oak Ridge converging with the fire from McIntosh and Pegram, which describes the predicament in which Union General Roy Stone's men found themselves. Stone reported that "the enemy opened fire on us from two batteries on the opposite ridge [Herr's Ridge]." Then, "between 12 and 1 o'clock...a new battery upon a hill on the extreme right [Oak Hill] opened a most destructive enfilade of our line." A half hour later, "the grand advance of the enemy's infantry began." O.R. 27.1: 329–330. Stone was subject to the same limitations of time that Pendleton was, but he gives a range of noon to one o'clock. Since Pendleton is equally unspecific—"perhaps" two o'clock—it seems reasonable to conclude that the batteries on Oak Hill rolled up a little before one o'clock. For our purposes, the exact time is not particularly important.

314   Fremantle, *Three Months in the Southern States*, 254.

315   O.R. 27.2: 348; Maurice, ed., *Lee's Aide-de-Camp*, 227–228.

316   O.R. 27.2: 348. Pendleton wrote that after "arriving near the crest of an eminence more than a mile west of the town," they dismounted and left the horses "under cover." McIntosh's and Pegram's Confederate artillery battalions were positioned on either side of the road by the tavern. To be on an eminence behind the guns meant that they had to be on the western part of Herr's Ridge, which does offer a view of the field in front of the artillery. There is a swale of approximately 400 yards between the two crests, much of which would have been filled with artillery horses and caisson. The western crest of Herr's Ridge is just under a mile and a half west of the outskirts of town. Despite the oversimplification of terminology, the standard names are used throughout.

317   For a readable and engaging overview of the fighting on July 1, see Pfanz, *Gettysburg: The First Day*.

318   Black Horse Tavern, GNMP Vertical Files, Va-21.

319   O.R. 27:2: 349. Though Pendleton may not have realized it, Johnson was not the only battery there. He was joined by Capt. W.B. Hurt's battery. Hurt had two rifled guns (the other two being Whitworths, used elsewhere on the field at this time). With Hurt only having the two guns, Pendleton probably didn't realize there were guns from two batteries there.

      Johnson and Hurt had originally been posted much closer to Bream's Hill, on the Adam Butt farm, but had been moved up to support the attack if possible. McIntosh reported that two unnamed batteries had been "advanced…to the intervening hollow, and followed close upon the enemy as he left the hills." O.R. 27.2: 675. This was probably Johnson and Hurt, as Pendleton reported Johnson had "been sent for from McIntosh's battalion." O.R. 27.2: 349. Philip Laino has a good explanation of the various interpretations in his *Gettysburg Campaign Atlas*, 158, n. 45.

      As to Peterkin's presence, he notes in his diary that he "went first to the centre + then to the right." Peterkin to Pendleton, Dec. 6, 1875, in Pendleton Papers, UNC Wilson Library. Sam Johnston always insisted he accompanied Pendleton and Long (both of whom conducted recons on the right flank of the Confederate army on July 1st). In 1878, Johnston wrote to Fitz Lee that Pendleton's claimed July 2nd reconnaissance was "doubtless the reconnaissance made the evening of the 1st by Genls. Pendleton + Long and myself," which was "made with a view to selecting a position for Genl. Pendleton's artillery to cover Gen. Hill's right against a flank movement. It did not extend further than three quarters of a mile from the Chambersburg" Pike. Johnston to F. Lee, Feb. 16, 1878, in S.R. Johnston Papers, VHS. Then in 1895, he wrote Peterkin directly, telling him that "I was with General A.P. Hill during General Ewell's attack on the enemy's right on the evening of the first day when General Lee rode up. After seeing that General Ewell had driven the enemy back, General Pendleton, General Long, Colonel Walker and myself made a reconnaissance on our right. I supposed that this reconnaissance was to be ready for a flank movement on the part of the enemy." Johnston to Peterkin, Dec. 1895, in S.R. Johnston Papers, VHS.

320   O.R. 27.2: 349. Bachelder's afternoon map series for July 1 shows Johnson's battery near the Adam Butt farm throughout the afternoon. Likewise, the map shows the Eighth Illinois with skirmishers from Willoughby Run to Bream's Hill along the Fairfield Road around 3:30 p.m., when Pendleton was reconnoitering. Bachelder's map shows the Seventh North Carolina facing off against them. Brig. Gen. Lane reported he "ordered the Seventh Regiment to deploy as a strong line of skirmishers some distance to my right...to protect our flank, which was exposed to the enemy's cavalry." O.R. 27.2: 665. Buford reported that once the First Corps arrived and his troopers were able to pull back, he ordered Gamble's men to the left of the line. O.R. 27.1: 927.

321   O.R. 27.2: 348–349.

322   O.R. 27.2: 469. Rodes experienced the same problem in his division: "In the pursuit, the division captured about 2,500 prisoners – so many as to embarrass its movements materially." O.R. 27.2: 555. The word embarrass in 1860's parlance meant "to perplex; to render intricate; to entangle." Webster, *American Dictionary*, 388.

323   Sickles and Berman, 1974 NRHP Nomination Form for Adams County Courthouse; Buehler, *Recollections of the Rebel Invasion*, 5, in ACHS. James Power Smith described the scene in town in a 1905 paper read before a northern veterans' society. "The square was filled with Confederate soldiers," Smith recalled. "With them were mingled many [Federal] prisoners." Smith, *General Lee at Gettysburg*, 12.

324   Campbell Brown, General Ewell's son-in-law and staff officer, remembered troops from both Early's and Rodes's divisions "mingling in their advance" into the town. Jones,ed., *Campbell Brown's Civil War*, 211.

     Early remembered sharpshooters in the southern end of town (or around Cemetery Hill), as well: "[Ewell] then asked me to ride with him up the street towards [Cemetery] hill to reconnoitre; but, as we were proceeding that way, we were stopped by a fire from the enemy's sharpshooters in that end of the town." Early, "A Review by General Early," in *SHSP*, vol. 4, 256.

     Tillie Pierce, a young girl living on Baltimore Street during the battle who later wrote a famous account of her experiences, recalled the house across the street being hit by an artillery shell as a small girl looked through the window. The girl survived unharmed but stayed away from the window. Alleman, *At Gettysburg*, 96–97. Another civilian, Nellie Aughinbaugh, recalled the sharpshooter activity on the first day, as well: "Sharp shooters were stationed all through the town to do their deadly work." She describes a Union soldier standing in the doorway talking with them when a bullet snaps a button off his coat. Though the example she gives seems embellished, the fundamental story is likely true. On the first day, it is unlikely a Federal soldier was simply talking with the family during the confusion. If it was after the first day, a Confederate sharpshooter was likely not firing behind Confederate lines. Aughinbaugh, *Personal Experiences of a Young Girl During the Battle of Gettysburg*, 10, 96–97.

325   O.R. 27.2: 469.

326   Taylor, "Second Paper by Walter H. Taylor, of General Lee's Staff," in *SHSP,* vol. 4, 127. The wording of the order is the source of one of Gettysburg's most heated controversies. Major Charles Marshall, the staff officer who penned Lee's report, wrote that "Ewell was…instructed to carry the hill occupied by the enemy, if he found it practicable, but to avoid a general engagement until the arrival of the other divisions of the army." O.R. 27.2: 318. Though as we see here, the officer who delivered the order used the word "possible." Ewell did not take the hill (it probably was neither possible nor practicable, given the state of the Confederate troops and the defenses the Federals had quickly established on the hill).

327   O.R. 27.2: 349. The War Department's *Instruction for Field Artillery*, printed in 1863, called for fourteen yards between each gun, meaning Garnett's fifteen guns needed approximately a 240-yard front (accounting for the two-yard width of the cannon carriage). An artillery piece also needed nearly fifty yards of depth, as well, for horses, limber, and caisson. U.S. War Department, *Instruction for Field Artillery*, 185; Teague, *Gettysburg By The Numbers*, 50. Field conditions often dictated variations in the distances, but regardless, Pendleton needed to find a large area suitable for artillery.

328   O.R. 27.2: 349; O.R. 27.2: 652. Garnett reported that he was posted "in the rear of the line of battle nearly opposite Cemetery Hill, where they remained in park until the following morning, protected from the enemy's fire by a high hill." As with many Confederate positions on the night of July 1 and morning of July 2, there is conjecture about exactly where Garnett was positioned. James A. Woods, in his *Gettysburg July 2: The Ebb and Flow of Battle*, places Garnett closer to the Chambersburg Pike. He notes the imprecise nature of placing the battery, but ultimately relies on Bachelder's map. Woods, *Ebb and Flow of Battle*, 2, 5, 14–15. Garnett's report, read in conjunction with Pendleton's, suggests the placement was closer to the Fairfield Road.

329   O.R. 27.2: 349. After his meeting with Ramseur, Pendleton reported the following: "Having further examined this ridge, and communicated with Colonel Walker, chief of artillery Third Corps, I returned across the battlefield, and sent to inform the commanding general of the state of facts, especially of the road to the right, believed to be important toward a flank movement against the enemy in his new position." George Peterkin corroborates this in a postwar publication of his purported diary. Peterkin noted that after arriving on the field he "went first to the center and then to the right. Saw Gen'l Ramseur." Strider, ed., *Life and Work of Peterkin*, 62. Peterkin's letter to Pendleton in 1875 corroborates the printed version of the diary on this point. Peterkin to Pendleton, Dec. 6, 1875, UNC Wilson Library. The diary entries are copied into a letter and again repeated (slightly differently) elsewhere. The location of the original diary is not known.

        Pendleton wrote that after he talked with Walker he "returned across the battlefield," meaning he was traveling (a) to somewhere he had left earlier and (b) he traveled over the day's battlefield. That means he almost certainly went back to Herr's Ridge. Peterkin remembered he "camped in an orchard about 2 ½ miles from G[et-tysburg], which is most likely the Spangler residence on the Chambersburg Pike. Peterkin to Pendleton, Dec. 6, 1875, in Pendleton Papers, UNC Wilson Library.

The McMillan farm is where the Second Corps artillery extended to the next morning, placed overnight by Pendleton, his staff and probably Walker. Pendleton may have gone a little further than McMillan's farm, but not much. As he stated in his report of the afternoon's reconnaissance, he didn't travel far beyond the lines, if he went past them at all. Page, *Reminiscences*Shields Collection, W&L Leyburn Library. A more accessible version is found in Elmore, "Revelations of a Confederate Artillery Staff Officer" *Gettysburg Magazine* No. 54, 73.

330   James Power Smith to Major Brown, undated copy in Jubal Early Papers, LOC; O.R. 27.2: 445.

331   James Power Smith to Major Brown, undated copy in Jubal Early Papers, LOC. Arthur Fremantle noted this request, as well. He wrote in 1864 that he and Longstreet rode up to Lee, who was talking with A.P. Hill, most likely on Seminary Ridge (Fremantle placed the conversation around 4:30 p.m. and noted the Federals had already retreated to Cemetery Hill). "Whilst we were talking, a message arrived from General Ewell, requesting Hill to press the enemy in the front, whilst he performed the same operation on his right." Fremantle, *Three Months in the Southern States,* 254–255. If Smith is right, this is Cemetery Ridge. It's also very possible Smith has combined several memories, both his own and picked up from others, unconsciously conflating the occupations of Cemetery Ridge on July 1 with the occupation of Little Round Top on July 2. In hindsight, which is where Smith is operating, Little Round Top is, indeed, an eminence on the Confederate right—but not as it was constituted in the late afternoon of July 1.

332   James Power Smith to Major Brown, undated copy in Jubal Early Papers, LOC; Long to Early, April 5, 1876, in *SHSP*, vol. 4, 66–67.

333   James Power Smith to Major Brown, undated copy in Jubal Early Papers, LOC. In a speech forty-two years after the battle, Smith said "the elevated position in front" of him was the hill Early and Ewell had seen. Smith, "General Lee at Gettysburg," 13. The paper is published in a more accessible volume of speeches compiled by Ken Bandy and Florence Freeland.

See Smith, "General Lee at Gettysburg," in Bandy and Freeland, *The Gettysburg Papers* 2:1047.

Campbell Brown, of Ewell's staff, supports Smith's version. Brown makes it clear that Lee was noncommittal and left the decision to attack on that front entirely with Ewell, without promise of support. Ewell had ordered Early to investigate "Extra Billy" Smith's report of infantry and cavalry, while telling Rodes to "get into position & communicate with Hill." In the meantime, "a Staff Officer sent to him (I forget whom, but have an idea it was [Alexander "Sandie"] Pendleton or Jas. Smith,) brought word that Hill had not advanced & that Gen'l Lee who was with him, left it to Gen'l Ewell's discretion whether to advance alone or not." Jones, ed., *Campbell Brown's Civil War*, 211. Fremantle supports this, too. "The pressure was accordingly applied in a mild degree, but the enemy were too strongly posted, and it was too late in the evening for a regular attack." Fremantle, *Three Months in the Southern States*, 255.

In his 1905 speech, Smith noted that "some of 'those people' were there" on the eminence. According to this version, "a few mounted men, apparently reconnoitering," were seen on the rise of ground, though it was probably Robinson's First Corps division, which had been positioned near the Abraham Brien farm and Ziegler's Grove. In his report, Robinson stated that "after withdrawing from this contest [the fight west of town], I took up a position on a ridge to the left of the cemetery, facing the Emmitsburg road, and remained there until...relieved by a division of the Second Corps" the next day. Smith, "General Lee at Gettysburg," 13; O.R. 27.1: 290. Bachelder's map of the evening of July 1 placed Robinson's troops at the Angle. See also Laino, *Gettysburg Campaign Atlas*, Map 1-71, 155. Armistead Long, on the other hand, remembered "the ridge was occupied in considerable force." Long, *Memoirs of Robert E. Lee*, 277. The difference in Long's and Smith's versions might be accounted for by the times they viewed the ridge, skewed by the length of time between writing down their thoughts.

It's tempting to think Lee, Early, and Ewell were referring to the Peach Orchard, but this is unlikely. From their positions, Rodes and Early would not have been able to tell the Peach Orchard "commanded" Cemetery Hill. The orchard was also unoccupied during the time Smith is describing. The first Federals to report there were of Graham's Third Corps brigade, who reported arriving around 7 p.m. O.R. 27.1: 502. The rest of the corps reported arriving after dark. O.R. 27.1: 493; O.R. 27.1: 513. (Though Birney reported the corps' arrival at 5:30, no one else did. Birney was temporarily in charge of the Third Corps and a supporter of Sickles; Meade had been unimpressed with the Third Corps' marching prowess during the campaign and made a point of letting Sickles know, so Birney had reason to note the earliest possible time and that the corps marched "with enthusiasm and alacrity" over the "almost impassible" roads.) O.R. 27.1: 482. Buford's men were sent to the "extreme left" after the Federals fell back to Cemetery Hill, but there's no evidence Lee had examined the Peach Orchard ground quite yet.

Other possibilities are that Smith is referring to the Round Tops, falling into the postwar emphasis on the hills that simply didn't exist on July 1, or that Smith is just incorrect in his memory and Lee didn't actually make such a statement. Given the knowledge available to the Confederate command that afternoon and evening, and looking at their focus, i.e. Cemetery Ridge and Culp's Hill, and their own positions that evening (McMillan's Orchard, etc.), it's more likely that the "commanding" ground Smith spoke of was Cemetery Ridge and/or Emmitsburg Road Ridge, as these ridges (1) provided command of Cemetery Hill via enfilade capabilities and (2) were actually occupied by Federal troops by the end of the evening.

Regarding Confederate supports for an evening attack, there was a fresh division on Knoxlyn Ridge under General Richard H. Anderson, but that was over two miles from the center of town. By the time they could be ready for an attack, it would be too late. "Upon approaching Gettysburg," Anderson wrote, "I was directed to occupy the position in line of battle which had just been vacated by Pender's division.... We continued in this position until the morning of the 2d, then I received orders to take up a new line of battle on the right of Pender's division, about a mile and a half farther forward." O.R. 27.2: 613.

334   Jones, ed., *Campbell Brown's Civil War*, 211–212. Ewell notes in his report that "I could not bring artillery to bear" on Cemetery Hill and "all the troops with me were jaded by twelve hours' marching and fighting." O.R. 27.2: 445. Hancock noted that by about 5:30, the Federals "have now taken up a position in the cemetery, and cannot well be taken. It is a position, however, easily turned." O.R. 27.1: 366. The Confederates saw this, as well, which is precisely why they wanted Hill's assistance that evening, why they spent so much time focusing on the "commanding" eminence, and as we will see, why Lee wanted to pull Ewell's Corps to the Confederate right.

    The version here is taken primarily from Ewell's staff, who had a vested interest in protecting Ewell's reputation. In the postwar years, Ewell took his share of blame for not taking Cemetery Hill on July 1. Some of the details are probably skewed into representing Ewell in a more favorable light. But the basic elements do align with contemporary accounts, such as Lee's report. For example, Lee wrote "without information as to [the rest of the Federal army's] proximity, the strong position which the enemy had assumed could not be attacked without danger of exposing the four divisions present, already weakened and exhausted by a long and bloody struggle, to overwhelming numbers of fresh troops. General Ewell was, therefore, instructed to carry the hill occupied by the enemy, if he found it practicable, but to avoid a general engagement until the arrival of the other divisions of the army, which were ordered to hasten forward." O.R. 27.2: 317–318. Lee had no fresh troops, didn't know the position of the Federal reinforcements, and gave Ewell discretion whether to attack or not. This is, in essence, the same story J.P. Smith and Campbell Brown told. Rodes also mentions the meeting in town in his official report. O.R. 27.2: 555.

335   Jones, ed., *Campbell Brown's Civil War*, 211.

336   O.R. 27.2: 469. In calculating the force that was sent up the York Road, Smith was not engaged and brought approximately 800 men to the field. Gordon reported bringing 1,200 men into battle (one regiment was detached) and he suffered approximately 350 casualties. Due to inaccurate reporting, straggling, etc., the numbers can be rounded to roughly

800 for Gordon's brigade. The combined force is therefore approximately 1,600 men.

337   O.R. 27.2: 349.

338   Long to Early, April 5, 1876, in *SHSP* vol. 4, 66–67. Long continued by saying "after making my report no mention was made of a renewal of the attack that evening."

339   Ewell reported that he "received orders soon after dark to draw my corps to the right, in case it could not be used to advantage where it was; that the commanding general thought from the nature of the ground that the position was a good one on that [the south] side." O.R. 27.2: 446. Marshall to Early, March 13, 1878, Early Papers, LOC.

340   Charles Marshall to Jubal Early, March 23, 1870, in Early Papers, LOC; Gilmor, *Four Years in the Saddle*, 98. The inference that Turner was present is taken from his later account of the conversation. Turner, *Gettysburg*, Early Papers, LOC. Ewell uses the same language—"used to advantage"— in his report. O.R. 27.2: 446.

341   Marshall to Early, March 23, 1870, Early Papers, LOC; Turner, *Gettysburg*, Early Papers, LOC. Early always maintained that he insisted on pressing the attack on July 1. In his report, submitted August 22, 1863, he wrote that "meeting with an officer of Major-General Pender's staff, I sent word by him to General Hill that if he would send up a division, we could take the hill to which the enemy had retreated; and shortly after meeting with General Ewell, I communicated my views to him . . ." O.R. 27.2: 469. In an 1876 article for the *Southern Historical Society Papers*, Early remembered he was "exceedingly anxious for the advance against the heights, and would have made it with my own division, immediately after the enemy was driven through the town, if Smith had come to me with his brigade when sent for, as soon as Gordon's ammunition was replenished." After learning all of the facts, though (mostly after the war), Early changed his mind. "I must confess that, though my opinion at the time was different, subsequent developments have satisfied me that [Ewell's] decision was right. Johnson did not arrive in time to make the assault with a prospect of success…There is, then, no good reason for imputing to Ewell an intentional disregard of the wishes or instructions of General Lee. Early, "A Review by General Early," in *SHSP* vol. 4, 257. Early, like so many writers after the war, also had a vested interest in convincing readers that the Second Corps was not at fault for not taking Cemetery Hill. But, given the fact that Early always maintained he *did* wish to attack, his own

personal reputation was relatively safe in that regard, meaning his change of heart is probably more sincere than otherwise. Early's statement that it would cost 10,000 lives to get up the hill in the morning can be found in Lt. Turner's account of the meeting. Turner, *Gettysburg*, Early Papers, LOC. Jubal Early's nephew, John Cabell Early, left an account of the meeting, as well, but it wasn't published until 1911 and its contents offer quite a few inaccuracies, such as a conversation about taking the Round Tops that night. Early, "A Southern Boy's Experience at Gettysburg."

Though some postwar accounts refer to a meeting between various officers of the Second Corps and Lee, there's little contemporary evidence that this occurred. Most information places Lee on Herr's and Seminary Ridges, with Second Corps officers riding to the west side of town to meet with Lee, not vice versa.

342   O.R. 27.2: 446. Ewell reported that "I represented to the commanding general that the hill above referred to was unoccupied by the enemy, as reported by Lieutenants Turner and Early, who had gone upon it, and that it commanded their position and made it untenable, so far as I could judge."

343   O.R. 27.2: 445–446. In his report, Ewell said that his orders to "draw my corps to the right" were received just after dark, which jibed with Marshall's account.

344   McLaws, "Gettysburg," in *SHSP*, vol. 7, 67; O.R. 27.1: 358.

345   E.P. Alexander later recalled marching "over a fairly good pike by a bright moon" that night. Gallagher, ed., *Fighting for the Confederacy*, 235.

346   Fremantle, *Three Months in the Southern States*, 254. Fremantle placed the time at 4:30 that afternoon. In his first article on the battle, Longstreet thought it was 5 p.m. Longstreet, "Lee in Pennsylvania," in *Annals of the War*, 420.

347   In his article for *Century* in the 1880s, Longstreet noted that Lee was on Seminary Ridge. Longstreet, "Lee in Pennsylvania," in *Annals of the War*, 420–421. Confederate confusion as to ridge names west of town on July 1 was a common occurrence, though. For example, Charles Marshall recalled Lee's headquarters on Seminary Ridge at 2 p.m. on July 1, which was simply not possible since the Federal line stood atop it. Maurice, ed., *Lee's Aide-De-Camp*, 227–228, 233. McLaws, remember, also had a hard time distinguishing the names of the ridges west of town. McLaws to Longstreet, June 10, 1873 (draft), UNC Wilson Library. Longstreet also noted that the troops were retreating up *one* of the opposite ridges,

a subtle indication that there was another ridge between them and the Federals. Likewise, with the Federal retreat from Seminary Ridge having just begun in earnest, it was unlikely Lee had moved up that far at that time.

348   Longstreet, "Lee in Pennsylvania," in *Annals of the War*, 421.

349   In his 1873 letter to McLaws, he calls the offensive strategy with defensive tactics the "ruling idea of our campaign." Longstreet to McLaws, July 25, 1873, in McLaws Papers, UNC Wilson Library. Longstreet held fast to this position throughout his life. Longstreet, "Lee's Invasion of Pennsylvania," in *Battles & Leaders* 3:246–247; Longstreet, *From Manassas to Appomattox*, 358.

350   Longstreet, "Lee in Pennsylvania," in *Annals of the War*, 416–417.

351   Swinton, *Campaigns of the Army of the Potomac*, 340. These are Swinton's words, but Swinton noted his impressions all came directly from Longstreet. In *Annals of the War*, Longstreet wrote that he had gotten "a taste of victory." Longstreet, "Lee in Pennsylvania," in *Annals of the War*, 421.

352   Longstreet, "Lee's Right Wing at Gettysburg," in *Battles & Leaders* 3: 340. In his memoirs, Longstreet took this quite a bit further, perhaps evidence of the bitterness of the last twenty years locked in verbal combat. "That [Lee] was excited and off his balance was evident on the afternoon of the 1st, and he labored under that oppression until enough blood was shed to appease him." Longstreet, *From Manassas to Appomattox*, 384.

353   Though the order was initially given that morning, Rodes's report suggests there may have been some confusion as to whether the order was meant to be a standing one or its time had passed. Rodes said the afternoon attack had already begun when he received the order not to bring on a general engagement. By that time it was too late to obey it. After the Federal retreat, Rodes concluded that he couldn't attack Cemetery Hill without bringing on another general engagement; he says he decided to follow what he considered a standing order not to bring on another general engagement. O.R. 27.2: 555. Whether the report is an accurate reflection of his thoughts or simply a self-serving explanation of why he didn't press the attack, it's a plausible explanation and supported by Lee's report.

354   Longstreet, "Lee in Pennsylvania," in *Annals of the War*, 421.

355   Lawley, *The Times* (London), Aug. 18, 1863. Emphasis added.

356   Fremantle, *Three Months in the Southern States*, 256.

357   Ross, *A Visit to the Cities and Camp Camps of the Confederate States, 1863-64*, 49.

358 Lawley, *The Times* (London), Aug. 18, 1863.

359 Maurice, ed., *Lee's Aide-de-Camp*, 232. In a letter to Jubal Early in 1878, Marshall connects Lee's statements about inability to forage to Lawley's statement about lack of cavalry: "Genl Lee in his report, in assigning reasons for attacking the enemy at Gettysburg, mentions the very apparent one, that the enemy's superiority in cavalry rendered it impossible for him to support his army by foraging in a hostile country in the presence of such a force and also to withdraw from that proximity with our trains in safety." This would prevent Longstreet's plan of moving to the right, "because if we could not forage, the enemy need not have troubled himself to drive us from the strongest position that ingenious Longstreet could have selected." Marshall to Early, March 13, 1878, Early Papers, LOC.

360 Armistead Long, for example, wrote in his memoir of the war that "Longstreet gave it as his opinion that the best plan would be to turn Meade's left flank and force him back to the neighborhood of Pipeclay Creek. To this General Lee objected, and pronounced it impracticable under the circumstances." Long, *Memoirs of Robert E. Lee*, 277. Lawley, on the other hand, gives the impression that Lee and Longstreet were both of the mindset, after examination of the ground, that moving to the right was impractical. This is important, given Lawley's postwar correspondence with Early.

361 Lawley, *The Times* (London), Aug. 18, 1863.

362 Lawley couldn't help but notice the "undue contempt" the Confederates had for their opponents in the clamoring for action the next day. Fremantle remembered the disdain for the northern army, too. Though Longstreet was concerned about the Federal position, his staff "spoke of the battle [on July 2] as a certainty, and the universal feeling in the army was one of profound contempt for an enemy whom they have beaten so constantly, and under so many disadvantages." Lawley, *The Times* (London), Aug. 18, 1863; Fremantle, *Three Years in the Southern States*, 256.

  Likewise, Lee reported that although a battle may have been "unavoidable," the "success already gained gave hope of a favorable issue." O.R. 27.2: 318. Read in conjunction with Lawley's contemporary article, this can be construed as Lee's diplomatically oblique way of saying the same thing.

363 Lawley, *The Times* (London), Aug. 18, 1863.

364 Lawley, *The Times* (London), Aug. 18, 1863; O.R. 27.2:318.

365   Lawley, *The Times* (London), Aug. 18, 1863.

366   O.R. 27.2: 318.

367   Pendleton's report indicated he inspected the lines in the vicinity of Seminary Ridge and by Ramseur's evening position. Given the ultimate placement of the guns, it's likely his reconnaissance brought him there (not to mention the fact that the area is the highest point opposite Cemetery Hill). O.R. 27.2: 349. Long performed a reconnaissance of the Federal position "on Cemetery Ridge." Long, *Memoirs of Robert E. Lee*, 277. The placement of the troops, especially artillery, which both Long and Pendleton were tasked with, strongly suggests McMillan's farm was a well-visited area on the evening of July 1. Likewise, J.P. Smith's description indicates Lee and Longstreet also spent time observing the Federal line, and especially the approach from the south, from the farm.

368   In his memoirs, Long wrote that he had a conversation with Lee on the evening of July 1. Lee asked Long's opinion as to whether they should attack without Stuart or wait for him. According to Long, he told Lee it was "best not to wait for Stuart. It is uncertain where he is or when he will arrive. At present only two or three corps of the enemy's army are up, and it seems best to attack them before they can be greatly strengthened by reinforcements." Long, *Memoirs of Robert E. Lee*, 278. Lee explained the desire to attack quickly due to the lack of ability to forage and the presence of the Federal cavalry (and presumably the lack of his own ability to counter anti-foraging efforts). O.R. 27.2: 318.

369   While Longstreet's accounts in the 1870s and 1880s are not spun from whole cloth, they do take significant artistic license. *Both* Lee and Longstreet seriously considered a strategic movement south. Both were also opposed to a direct assault on Cemetery Hill. Though Lee eventually resigned himself to attack, it was only after careful deliberation of the ground and his available options.

370   McLaws, "Gettysburg," in *SHSP*, vol. 7, 67–68. McLaws wrote in his 1878 speech that he met Longstreet at 10 p.m. a few miles west of Marsh Creek, reaching the creek at about midnight. This is supported by Kershaw's report. O.R. 27.2: 366. But Hood's men also said they reached the creek at midnight and they were behind McLaws; they obviously both could not have arrived at the same time. O.R. 27.2: 420. Col William Shepherd, Second Georgia, in Benning's Brigade of Hood's Division, reported his regiment "arrived at 12 p.m. [sic] in the neighborhood of the scene of an engagement took place on the 1st instant, where it was permitted to

bivouac for a few hours." Col. Wesley Hodges of the 18th Georgia remembered the same. O.R. 27.2: 424.

That McLaws met Longstreet at or very near Marsh Creek is also supported by other contemporary accounts. Fremantle, for example, remembered Longstreet leaving the battlefield at dark, or after 8 p.m. Cashtown was eight miles away, which was about a two-hour horseback ride at the normal gait of four mph. The most probable scenario is that Longstreet left Gettysburg between 8 and 9 p.m., after it was fully dark and the firing had stopped, as Fremantle indicated. That would place him a little west of Marsh Creek when he met McLaws about 10 p.m., roughly halfway to Cashtown. With orders to rest at Marsh Creek, McLaws would have arrived around 10–10:30 and settled in by 10:30–11. This timeline allows Hood to reach the vicinity of the creek and be fully settled in by around midnight. Fremantle, *Three Months in the Southern States*, 255. Likewise, Longstreet's report states that "McLaws' division...reached Marsh Creek, 4 miles from Gettysburg, a little after dark, and Hood's division got within nearly the same distance of the town about 12 o'clock that night." A little after dark cannot reasonably be interpreted to mean "midnight." And if Longstreet left the field between 8 and 9 p.m., he would have met with McLaws, just west of Marsh Creek, a little over an hour later, or 9–10 p.m. O.R. 27.2: 358.

Kershaw reported his brigade's orders were to be on the road at 4 a.m. that morning. O.R. 27.2: 366. The First Corps medical director remembered the order to march at "daybreak." J.S.D. Cullen to Longstreet, May 18, 1875, quoted in Longstreet, *From Manassas to Appomattox*, 383–384.

371   Marshall to Early, March 23, 1870, Early Papers, LOC; Marshall to Early, March 13, 1878, Early Papers, LOC. Campbell Brown confirms Ewell went to see Lee, but states Marshall returned with another dispatch while Ewell was gone. Jones, ed., *Campbell Brown's Civil War*, 214. Given the discrepancy in accounts, it seems more reasonable to assume Marshall is correct, since he personally rode with Ewell back to army headquarters. Marshall's and Brown's accounts were written only a few months apart.

372   O.R. 27.2: 446; Marshall to Early, March 23, 1870, Early Papers, LOC; Marshall to Early, March 13, 1878, Early Papers, LOC; Campbell Brown

notes, July 2 + 3, 1878, in Polk, Brown, Ewell Papers, UNC Wilson Library.

373 O.R. 27.2: 446; Jones, ed., *Campbell Brown's Civil War*, 214. Ewell's report supports this, though it is an oblique reference. Ewell reported the order delaying the attack, which orders came at daylight. O.R. 27.2: 446.

374 O.R. 27.2: 446.

375 Sorrel, *Recollections of a Staff Officer*, 167–168. In his memoirs, Longstreet recalled that he left the battlefield around 7 p.m. and that Lee had already decided to let Ewell take the position on Culp's Hill. Longstreet also gets the troop placements on July 1 a bit wrong (such as placing Anderson on Seminary Ridge that evening). But if Longstreet left the field at 7, then Fremantle is wrong (it wouldn't have been dark, much less *after* dark) and Marshall, Ewell, and Campbell Brown are wrong about the time Ewell met with Lee (which was well after dark). More likely, after thirty-two years of reading and writing about the battle, Longstreet's memory was tainted by the narrative playing out, not to mention the effect on his memory that his own role in that discussion played. Longstreet, *From Manassas to Appomattox*, 360–361.

376 Long to Longstreet, May 31, 1875, Longstreet Papers, UNC Wilson Library. Long wrote the same thing in his memoirs. *Memoirs of Robert E. Lee*, 277.

377 O.R. 27.2: 420; O.R. 27.2: 42; O.R. 27.2: 366.

378 D.H. Hill, "McClellan's Change of Base and Malvern Hill," in *Battles & Leaders* 2:391.

379 McLaws to Wife, July 7, 1863, McLaws Papers, UNC Wilson Library.

380 "The Great Battle of Gettysburg," *Savannah (GA) Republican*, July 19, 1863. The dispatch from correspondent P.W.A. is dated July 4, 1863. "The attack was renewed…on the 2d, without proper reconnoiassances," the correspondent wrote. Reinforcing this point, the correspondent wrote that "little disposition was shown to undertake a proper reconnaissance of the ground – an omission which every man in the army now deeply regrets." The letter was reprinted in the July 20 edition, too, and distributed to other papers, such as the July 23 edition of the *Charleston (SC) Mercury.*

Another submission to the *Republican* by a frequent soldier correspondent calling himself "Tout le Monde" (French for "everyone") appeared in the July 23 issue. In addition to excoriating Lee for his decision to continue the fight after the first and second day, he appears to also fault Lee for failing to reconnoiter. "What General ever makes a battle without understanding the ground? Gen. Lee must have been deceived and to that extent was greatly culpable," he wrote. "Letter from the Army – July 13th," *Savannah (GA) Republican*, July 23, 1863.

    McLaws's alleged lack of reconnaissance certainly became a major piece of his postwar writings and he complained bitterly about it to his wife after the battle.

381   "The Pennsylvania Campaign – A Review of Its Movements and Results," *The Savannah (GA) Republican*, reprinted in *The Charleston (SC) Mercury*, July 28, 1863. The delay was not the only reason. The long wait to allow Ewell's trains to pass was also given as a reason (another of McLaws's gripes, evident in all of his postwar writings), as was a failure to concentrate the army sooner and a failure to push Anderson and Johnson to the front. Notably, however, there is no blame laid at Longstreet's feet. Rather, the correspondent is more critical of Lee than anyone (which makes sense, since McLaws was presumably upset with Lee, as well, having been publicly called out on his performance in Lee's reports).

382   "It was deemed advisable to make an effort to turn the enemy's left flank, and Longstreet was charged with that important duty. For this purpose, McLaws' and Hood's divisions were put in motion, but the latter discovered, after proceeding some distance by a circuitous route, that he could go no further in that direction without bringing his column within view of the enemy, and thus disclosing the whole movement. It became necessary therefore for him to retrace his steps, and to advance by another route. In this way much time was lost before the movement upon the enemy's flank could be executed, and which might have been avoided by a previous examination of the ground." "The Great Battle of Gettysburg," *Savannah (GA) Republican*, July 19, 1863.

383   "From Gen. Lee's Army – The Battle of Gettysburg," *Richmond (VA) Dispatch*, reprinted in *The Charleston (SC) Mercury*, July 16, 1863.

384   "Rebel Generals," *St. Louis (MO) Republican*, reprinted in *Memphis (TN) Bulletin*, July 10, 1863. Though the *Charleston Mercury* reprinted the *Savannah Republican's* correspondence and published vicious diatribes against Longstreet during Reconstruction, it also reprinted correspondence about Gettysburg that was much more favorable to Longstreet – the *Republican* bears responsibility for the "sly undercurrents" Longstreet mentioned.

385   James Longstreet to Augustus Longstreet, July 24th, 1863, cited in Longstreet, "Lee in Pennsylvania," in *Annals of the War*, 414–415. To date, no original (or even facsimile or typescript) of the letter has been located. Early hints at a belief that the letter was written later as forged evidence to support Longstreet. Early, "Rely to General Longstreet," in *SHSP* vol.4.

386   Goggin to Longstreet, Aug. 15, 1887, in GNMP V7-SC-Brigades. Original in USAMHI. Emphasis in original.

387   Longstreet submitted his report even before the regimental reports were in. Major R.C. Maffett submitted his report to Kershaw on July 31, four days after Longstreet completed the First Corps report. O.R. 27.2: 373.

388   Longstreet to Pendleton, April 4, 1875, Pendleton Papers, UNC Wilson Library.

389   Pendleton to Longstreet, April 1875, Pendleton Papers, UNC Wilson Library.

390   Longstreet to Pendleton, April 19, 1875, Pendleton Papers, UNC Wilson Library.

391   "As I have never applied myself to politics, I cannot claim to speak to the wise statement of the country, who are devoting their energies to the solution of the problem which agitates the public mind," Longstreet admitted. "I can only speak the plain, honest convictions of a soldier." "Gen. James Longstreet on the Situation," in *New Orleans Times*, March 19, 1867.

392   Pendleton replied to Longstreet that while the letter's "tenor might warrant me in treating it with silence, I chose to reply." Pendleton to Longstreet, April 1875, Pendleton Papers, UNC Wilson Library.

393   Pendleton to Long, Oct. 5, 1875, Long Papers, UNC Wilson Library. A transcribed version is located in GNMP V5-Pendleton, Wm. N.

394   Jones, ed., *Campbell Brown's Civil War*, 214. Walter Taylor also remembered that the plan, as of the night of July 1, was for Ewell to attack at dawn on July 2. Taylor, "Memorandum by Colonel Walter H. Taylor," in *SHSP*, vol. 4, 83. Though Taylor's memorandum isn't entirely accurate, it's helpful in showing the collective memory from which Pendleton would be drawing.

395   "I think Genl Pendleton confuses the 2nd + 3rd July, probably," Marshall confided to Longstreet. Marshall to Longstreet, May 7, 1875, Longstreet Papers, UNC Wilson Library.

396   Campbell Brown Diary. Polk, Brown, and Ewell Family Papers, UNC Wilson Library. The entry appears in the early March section of the diary. In the July entries describing Gettysburg, Brown directs himself back to

this space, which was blank when he needed more space to describe the battle.

397   O.R. 27.2: 320.

398   Venable to Longstreet, 1875, Longstreet Papers, Emory University Rose Library. According to Venable, the Washington & Lee faculty refused to print it "because they were aware of his condition," which is why it ended up in the *Southern Magazine*. Pendleton's "whole statement with regard to Gettysburg is full of mistakes + there are many other things needing correction in other parts of his address," Venable went on to say. He was referring to Pendleton's postwar account.

399   Longstreet to Long, May 20, 1875, Long Papers, UNC Wilson Library.

400   Long to Longstreet, May 31, 1875, Longstreet Papers, UNC Wilson Library.

401   Long to Longstreet, April 19, 1876, Long Papers, UNC Wilson Library.

402   Loftus, *Memory*, 40.

403   Loftus, *Memory*, 37. Loftus writes, "Memory is imperfect. This is because we often do not see things accurately in the first place." Then the memories are subjected to both internal and external factors that distort it.

404   Lawley, *The Times* (London), Aug. 18, 1863.

405   Carrington, "Inspirational Quotes," https://www.leocarrington.com/quotes-citas.html.

406   "Only the dead have seen an end to war" is a quote commonly attributed to Plato, though it doesn't appear in any of his known written works. It's been used in speeches, movies, war memorials, etc. without any particular attribution to a particular work, so it's doubtful the quote originated with him. But since the quote is so widely attributed to the Greek philosopher and recognized as his quote, the connection is used here.

407   O.R. 27.2: 446; Jones, ed., *Campbell Brown's Civil War*, 214.; Turner, *Gettysburg*, Early Papers, LOC. Turner remembered the dispatch as saying the Fifth Corps would be *in position* by 2 a.m., but Ewell probably still had the order with him when he wrote the report (and even if he didn't, he was still writing in 1863, not after the war). Ewell's account is probably more accurate.

408   Jones, ed., *Campbell Brown's Civil War*, 214.

409   O.R. 27.2: 446.

410   Jones, ed., *Campbell Brown's Civil War*, 214; O.R. 27.2: 446.

411   O.R. 27.2; 456.

412   O.R. 27.2: 470.

413   O.R. 27.2: 480

414   For example, Brig. Gen. George Steuart simply reported that he formed
       his line of battle that evening and his men "slept on our arms that night."
       His pickets were thrown 300 yards to the front. O.R. 27.2: 509. Brig.
       Gen. James Walker, commanding the Stonewall Brigade, reported that
       "after nightfall [they] took position on the southeast side of the town…
       and, throwing forward skirmishers, we remained for the night." O.R.
       27.2: 518. Brig. Gen. John Jones "formed line of battle about dark on
       the left of Nicholl's brigade.…As soon as the line was formed, pickets
       were thrown well to the front, and the brigade lay upon their arms during
       the night. Nothing of importance so far as my brigade was concerned
       occurred during the night." O.R. 27.2: 531.

415   Jones, ed., *Campbell Brown's Civil War*, 214.

416   O.R. 27.1: 283.

417   Thomson, *From Philippi to Appomattox*, 165. Thomson is also quoted by
       battlefield guide John Archer in his fine book and guide on Culp's Hill.
       Archer's book is more accessible than Thomson's. Archer, *Culp's Hill at
       Gettysburg*, 18.

418   O.R. 27.2: 536; O.R. 27.2: 446. Richardson was severely wounded and
       captured, though it appears he was initially within Confederate lines and
       cared for in a Confederate hospital, left behind as too severely wounded
       to take with the army on the retreat. Proctor Smith noted that Richardson
       was "severely wounded + left in the hands of the enemy," while Ewell
       echoed this in his report. Report of Col. William Proctor Smith, William
       Proctor Smith, Letter Book 1863-1864; O.R. 27.2: 452.

419   O.R. 27.1: 284.

420   "At Gettysburg: How a Proposed Night Attack By the Enemy Was Foiled,"
       National Tribune, Feb. 11, 1886, in Thomson, *From Philippi to Appo-
       mattox*, vii.

421   Thomson, *From Philippi to Appomattox*, 165. There were no captains or
       lieutenants listed as captured in the Forty-second Virginia, according
       to Busey's volume on Confederate casualties. O.R. 27.2: 537.

422   Turner, *Gettysburg*, Early Papers, LOC.

423   O.R. 27.2: 536; Busey and Busey, *Confederate Casualties at Gettysburg*
       3:1643. The July 28, 1863 *Staunton Spectator* also listed Lt. Dryer (spelled
       Dyer in the paper) as missing in its casualty list.

424   O.R. 27.2: 446.

425   Campbell Brown notes, July 2 + 3, 1878, in Polk, Brown, Ewell Papers, UNC Wilson Library.

426   O.R. 27.2: 470.

427   O.R. 27.2: 318.

428   Venable to Longstreet, May 11, 1875, in Early, "Reply to General Longstreet," in *SHSP* vol. 4, 289. Campbell Brown supports this, for he wrote that the Second Corps was "ready at daylight – but an order soon came postponing the attack till 9 a.m." Jones, ed., *Campbell Brown's Civil War*, 214.

429   Long to F. Lee, Jan. 17, 1878, in F. Lee, "Review of First Two Days and Reply to Longstreet," in *SHSP* vol. 5, 180–181.

430   In his report, Ewell wrote that "orders had come from the general commanding for me to delay my attack until I heard General Longstreet's guns open on the right." At some point during the morning, "I received a communication from the commanding general, the tenor of which was that he intended the main attack to be made by the First Corps." O.R. 27.2: 446. Campbell Brown noted that the corps was ready to attack at daylight, but "an order soon came postponing the attack till 9 a.m. - & finally another put it off till 4 p.m. Our movements were in any event to depend on Longstreet." Jones, ed., *Campbell Brown's Civil War*, 214.

431   Page, *Reminiscences*, in Shields Collection, W&L Leyburn Libary, 5; O.R. 27.2: 610. Walker is not specific with the time he placed the batteries on the ridge, but others like Pendleton were. If he was placing the batteries, he was with Pendleton before dawn.

432   Jones, ed., *Campbell Brown's Civil War*, 214.

433   O.R. 27.2: 446; Jones, ed., *Campbell Brown's Civil War*, 214.

434   Long, *Memoirs of Robert E. Lee*, 277.

435   Early, "Reply to General Longstreet," in *SHSP* vol. 4, 285–286. Early still maintained the order was for *Longstreet* to attack at dawn, however.

436   Longstreet, "Lee in Pennsylvania," in *Annals of the War*, 422; Longstreet, *From Manassas to Appomattox*, 362.

437   Black, *Crumbling Defenses*, 36–37. Captain James Hart, who commanded the horse artillery in Black's command, also remembered arriving at "sunrise." Hart to Bacheler, March 3, 1886, in Ladd, *The Bachelder Papers*, 2:1215.

438   Page, *Reminiscences*, in Shields Collection, W&L Leyburn Library, 4–5. Pendleton reported that Walker was posting the batteries that morning.

O.R. 27.2: 350. If Page is right and Pendleton was assisting in posting the batteries, then Walker was there, too.

439 O.R. 27.2: 665.

440 O.R. 27.2: 671; Pfanz, *Gettysburg: The First Day*, 307–308.

441 O.R. 27.2: 671.

442 O.R. 27.2: 350.

443 Perry, "Lee and Longstreet: Which Was Responsible for the Gettysburg Defeat?" *New York Sun*, Nov. 10, 1895.

444 Jones, "Gettysburg – Longstreet vs. Lee," *New York Sun*, Dec. 15, 1895. One of Jones's many points was that "Bishop George W. Peterkin…who was with him at the time, fully confirms Gen. Pendleton's statements as to the reconnoissance [sic], &c., and says that as they left Gen. Lee on the night of the 1ˢᵗ, Gen. Pendleton told him that 'Gen. Longstreet was to attack very early in the morning.'"

445 Johnston to Peterkin, Dec. 1895, in S.R. Johnston Papers, VHS.

446 This wasn't the first time Johnston brought this up. Responding to Fitz Lee in 1878, Johnston wrote that he was "confident that the reconnaissance that Maj. Clarke and myself made was the first one made on the enemy's left. The one referred to by Genl. Pendleton [in his speech] is doubtless the reconnaissance made the evening of the 1ˢᵗ by Genls. Pendleton and Long and myself." That reconnaissance "did not extend further than three quarters of a mile from the Chambersburg Pike." Johnston to F. Lee, Feb. 16, 1878, in S.R. Johnston Papers, VHS.

447 Noah Webster's 1862 dictionary defines "reconnoitre" as "to view; to survey." *An American Dictionary of the English Language*, 920.

448 Pendleton, "Personal Recollections of General Lee," in *Southern Magazine*, 625.

449 Johnston to Peterkin, Dec. 1895, in S.R. Johnston Papers, VHS.

450 Long to Early, April 5, 1876, in *SHSP* vol. 4, 67.

451 Long to Early, in *SHSP* vol. 4, 67. He reiterated this account in a private letter to Longstreet the same year, telling the Old War Horse that he "observed the enemy's position on Cemetery hill about sunrise" on the second. Long to Longstreet, April 19, 1876, Long Papers, UNC Wilson Library.

452 O.R. 27.2: 350. Pendleton noted "So far as judgment could be formed from such a view, assault on the enemy's left by our extreme right might succeed."

453 Long to Early, April 5, 1876, in *SHSP* vol. 4, 67.

454 Obituary, in S.R. Johnston Papers, VHS.

455 *Eminent and Representative Men of Virginia and the District of Columbia, of the Nineteenth Century*, 485–487.

456 *Virginia Gazette*, June 13, 1777 (no. 124), p.4, c.2 https://research. history.org/DigitalLibrary/va-gazettes/VGSinglePage.cfm?issueID-No=77.P.41&page=3&res=LO

457 Maeva, *The Documentary History of the Supreme Court of the United States, 1789 – 1800* 1:31.

458 *Alexandria Gazette*, July 24, 1852.

459 Deed, Fairfax County Circuit Court, Book U-3, pg. 229; Deed, Fairfax County Circuit Court, Book U-3, pg. 227; Deed, Jan. 25, 1859, Fairfax County Circuit Court, Book A-4, pg. 377. Where Sam spent the three years between selling his inherited property and buying his interest in West Grove is unknown.

460 *Alexandria Gazette and Virginia Advertiser,* June 24, 1859; Marriage License, Sam R. Johnston and Mary G. Ege, June 21, 1859, in Fairfax County Historical Records Center; Buie, "Carroll Yesteryears" *Carroll County Times*, Aug. 23, 2020. The iron business was booming in the mid-nineteenth century. Even Thaddeus Stevens, the prominent abolitionist Congressman from Gettysburg, tried his hand in the iron business (though Jubal Early burned the foundry down on the way to Gettysburg in June 1863). Hoke, *The Great Invasion*, 170–171, n. 171.

461 Ege, *Ege Family in the United States,* 130; Coddington & Batalo, "Fallout from the Johnston Reconnaissance," *Military Images*, 36–37.

462 Obituary, in S.R. Johnston Papers, VHS. The story is probably apocryphal, as the *Alexandria Gazette* reported Johnston helping to form the Fairfax cavalry company in January 1861. Virginia seceded in April. *Alexandria Gazette*, Jan. 15, 1861.

463 Samuel R. Johnston File, NARA, M258, RG109, Roll 0067; "New Fairfax Cavalry Company," *Alexandria Gazette*, Jan. 15, 1861.

464 Millard may not have been a tax collector yet, but he's documented to have been by at least 1863. Either way, he was a prominent unionist who only moved to Loudoun County for his wife's health. During and after the war, when the most documentation on his activities exists, he was no quiet supporter of the Union. *The Baltimore Sun*, August. 27, 1912.

465 Complaint, *Millard v. Johnston,* Fairfax Circuit, Historic Records Court, 1866-020; Sheriff Attachment, July 21, 1862, *Millard v. Johnston,* Fairfax Circuit Court, Historic Records 1866-020; Complaint, *Millard v. John-*

ston, Fairfax Circuit Court, Historic Records Center, Folder X-I-0749. Millard was originally from Massachusetts, as was his father-in-law Lirlauslet Karner, who was also captured. In the New England papers, Karner was reported to have been "killed in his own house by a party of rebels a few days since, and his dwellings and barns plundered by the murderers." *New England Farmer,* July 6, 1861.

466   Complaint, *Millard v. Johnston,* Fairfax Circuit, Historic Records Court, 1866-020.

467   Samuel R. Johnston file, NARA, M258, RG 109, Roll 0107.

468   Recommendation, in Samuel R. Johnston file, NARA, M258, RG109, Roll 0107.

469   Keith Armistead file, NARA, M382, RG 109.

470   OR 11.2: 519. Stuart reported that "Major Meade and Lieut. Samuel R. Johnston, of the Engineers...had just made, in the drenching rain, a personal examination of the enemy's position and found it abandoned."

471   OR 12.3: 945. Lee wrote Col. Jeremy Gilmer on August 25, 1862, that "there are no engineer officers with this army except those around Richmand and one (Captain Johnston) just arrived here."

472   O.R. 12.2: 586. Longstreet thanked Johnston and much of Lee's staff personally "for great courtesy and kindness in assisting me on the different battle-fields" in his report of October 10, 1862.

473   OR 21.1:556.

474   OR 21.1:552.

475   OR 21.1:569.

476   Gallagher, ed., *Fighting for the Confederacy,* 167–168.

477   OR 25.2:664. In March, Lee sent him to a river crossing at Rapidan Station "to see if rifle-pits can be constructed there to protect the bridge."

478   William Proctor Smith, Report of the Battle of Gettysburg, Letter Book 1863-1864, KHS; *Staunton (VA) Spectator and General Advertiser,* Sept. 4, 1895.

479   William Proctor Smith, Report of the Battle of Gettysburg, Letter Book 1863-1864, KHS.

480   OR 25.1:825

481   Typescript, S.R. Johnston Papers, VHS.

482   OR 25.1:879–880.

483   OR 25.1:821.

484   OR 25.1:831; William Proctor Smith, Report of the Battle of Gettysburg, Letter Book 1863-1864, KHS.

485   Hotchkiss Diary, June 29, 1863, LOC; William Proctor Smith, Report of
       the Battle of Gettysburg, Letter Book 1863-1864, KHS.

486   In his letter to Peterkin in 1895, Johnston wrote "I was with General
       A.P. Hill during General Ewell's attack on the enemy's right on the
       evening of the first day when General Lee rode up. After seeing
       that General Ewell had driven the enemy back, General Pendleton,
       General Long, Colonel Walker and myself made a reconnaissance
       on our right." It's also possible Johnston returned to headquarters
       west of the mountains and rode ahead to assist Hill during what was
       initially anticipated to be a reconnaissance in force that morning.

487   Gettysburg National Park Ranger Troy Harman, for example, leads a
       program called "Capt. Samuel Johnston's Sunrise Reconnaissance."

488   Johnston to F. Lee, Feb. 11, 1878, in S.R. Johnston Papers, VHS.

489   Johnston to F. Lee, Feb. 16, 1878, in S.R. Johnston Papers, VHS.

490   "Borough of Gettysburg, Pennsylvania, USA – Sunrise, Sunset,
       and Daylength, July 1863," https://www.timeanddate.com/sun/
       @4558191?month=7&year=1863

491   Johnston wrote that "it was about 4 a.m. when I started out" in his letter
       to McLaws on June 27, 1892. S.R. Johnston Papers, VHS. In his letter to
       George Peterkin, he wrote that "about four o'clock next morning [July 2]
       General Lee called me and directed that I go at once and make reconnais-
       sance as far as practicable on our right." Johnston to Peterkin, Dec. 1895,
       in S.R. Johnston Papers, VHS.

492   U.S. Dept. of the Interior, *Cultural Landscape Report*, ROT Maps, 9, 12.

493   Johnston to F. Lee, Feb. 11, 1878, in S.R. Johnston Papers, VHS. In his
       letter to McLaws in 1892, Johnston wrote that Lee "wanted me to recon-
       noiter along the enemy's left and return as soon as possible." Johnston to
       McLaws, June 27, 1892, in S.R. Johnston Papers, VHS. Finally, in his
       1895 letter to George Peterkin, he wrote that Lee "directed that I go at
       once and make reconnaissance as far as practicable on our right." Johnston
       to Peterkin, Dec. 1895, in S.R. Johnston Papers, VHS.

494   John J. Clarke, NARA, M331 RG 109, Roll 0057. Clarke's National
       Archives file shows an assignment to Longstreet's staff on June 3, 1863,
       the day the Gettysburg Campaign began. But Proctor Smith's report indi-
       cates Clarke was assigned to Longstreet's command soon after Longstreet
       returned from Suffolk, just after the Battle of Chancellorsville. Smith
       reports that Clarke tended to several assignments in May, suggesting he
       was with the army a few weeks earlier than the National Archives paper-

work shows. William Proctor Smith, Report of the Battle of Gettysburg, Letter Book 1863-1864, KHS.

495   William Proctor Smith, Report of the Battle of Gettysburg, Letter Book 1863-1864, KHS; Hotchkiss Diary, June 29, 1863, LOC.

496   Fremantle, *Three Months in the Southern States*, 256–257. Fitzgerald Ross also remembered Clarke giving Fremantle a horse, but thought it was the night before. Ross, *A Visit to the Cities and Camps of the Confederate States*, 49. Either way, Clarke was at headquarters that night.

497   Johnston to Peterkin, Dec. 1895, in S.R. Johnston Papers, VHS.

498   Black, *Crumbling Defenses*, 36–37; Longstreet, "Lee in Pennsylvania," in *Annals of the War*, 422; Fremantle, *Three Months in the Confederate States*, 256.

499   Other evidence suggests this, too. Fremantle and Captain Justus Scheibert, another foreign observer, famously spent the morning meeting in a tree, a scene that has been depicted in more than one painting. According to Fremantle, the headquarters entourage arrived with Longstreet around 5 a.m. "at the same commanding place we were on yesterday." Fremantle remembered that he "climbed up a tree in company with Captain Schreibert...Just below us were seated Generals Lee, Hill, Longstreet, and Hood, in consultation."

The evening before, while Fremantle stood on Seminary Ridge watching "the enemy retreating up one of the opposite ridges" and talking with Lee and Hill, "a message arrived from General Ewell, requesting Hill to press the enemy in the front, whilst he performed the same operation on his right." That put the location in the area of McMillan's Hill, for that's where J.P. Smith found Lee with the same message from Ewell. Fremantle "climbed up a tree in the most commanding place I could find, and could form a pretty good general idea of the enemy's position." Fremantle, *Three Months in the Southern States*, 254–257. If Fremantle's July 2 arboreal lookout was the same as the one on July 1, then it was probably on or near McMillan's Hill.

500   Fremantle, *Three Months in the Southern States*, 256–257. Since both Clarke and Fremantle can be placed at Seminary Ridge at daylight, it's reasonable to conclude they rode together. And since Clarke was at Seminary Ridge at just the time Johnston was heading off to the Emmitsburg

Road, this seems to be the best estimate for when they met. A discussion of Johnston's route begins at page 204.

501   O.R. 27.2: 358. Longstreet reported that "engineers, sent out by the commanding general and myself, guided us by a road which would have completely disclosed the move."

502   John J. Clarke, NARA, M331, RG 109, Roll 0057; *The Baltimore Sun*, Sept. 17, 1880; *The Brooklyn Daily Eagle*, Sept. 17, 1880.

503   "Funeral of the Late Colonel John G. Clarke," *Richmond Dispatch*, Sept. 18, 1880. Manchester is now a section of Richmond, Virginia, but at the time was an independent city.

504   In addition to the $3,000 judgment Josiah Millard ultimately won against him, pre-war creditors won default judgments of close to $2,000 (for context, remember he purchased his half interest in West Grove for $9,000). He had also lost (temporarily, as it turned out) his rights in West Grove, which had been purchased by an understandably vindictive Millard. *Admin. Of John R. Johnston's Estate v. Millard*, Fairfax County Circuit Court, Historic Records, 1879-008. The file covers both the cases against Millard and Johnston by the Johnston Estate. "Property Sale," *Alexandria Gazette and Virginia Advertiser*, March 14, 1868 advertised the sale of half of West Grove to George Johnston. Several cases appear in the record against Sam Johnston for debts just after the war: *Farmers Bank of Virginia v. Johnston*, Fairfax County Circuit Court, Box 071, folder 1868-132, Box 074, folder 1869-100; *Willis Henderson v. Johnston*, Fairfax County Circuit Court, Box 061, folder 1865-180, and *Thomas Ogden v. Johnston*, Box 056, folder 1864-024; "Negro Games," *Alexandria Gazette and Virginia Advertiser*, Aug. 22, 1866; "Auction Sales," *Washington, D.C. Evening Star*, June 29, 1864, listing "Samuel R. Johnston's West Grove farm" for sale at auction by the "United States Marshal's Sale of Confiscated Property in the Eastern District of Virginia."

505   *Alexandria Gazette*, July 7, 1868; *Alexandria Gazette*, August 17, 1868; *Alexandria Gazette*, June 16, 1870.

506   *The Baltimore Sun*, April 15, 1870; http://www.abandonedrails.com/Valley_Railroad.

507   *Alexandria Gazette*, June 12, 1871.

508   *Cincinnati Enquirer*, July 25, 1877.

509   Johnston to McLaws, June 27, 1892, in S.R. Johnston Papers, VHS.

510   Goggin to Longstreet, Aug. 15, 1887, USAMHI, in GNMP V7-SC-Brigades. Original in USAMHI. Goggin, McLaws's division adjutant,

remembered that at some point during the march, "the sharpshooters of Wofford's brigade were kept well to the front."

511   Johnston to McLaws, June 27, 1892, in S.R. Johnston Papers, VHS; McLaws to Johnston, June 8, 1892, in S.R. Johnston Papers, VHS. After a series of direct questions more akin to a legal interrogatory than a friendly letter, McLaws bluntly wrote Johnston that "the delay in not making the movements undoubtedly must be laid either upon your shoulders or upon Gen. Longstreet."

512   O.R. 27.2: 350.

513   Cullum, *Officers and Graduates of the U.S. Military Academy*, vo. 2, 675–690.

514   William Proctor Smith, NARA, M258, RG 109, Roll 0109.

515   William Proctor Smith, Report of the Battle of Gettysburg, Letter Book 1863-1864, KHS. "At Bunker's Hill after we had crossed the Potomac [on the retreat] Genl. Lee issued an order postponing the organization… because his army had been much reduced by the losses at Gettisburg [sic]."

516   William Proctor Smith, Report of the Battle of Gettysburg, Letter Book 1863-1864, KHS.

517   William Proctor Smith, Report of the Battle of Gettysburg, Letter Book 1863-1864, KHS.

518   William Proctor Smith Obituary, newspaper clipping, KHS.

519   Johnston to F. Lee, Feb. 11, 1878, in S.R. Johnston Papers, VHS.

520   Johnston to McLaws, June 27, 1892, in S.R. Johnston Papers, VHS.

521   McLaws, "The Battle of Gettysburg,", 71-73, in GNMP, V5-McLaws, Lafayette.

522   "White Sulpher Springs," *The New York Times*, Aug. 25, 1877.

523   "Jackson's Widow – Correspondence with Acting Mayor Meredith – Visiting Military," *The Richmond Dispatch*, Oct. 26, 1875. Smith also attended the reinterment of Jefferson Davis in 1893, just a year and a half before his death and was on the finance committee for the City of Richmond's Committee in Charge of the Davis funeral. *New York World*, May 28, 1893. A short obituary in the *Baltimore Sun* notes that he "attended the last banquet of the Confederate Army and Navy Society in Maryland…January last [1895]." William Proctor Smith Obituary, newspaper clipping, in William Proctor Smith Papers, KHS.

524   Taylor to Longstreet, Aug. 15, 1879, in GNMP V5-Longstreet, James. Longstreet had written to Taylor asking if he could provide information

on which engineer guided his corps from Gordonsville to the Wilderness. Both Sam Johnston's and Proctor Smith's names came up, but Taylor could definitively say it wasn't Johnston (in a letter that hasn't survived, apparently, Johnston wrote to Taylor and said it wasn't him). "I regret that I do not know Col. Smith's address at this time," Taylor wrote Longstreet. Smith was noted as having a "national reputation" and "for several years has been employed on government work on Kanawha and New Rivers… as assistant engineer." "Death of Col. William Proctor Smith," *The Baltimore Sun*, Aug. 29, 1895.

525   O.R. 27.2: 363.

526   Black, *Crumbling Defenses*, 36–37. Johnston was already surveying the field on Seminary Ridge with Long, Pendleton, and Walker. Black knew Rogers so it's unlikely he is misremembering which engineer he saw at headquarters.

527   Rogers to Hon. Secretary of War of the Confederate States, Sept. 12, 1861, in Henry J. Rogers file, NARA, M258, RG 109, Roll 0109 ,; Krick, *Staff Officers in Gray*, 337. Rogers spent his antebellum military career surveying land in Minnesota, but came back to Virginia and joined the Confederate army when hostilities broke out. He knew John Black from service in South Carolina near Adams Run, where there was skirmishing in the first half of 1862. He was captured while Longstreet was in Suffolk and had only recently been released. Black, *Crumbling Defenses*, 37; Krick, *Staff Officers in Gray*, 257.

528   Henry J. Rogers file. NARA, M258, RG 109,Roll 0109.

529   Walker, *Biographical Sketches*, 458.

530   Walker, *Biographical Sketches*, 458; Templeman, "Benjamin Hallowell, Dedicated Educator," 24–33.

531   Henry J. Rogers file, NARA, M258, RG 109, Roll 0109.

532   In an online presentation on the reconnaissance, Gettysburg National Park Ranger Troy Harman says "we know only one other name in that group and that was a major of artillery and his name was John Cheves Haskell, from South Carolina." Troy D. Harman, "Gettysburg: Robert E. Lee Reconnoiters Little Round Top, July 2, 1863," April 2020, https://www.youtube.com/watch?v=ltD1j48qdYM. Reference to Haskell can be found approximately twelve minutes into Mr. Harman's presentation.

533   Major Henry has sometimes been referred to as "Mathias," but Heitman's *Historical Register and Dictionary of the United States Army* calls him Mathis, 1: 524.

534   Haskell, *Reminiscences of the Confederate War*, 67–68, in John Cheves Haskell Papers, UNC Wilson Library. Haskell's reminiscences have been published many times since and are easily found for sale online. He inadvertently wrote that they marched toward the battlefield on the evening of July 2.

535   Haskell, *Reminiscences of the Confederate War*, 80, in John Cheves Haskell Papers, UNC Wilson Library.

536   For a concise overview of Federal troop positions in the early afternoon, see Woods, *Ebb and Flow of Battle*, 122-130; O.R. 27.1: 518. Philip Laino's *Gettysburg Campaign Atlas* also provides fantastic maps detailing the movements that day.

537   Gallagher, ed., *Fighting for the Confederacy*, 235–236. Alexander probably consolidated several shorter recons into one when he tried to remember the order of events many later.

538   Johnston to Peterkin, Dec. 1895, S.R. Johnston Papers, VHS; Sears, *Gettysburg*, 253; Guelzo, *Gettysburg: The Last Invasion*, 242–243. Harry Pfanz doesn't quite say that Johnston didn't make it to Little Round Top, but wonders how he missed two Federal corps, concluding that at the very least, Johnston's team "was somehow the victim of grave misfortune." *Gettysburg: The Second Day*, 107.

539   Fitz Lee published Johnston's letter against his express wishes in 1879. Lee, F. "A Review of the First Two Days' Operations," in *SHSP* vol. 5, 183–184. McLaws published Johnston's 1892 letter four years after he sent it, in the last article he wrote on the battle. McLaws, "The Battle of Gettysburg," in GNMP, V5-McLaws, Lafayette.

540   Johnston to McLaws, June 27, 1892, in S.R. Johnston Papers, VHS.

541   Johnston to F. Lee, Feb. 16, 1878, in S.R. Johnston Papers, VHS.

542   Johnston to Peterkin, Dec. 1895, in S.R. Johnston Papers, VHS.

543   Campbell Brown notes, July 2 and 3, 1878, in Brown, Polk, Ewell Papers, UNC Wilson Library.

544   Ross, "Egocentric Biases," 323.

545   U.S. Dept. of the Interior, *Cultural Landscape Report*, ROT Maps 9, 12, 15. Warren Map, 1876.

546   Kershaw to Bachelder, in Ladd, *The Bachelder Papers*, 1: 453–454.

547   McLaws notes, in GNMP V5-McLaws, Lafayette.

548   Bachelder, *Gettysburg Battlefield* map, 1863.

549   Johnston to McLaws, June 27, 1892, in S.R. Johnston Papers, UNC Wilson Library.

550   Frassanito, *Early Photography at Gettysburg*, 243–245. 1858 Frederick County, MD Wall Map. 1858 Franklin County, PA Wall Map.

551   "Making War History: Second Day of the Remarkable Reunion at Gettysburg," *The Philadelphia Times*, May 1, 1893.

552   Sears, *Gettysburg*, 253.

553   Johnston to McLaws, June 27, 1892, in S.R. Johnston Papers, VHS.

554   Oates, "Gettysburg – The Battle on the Right," in *SHSP* vol. 6, 182. Oates wrote that "on the third day, Law's brigade, still on the right, lay along the southern foot of Round Top. Our picket line extended considerably to the rear and nearly at right angles with the line of battle;" Oates to Alexander, Aug. 25, 1868, in E.P. Alexander Papers, UNC Wilson Library; Lt. Col. L.H. Scruggs of the Fourth Alabama reported that after falling back and giving up the attack that afternoon, "we remained in the enemy's front, some 200 yards distant, during the night." O.R. 27.2: 391. Bachelder, *Map of the Battle Field*, July 3 (1883). Col. W.W. White, Seventh Georgia, "retired in good order across the ravine, and went into bivouac for the night." O.R. 27.2: 397. Captain George Hillyer of the Ninth Georgia reported his regiment "retired to the point where we first encountered the enemy's main position." O.R. 27.2: 400. Gen. Jerome Robertson, commanding a brigade in Hood's Division, reported that "about 2 o'clock that night" his brigade began to shift. O.R. 27.2: 406. Gen. Henry Benning, commanding another of Hood's brigades, wrote that he "employed the night in arranging my line." O.R. 27.2 416. Jeffry Wert also has a concise description of the Confederate position during the cavalry attack. *Gettysburg: Day Three*, 273–275. Bachelder, *Map of the Battle Field*, July 3 (1883). See Black, *Crumbling Defenses*, 40–41, for cavalry movements.

555   Law to Bachelder, June 13, 1876, in Ladd, *The Bachelder Papers*, 1: 495. Law told Bachelder that he "divin[ed] that the motive was to so weaken my force in front of Genl. Farnsworth…as to enable him to break through & place himself in rear of our line on the mountain & possibly capture our guns."

556   Law to Bachelder, June 13, 1876, in Ladd, *The Bachelder Papers*, 1: 495–498; O.R. 397; O.R. 400; General Alfred Pleasonton, commanding the Federal Cavalry Corps, gave high praise to Farnsworth in his report. O.R. 27.1: 916.

557   Law went into great detail about his efforts to fend off the Federal cavalry, primarily describing Farnsworth's attack, in a letter to John Bachelder in

1876. Law to Bachelder, June 13, 1876, in Ladd, *The Bachelder Papers*, 1:495–499. Oates also wrote extensively about the fight, for he was directly involved in it. Oates to Alexander, Aug. 25, 1868, in E.P. Alexander Papers, UNC Wilson Library; Oates, "Gettysburg – The Battle on the Right," in *SHSP* vol. 6, 182. O.R. 27.2: 391-392; O.R. 27.2: 396; O.R. 27.2: 397; O.R. 27.2: 400.

558   Johnston to McLaws, June 27, 1892, in S.R. Johnston Papers, VHS. (Emphasis added).

559   Johnston to McLaws, June 27, 1892, in S.R. Johnston Papers, VHS.

560   Johnston to McLaws, June 27, 1892, in S.R. Johnston Papers, VHS.

561   Johnston to F. Lee, Feb. 11, 1878, in S.R. Johnston Papers, VHS.

562   "The delay of several hours cannot be attributed to Gen'l Longstreet having taken the wrong road, (whether he or I is to blame for that)," Johnston concluded, "but to the delay in getting under way; to the slowness of the march; to the time unnecessarily lost by halting McLaws, and to the time lost in beginning the fight after the line was formed." Johnston to F. Lee, Feb. 11, 1878, in S.R. Johnston Papers, VHS.

563   Caldwell's division was safely on Cemetery Ridge by that point and most of the trains had been directed to Westminster, so they wouldn't have been trailing the infantry column. Only ammunition wagons and ambulances were authorized to accompany the infantry columns. Hancock reported that "the trains of all the troops under my command were ordered to the rear" on the night of July 1. O.R. 27.1: 368. "Upon receiving orders to march against the enemy…trains (ammunition wagons excepted) must be parked in the rear of the place of concentration)." O.R. 27.2: 417; Meade told Sickles that "your trains will remain parked here until further orders." O.R. 27.2: 42; Meade directed the Sixth Corps to "move your command up to Taneytown to-night [July 1]; your train, excepting ambulances and ammunition, to Westminster." O.R. 27.3: 465. See also O.R. 27.3: 457–458, 468. See also Dr. Jonathan Letterman's report in O.R. 27.1: 195–196.

It doesn't appear that much, if any, of the artillery was following Caldwell, either. See Woods, *The Ebb and Flow of Battle*, 37, quoting a member of Battery B, First New York that the battery was positioned on Cemetery Ridge in the "early morning." Captain John Hazard reported that the artillery "brigade moved with the corps at daylight." O.R. 27.1: 478.

564   U.S. Dept. of the Interior, *Cultural Landscape Report*,vol. 2, 145; ROT Map 21.

565   Johnston to McLaws, June 27, 1892, in S.R. Johnston Papers, VHS.

566   Both Birney and Humphreys reported that de Trobriand's Brigade arrived at 9 a.m., though de Trobriand and one of his regimental commanders, Lt. Col. Charles Merrill of the Seventeenth Maine, remembered "arriving on the battlefield about 10 o'clock." O.R. 27.1: 482; O.R. 27.1: 531; O.R. 27.1: 519; O.R. 27.1: 522. Burling, curiously, *also* remembered arriving at 9 a.m., though two of his regimental commanders thought it was 10. O.R. 27.1: 570; O.R. 27.1: 575.

567   Johnston to McLaws, June 27, 1892, in S.R. Johnston Papers, VHS.

568   Longstreet, "Lee in Pennsylvania," in *Annals of the War*, 423.

569   Johnston to McLaws, June 27, 1892, in S.R. Johnston Papers, VHS. His letter to Peterkin is shorter on detail, but lines up with his recollections from 1892. In his two letters to Fitz Lee in 1878, Johnston also describes giving his report in the presence of Hill and Longstreet. The fact that Johnston stood by the generals is inferred from his statement that he sat down next to Lee after giving his report, implying he was standing when he delivered it.

570   Pfanz, *Gettysburg: The Second Day*, 107.

571   Sears, *Gettysburg*, 253–254.

572   Guelzo, *Gettysburg: The Last Invasion*, 238. Other authors have concluded the same. Noah Trudeau, in his fine volume on the battle, wrote that Johnston "truly believed there were no Federals near Little Round Top, and though the reality was otherwise, his account helped confirm Lee's notion of the Union position." *Gettysburg: A Testing of Courage*, 289. Coddington thought Johnston and his team should have moved further north to investigate the woods in which some of the Third Corps men were bivouacked, but concluded Johnston "and his party were satisfied with having found no one on Little Round Top." *Gettysburg: A Study in Command*, 373.

573   Johnston to McLaws, June 27, 1892, in S.R. Johnston Papers, VHS.

574   Wainwright, *A Diary of Battle*, 239.

575   O.R. 27.3: 420.

576   O.R. 27.1: 482.

577   O.R. 27.1: 502; O.R. 27.1: 513.

578   O.R. 27.1: 531.

579   O.R. 27.1: 531; O.R. 27.1: 543. Humphreys reported they arrived at 1 a.m., as did the commander of the Sixteenth Massachusetts. O.R. 27.1: 531; O.R. 27.1: 551. Col. William Brewster, of the Seventy-third New York, reported it was closer to midnight. O.R. 27.1: 558. The commanders of the Eleventh Massachusetts and Twenty-sixth Pennsylvania both thought it was 2 a.m. when they arrived, while Lt. Col. Clark Baldwin of the First Massachusetts remembered arriving at 2:30 that morning. O.R. 27.1: 548; O.R. 27.1: 556; O.R. 27.1: 547. In addition to the problems of accurate timekeeping in the mid-nineteenth century, the order of march would affect when a particular regiment arrived, for a regiment at the front of the column would arrive well before the last regiment in line. Adolfo Cavada remembered that "overcome with fatigue and sleepiness I threw myself under the nearest tree amid the wet grass, and in spite of rain & mud was soon lost to everything around me." Cavada Diary, GNMP, V5-Cavada, Adolfo.

580   Tremain, *Two Days of War*, 37. Tremain was a lifelong friend of Sickles and it did no favors to his old commander to mention that they weren't in any particular order that night.

581   Strouss, "Address," in *Pennsylvania at Gettysburg*, 1: 329.

582   Craft, "Address," in *Pennsylvania at Gettysburg*, 2: 676.

583   U.S. Dept. of the Interior, *Cultural Landscape Report*, ROT Map 16.

584   O.R. 27.1: 500. Major John Moore of the Ninety-ninth Pennsylvania of Ward's Brigade, also remembered camping a mile south of town. O.R. 27.1: 513.

585   O.R. 27.2: 531. Humphreys reported camping a mile south of town. Birney's Division was camped in the Trostle and Weikert farm fields, which were approximately 1.3 miles from town. Measurements for this study used the Emmitsburg Road/Taneytown Road intersection as the general demarcation point for the southern end of town. If Humphreys camped a mile south of town, then he had to be north of Birney's Division. Tremain suggests this as well: "General Humphreys' division had arrived last upon the ground, and…had doubtless picketed his own front. So he was given the right [northern] front, and Birney the left [southern] front and flank." *Two Days of War*, 37.

It should be noted that some of Humphreys' regimental commanders thought they camped anywhere from two to three miles from Gettysburg that night, but this is more likely due to the confusing and harrowing night march, for camping at that distance would have put them over a mile outside their lines. O.R. 27.1:551; O.R. 27.1: 552.

586   O.R. 27.1: 511.

587   O.R. 27.1: 549; O.R. 27.1: 551.

588   Cavada Diary, GNMP V5-Cavada, Adolfo.

589   Troop strengths are rounded and taken from Floyd, *Commanders and Casualties at the Battle of Gettysburg*, 18-21. Henry Tremain wrote in his memoir that "Birney's task at this juncture was quite simple. His division, then depleted by the detachment left at Emmitsburg, was rather in reserve." *Two Days of War*, 38. Both divisions, in fact, had left a brigade at Emmitsburg. Other regiments were detached on various duties, such as the Eighty-fourth Pennsylvania, which guarded the corps' wagon train. O.R. 27.1: 557.

590   U.S. Dept. of the Interior, *Cultural Landscape Report*,ROT Maps 13 and 16.

591   O.R. 27.1: 369.

592   Captain Henry Coates of the First Minnesota, in Gibbon's Division, reported that he was ordered to march at 3 a.m. O.R. 27.1:424. Likewise, one of Hays's regimental commanders, Captain Aaron Selley of the 111th New York reported the regiment began its march to Gettysburg at 3 a.m. O.R. 27.1:475. Nearly all the commanders remembered camping about three miles south, but for some examples, see Hays's report (O.R. 27.1: 455), artillery Captain John Hazard's report (O.R. 27.1: 478), and Col. John Reynolds's report (O.R. 27.1: 413).

593   Major L.W. Bradley, of the Sixty-fourth New York in Caldwell's Division, reported that they camped three miles south of Gettysburg on July 1, were ordered to make coffee and be ready to march at 2:30 a.m., waited until 4:10 to move (likely waiting on Gibbon's and Hays's divisions to clear the road ahead of them), and then moved "about 1 mile to the front." This would place them on the Taneytown Road just behind the Round Tops, when "at 6:10 am we marched with the brigade out of the wood across the Taneytown road" and formed with the brigade in line around 7 a.m. O.R. 27.1: 407. Bradley's times are quite specific and, like all precise times, need to be looked at as *general* times.

594   Col. Devereaux reported Gibbon's Division formed "in columns of regiments by brigade" on the east side of the Taneytown Road. O.R. 27.1: 442. Caldwell reported that he was placed "on the left of the Second Division, in columns or regiments by brigades." O.R. 27.1: 379. Col. Boyd

McKeen, who commanded Zook's Brigade when that officer was killed in the Wheatfield, reported that "early in the morning of the 2d, the brigade was massed in the woods to the left and rear of the position occupied by the corps when in line." O.R. 27.1: 381. The famous Irish Brigade's commander, Col. Patrick Kelly, remembered marching to Gettysburg around 4:30 a.m. (around daylight) and arrived "on the heights near the village, and in view of the enemy's pickets," where the brigade "took a position in two lines on the right of the First Brigade [Cross's], stacked arms, and allowed the men to rest." O.R. 27.1: 386.

595   Forster, "Address," in *Pennsylvania at Gettysburg*, 2: 714.

596   O.R. 27.1: 442.

597   O.R. 27.1: 456.

598   Long to Early, April 5, 1876, in *SHSP* vol. 4, 67.

599   O.R. 27.1: 409, 411; O.R. 27.1: 463.

600   O.R. 27.1: 407.

601   The far left of the Second Corps (Caldwell's Division) wasn't formed in any battle line until around 10 a.m. Lt. Col. John Fraser, who took command of the Third Brigade when Zook went down later in the day, reported arriving at 10 a.m. (O.R. 27.1: 395), but based on the rest of the division's reports, he probably meant they formed in line at 10. Patrick Kelly reported that "about 10 am" his Irish Brigade was "placed in position in line of battle," (O.R. 27.1: 388), while Cross's Brigade reported that "at 10 am the brigade massed in column of regiments on the left of the division." (O.R. 27.1: 381).

602   McLaws to wife, July 7, 1863, McLaws Papers, UNC Wilson Library.

603   Sears, *Gettysburg*, 253.

604   Harry Pfanz wrote that "Geary's division had started from that area at daybreak and might have cleared it before they [Johnston's party] arrived." *Gettysburg: The Second Day*, 107. Coddington agreed. "By chance they must have come to that natural stronghold just as there was a change of guard, so to speak, for they saw none of the enemy. Perhaps only minutes before they got there around 5:30 a.m. the two brigades of Geary's division...had left to occupy positions on Culp's Hill." *Gettysburg: A Study in Command*, 373.

605   O.R. 27.1: 825.

606   O.R. 27.1: 836.

607   O.R. 27.1: 839.

608   O.R. 27.1: 825.

609   O.R. 27.1: 839.

610   O.R. 27.2: 927. Colonel Thomas Devin, commanding one of Buford's brigades, reported the same thing. O.R. 27.1: 939.

611   Moyer, *History of the Seventeenth Regiment*, 398.

612   Cavada Diary, GNMP V5-Cavada, Adolfo.

613   Cheney, *History of the Ninth Regiment, New York Cavalry*, 114.

614   Johnston to McLaws, June 27, 1892, in S.R. Johnston Papers, VHS. Johnston to Peterkin, Dec. 1895, in S.R. Johnston Papers, VHS.

615   Campbell Brown remembered getting a message delaying the attack until 9 a.m., indicating Lee still intended to try to salvage Ewell's attack for at least a portion of the morning. Jones, ed., *Campbell Brown's Civil war*, 214. For Venable being the messenger, see F. Lee to Venable, July 30, 1894, Venable Papers, UNC Wilson Library; Longstreet, "Lee's Right Wing at Gettysburg," in *Battles & Leaders*, 3: 340.

616   Maurice, ed., *Lee's Aide-de-Camp*, 233–234. "General Lee rode to the right...to ascertain whether a reconnaissance made of Cemetery Hill in daylight shewed [sic] that an attack on that position would be more promising." Though Fitz Lee wasn't present for the decision, he had heard the same thing. "I see it stated that General Lee and Longstreet were together early in the morning of the second of July at Gettysburg, that he sent you [Venable] to General Ewell first, and afterwards went himself, to see if he could commence the battle on that flank, all of which I know to be true." F. Lee to Venable, July 30, 1894, Venable Papers, UNC Wilson Library.

617   In his report, Pendleton mentioned he sent back "two of the three members of my staff present." OR 27.2:350.

618   Long to Early, April 5, 1876, in *SHSP*, vol. 4, 67.

619   Long wrote that when he and Lee returned from the Cemetery Hill reconnaissance, "the ridge to which [Walker's] attention had been called in the morning was still unoccupied; but as this ground was to be the position of Longstreet's corps...[among other reasons] its occupation was therefore delayed until the occurrence of that event." Long to Early, April 5, 1876, in *SHSP* vol. 4, 68.

620   O.R. 27.2: 350.

621   Page, *Reminiscences*, in Shields Collection, W&L Leyburn I, 5–6. George Peterkin simply remembered they "left camp very early + reconnitered the right." Peterkin to Pendleton, Dec. 6, 1875. Pendleton Papers, UNC Wilson Library.

622   Page, *Reminiscences*, in Shields Collection, W&L Leyburn Libary, 5–6.

623   Emanuel Pitzer Damage Claim, in Georg, *Summary of Damage Claims*,
      ACHS. Pitzer claimed "$5,000 in gold, silver and bank notes taken July
      2" and that "Rebels were all over the premises…and ransacked the house
      from garrett to celler." Other documents show "only" $2,000 as having
      been taken. As part of Pitzer's damage claim, he called his neighbor
      George Culp as a witness.

624   Beard, Elizabeth Plank, unpublished memoir, ACHS; Coco, *A Vast Sea of
      Misery*, 141–143.

625   Pendleton wrote that "these [Pitzer] woods having been thus cleared of
      the enemy, some view of the ground beyond them, and much further to
      the right than had yet been examined, seemed practicable." Noting that
      he was able to scout further to the right after the Pitzer fight, Pendleton
      was taken to the "farm-house at the summit, where the cross-road from
      Fairfield, etc. emerges." O.R. 27.2: 350. This could be the Warfield or
      Snyder house, too, but those are only a half mile up the slope from the
      Pitzer farm. If it was safe to ride to the Pitzer farmhouse, it was probably
      safe to reach the summit of the ridge.

626   O.R. 27.2: 350.

627   Page, *Reminiscences*, in Shields Collection, W&L Leyburn Libary, 6–7.

628   O.R. 27.2: 350.

629   Cheney, *History of the Ninth Regiment, New York Cavalry*," 115; George
      Barber file, New York, Civil War Muster Roll Abstracts, 1861 – 1900,
      New York State Archives, Roll 31514_220237.

630   Devin reported that his men reconnoitered "in rear of the enemy's right"
      that morning. Pendleton's prisoners were certainly behind Confederate
      lines and undoubtedly word of the capture of at least one trooper made
      it back to headquarters. Though he mentions encountering Anderson's
      movement into position while he was doing so, Devin implies he was
      engaged in reconnoitering all morning, which also agrees with Buford's
      report. O.R. 27.1: 939. Buford, remember, had pickets extended to Fair-
      field. O.R. 27.1: 927. Long remembered stumbling upon a captured
      Federal cavalry non-commissioned officer in the general vicinity, too.
      Long to Early, April 5, 1876, in *SHSP* vol. 4, 68.

631   O.R. 27.2: 350.

632   Page, *Reminiscences*, in Shields Collection, W&L Leyburn Libary, 7. Page
      told his prisoners that "I will try and get your paroles when we reach Gen.
      Lee's headquarters."

633   O.R. 27.2: 350.

634 Page, *Reminiscences*, in Shields Collection, W&L Leyburn Libary, 8–9.

635 Hood to Longstreet, June 28, 1875, in *SHSP* vol. 4, 147. If Hood arrived when he said he did (and all evidence suggests that he did), then he arrived shortly after Lee arrived at Hill's headquarters.

636 G.T. Anderson to Bachelder, March 15, 1876, in Ladd, *The Bachelder Papers*, 1: 449. Anderson noted they waited here for hours, indicating this was the morning position rather than the line of battle east of the Emmitsburg Road.

637 Johnston to F. Lee, Feb. 16, 1878, in S.R. Johnston Papers, VHS. Johnston initially wrote that "my impression is that they had crossed Willoughby run and were at the slope near HeadQ." But then he crossed out "had crossed Willoughby run."

638 Law to Bachelder, Feb. 2, 1891, in Ladd, *The Bachelder Papers*, 3: 1790. For reference, the McPherson farm is about one mile from the 1863 town limits. Law was consistent in this. In his article for *Century*, he wrote that "on my arrival I found the other brigades of Hood's division resting about a mile from the town." Law, "The Struggle for 'Round Top,'" in *Battles & Leaders*, 3: 319.

639 In an 1896 letter to Thomas Munford, McLaws wrote that Hood "arrogated to himself the claim that there was no other command in the battle [of Antietam], and that everything depended on the two brigades which were under his orders." Hood, in McLaws's mind, "practiced the same with Longstreet and the same with Gen. Johnston." McLaws to Munfod, Jan. 6, 1896, in McLaws Papers, UNC Wilson Library. For McLaws, anyway, Hood deliberately "cutting him off," so to speak, wouldn't be hard to imagine.

640 Hood to Longstreet, June 28, 1875, in *SHSP* vol. 4, 147.

641 Kershaw to Bachelder, March 20, 1876, in Ladd, *The Bachelder Papers*, 1: 453. Fremantle remembered Longstreet "disposing of McLaws's Division for to-day's fight" around 7 a.m. Fremantle, *Three Months in the Southern States*, 257. This indicates Kershaw is pretty accurate, at least as to this particular time. At a normal marching speed of two miles per hour, the distance could be covered in about an hour, meaning a 6 o'clock arrival. If Kershaw, as the head of McLaws's column, arrived between 5:30 and 6 a.m. (just after sunrise), then 7 a.m. is a reasonable time for Longstreet to be "disposing" of them and telling McLaws the general position he should occupy. It's also worth noting that Fremantle first saw Longstreet

"disposing" of McLaws's Division at around 7. This doesn't necessarily mean, though, that Longstreet had just started to do so.

642   O.R. 27.2: 366; O.R. 27.2: 343. The Twenty-sixth North Carolina's report indicates the brigade slept in these woods that night. "That night the brigade bivouacked in the woods they had occupied previous to making the charge," which would put them in the woods on Herr's Ridge. If that's the case, then Kershaw would be correct in reporting he moved to their right. Long mentioned Anderson's position "in reserve" of the existing line. Long to Longstreet, April 19, 1876, in Long Papers, UNC Wilson Library.

643   Kershaw to Bachelder, March 20, 1876, in Ladd, *The Bachelder Papers*, 1: 453. In his *Century* article written about ten years later, Kershaw remembered that the column "was halted at the end of the lane leading to the Black Horse Tavern, situated some five hundred yards to our right." Kershaw, "Kershaw's Brigade at Gettysburg," in *Battles & Leaders* 3: 331. If the brigade was a mere five hundred yards from the Black Horse Tavern, then it was sitting on the southern end of Bream's Hill. None of the accounts support this position, including Kershaw's prior statements. His 1876 letter to Bachelder is probably more reliable, for not only was it written ten years earlier than the *Century* article, it was written before Longstreet's or McLaws's accounts were published. Kershaw was also writing in response to Bachelder's request for information and was looking at the map Bachelder forwarded with his request for information. Kershaw to Bachelder, March 20, 1876, in Ladd, *The Bachelder Papers*, 1: 458. In contrast, Kershaw may have used any number of maps in the 1880s, which may or may not have been to scale. The accuracy of Kershaw's statement that his brigade was a mere five hundred yards from the Black Horse Tavern is doubtful. More likely, based on all the other available information, Kershaw simply remembered being *near* the tavern and used a general measurement that got the point across. Or…he simply measured wrong on the map (if indeed the map he used was to proper scale. He may have measured correctly on an inaccurate map).

Kershaw's *Century* article also included other mistakes related to time and distance. He wrote that the column's position on Herr's Ridge "commanded a view of the Emmitsburg road about Kern's house," and that the column marched from Herr's Ridge into position around noon or 1 p.m. Kershaw, "Kershaw's Brigade at Gettysburg," in *Battles & Leaders* 3: 331. The position on Herr's Ridge did not command a view of the Emmitsburg Road "about Kern's house," but the brigade's position at the end of July 3 did. The brigade concluded the battle with its right flank resting on the Emmitsburg Road only half a mile from Kern's house. See Bachelder's 1883 map, July 3, 1863 5 p.m.

644   Fremantle, *Three Months in the Southern States*, 257.

645   Kershaw to Bachelder, March 20, 1876, in Ladd, *The Bachelder Papers*, 1: 453.

646   Gilhams' Manual, though most likely not used by McLaws's men, describes a "Change of front perpendicularly to the rear." The right company in a battle line faces to the right, then each company behind it about faces and wheels to their left, which results in the unit facing forty-five degrees to the right and shifted to the right. In this case, they didn't change front, but simply shifted their line by using a similar maneuver. Most of the military manuals were based on the same theories and methods of movements, with slight variations. Gilham's uses the specific term "perpendicular to the rear," whereas other manuals do not, hence its inclusion here. Gilham, *Manual for Volunteers and Militia*, 238–239.

647   McLaws, "The Battle of Gettysburg,", 76, in GNMP, V5-McLaws, Lafayette.

648   In battle line, the division was about 1.3 miles long. Kershaw took up 715 yards, Semmes only 433, Barksdale another 533 yards, and finally Wofford consumed 532 yards. The length of a battle line is determined simply by converting the number of men to linear feet. Each file was granted 2 feet of space, so each person in the brigade counts for 2 feet. The ranks are double ranks, so that number is divided in half. Doubling, then halving, results in the original number. Kershaw's brigade, for example, had approximately 2150 men in it, so it consumed 2150 feet of space, or 715 yards. Using the same calculations for each brigade, we can find that the brigade used up approximately 2300 yards, or 1.3 miles.

We also have to consider that a number of the men were non-commissioned officers, file closers, and officers, who did not necessarily take up space in the line. Irregularities will skew the distance, too, for example not keeping intervals between units, stragglers, men out of the ranks due to illness, etc. These calculations are based on full strength numbers to estimate the length of the column.

649   Dr. Hall's first name appears on Bachelder's Isometric Map. Bachelder, *Gettysburg Battlefield* map, 1863.

650 "Gen. Lee was at our quarters in the morning and there planned the movement." Hotchkiss Diary, July 2, 1863, LOC.

651 Long to Longstreet, April 19, 1876, Long Papers, UNC Wilson Library. Long wrote that after the sunrise survey, "subsequently about ten o'clock a.m. on the 2nd of July I accompanied Genl Lee on a reconnaissance of Genl Meade's position from the heights occupied by the [Confederate] 3rd corps." Charles Marshall remembered that after viewing Cemetery Hill from Ewell's headquarters, "Lee thereupon returned to Seminary Ridge" and later issued orders for the attack. Maurice, ed., *Lee's Aide-de-Camp*, 233–234. For the time, see Long to Longstreet, April 19, 1876, Long Papers, UNC Wilson Library.

652 Long to Early, April 5, 1876, in *SHSP* vol. 4, 68. In his memoirs, he wrote that "the enemy was gradually strengthening his position by fresh arrivals of troops, and that the advantage in numbers and readiness which the Confederate army possessed was rapidly disappearing." Long, *Memoirs of Robert E. Lee*, 281; Maurice, ed., *Lee's Aide-de-Camp*, 233.

653 Armistead Long remembered this general scenario in his memoir. In a conversation with Lee on the evening of July 1, Long thought that "at present only two of three corps of the enemy's army are up, and it seems best to attack them before they can be greatly strengthened by reinforcements. . . General Lee evidently agreed with me in this opinion." Long, *Memoirs of Robert E. Lee*, 278.

654 Lawley, *The Times* (London), Aug. 18, 1863.

655 Hood to Longstreet, June 28, 1875, in *SHSP* vol. 4, 148.

656 Long to Early, April 5, 1876, in *SHSP* vol. 4, 68. Long wrote "It was now about ten o'clock, and the Federals had considerably increased in numbers and extended their left." Then he proclaimed Lee's exasperation.

657 Walker to F. Lee, in *SHSP* vol. 5, 181.

658 Walker didn't have any more artillery to place, but Long was initially frustrated that Walker hadn't listened to his earlier orders to put guns on the rise of ground to the right.

659 Long, *Memoirs of Robert E. Lee*, 281.

660 Trudeau, *Gettysburg: A Testing of Courage*, 323; Laino, *Gettysburg Campaign Atlas*, 179. Pfanz wrote that the "immediate objective was to gain the high ground between Seminary and Cemetery ridges.... Hood's and McLaws's divisions were to envelop the enemy left and drive it in" with Hill supporting while Ewell was to demonstrate against the Federal right

and attack in full force if an opportunity presented itself. Pfanz, *Gettysburg: The Second Day*, 113.

661 Pfanz, *Gettysburg: The Second Day*, 113.

662 McLaws, "Gettysburg," in *SHSP*, vol. 7, 69.

663 In notes of his conversations with Lee after the war, Ewell's former staff officer William Allan wrote that Lee thought "victory [would] have been won if he could have gotten one decided simultaneous attack on the whole line. This he tried his utmost and failed." Allan, "Memoranda," in Gallagher, *Lee the Soldier*, 14.

664 O.R. 27.2: 366.

665 O.R. 27.2: 372.

666 McLaws, "Gettysburg," in *SHSP*, vol. 7, 70–71. McLaws wrote that initially he was to march his division in columns of companies, face left (which formed a battle line), and attack the left flank. This would put McLaws across the road, as he said, and also avoid the rough ground south of the Rose farm. Then, when the Federals were spotted in the Peach Orchard, Longstreet issued the order to hit the orchard and then wheel to the left.

667 OR 27.2: 380.

668 Longstreet, "Lee's Right Wing at Gettysburg," in *Battles & Leaders*, 3: 341.

669 O.R. 27.2: 404.

670 Longstreet to McLaws, Dec. 11, 1887, in McLaws Papers, UNC Wilson Library. Alexander's descriptions of his routes, reviewed in detail later, also suggest he followed the Ravine Road. See "Gettysburg's Field: The Visit of the Union and Confederate Generals," *The Philadelphia Times*, April 30, 1893; Alexander to Jones, March 17, 1877, in *SHSP* vol. 4, 101; Gallaghered., *Fighting for the Confederacy*, 236.

671 In 1877, Walter Taylor wrote "General Longstreet clearly admits that he assumed the responsibility of postponing the execution of the orders of the commanding general." Taylor argues, convincingly enough on its face, that Longstreet "received instructions to move *with the portion of his command that was then up*, to gain the Emmettsburg [sic] road on the enemy's left; but fearing that his force was too weak to venture to make an attack, he delayed until Law's brigade joined its division, about noon on the 2d." Taylor, *Four Years with General Lee*, 98.

Armistead Long made the same argument in his memoir. Long, *Memoirs of Robert E. Lee*, 281–283.

672   Longstreet explicitly asked Armistead Long where Anderson's division was at the time the orders were issued. Long answered that "about 10 o'clock a.m. on the 2d of July I accompanied General Lee on a reconnaissance of Genl Meade's position from the heights occupied by the Third Corps. At that time R.H. Anderson's division was in reserve a little to the rear and right of the other…divisions of Hill's Corps and so remained until it was ordered to support your attack in the afternoon." Long to Longstreet, April 19, 1876, in Long Papers, UNC Wilson Library. Longstreet's letter to Long is dated April 11, 1876, and also located in Long's papers at UNC Wilson Library. Longstreet, for what it was worth, always maintained that he didn't receive orders any earlier than 10 a.m. In his *Battle & Leaders* article, he wrote that Anderson "advanced on the morning of the 2d at 10 am to find its position on the right of Hill's Corps."

673   O.R. 27.2: 630.

674   O.R. 27.2: 614.

675   O.R. 27.2: 671.

676   Purifoy, "Battle of Gettysburg, July 2, 1863," in *Confederate Veteran*, vol. 31, 416

677   Alexander, *Military Memoirs*, 391.

678   Alexander, "Report," in *SHPS* vol. 4, 235.

679   O.R. 27.2: 617.

680   O.R. 27.2: 622. When Wright stepped out for his illness, Colonel William Gibson of the Forty-eighth Georgia took over. Gibson told Wright that "between 4 and 5 p.m. the brigade reached a position three-fourths of a mile to the right of the turnpike, and about 2 ½ or 3 miles from Gettysburg, where they remained until next morning, and where I found them in line of battle on returning to the command at 7 a.m. on July 2."

681   O.R. 27.2: 613.

682   O.R. 27.1: 607.

683   For reference, the First Shot Marker is 1.9 miles from the Park Service's Stone-Meredith Avenue.

684   O.R. 27.2: 613.

685   Park Ranger Karlton Smith, who penned a fantastic analysis of the reconnaissance and countermarch for the 2006 Gettysburg National Park Seminar, concluded this, as well. Smith, "To Consider Every Contingency," in *Papers of the 2006 Gettysburg National Military Park Seminar*, 109.

686   Longstreet, "Lee in Pennsylvania," in *Annals of the War*, 422. In his *Battles & Leaders* article, he wrote it was "about 11 o'clock" when Lee "ordered

the march." Longstreet, "Lee's Right Wing at Gettysburg," *Battles & Leaders*, 3: 340. Finally, in his memoirs, he wrote "it was eleven o'clock when General Lee's orders were issued." Longstreet, *From Manassas to Appomattox*, 365.

687   Maurice, ed., *Aide-de-Camp of Lee*, 233–234.

688   Alexander, *Military Memoirs*, 391.

689   Alexander, "Report," in *SHPS* vol. 4, 235. Emphasis added. Alexander initially reported a 9 a.m. arrival time in his report dated August 3, 1863. But Osmond Taylor reported to *him* on August 3, too, and a week later, Alexander used Taylor's time as the battalion's arrival time. All of Alexander's accounts vary as to the time of arrival, so it's not unreasonable to assume he didn't have accurate notes and simply reported what his subordinate reported to him. Either way, it appears Alexander arrived around 10 a.m. and began marching around 11 a.m., in line with Longstreet's and Marshall's recollections.

690   O.R. 27.2: 432.

691   Johnston to F. Lee, Feb. 11, 1878, in S.R. Johnston Papers, VHS.

692   McLaws, "Gettysburg," in *SHSP* vol. 7, 68.

693   Fremantle, *Three Months in the Confederate States*, 233–234, 236, 238.

694   Fremantle, *Three Months in the Southern States*, 256–257, 290, 303. Longstreet also corroborates the timeline in his first article for the *Philadelphia Weekly Press*. He writes "On the morning of the 2d, I went to General Lee's headquarters at daylight, and renewed my views against making an attack." Longstreet, "Lee in Pennsylvania," in *Annals of the War*, 422. The contents of Longstreet's discussion with Lee are debatable, but there is enough contemporary evidence that he arrived at daylight to believe that aspect of his account.

695   Black, *Crumbling Defenses*, 7–9, 36–37. Black then goes on to describe the troops "massed in brigades" and resting, or cleaning their rifles, eating, and otherwise "preparing for action." *Crumbling Defenses*, 38. Black seems to have passed through Hood's Division first, as he describes the resting troops eating and cleaning weapons. If Hood arrived first and McLaws was just arriving ("his corps [was] still marching up and massing in Brigades"), then Black saw McLaws arriving. He recalls seeing Barksdale during this tour of Longstreet's Corps, indicating a significant portion of McLaws's Division had arrived, for Kershaw was first in line.

696   Fremantle, *Three Months in the Southern States*, 257.

697   "I never saw him use a note-book or any scrap of paper as an aid to memory, and yet his book puts down things with much accuracy." Sorrel, *Recollections of a Staff Officer*, 180.

698   Longstreet wrote two articles for the *Philadelphia Weekly Press* which appeared in the anthology titled *Annals of the War*. One of the articles was a detailed account of his actions, while the other served more as an argument paper in his own defense. He then published an article appearing in the *Battles & Leaders* collection, followed by his memoir, *From Manassas to Appomattox*.

699   Longstreet, "Lee in Pennsylvania," in *Annals of the War*, 422. McLaws told Longstreet that he thought his division arrived "between 8 & 9 o'clock or earlier." McLaws to Longstreet, June 12, 1873, in McLaws Papers, UNC Wilson Library. Johnston's recollection supports Longstreet's in that they both remembered a delay that morning. Longstreet left Lee's activities between 9 a.m. and 11 a.m. unstated. Johnston remembered being ordered to assist Longstreet at about 9 a.m., and then waiting for quite some time. In an 1878 letter to Fitzhugh Lee in direct response to Longstreet's *Weekly Press* article, Johnston wrote that "after I made my report I withdrew, leaving the Generals in conference; soon after I was ordered to ride with General Longstreet. After no little delay the column got in motion…. The delay of several hours cannot be attributed to Gen'l Longstreet having taken the wrong road…but to the delay in getting under way," etc. Johnston to F. Lee, Feb. 11, 1878. S.R. Johnston Papers, VHS. Then in 1892, he wrote McLaws "I am not sure but I think it must have been 9 a.m. when I joined General Longstreet. We did not move off very promptly." Johnston to McLaws, June 27, 1892. S.R. Johnston Papers, VHS.

700   Tagg, *The Generals of Gettysburg*, 210, 252.

701   Larry Tagg suggests McLaws *was* upset by the slight. *The Generals of Gettysburg*, 211.

702   Fremantle recalled Longstreet riding in front of Wofford's Georgia brigade, "hat in hand, and in front of everybody." *Three Months in the Southern States*, 261; McLaws, "Gettysburg," in *SHSP* vol. 7, 74. Kershaw recalled his instructions coming from both Longstreet and McLaws in rapid succession. Kershaw, "Kershaw's Brigade at Gettysburg," *Battles & Leaders*, 3: 332–333. McLaws also relates that Longstreet questioned his artillery placement: "General Longstreet then came up in person and I met him. His first words were, 'Why is not a battery placed here?'"

McLaws explained that it would draw fire to the infantry, but Longstreet issued a "peremptory order for a battery." General Barksdale famously wanted to charge, but McLaws had to wait for Longstreet's permission. "General Barksdale two or three times came to me and said, 'General, let me go; General, let me charge!' But, as I was waiting General Longstreet's will, I told General Barksdale to wait." McLaws, "Gettysburg," in *SHSP* vol. 7, 72–73.

703   McLaws to Wife, July 7, 1863, in McLaws Papers, UNC Wilson Library.

704   "Biography of Thomas J. Moncure," *Richmond Times*, June 12, 1901; Thomas J. Moncure file, NARA, M258, RG 109. The only evidence Moncure was at Gettysburg, aside from McLaws's account, is a statement in his 1912 obituary: "He was in Pickett's charge at Gettysburg . . ." "In Memoriam: Thomas J. Moncure," *The (Fredericksburg, VA) Daily Star*, Sept. 2, 1912. This is suspect, for an engineer would not be in the attack and McLaws's Divisions did not participate in Pickett's Charge. While commanders routinely thanked their staff in their official reports, the lack of any surviving reports from McLaws's headquarters frustrates the efforts to place Moncure at Gettysburg. Neither spelling of his name appears in the Gettysburg volume of the *Official Records*. The *Washington Post* ran a short biography in 1901 when Moncure was a delegate in Virginia's constitutional convention in 1902, in which it said "He was with McLaws's division at Gettysburg and at Chickamauga." "Delegate Thomas J. Moncure," *The Free Lance (Fredericksburg, VA)*, July 13, 1901. But that was well after he had become a key component in McLaws's articles, all of which had been published by then. Anyone doing biographical research would have McLaws's accounts readily available, as they appeared in large newspapers and the *Southern Historical Society Papers*.

      On June 9, 1863, less than a week after Lee made his first steps in what became the Gettysburg Campaign, Moncure was nominated for First Lieutenant of Engineers by Jeremy F. Gilmer, chief of the Engineer Bureau. Thomas J. Moncure file, NARA, M258, RG 109.

705   O.R. 31.1: 508.

706   William Proctor Smith, Report of the Battle of Gettysburg, Letter Book 1863-1864, KHS.

707   William Proctor Smith, Report of the Battle of Gettysburg, Letter Book 1863-1864, KHS.

708 William Proctor Smith, Report of the Battle of Gettysburg, Letter Book 1863-1864, KHS. Capt. Collins is Captain Charles Reed Collins, who was an engineer officer with the Army of Northern Virginia and served with Kershaw until transferring to the cavalry as a Major in April 1863, shortly after Proctor Smith arrived. Krick, *Staff Officers in Gray*, 101; Charles R. Collins file, NARA, M324, RG 109. Smith notes the departure of Collins for the cavalry in his report, as well.

709 William Proctor Smith, Report of the Battle of Gettysburg, Letter Book 1863-1864, KHS.

710 "There were many halts, the question arising as to the proper route to be pursued, so as to avoid the observation of the enemy, as we had no guide." Goggin to Longstreet, Aug. 15, 1887, in GNMP V7-SC-Brigades. Original in USAMHI.

711 McLaws also could not have watched the Federal troops march up the Emmitsburg Road for hours upon hours as he waited for orders. The topography and foliage has changed dramatically since the battle, disrupting the modern viewshed, and modern viewers cannot see much of what McLaws would have seen on the morning of July 2. It's certainly possible a high point along the ridge allowed McLaws to see the Emmitsburg Road with the aid of field glasses. But what he claimed to have seen simply wasn't there. Only two brigades of infantry, perhaps 3,000 men, marched up the Emmitsburg Road that morning. All had arrived at their destination by 10 a.m. There simply weren't hordes of Yankee troops funneling along the Emmitsburg Road for hours that morning.

 Col. Regis de Trobriand arrived with his brigade, which had been left behind with Col. George Burling's New Jersey Brigade, at 10 a.m. the morning of the second. O.R. 27.1:519. Burling reported arriving at about 9 a.m. O.R. 27.1: 570. General Andrew Humphreys's adjutant, Major Charles Hamlin, wrote to Humphreys barely a month after the battle that Burling's Brigade "came up at about 9 o'clock July 2d." Hamlin to Humphreys, Aug. 11, 1863, in GNMP V5-Humphreys, A.A.

 Glenn Tucker, relying on McLaws and Longstreet, wrote that the First Corps "groped for a good route by which to reach Meade's flank undetected." *High Tide at Gettysburg*, 235.

712 McLaws to Longstreet, June 10, 1873, in McLaws Papers, UNC Wilson Library.

713 Johnston to F. Lee, Feb. 11, 1878, in S.R. Johnston Papers, VHS.

714   McLaws to Longstreet, June 12, 1873, in McLaws Papers, UNC Wilson Library.

715   McLaws to Longstreet, June 12, 1873, in McLaws Papers, UNC Wilson Library. (Emphasis added).

716   In his 1879 *Southern Historical Society Papers* article, he follows Longstreet's lead and says Lee specifically mentioned Johnston's name to McLaws as the officer who had reconnoitered. McLaws, "Gettysburg," in *SHSP* vol. 4, 68. Longstreet says Johnston was ordered to lead the column. Longstreet, "Lee in Pennsylvania," in *Annals of the War*, 422. McLaws alone connects the dots to the conclusion that Johnston was the reconnoitering officer they were waiting on.

717   Johnston to F. Lee, Feb. 11, 1878, in S.R. Johnston Papers, VHS.

718   Longstreet, "Lee in Pennsylvania," in *Annals of the War*, 422.

719   F. Lee, "A Review of the First Two Days' Operations at Gettysburg," in *SHSP* vol. 5, 183–184. Fitzhugh Lee was somewhat fair to Longstreet in the article, recognizing Longstreet's contribution to "the cause" and even acknowledging the right to political disagreement, while vehemently disagreeing with his treatment of Lee since the end of the war.

720   McLaws, "Gettysburg," in *SHSP* vol. 7, 68–69.

721   Johnston to F. Lee, Feb. 11, 1878, in S.R. Johnston Papers, VHS; Johnston to McLaws, June 27, 1892, in S.R. Johnston Papers, VHS.

722   "For the sake of tracing more exactly the mode of approach, I proceeded some distance along the ravine road." O.R. 27.2: 350.

723   Alexander, *Military Memoirs*, 391.

724   In his report in the *Official Records*, Alexander says he arrived at 9 a.m. O.R. 27.2: 429. In his revised report a week later, he wrote that he arrived at 10 a.m. Alexander "Report," in *SHSP* vol. 4, 235.

725   Page, *Reminiscences*, in Shields Collection, W&L Leyburn Libary, 7.

726   West to "My Dear Little Man," July 8, 1863, in West, *A Texan in Search of a Fight*, 85. The July 8, 1863 letter is also available at the Gettysburg National Military Park Library and Research Center, V7-TX4.

727   Sims, *Recollection of A.C. Sims*, in GNMP V7-TX1.

728   Johnston to F. Lee, Feb. 11, 1878, in S.R. Johnston Papers, VHS.

729   McLaws, "Gettysburg," in *SHSP*, vol. 7, 69.

730   Page had been "disgusted," remember, when he found Longstreet's men at rest after he had delivered his prisoners. But Page had arrived when Lee was still scouting Cemetery Hill from Ewell's position. Page, *Reminiscences*, in Shields Collection, W&L Leyburn Libary, 9. George Peterkin

thought Pendleton was absolutely right in his recollections. "What you say of the lateness of Genl Longstreet's arrival + attack is unquestionably true." Peterkin to Pendleton, Dec. 6, 1875, in Pendleton Papers, UNC Wilson Library. Long, in his memoir, remembered "Lee's impatience increased after this reconnaissance [of Cemetery Hill], and he proceeded in search of Longstreet, remarking, in a tone of uneasiness, 'What *can* detain Longstreet? He ought to be in position now.' This was about 10 A.M." Long, *Memoirs of Robert E. Lee*, 281.

731   Pfanz points this out in *Gettysburg: The Second Day*, 113–114.

732   James Henry Hendrick to Mother, July 8, 1863, in GNMP V7-TX1. This could just be Hendricks attributing the actual time to the intended time, but there was no real reason for him to mention that they were *supposed* to attack when they did. Given that he wrote the letter a mere six days after the attack, it's strong evidence to support an argument that Lee intended to attack in the mid-afternoon.

733   Jones, ed., *Campbell Brown's Civil War*, 214.

734   O.R. 27.2: 470.

735   O.R. 27.2: 605.

736   Ross, *A Visit to the Cities and Camps of the Confederate States*, 50.

737   O.R. 27.2: 613. Anderson reported "I received orders to take up a new line of battle on the right of Pender's division, about a mile and a half farther forward."

738   Though marching on good roads could see marching speeds of three mph, more likely the farm lanes and terrain slowed it a bit. In estimating times (and it should be stressed that they can only be estimates), a two mph speed is probably more accurate.

739   Black, *Crumbling Defenses*, 38–39. Black said Horsey got back a little before eight. The bridge was the one crossing Marsh Creek on the Fairfield Road.

740   Lee "introduced me to Gen L[ongstreet] & said "…I commend Col. B[lack] to you as once a cadet under me at West Point." Black, *Crumbling Defenses*, 37. Though no one suggested Black led the column, could Longstreet be alluding to him as "one of the engineers" that led them down the wrong road?

    Horsey wouldn't have seen Berdan's men, either, for his reconnaissance would have reported before McLaws left. Berdan's men headed into Pitzer's Woods between 11 a.m. and 11:30 a.m., when McLaws was well on his way.

741   Kershaw to Bachelder, March 20, 1876, in Ladd, *The Bachelder Papers*, 1: 453.

742   O.R. 27.2: 366.

743   McLaws, "Gettysburg," in *SHSP* vol. 7, 69.

744   O.R. 27.1: 515. Berdan reported that his assignment was to send forward a detachment of one hundred sharpshooters to discover, if possible, what the enemy was doing."

745   O.R. 27.1: 515.

746   O.R. 27.1: 516–571. Berdan corroborated the route, but without the condescension, in his own report.

747   O.R. 27.1: 515.

748   O.R. 27.1: 515. Berdan wrote that the Confederates were "changing direction, as it were, by the right flank." It may seem counterintuitive that Berdan saw the Confederates facing right, since one would have to face left to get into position if the column was heading south. But an unknown author from the Eighth Alabama clarifies. Writing to Porter Alexander as part of his response to Alexander's circulars after the war, the anonymous soldier noted that the sharpshooters attacked them as they were "moving diagonally across the field to the left." The Eighth Alabama, meanwhile, *was* "moving by the right flank to a point still farther on the left." This meant the regiment followed the one that would be to its left in line, then turned right to move further down the ridge into its place in line.

The three columns Berdan saw were not three divisions, but rather three columns of Anderson's Division as each brigade and regiment separated to get into line. Author unknown, *A Short History of the 8th Alabama*, E.P. Alexander Papers, UNC Wilson Library. The piece is included in Folder 25b, which covers the end of 1869. Lt. Col. Hilary Herbert, commanding the Eighth Alabama, also remembered that "Wilcox's brigade was marching by the flank when [the 10th Alabama], leading, became engaged with troops in front of us." Herbert to Bachelder, July 9, 1884, in Ladd, *The Bachelder Papers*, 2: 1055–1057.

749   O.R. 27.2: 613.

750   O.R. 27.2: 631.

751   Herbert to Bachelder, July 9, 1884, in Ladd, *The Bachelder Papers*, 2: 1055–1057.

752   O.R. 27.1: 515.

753   Herbert to Bachelder, July 9, 1884, in Ladd, *The Bachelder Papers*, 2: 1055–1057.

754   Herbert to Bachelder, July 9, 1884, in Ladd, *The Bachelder Papers*, 2: 1055–1057; O.R. 27.1: 507.

755   O.R. 27.1: 507. Lakeman reported forty-eight casualties in the brief encounter.

756   Cheney, *History of the Ninth Regiment, New York Cavalry*, 114–115.

757   O.R. 27.1: 939.

758   The Sixth New York's regimental historian wrote that "two squadrons of the Sixth New York were dismounted and deployed in support of the Berdan sharpshooters. Hall, et al., *History of the Sixth New York Cavalry*, 142; A Lieutenant Whittemore was sent with the twenty troopers to support Bradshaw, according to the Ninth New York's regimental history. Cheney, *History of the Ninth Regiment, New York Cavalry*, 114–115

759   O.R. 27.2: 617.

760   O.R. 27.1: 507.

761   O.R. 27.1: 507; Herbert to Bachelder, July 9, 1884, in Ladd, *The Bachelder Papers*, 2: 1055–1057.

762   O.R. 27.1: 507.

763   O.R. 27.1: 507.

764   Batchelder, "The Washington Elm Tradition," *Bits of Cambridge History*, 247.

765   O.R. 27.2: 489.

766   Jerome's first message, at 11:45 a.m., reported that the "enemy's skirmishers are advancing from the west, 1 mile from" his position. O.R. 27.2: 489. Wilcox reported that his skirmishers were out in front of the column and greeted by the fire from the sharpshooters. O.R. 27.2: 617.

767   O.R. 27.1: 202.

768   O.R. 27.1: 202; Brown, *Signal Corps in the War of the Rebellion*, 370.

769   O.R. 27.3: 485. Norton signaled Butterfield that "communication with Emmitsburg is still open, but no communication yet with Gettysburg."

770   O.R. 27.1: 201. Norton reported that the Seminary, town courthouse, and Cemetery Hill were all used as signal stations on July 1; Brown, *Signal Corps in the War of the Rebellion*, 359.

771   Brown, *Signal Corps in the War of the Rebellion*, 370.

772   On June 30, for example, General Reynolds, commanding the left wing of the army, sent a message to General Oliver O. Howard to "be ready to move to [Reynolds's] left, in case [the Confederates] move on him

from Fairfield and the mountain road." O.R. 27.3: 418. On the morning of July 1, Howard told Reynolds that he would move up to supporting distance at Gettysburg, stopping two miles south to cover the intersection of the Millerstown Road and Emmitsburg Road at the Peach Orchard. O.R. 27.3: 457. For further discussion on this, see Thompson, "It Was the Intention to Defend the Place," *Gettysburg Magazine* no. 65, 7–8.

773   Acken, ed., *Service with the Signal Corps*, 248; Brown, *Signal Corps in the War of the Rebellion*, 370.

774   Acken, ed., *Service with the Signal Corps*, 248–250.

775   Acken, ed., *Service with the Signal Corps*, 251.

776   Acken, ed., *Service with the Signal Corps*, 251; Fortescue Diary, UNC Wilson Library.

777   O.R. 27.1: 202. The reference to "Round Top Mountain" may have been an error in terminology by Norton, since he was writing after the events all took place. Or it may simply have been a transcription error by the compilers of the *Official Records*. It wouldn't be the first. For example, the editors of the *Records* designate a message from Jerome to Oliver Howard regarding a flanking movement *on the right* as July 2, when it's almost certainly referring to Ewell's troops on July 1. O.R. 27.3: 488

778   O.R. 27.1: 202.

779   O.R. 27.3: 489.

780   O.R. 27.3: 486.

781   "At nine o'clock we succeeded in locating a flag flying on the Taneytown Road," Fortescue wrote. But "about 11 a.m. we were informed by the station on the Taneytown Road that they had been ordered up to head-quarters…and we are therefore again in the air without communication." Acken, ed., *Service with the Signal Corps*, 251–252.

782   Fortescue wrote that he sent written messages via courier in addition to the flag signals. Acken, ed., *Service with the Signal Corps*, 251.

783   Acken, ed., *Service with the Signal Corps*, 251–252.

784   Acken, ed., *Service with the Signal Corps*, 253. In his pocket diary, he doesn't mention the morning attempts, but curiously refers to Little Round Top as "Pigeon Hill." "A very heavy battle commenced at Gettysburg," he scribbled in the diary. "Our line of battle extended from the town to Pigeon Hill a distance of four miles." Fortescue Diary, UNC Wilson Library.

785   Captain E.C. Pierce, one of the Sixth Corps signal officers, reported that on July 3, after suffering losses from sharpshooters picking off men on

Little Round Top, they decided it was impossible to use flag signals "and consequently we continued to report by orderlies." Brown, *Signal Corps in the War of the Rebellion*, 362.

786 Neither Devin's nor Buford's reports state a specific time, but Devin notes that shortly after the Pitzer Woods fight, they marched to Taneytown. "The enemy not pressing his advance, and the Third Corps coming into position, we were ordered to march to Taneytown." O.R. 27.1: 939. Historian Eric Wittenberg writes that Gamble left first, at 11 a.m., followed by Devin a little after noon. Wittenberg, *The Devil's to Pay*, 177–178. If that's the case, then Jerome left with Devin's men, since he was on Little Round Top during the Pitzer Woods fight and Devin acknowledged leaving after the fight was over.

787 O.R. 27.3: 488. The time stamp in the *Official Records* is 1:30 p.m.

788 Alexander, "Artillery Fighting at Gettysburg," in *Battles & Leaders*, 3: 358.

789 Longstreet, "Lee in Pennsylvania," in *Annals of the War*, 423; McLaws, "Gettysburg," in *SHSP* vol. 7, 69; Stephen Sears blames the signal station for stopping McLaws and forcing the countermarch. *Gettysburg*, 258. Harry Pfanz wrote that McLaws "halted when it appeared that his troops could be seen from Little Round Top. He and Captain Johnston, and possibly others, searched for a suitable alternate route out of sight of the signalmen." *Gettysburg: The Second Day*, 119. The "wig-wagging" description is taken from Gallagher, ed., *Fighting for the Confederacy*, 235.

790 Batchelder, "The Washington Elm Tradition," *Bits of Cambridge History*, 247.

791 McLaws, "Gettysburg," in *SHSP*, vol. 7, 69.

792 McLaws, "Longstreet at Gettysburg," *Philadelphia Weekly Press*, Feb. 15, 1888, inn GMNP V5-McLaws, Lafayette.

793 McLaws, "The Battle of Gettysburg," in GNMP, V5-McLaws, Lafayette.

794 McLaws to Longstreet, June 12, 1873, in McLaws Papers, UNC Wilson Library.

795 McLaws, "Gettysburg," in *SHSP* vol. 7, 70.

796 O.R. 27.2: 350.

797 Coxe, "The Battle of Gettysburg," *Confederate Veteran*, vol. 21, 433. Coxe's account was published in 1913 and he thought the firing was in the Peach Orchard. But the Peach Orchard isn't visible from the hill and there wasn't "desultory picket firing" at the Peach Orchard at that time.

798 Without getting into the many variables as to how the human eye discerns objects, "human-scale" objects (as opposed to light sources) can

be discerned at around two miles. Of course, various factors affect this, particularly the angle, which distorts perceived height. In order to be seen and recognized, an object should have an angle of at least 1 arcminute (1/60 of a degree). At 15,000 feet (nearly three miles) a six-foot object (such as a human or signal flag) has an angle of 1.37 arcminutes (.022918 degrees). The Little Round Top signal station is 2.85 miles from McLaws Hill. A calculator and formula can be found at https://www.1728.org/angsize.htm. For a short and accessible explanation, see Wolchover, "How Far Can the Human Eye See?" https://www.livescience.com/33895-human-eye.html?msclkid=0ac86ebdd0cb11eca00ec5cc6cf82a15

799   O.R. 27.1: 518.

800   McLaws to Longstreet, June 12, 1873, in McLaws Papers, UNC Wilson Library.

801   McLaws's first public statement referring to a signal station was in "Gettysburg," in *SHSP* vol. 7, 69.

802   Longstreet, "Lee in Pennsylvania," in *Annals of the War*, 423–424; Alexander, "Letter from General E.P. Alexander, late Chief of Artillery, First Corps, A.N.V. March 17th, 1877," in *SHSP*, vol. 4, 101. Swinton referenced a signal station on "the summit of the hill" in his *Campaigns of the Army of the Potomac*, but his reference is primarily to the signal station on the hill when Warren arrived just before the attack started. Swinton, *Campaigns of the Army of the Potomac*, 346.

803   O.R. 27.2: 366.

804   McLaws to Longstreet, June 12, 1873, in McLaws Papers, UNC Wilson Library; McLaws, "Gettysburg," in *SHSP* vol. 7, 69. The *Southern Historical Society Papers* account is substantially the same as the one he told Longstreet in 1873, with the exception of the signal station's prominence.

805   Longstreet, "Lee in Pennsylvania," in *Annals of the War*, 422–423.

806   Though Longstreet was initially vague about whether he actually rode to McLaws's column to see what caused the delay, by 1888, he acknowledged that he in fact "rode forward to ascertain the cause" of the delay, which is what Kershaw reported in 1863. Longstreet, "Lee in Pennsylvania," in *Annals of the War*, 423; Longstreet, "Lee's Right Wing at Gettysburg," in *Battles & Leaders*, 3: 340.

807   "The corps was not put under my charge to be taken where I saw fit, for certainly I had not received any instructions from either Gen'l Lee or Gen'l Longstreet as to where the latter was to go." Johnston to Fitz Lee, Feb. 11, 1878, in S.R. Johnston Papers, VHS. When he responded

to McLaws's letter in 1892, though, Johnston said that he stayed with Longstreet the whole time, telling the First Corps commander directly that McLaws would expose his troops to Federal observation. Johnston to McLaws, June 27, 1892, in S.R. Johnston Papers, VHS. "Around the neighborhood" quote comes from McLaws, "Gettysburg," in *SHSP* vol. 7, 69.

808   O.R. 27.2: 366.

809   Goggin to Longstreet, Aug. 15, 1887, in GNMP V7-SC-Brigades. Original in USAMHI.

810   Page, *Reminiscences*, in Shields Collection, W&L Leyburn Libary, 7.

811   Peterkin to Pendleton, Dec. 6, 1875, in Pendleton Papers, UNC Wilson Library.

812   O.R. 27.2: 350.

813   Page, *Reminiscences*, in Shields Collection, W&L Leyburn Libary, 10. The initial typescript reads "And when I reported to Gen. Pendleton on my return from Gen. Lee's headquarters about 10 A.M. and learned that Lieut. Peterkin had reported that he could not find Gen. Longstreet; and having seen his troops marching and counter-marching on my return, I was utterly amazed…" The time is crossed out in what appear to be self-edits and "had reported that he had met the head of McLaws' Division, but" is inserted between "had reported that he" and "could not find Gen. Longstreet." With the handwritten corrections, it reads, "And when I reported to Gen. Pendleton on my return from Gen. Lee's headquarters [about 10 A.M.] and learned that Lieut. Peterkin had reported [he had met the head of McLaws Division, but could not find Gen. Longstreet."

814   Ross, *A Visit to the Cities and Camps of the Confederate States*, 59; Lawley, *The Times* (London), Aug. 18, 1863. Lawley heard McLaws didn't attack with "sufficient promptitude." Part of this accusation almost certainly involved the claims that McLaws didn't begin his attack promptly enough to support Hood.

815   Ross, *A Visit to the Confederate Cities and Camps*, 54. Ross noted a "long consultation with the Commander-in-Chief" early in the afternoon, for he met Longstreet at 3 p.m. after the corps commander's meeting with Lee.

816   O.R. 27.2: 350. The farmhouse was probably the James Warfield house, but it may have been a small farmhouse inhabited by C. Shefferer.

817   Long, *Memoirs of Robert E. Lee*, 281. Long also mentioned Lee's trip to this portion of the field to Jubal Early in an 1876 letter, though as would be

expected in a letter to Early, Long blamed Lee's anxiety as to Longstreet's whereabouts as the reason for the trip. Long to Early, April 5, 1876, in *SHSP* vol. 4, 68.

818   Long to Early, April 5, 1876, in *SHSP* vol. 4, 68.

819   Alexander, *Military Memoirs*, 391. Alexander wrote that "about 10 [Lee] returned" from the Confederate left, "and presently received the report from Long and Pendleton who had reconnoitered on the right." Long and Pendleton didn't reconnoiter the right together, but they *were* together with Lee on the southern portion of Seminary Ridge at the same time Alexander was conducting his initial reconnaissance.

820   Walker to F. Lee, in Lee, F. "A Review of the First Two Days' Operations," in *SHSP* vol. 5, 181.

821   Gallagher, ed., *Fighting for the Confederacy*, xv–xvi; Certification of John Leconte, July 13, 1868, in Edward Porter Alexander Papers, UNC Wilson Library; Confidential letter to Alexander, March 5, 1870, in Edward Porter Alexander Papers, UNC Wilson Library.

822   Gallagher, "If the Enemy is There, We Must Attack Him," in *The Second Day at Gettysburg*, 15.

823   Alexander, "Colonel E.P. Alexander's Report of the Battle of Gettysburg," in *SHSP* vol. 4, 235.

824   Alexander, "Letter from General E.P. Alexander, late Chief of Artillery, First Corps, A.N.V. March 17th, 1877," in *SHSP*, vol. 4, 101; Alexander, "Artillery Fighting at Gettysburg," in *Battles & Leaders*, 3: 358; Gallagher, ed., *Fighting for the Confederacy*, 235. Herr's Ridge is broad and open where it meets the Chambersburg Pike. Herr's Ridge Woods begins about 400 yards to the south of the road. Most likely, Alexander, being the last of Longstreet's column to arrive, took a spot in the woods and open field along the Chambersburg Pike on Herr's Ridge. Alexander *was* consistent that his position was a mile from Seminary Ridge, placing him on Herr's Ridge.

825   Alexander, "Letter from General E.P. Alexander, late Chief of Artillery, First Corps, A.N.V. March 17th, 1877," in *SHSP*, vol. 4, 101.

826   Alexander, "Artillery Fighting at Gettysburg," in *Battles & Leaders*, 3: 358.

827   Gallagher, ed., *Fighting for the Confederacy*, 235. Alexander didn't discuss the specific movements of his battalion that morning in *Military Memoirs of a Confederate*. In his report, he says Longstreet gave him his orders "shortly after our arrival." O.R. 27.2: 429.

828   Alexander, "Letter from General E.P. Alexander, late Chief of Artillery, First Corps, A.N.V. March 17th, 1877," in *SHSP*, vol. 4, 101. His later recollections all agree on this point. Alexander, "Artillery Fighting at Gettysburg," in *Battles & Leaders*, 3: 358; Gallagher, ed., *Fighting for the Confederacy*, 235.

829   Alexander, "Letter from General E.P. Alexander, late Chief of Artillery, First Corps, A.N.V. March 17th, 1877," in *SHSP*, vol. 4, 101.

830   Gallagher, ed., *Fighting for the Confederacy*, 235.

831   Alexander, "Artillery Fighting at Gettysburg," in *Battles & Leaders*, 3: 358.

832   Gallagher, ed., *Fighting for the Confederacy*, 235–236.

833   O.R. 27.2: 350.

834   Gallagher, ed., *Fighting for the Confederacy*, 236.

835   Alexander, "Letter from General E.P. Alexander, late Chief of Artillery, First Corps, A.N.V. March 17th, 1877," in *SHSP*, vol. 4, 101.

836   Alexander, "Letter from General E.P. Alexander, late Chief of Artillery, First Corps, A.N.V. March 17th, 1877," in *SHSP*, vol. 4, 101.

837   Gallagher, ed., *Fighting for the Confederacy*, 236.

838   The "non-arrival" quote is from Alexander, *Military Memoirs of a Confederate*, 392; Alexander, "Artillery Fighting at Gettysburg," in *Battles & Leaders*, 3: 359.

839   "I immediately started my reconnaissance, and in about three hours had a good idea of all the ground, and had Cabell's, Henry's, and my own battalions parked near where our infantry lines were to be formed and the attack begun." Alexander, "Artillery Fighting at Gettysburg," in *Battles & Leaders*, 3: 359. Alexander refers to the valley by name in *Fighting for the Confederacy*, 236.

840   O.R. 27.2: 432; "Colonel E.P. Alexander's Report of the Battle of Gettysburg," in *SHSP* vol. 4, 235.

841   "Colonel E.P. Alexander's Report of the Battle of Gettysburg," in *SHSP* vol. 4, 235.

842   O.R. 27.2: 350.

843   Alexander, "Letter from General E.P. Alexander, late Chief of Artillery, First Corps, A.N.V. March 17th, 1877," in *SHSP*, vol. 4, 101.

844   Gallagher, ed., *Fighting for the Confederacy*, 235–236.

845   "About midday General Longstreet arrived and viewed the ground. He desired Colonel [E.P.] Alexander to obtain the best view he then could of the front. I therefore conducted the colonel to the advanced point of observation previously visited." O.R. 27.2: 350.

846 O.R. 27.2: 350.

847 Alexander, "Letter from General E.P. Alexander, late Chief of Artillery, First Corps, A.N.V. March 17th, 1877," in *SHSP*, vol. 4, 101. He wrote substantially the same thing in his personal memoir: "I don't think it took me much over an hour to get a very fair idea of the ground & roads & to find Cabell's & Henry's battalions, & give them what instructions were needed. Then I rode back to bring up my own battalion." Gallagher, ed., *Fighting for the Confederacy*, 236.

848 Alexander, "Artillery Fighting at Gettysburg," in *Battles & Leaders*, 3: 359. According to Alexander, reconnoitering and moving the artillery into position took a total of three hours.

849 Pfanz, *Gettysburg; The Second Day*, 117–118. "Alexander probably led his batteries over the road that runs from the Chambersburg Pike along Marsh Creek to Black Horse Tavern. The battalion crossed the Fairfield Road to the road leading south beyond it, climbed the hill, and in order to avoid being seen by the Federal signalmen, turned into the fields to bypass the exposed crest. It then returned to the road and followed it along Willoughby Run to Pitzer's Schoolhouse." Stephen Sears also places Alexander on the Black Horse Tavern Road. *Gettysburg*, 257–258. Noah Trudeau suggests the same, for he writes that McLaws was supposed to follow Alexander. *Gettysburg: A Testing of Courage*, 312. The suggestion is not that McLaws took the wrong route, but that Alexander went the Black Horse Tavern Road. Glenn Tucker also thought Alexander took the Black Horse Tavern Road. Tucker, *High Tide at Gettysburg*, 233.

Coddington, on the other hand, thought Alexander followed Willoughby Run the whole way. After he gathered his battalions, he "sent them down Willoughby Run to Pitzer's School House on the Fairfield crossroad." *Gettysburg: A Study in Command*, 375. Coddington uses the term "Fairfield crossroad" to describe the Eiker's Mill Road, or the modern-day Millerstown Road.

850 Alexander, "Letter from General E.P. Alexander, late Chief of Artillery, First Corps, A.N.V. March 17th, 1877," in *SHSP*, vol. 4, 101.

851 Gallagher, ed., *Fighting for the Confederacy*, 236.

852 Gallagher, ed., *Fighting for the Confederacy*, 236 n. 45, 585.

853 Pfanz, *Gettysburg; The Second Day*, 489. Interestingly, Coddington assumed Alexander turned out to the *right* based on Alexander's writings before the publication of his personal memoirs. Coddington published his magnum

opus in 1968, two decades before Alexander's memoirs were found and edited by Gary Gallagher.

854   "Gettysburg's Field: The Visit of the Union and Confederate Generals," *The Philadelphia Times*, April 30, 1893.

855   Though there are heights that could be called "precipitous" along Marsh Creek, Alexander's detour would have had to have been five times longer than he remembered for that to be the route. Following the Plank Road off to the right from McLaws Hill is a mile and a half, 2,500 yards. Likewise, some have proposed Alexander made it as far as the Crawford farm along Marsh Creek, if not beyond Marsh Creek. Alexander was consistently clear on two points: the road was "short and direct" and he cut around the hill through fields and meadows. The Marsh Creek route is neither short nor direct and it follows a *lane—not meadows—around* the hill and back to the road. Without any additional evidence, it's hard to justify such a deviation from his account. The modern—day Willoughby Run Road does not cross the creek.

     Not only do the Marsh Creek routes require a major departure from Alexander's description when taken as a whole, it would be seriously negligent and unlikely for Alexander to have gone that far away from his battle line. He had conferred with Pendleton that morning, who had encountered Federal cavalry much closer to the main line that morning, making it irresponsible in the extreme to take an unaccompanied and vulnerable battalion that far from its support.

856   In his *Battles & Leaders* account, he remembered the reconnaissance and march taking three hours. Alexander, "Artillery Fighting at Gettysburg," in *Battles & Leaders,* 3: 359. Elsewhere, he thought the reconnaissance took perhaps two hours. Alexander, "Letter from General E.P. Alexander, late Chief of Artillery, First Corps, A.N.V. March 17th, 1877," in *SHSP*, vol. 4, 101.

857   Pfanz, *Gettysburg: The Second Day*, 118.

858   Peterkin to Pendleton, Dec. 6, 1875, in Pendleton Papers, UNC Wilson Library.

859   O.R. 27.2: 366. Kershaw remembered that the "major-general commanding" (McLaws—Longstreet was a Lieutenant-General) returned, but was silent as to Longstreet's whereabouts. Though later accounts place Longstreet with McLaws when McLaws rode back to the column, other evidence, as we saw, suggests Longstreet tended to other matters while

McLaws executed the countermarch. "In a few minutes (not five) both returned," Kershaw wrote to Bachelder in 1876. Kershaw to Bachelder, March 20, 1876, in Ladd, *The Bachelder Papers,* 1: 454. Fitzgerald Ross, though, remembered Longstreet engaged in a "long consultation" with Lee. Ross, *A Visit to the Confederate Cities and Camps,* 54.

860 Casey, *Infantry Tactics,* vol. 1, 104–110; vol. 2, 95–96. Casey's tactical manual provides for platoon level maneuvering during the countermarch. Practically, this would involve the company.

861 McLaws to wife, July 7, 1863, in McLaws Papers, UNC Wilson Library.

862 McLaws to wife, August 14, 1863, in McLaws Papers, UNC Wilson Library.

863 Taylor to brother, July 17, 1863, in Tower, ed., *Lee's Adjutant,* 61.

864 Latrobe wrote that they "succeeded in driving the enemy far back but not being cooperated with by Hill had to be partially retired from the ground we had gained." Latrobe Diary, July 2, 1863, in Maryland Historical Society. Hotchkiss said that "we made a vigorous attack on the enemy – though not a simultaneous one + drove them from some of their positions." Hotchkiss Diary, July 2, 1863, LOC.

865 O.R. 27.2: 366–367.

866 O.R. 27.2: 372.

867 Longstreet's report mentions that the engineers from both Lee's staff and his own "guided us by a road which would have completely disclosed the move" and that "some delay ensued in seeking a more concealed route." O.R. 27.2: 358. But he doesn't give any details or describe a countermarch, per se.

868 Kershaw to Bachelder, March 20, 1876, in Ladd, *The Bachelder Papers,* 1: 454.

869 Kershaw, "Kershaw's Brigade at Gettysburg," *Battles & Leaders,* 3: 33–332. Kershaw also used the term "by-road" to describe Herr's Ridge Road. Kershaw to Bachelder, March 20, 1876, in Ladd, *The Bachelder Papers,* 1: 453.

870 O.R. 27.3: 488.

871 Longstreet remembered the march as slow, blaming the speed (or lack thereof) on "the conductor" of the march having to stop and find new ways to avoid the signal station. Longstreet, "Lee in Pennsylvania," in *Annals of the War,* 422–423. Johnston also thought "the slowness of the march" had something to do with the delay in the attack. Johnston to F. Lee, Feb. 11, 1878, in S.R. Johnston Papers, VHS. Describing the march

to McLaws, he said they didn't "move off promptly, nor was our march at all rapid." Johnston to McLaws, June 27, 1892, in S.R. Johnston Papers, VHS. And of course, there were the whispers that McLaws's lack of speed contributed to the loss.

872   Kershaw remembered that "McLaws halted the troops and with Longstreet went over the hill along the road we were on." Kershaw to Bachelder, March 20, 1876, in Ladd, *The Bachelder Papers*, 1: 454.

873   Peterkin told Pendleton in 1875 that when Longstreet's first route didn't pan out, "you sent me to put into use the knowledge of the other road which we had acquired in our early morning ride." His diary says that he was sent to "guide Genl McLaws by the road along the creek bottom." Peterkin to Pendleton, Dec. 6, 1875, in Pendleton Papers, UNC Wilson Library. Pendleton reported that he sent his staff back to Longstreet closer to McLaws's second halt, suggesting McLaws only needed directions from Herr's Ridge. Of course, he knew how to get back there.

874   In a letter to Bachelder in 1876, Kershaw remembered that "in a few minutes (not five) both returned." As we saw, Kershaw was probably mistaken as to Longstreet's return, but he gives a good indication of the time McLaws and Longstreet spent away from the column. Kershaw to Bachelder, March 20, 1876, in Ladd, *The Bachelder Papers*, 1: 454.

875   By all accounts, Law was allowed to rest briefly when he arrived. Law remembered that "in a short time after my brigade came up, the division was moved to our right." Law, "The Struggle for 'Round Top,'" *Battles & Leaders*, 3: 319. In his 1891 letter to John Bachelder, Law told the New England historian that he waited *two hours* before moving. That may not have been far off, for if he arrived at noon and Hood postponed his march to follow McLaws, then they didn't start any earlier than 1:30 (even though they may have been formed into columns and *prepared* to march earlier than that).

876   Longstreet reported that "as soon after [Law's] arrival as we could make our preparations, the movement was begun." O.R. 27.2: 358. It's tempting to interpret Longstreet's statement that the column started soon after Law arrived, but that's not quite what Longstreet said. He said they began the march as soon *as they could* once Law arrived, two very different statements.

877   For example, Walter Taylor wrote that "Longstreet clearly admits that he assumed the responsibility of postponing the execution of the orders of the commanding general" by waiting for Law. Taylor notes that his

orders were, according to his own report, "to move with the portion of his command that was then up, to gain the Emmettsburg [sic] road." Taylor, *Four Years with General Lee*, 98. Longstreet only had two of his three divisions on the field that afternoon – Hood's and McLaws's. Pickett was still miles away and unavailable for an attack on July 2. The "portion of my command that was then up" may have referred to Hood and McLaws more generally, rather than the specific brigades that were up. If that's correct, it's another example of Longstreet's imprecision with words causing problems for both himself and historians.

In Longstreet's report, he seems to say he *did* take it upon himself to wait for Law. "Fearing that my force was too weak to venture to make an attack," he wrote, "I delayed until General Law's brigade joined its division." O.R. 27.2: 358.

878 Law to Bachelder, Deb. 2, 1891, in Ladd, *The Bachelder Papers*, 3: 1790; West to "My Dear Little Man," July 8, 1863, in West, *A Texan in Search of a Fight*, 85.

879 Law to Bachelder, Deb. 2, 1891, in Ladd, *The Bachelder Papers*, 3: 1790.

880 Given the length of his column, about 1.3 miles, the head of McLaws's Division reached the Ravine Road around 1:30, when Capt. Hall saw the tail of his column passing along Herr's Ridge. Lt. Col. William Shepherd of the Second Georgia remembered that "at 1 p.m. it again took up the line of march, moving by a circuitous route to the right." O.R. 27.2: 420. Shepherd's recollection was likely of Hood's men preparing to march and lining up on the road. A little more than a half hour later, they'd be marching.

881 Longstreet, "Lee in Pennsylvania," in *Annals of the War*, 422–423.

882 Johnston to McLaws, June 27, 1892, in S.R. Johnston Papers, VHS; Johnston to F. Lee, Feb. 11, 1878, in S.R. Johnston Papers, VHS.

883 For a concise and easy to understand overview of columns and their tactical use, see Hess, *Civil War Infantry Tactics*, 49–53.

884 McLaws wrote that the fences lining the road didn't give enough room "for a company front, making it necessary to break files to the rear." McLaws, "Gettysburg," in *SHSP* vol. 7, 69.

885 Johnston to F. Lee, Feb. 11, 1878, in S.R. Johnston Papers, VHS.

886 Johnston to McLaws, June 27, 1892, in S.R. Johnston Papers, VHS.

887 Longstreet, "Lee's Right Wing at Gettysburg," in *Battles & Leaders*, 3: 340. Emphasis added. Ten years earlier, in his *Annals of the War* account, Longstreet wrote nearly the same thing. "Looking up toward Round Top

I saw that the signal station was in full view, and, as we could plainly see this station, it was apparent that our heavy columns was [sic] seen from their position, and that further efforts to conceal ourselves would be a waste of time." It was here that he suggested he had no control over McLaws, since Johnston was in charge of the column, but "I sent orders to Hood, who was in the rear and not encumbered by these instructions, to push his division forward by the most direct route." Longstreet, "Lee in Pennsylvania," in *Annals of the War*, 423. The notable omission is that this was the second stop, but the content of the account precludes its being at McLaws Hill. Also, Hood's column would now be toward the rear, as McLaws's column passed.

888   Sorrel to McLaws, January 30, 1888, in McLaws, "Longstreet at Gettysburg," Part Two, Feb. 29, 1888. In GMNP V5-McLaws, Lafayette.

889   Coxe, "The Battle of Gettysburg," *Confederate Veteran* vol. 21, 434.

890   Goggin to Longstreet, Aug. 15, 1887, in GNMP V7-SC-Brigades. Original in USAMHI. Emphasis in original. It *could* be interpreted that Goggin observed the discussion between Longstreet and McLaws further south, as McLaws was getting into position. But like Coxe, he thought McLaws's column had been stopped for the purpose of moving Hood forward. That suggests he saw McLaws's column while it was halted, indicating it was at Pendleton's Hill. If it were further south, then it would be Hood, not McLaws, that was stopped, since Kershaw remembered Hood passing behind him *after* he was in position.

An often quoted account by William Abernathy colorfully made the point about McLaws's anger. "McLaws was saying things I would not like to teach my grandson…to repeat," Abernathy wrote in a very fanciful memoir. But Abernathy's account was written well after the battle and he incorporates words and descriptions right out of McLaws's articles, indicating an awareness of the traditional story. Hood, who followed so closely "in his impetuous way" had "lapped" and "considerably mixed" with McLaws's Division, wrote Abernathy. Hoopes, "Confederate Memoir of William M. Abernathy," 22.

891   In addition to his insistence that Longstreet allowed him to retain the lead during the march, McLaws later said the following, indicating he was in position prior to Hood's movement past him: "To form line of battle by directing troops across the country broken by fences and ditches requires considerable time…. While this was going on I rode forward…. The firing on my command showed to Hood in my rear that the enemy

was in force in my front and right, and the head of his column was turned by General Longstreet's order to go on my right." McLaws, "Gettysburg," in *SHSP* vol. 7, 69–70. For Kershaw's account of Hood passing behind him, see O.R. 27.2: 367.

892   Johnston to F. Lee, Feb. 11, 1878, in S.R. Johnston Papers, VHS.

893   Johnston to F. Lee, Feb. 11, 1878, in S.R. Johnston Papers, VHS. Peterkin, remember, led Longstreet's column down the Ravine Road after the prior route "proved objectionable." This is a more reasonable interpretation of the road "Longstreet had to follow" than the Black Horse Tavern Road. Peterkin to Pendleton, Dec. 6, 1875. Pendleton Papers, UNC Wilson Library.

894   Kershaw wrote that "McLaws ordered me to countermarch, and in doing so we passed Hood's division." Kershaw, "Kershaw's Brigade at Gettysburg," in *Battles & Leaders*, 3: 331–332.

895   In his 1878 correspondence with Fitz Lee, Johnston related that he told Longstreet they "would have to pass in full view of the enemy" and that "our movement was discovered." Johnston to F. Lee, Feb. 11, 1878, in S.R. Johnston Papers, VHS. In his 1892 letter to McLaws, he wrote that "you would disclose your movements to the enemy" and that the "column got in full view of the enemy." Johnston to McLaws, June 27, 1892, in S.R. Johnston Papers, VHS.

896   "I read the paper referred to with some surprise," Johnston wrote Lee, meaning Longstreet's article. Johnston to F. Lee, Feb. 11, 1878, in S.R. Johnston Papers, VHS.

897   Alexander submitted two reports, remember, changing his time of arrival after his subordinate's report indicated a different time. O.R. 27.2: 429; "Colonel E.P. Alexander's Report of the Battle of Gettysburg," in *SHSP* vol. 4, 235. In his personal memoir, he explained that "when one is up long before day & marching he is very apt to think it much later than it really is. I don't remember consulting my watch." Gallagher, ed., *Fighting for the Confederacy*, 235.

898   "It seemed to me useless, therefore, to delay the troops any longer with the idea of concealing the movement, and the two divisions advanced." Longstreet, "Lee's Right Wing at Gettysburg," in *Battles & Leaders*, 3: 340. In his first article, he wrote that it was apparent that our heavy columns was [sic] seen from their position, and that further efforts to conceal ourselves would be a waste of time." Longstreet "Lee in Pennsylvania," in *Annals of the War*, 424.

899   Sorrel, *Recollections of a Confederate Staff Officer*, 168.

900   See Laino, *Gettysburg Campaign Atlas*, 183. Precisely when Sickles moved forward isn't known, but General Andrew Humphreys remembered he pushed part of his force up to the Emmitsburg Road "shortly after midday." O.R. 27.1: 31.

901   Goggin to Longstreet, Aug. 15, 1887, in GNMP V7-SC-Brigades. Original in USAMHI.

902   O.R. 27.2: 367. The fact that Longstreet's orders were to first push the Federals out of the Peach Orchard were issued while Kershaw was marching down the Ravine Road means Longstreet knew about Sickles's move before McLaws formed on the ridge.

903   This all has to be divined from circumstances. As we saw, little direct documentation exists as to the original plan, but all evidence suggests a last-minute change. Harry Pfanz notes this gap in the documentary record in his usual clear and succinct way. *Gettysburg: The Second Day*, 153. But all existing evidence does suggest the plan was altered and as it turned out, Hood ended up on the far right of the Confederate line and McLaws's attack depended on the success and timing of Hood's.

904   Goggin to Longstreet, Aug. 15, 1887, in GNMP V7-SC-Brigades. Original in USAMHI.

905   Goggin to Longstreet, Aug. 15, 1887, in GNMP V7-SC-Brigades. Original in USAMHI.

906   Kershaw to Bachelder, March 20, 1876, in Ladd, *The Bachelder Papers*, 1: 453–454.

907   Kershaw, "Kershaw's Brigade at Gettysburg," in *Battles & Leaders*, 3: 331.

908   In his letter to Fitz Lee, Johnston said the column "moved under cover of the ridge and woods…here the road turned to the right and led over a high hill where it intersected a road leading back in the direction of the Round Top, the one that Gen'l Longstreet had to follow." It was here that Johnston pointed out to Longstreet that passing over the "high hill" would cause the column "to pass in full view of the enemy." Johnston to F. Lee, Feb. 11, 1878, in S.R. Johnston Papers, VHS. In his letter to McLaws, Johnston simply said he alerted Longstreet to the hill, without any mention of riding with McLaws. Johnston to McLaws, June 27, 1892, in S.R. Johnston Papers, VHS.

909   Pendleton "would select a position, one of his staff was left to remain there, so as to designate to the officer of artillery assigned to that position, the exact location for his gun, or guns, and thus prevent any mistakes

being made." Page, *Reminiscences*, in Shields Collection, W&L Leyburn Libary.

910 Peterkin to Pendleton, Dec. 6, 1875, in Pendleton Papers, UNC Wilson Library.

911 McLaws, "Gettysburg," in *SHSP* vol. 7, 69.

912 Alexander to McLaws, Jan. 30, 1888, in McLaws, "Longstreet at Gettysburg," *Philadelphia Weekly Press*, Feb. 15, 1888. In GMNP V5-McLaws, Lafayette.

913 Alexander, *Military Memoirs*, 391.

914 Longstreet, *From Manassas to Appomattox*, 366.

915 Longstreet, "Lee in Pennsylvania," in *Annals of the War*, 423.

916 Johnston interpreted Longstreet's *Annals of the War* article as Longstreet riding at the tail end of the column, when as we saw, he meant that Longstreet rode with the rear division.

917 Johnston to F. Lee, Feb. 11, 1878, in S.R. Johnston Papers, VHS. Emphasis added.

918 Johnston to McLaws, June 27, 1892, in S.R. Johnston Papers, VHS.

919 Though *less* affected, Johnston's memories were still somewhat tainted by others'. In his letter to Peterkin in 1895, he made a point to compare his recollections with McLaws's. "General McLaws in a letter to me says: 'I found Gen'l Lee sitting on a log near the seminary . . .' I have said that I found Gen'l Lee sitting on a log near the seminary." Johnston to Peterkin, Dec. 1895, in S.R. Johnston Papers, VHS. That may well be where Johnston found Lee, but he still felt the need to try to conform his own memory with McLaws's.

920 Peterkin to Pendleton, Dec. 6, 1875. Pendleton Papers, UNC Wilson Library.

921 O.R. 27.2: 350.

922 Johnston to F. Lee, Feb. 11, 1878, in S.R. Johnston Papers, VHS.

923 So where was Clarke? Longstreet's engineer disappears from the battle's record after Johnston's mention of him on the recon, only showing up in ancillary documents (Longstreet's report in the litany of praise, the diaries of foreign observers, Col. Smith's report of the engineers, and in service records). Longstreet doesn't mention either engineer who led the column down the wrong road by name. Without additional documentation, we can't be sure of Clarke's role after the reconnaissance.

924 McLaws to Thomas Munford, Jan 8, 1896, in McLaws Papers, UNC Wilson Library.

925   McLaws, "Gettysburg," in *SHSP*, vol. 7, 69.

926   According to Coxe, Hood's column was "riding forward parallel to us about fifty yards to the left," or east. Coxe, "The Battle of Gettysburg," *Confederate Veteran* vol. 21, 434. Willoughby Run is not a wide stream, with banks only about thirty yards apart at the wider points.

927   Kershaw reported in October 1863 that just after he positioned his men, he saw that "Hood's division was then moving in our rear toward our right." O.R. 27.2: 367. McLaws remembered this too. In his July 7, 1863 letter to his wife, he wrote that "Gen H[ood] had gone around above me to the right." McLaws to Wife, July 7, 1863, in McLaws Papers, UNC Wilson Library.

928   Sims, *Recollection of A.C. Sims*, in GNMP V7-TX1. Sims may have remembered being moved into the woods near George Culp's farm or further down near Pitzer's schoolhouse. In the crook where Pitzer and Willoughby Runs meet is another patch of woods. Any of these could have been the woods Sims remembered.

929   Law, "The Struggle for 'Round Top,'" in *Battles & Leaders*, 3: 320. Law attributed this to the signal station, but by the time he was writing, that narrative had become firmly entrenched. As a brigade commander at the end of the column, he may not have ever been informed *why* the column was stopping. Stevens, *Reminiscences*, 113.

930   Longstreet to McLaws, July 25, 1873. McLaws Papers, UNC Wilson Library. Emphasis added.

931   McLaws to Wife, July 7, 1863, in GNMP, V5-Longstreet, James.

932   Fremantle saw Longstreet ride out in front of Wofford's brigade. *Three Months in the Southern States*, 261. Even McLaws wrote about Longstreet accompanying Wofford's advance, perhaps mollifying his corps commander: "At the commencement of the charge, General Longstreet went forward some distance with Wofford's brigade, urging them on by voice and his personal example to the most earnest efforts." McLaws, "Gettysburg," in *SHSP* vol. 7, 74. Kershaw wrote in his *Battles & Leaders* article that when "the brigade moved off…General Longstreet accompanied me in this advance on foot, as far as the Emmitsburg road. All the field and staff officers were dismounted on account of the many obstacles in the way." Kershaw, "Kershaw's Brigade at Gettysburg," in *Battles & Leaders*, 3: 334.

     For the account of the unwanted battery, see McLaws, "Gettysburg," in *SHSP* vol. 7, 72–73.

933 O.R. 27.2: 399.

934 Johnston to F. Lee, Feb. 11, 1878, in S.R. Johnston Papers, VHS.

935 Kershaw to Bachelder, April 1, 1876, in Ladd, *The Bachelder Papers*, 1: 470. The implication is that accounts of the hard and effective fighting by McLaws's men would show that the division contributed, belying any claims from Hood's men that they were ineffective or slow in providing support.

936 McLaws, "Gettysburg," in *SHSP* vol. 7, 73.

937 O.R. 27.2: 401. Since the march was under a "burning sun" and they came under fire, he couldn't have been referring to the several mile march from the Marsh Creek bivouac to the battlefield that morning.

938 Even Moxley Sorrel remembered that Longstreet's column was only "partially countermarched." Sorrel to McLaws Jan. 30, 188, in McLaws, "Longstreet at Gettysburg," Part Two, Feb.29, 1888, in GNMP V5-Mc-Laws, Lafayette.

939 Sims, *Recollection of A.C. Sims*, in GNMP V7-TX1.

940 Parker to Friend Sallie, Aug. 3, 1863, in *Galveston Weekly News*, Oct. 21, 1863, in GNMP V7-TX1.

941 If Hood was on McPherson's Ridge facing east, then by facing to the right they would be looking south along Willoughby Run.

942 Tout le Monde, "Letter from the Army - Hagerstown, July 7, 1863," in *Savannah (GA) Republican*, July 22, 1863. GNMP V7-GA17. Original in Brake Collection, USAMHI.

943 O.R. 27.2: 420.

944 O.R. 27.2: 424. The word appears again in "P.W.A.'s" column for the *Savannah (GA) Republican*. But more curiously, he noted that *Hood's* Division was the one that had to countermarch. He then notes that "McLaws's proper position was on the extreme right, but in the hurry to make the attack Hood was placed on the right and McLaws next to him." P.W.A.'s account is interesting in that it offers a hint of the "sly undercurrents" and also stands as the earliest mention of a countermarch and delay in the attack. This was probably among McLaws's first attempts to vicariously counter what he already felt was an unjust attack against his performance in the battle. Ross, Johnston, and Fremantle, remember, had all picked up on the rumors that McLaws was too slow during the battle and that *that* had something to do with the loss. "The Great Battle of Gettysburg," July 4,

1863 in *Savannah Republican* July 19, 1863. If nothing else, P.W.A. was unilaterally defending the division from those rumors.

945   O.R. 27.2: 414.

946   Webster, *An American Dictionary of the English Language*, 206. The 1862 entry for CIRCUITOUS reads "going round in a circuit; not direct; as, a *circuitous* road or course."

947   O.R. 27.2: 425. Col. Waddell wrote that "before reaching the point from which to make the attack, it was necessary to move by the right flank a distance of nearly 3 miles."

948   Colonel Shepherd called the march to the field "tiresome," O.R. 27.2: 420, while Col. Hodges called the heat "excessive." O.R. 27.2: 424. Major McDaniel also noted the sun was "burning" that afternoon. O.R. 27.2: 401. John M. Bowden, a private in Hood's Division, didn't remember all of the details well, but he *did* remember that the "march was awful, and the soldiers were exhausted." Bowden Memoir, in MSS 537f, Atlanta History Center, James G. Kenan Research Center.

949   Alexander, "Artillery Fighting at Gettysburg," in *Battles & Leaders*, 3: 359.

950   O.R. 27.2: 351.

951   O.R. 27.2: 367.

952   Haskell, *Reminiscences of the Confederate War*, 67–68, in John Cheves Haskell Papers, UNC Wilson Library.

953   Alexander, "Letter from General E.P. Alexander, late Chief of Artillery, First Corps, A.N.V. March 17th, 1877," in *SHSP*, vol. 4, 101–102. In his personal memoir, he wrote that he didn't remember why he went back, but found Longstreet's men stopped at the hill, waiting for a guide or more orders, one of the reasons this is usually interpreted as McLaws Hill. Though Alexander says *this* is where the guide was summoned, it was probably simply where *he* heard about Peterkin arriving to take McLaws along the Ravine Road. Likewise, Longstreet and Johnston both indicate McLaws *didn't* require a guide at Pendleton's Hill, for they simply pushed on ahead regardless of the signal station.

954   "My own recollection," Longstreet wrote to McLaws, "is that Alexander was with Hood, as you mention." Longstreet's reply indicates McLaws had suggested the same. Longstreet to McLaws, Dec. 11, 1887, in McLaws Papers, UNC Wilson Library.

955   Cabell's report simply mentions that it "moved up with the division." O.R. 27.2: 375. This was likely when McLaws moved up the Ravine Road, since the brief mention belies a long countermarch.

956   Kershaw also reported that the artillery was arriving as he was going into position, further suggesting that the First Corps artillery wasn't far out in front and waiting for hours. Kershaw wrote that as he reached the cross-road by Pitzer's schoolhouse, Longstreet ordered him up the ridge and to attack the enemy in the Peach Orchard. "At the same time a battery of artillery was moved along the road parallel with my line of march." This was about 3 p.m. O.R. 27.2: 367. Cabell's report suggests that it may have been his that Kershaw saw on the parallel road. "When we commenced to ascend the road leading to the crest of the hill, where the battle was subsequently fought, my battalion moved to the head of the column." O.R. 27.2: 375. Kershaw, of course, was leading the column.

957   In his two reports from August 1863, Alexander only discusses placing these two battalions, while Henry is left to place his own, consistent with Hood's independence exhibited throughout the fighting. In his first report, dated August 3, 1863, he wrote that "about 4 p.m. I placed four batteries (those of Captains Moody, Parker, Taylor, and Rhett...)." These were the various batteries in his own command, which was overseen by Major Frank Huger while Alexander exercised control over all the battalions. O.R. 27.2: 429. In his revised report of August 10, 1863, he wrote that "about 4 p.m....I placed in position against [the enemy] the eighteen guns of Cabell's battalion and eighteen of my own battalion, to fire upon the 'Peach Orchard' position, while Henry's battalion accompanied and fought with Hood's division in its attack upon 'Round Top.'" Alexander, "Report," in *SHSP*, vol. 4, 235–236. With Hood so far to the right, it made more sense for Alexander to keep personal control over the batteries on his side of the road and allow Henry to operate more independently east of the road. Alexander was correct in his first report, for he placed *his own guns* around 4 p.m., while Cabell had already begun firing around 3 p.m. It seems he simply carried the 4 p.m. time over in his revised report, without clarifying.

958   J. Willard Brown credits Hall's signal station with spotting Hood's men crossing the Emmitsburg Road and "massing upon Gen. Sickles's left." Brown, *Signal Corps in the War of the Rebellion*, 365. General Charles Graham, whose troops occupied the Peach Orchard, noticed Hood's column, too. "With intense and justifiable excitement," Graham pointed the Confederate column out to Henry Tremain, Sickles's aide-de-camp. Tremain, *Two Days of War*, 55.

959   O.R. 27.2: 351. P.W.A., the correspondent for the *Savannah (GA) Republican*, also wrote that Henry's artillery "announced that the assault had commenced on the extreme right. Cabell's battalion, of McLaws's division, opened next." No mention is made of Alexander, indicating he really was in reserve at this point. "The Great Battle of Gettysburg," *Savannah (GA) Republican*, July 19, 1863. A more accessible version is available in Styple, *Writing & Fighting the Confederate War*, 161–166.

960   "The fire from our lines and from the enemy became incessant, rendering it necessary for us sometimes to pause and allow the smoke to clear away, in order to enable the gunners to take aim." O.R. 27.2: 375.

961   Major Maffett, whose report is the only regimental report from McLaws's Division that survived long enough to make it into the *Official Records*, said the cannonade started at 3 p.m., and ended just before the infantry went in at 4 p.m. O.R. 27.2: 372. Kershaw also remembered getting the order to advance at 4 p.m. O.R. 27.2: 367. See also Murray, *E.P. Alexander and the Artillery Action in the Peach Orchard*, 75.

962   "Henry's battalion moved out with Hood and was speedily and heavily engaged," Alexander wrote in his *Century* article. "Cabell was ready to support him…. The ground at Cabell's position gave little protection, and he suffered rapidly in both men and horses. To help him I ran up Huger with 18 guns of my own 26, to Warfield's house, within 500 yards of the Peach Orchard, and opened upon it." Alexander, "Artillery Fighting at Gettysburg," in *Battles & Leaders*, 3: 359.

963   West to "My Dear Little Man," July 8, 1863, in West, *A Texan in Search of a Fight*, 85.

EPILOGUE

964   Pendleton, "Personal Recollections of General Lee," in *Southern Magazine* 15, 625.

965   McLaws to Longstreet, June 12, 1873, in McLaws Papers, UNC Wilson Library.

966   Hunt to Long, Sept. 4, 1884, in Long Papers, UNC Wilson Library.

967   Kershaw to Bachelder, Aug. 7, 1882, in Ladd, *The Bachelder Papers*, 2: 901.

MAPS

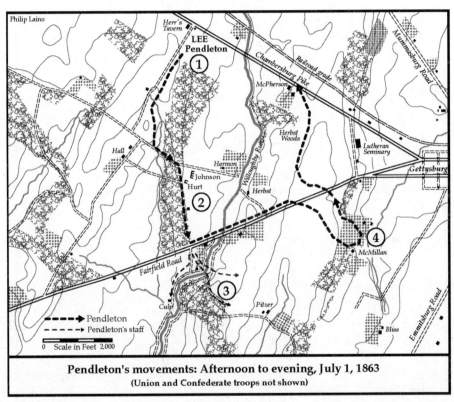

Pendleton's movements: Afternoon to evening, July 1, 1863
(Union and Confederate troops not shown)

Pendleton's reconnaissance on the afternoon of July 1, 1863. Map by Philip Laino.

461

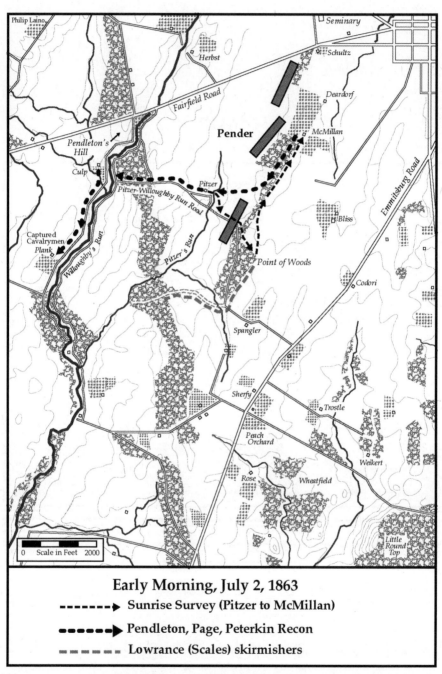

Early Morning, July 2, 1863

-------▶ Sunrise Survey (Pitzer to McMillan)

■■■■■■▶ Pendleton, Page, Peterkin Recon

▬ ▬ ▬ ▬ ▬ Lowrance (Scales) skirmishers

The sunrise survey and Pendleton's subsequent reconnaissance. Map by Philip Laino.

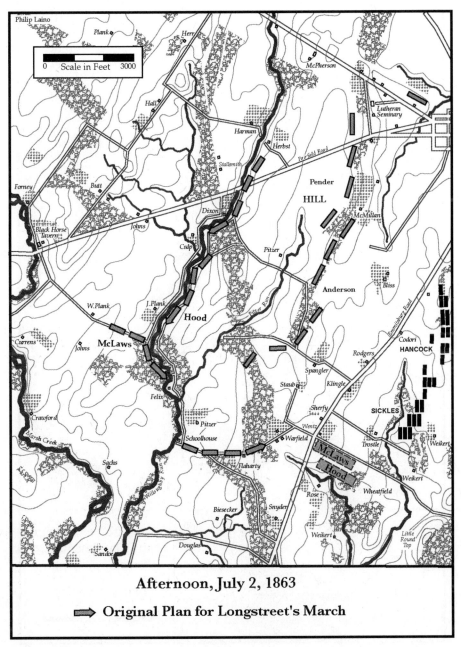

Afternoon, July 2, 1863

➡ **Original Plan for Longstreet's March**

The original plan for Longstreet's march into position on July 2, 1863. Map by Philip Laino.

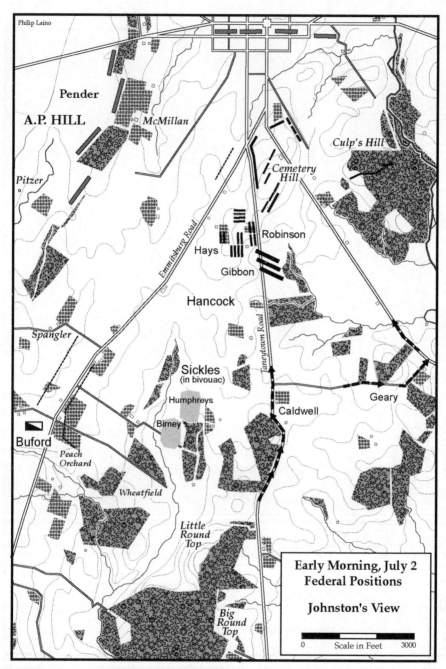

The Federal position south of Cemetery Hill as Johnston would have seen it from Little Round Top on the morning of July 2, 1863. Map by Philip Laino.

464

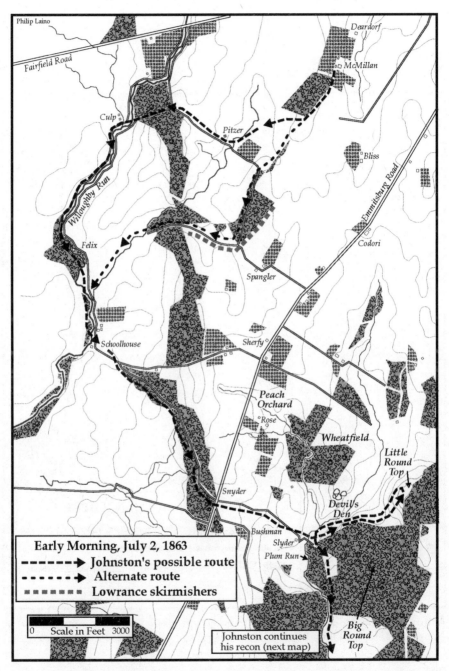

Early Morning, July 2, 1863
------▸ Johnston's possible route
------▸ Alternate route
▪▪▪▪▪▪▪ Lowrance skirmishers

0 Scale in Feet 3000

Johnston continues
his recon (next map)

Johnston's probable route, showing potential alternatives and the more traditional return trip. Map by Philip Laino.

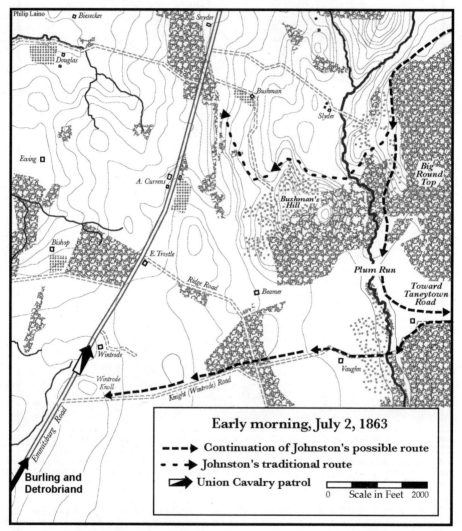

Johnston's probable route, showing potential alternatives and the more traditional return trip. Map by Philip Laino.

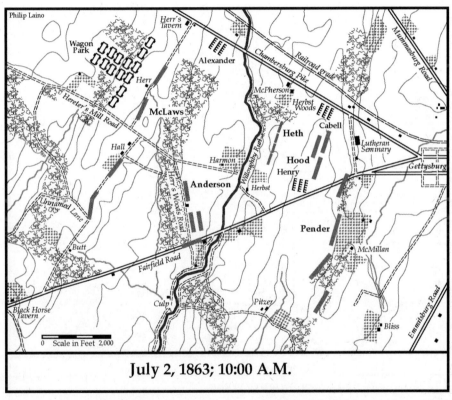

July 2, 1863; 10:00 A.M.

The position of the Confederate First Corps and Anderson's division at about 10:00 a.m. Until Lee determined exactly where to attack, the Army of Northern Virginia's fresh troops couldn't get much closer to the front. Map by Philip Laino.

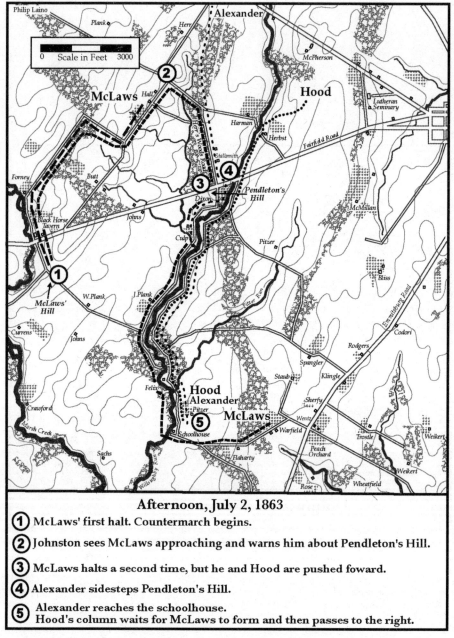

Afternoon, July 2, 1863

① McLaws' first halt. Countermarch begins.

② Johnston sees McLaws approaching and warns him about Pendleton's Hill.

③ McLaws halts a second time, but he and Hood are pushed foward.

④ Alexander sidesteps Pendleton's Hill.

⑤ Alexander reaches the schoolhouse.
Hood's column waits for McLaws to form and then passes to the right.

The march of the First Corps into position on July 2, 1863. Map by Philip Laino.

BIBLIOGRAPHY

AN INTERACTIVE BIBLIOGRAPHY CAN BE FOUND AT
www.AllenRThompson.com

MANUSCRIPTS & UNPUBLISHED SOURCES

Adams County Historical Society
> Beard, Elizabeth Plank. Unpublished and Untitled Memoir.
> Buehler, Fannie J. *Recollections of the Rebel Invasion and One Woman's Experience During the Battle of Gettysburg.* 1896.
> Miller (Harman), Amelia E. "Burning of McLean Home on the First Day's Battle of Gettysburg, Told by a Young Girl When the House Was Set on Fire." In *Gettysburg Compiler.* July 15, 1915.
> Georg, Kathleen R. *Summary of Damage Claims from the Battle of Gettysburg for Adams County, PA.*

Atlanta History Center, James G. Kenan Research Center
> *John Bowden Malachi Civil War Memoirs.* Atlanta: MSS 537f, as presented in the Digital Library of Georgia.

Commissioners' Correspondence, 1893–1921 (GETT 41143), Gettysburg National Park Commission, Office of the Commissioners.
> John Nicholson Diary.

Emory University, Stuart A. Rose Library

Charles Venable to James Longstreet, 1875. James Longstreet Papers. Collection no. 210.

Fairfax County (VA) Circuit Court, Historic Records Center

Administrator of John R. Johnston Estate v. Millard, folder 1879-008.

Deed Books

A-4

U-3

Farmers Bank of Virginia v. Johnston, Fairfax County Circuit Court, Box 071, folder 1868-132, Box 074, folder 1869-100.

Willis Henderson v. Johnston, Fairfax County Circuit Court, Box 061, folder 1865-180.

Millard v. Johnston, Fairfax Circuit Court, folder X-I-0749.

Millard v. Johnston, Fairfax Circuit Court, folder 1866-020. "Sheriff Attachment."

Millard v. Johnston, Box 060, folder 1865-040.

Thomas Ogden v. Johnston, Box 056, folder 1864-024.

"Sam R. Johnston and Mary G. Ege." Marriage License, June 21, 1859.

Gettysburg National Military Park Library

V5-Cavada, Adolfo

Cavada Diary.

V5-Humphreys, A. A.

Charles Hamiln to Andrew A. Humphreys, Aug. 11, 1863.

V5-Longstreet, James

James Longstreet to Lafayette McLaws, July 25, 1873. Typescript.

Walter H. Taylor to James Longstreet, Aug. 15, 1879.

V5-McLaws, Lafayette

Notes taken regarding S.R. Johnston letter (c. 1892).

McLaws, Lafayette. "The Battle of Gettysburg." Paper Read Before the Confederate Veterans Association, April 27, 1896.

V5-Pendleton, Wm. N.

Armistead Long to William Pendleton, Oct. 5, 1875. Typescript. Original in UNC Wilson Library.

V7-GA17.

Tout le Monde, "Letter from the Army - Hagerstown, July 7, 1863," in *Savannah (GA) Republican*, July 22, 1863. Original in Brake Collection, USAMHI.

V7-MS-Brigades B11 Barksdale's Brigade

Benjamin Humphreys to Lafayette McLaws, Jan. 6, 1878. Typescript. Original in UNC Wilson Library.

V7-MS-21

Everett, Jr, Frank E. "Delayed Report of an Important Eyewitness to Gettysburg Benjamin G. Humphreys." *The Journal of Mississippi History* 46, no. 4 (Nov. 1984).

V7-SC-7A

D. Wyatt Aiken to Joseph Kershaw, June 16, 1882, printed as "An Open Letter from Col. D. Wyatt Aiken to Gen. J.B. Kershaw," *Charleston (SC) News and Courier*, June 21, 1882.

Goggin to Longstreet, Aug. 15, 1887. Typescript. Original in USAMHI.

V7-TX1

James Henry Hendrick to Mother, July 8, 1863.

Parker to Friend Sallie, Aug. 3, 1863, in *Galveston Weekly News*, Oct. 21, 1863.

Sims, A.C. *Recollection of A.C. Sims (Pvt. Co. F, 1 Texas) at the Battle of Gettysburg.*

V7-TX4

West to "My Dear Little Man," in West, *A Texan in Search of a Fight: Being the Diary and Letters of a Private Soldier in Hood's Texas Brigade,* July 8, 1863.

Va-21

Black Horse Tavern

Library of Congress

Jubal A. Early Papers

Captain Turner, *Gettysburg*, n.d.

Robert E. Lee to Jubal Early, March 30, 1865.

Robert E. Lee to Jubal Early, March 16, 1865.
Jubal Early to Brother, July 15, 1867.
Charles Marshall to Jubal Early, March 23, 1870.
Francis Lawley to Jubal Early, May 14, 1872.
Braxton Bragg to Jubal Early, June 27, 1872.
Charles Marshall to Jubal Early, March 13, 1878.
J. William Jones to Jubal Early, May 2, 1878.
James Power Smith to Major Brown (n.d.)
Jedediah Hotchkiss Papers: Diaries, 1845–1899.
Kentucky Historical Society, Martin F. Schmidt Research Library
William Proctor Smith, Letter Book 1863-1864.
Newspaper Clippings.
William Proctor Smith Obituary.
Maryland Historical Society
Osmun Latrobe Diary, MS 526.
National Archives
Record Group 109: War Department Collection of Confederate Records 1825–1927
Armistead, Keith.
Collins, Charles R.
Haskell, John Cheves.
Johnston, Samuel R.
Moncure, Thomas.
Rogers, Henry J.
Smith, William Proctor.
Youngblood, William.
New York State Archives
Civil War Muster Roll Abstracts
George Barber.
Robert E. Lee Memorial Foundation Archives.
Lee Family Papers.
Charles Venable to Walter H. Taylor, Aug. 21, 1869.
Walter Herron Taylor Papers, Box 8, M2009.297
Jubal Early to Walter H. Taylor, April 9, 1871.
University of North Carolina, Louis Round Wilson Special Collections Library, Southern Historical Collection

Edward Porter Alexander Papers. Collection no. 00007.
    Winfield Featherston to E.P. Alexander, Nov. 10, 1867.
    Certification of John Leconte, July 13, 1868.
    William Oates to E.P. Alexander, Aug. 25, 1868.
    Confidential Letter to E.P. Alexander, March 5, 1870.
    A Short History of the 8th Alabama.
    Abstract Report Questionnaire, Folder 113.
William Allan Papers. Collection no. 02764.
    "Conversations with General Lee"
Louis R. Fortescue Diary, 1863-1864. Collection no. 03404-z.
John Cheves Haskell Papers. Collection no. 02549-z.
    Memoirs of the Confederate War, 1861–1865.
Armistead L. Long Papers. Collection no. 02503-z.
    James Longstreet to Armistead Long, May 20, 1875.
    William Pendleton to Armistead Long, Oct. 5, 1875.
    Armistead Long to James Longstreet, April 19, 1876.
    Henry Hunt to Armistead Long, Sept. 4, 1884.
    Charles Marshall to Armistead Long, June 3, 1886.
James Longstreet Papers. Collection no. 03081-z.
    Robert E. Lee to Jubal Early, March 30, 1865.
    James Longstreet to "My Dear General," June 8, 1867.
    Charles Marshall to James Longstreet, May 7, 1875.
    Armistead Long to James Longstreet, May 31, 1875.
    William Youngblood to James Longstreet, Sept. 5, 1892.
    Charles Pickett to James Longstreet, Oct. 12, 1892.
Lafayette McLaws Papers. Collection no. 00472.
    James Longstreet to Lafayette McLaws, June 3, 1863.
    John Bell Hood to Lafayette McLaws, June 3, 1863.
    Lafayette McLaws to wife, July 7, 1863.
    Lafayette McLaws to wife, Aug. 14, 1863.
    Nicholas Davis to Lafayette McLaws, July 30, 1863.
    G. Moxley Sorrel to Lafayette McLaws, Dec. 17, 1863.
    Benjamin Humphreys to "General," Feb. 16, 1864.
    McLaws to General, April 22, 1864.
    Statement of J.J. Middleton, March 1864.

Lafayette McLaws to James Longstreet, June 10, 1873. Draft.

Lafayette McLaws to James Longstreet, June 12, 1873.

James Longstreet to Lafayette McLaws, July 25, 1873.

John Bachelder to Lafayette McLaws, Dec. 23, 1874.

Benjamin Humphreys to Lafayette McLaws, Jan. 6, 1878.

Lafayette McLaws to James Longstreet, Nov. 30, 1885.

James Longstreet to Lafayette McLaws, Sept. 24, 1886.

"McLaws's Division at Gettysburg, Oct. 7, 1886." *Army and Navy Journal*, issue n.d.

James Longstreet to Lafayette McLaws, June 17, 1887.

James Longstreet to Lafayette McLaws, Dec. 11, 1887.

Joseph Kershaw to Lafayette McLaws, May 25, 1888.

"Longstreet at Gettysburg," *Philadelphia Weekly Press*, Feb. 15, 1888.

"The Capture of Harper's Ferry: An Interesting Narrative of the Maryland Campaign of 1862 - A Confederate Success Not Due to Stonewall Jackson," *Philadelphia Weekly Press*, Sept. 19, 1888.

McLaws, Lafayette. "The Maryland Campaign." Speech Given Before the Georgia Historical Society.

James Longstreet to Lafayette McLaws, Oct. 20, 1892.

Lafayette McLaws to Thomas Munford, Jan. 6, 1896.

William Nelson Pendleton Papers. Collection no. 01466

William Pendleton to "My Darling Love," Nov. 13, 1863.

William Pendleton to Charles A. Davidson, May 29, 1873.

James Longstreet to William Pendleton, April 4, 1875.

William Pendleton to James Longstreet, April 1875.

James Longstreet to William Pendleton, April 19, 1875.

William Pendleton to Editor-in-Chief of *Johnston's Universal Cyclopedia*, Dec. 21, 1875.

George Peterkin to William Pendleton, Dec. 6, 1875.

Polk, Brown, and Ewell Family Papers. Collection no. 00605

Campbell Brown Diary.

D.H. Maury to Campbell Brown, May 16, 1874.

Campbell Brown Notes, July 2–3, 1878.

Charles Venable Papers

Fitzhugh Lee to Charles Venable, July 30, 1894.

Virginia Historical Society

Helen M. Taylor Collection, Mss1 T2144a. Section 6.

Robert E. Lee to James Longstreet, Oct. 29, 1867.

S.R. Johnston Papers, Mss2 J6475 b 1-14.

Samuel Johnston to Fitzhugh Lee, Feb. 11, 1878.

Samuel Johnston to Fitzhugh Lee, Feb. 16, 1878.

Lafayette McLaws to J. Roy Baylor. n.d., [June 8/9, 1892].

Lafayette McLaws to Samuel Johnston, June 8, 1892.

J. Roy Baylor to Samuel Johnston, June 9, 1892.

Samuel Johnston to Lafayette McLaws, June 27, 1892.

Samuel Johnston to George Peterkin, Dec. 1895.

S.R. Johnston Papers, Mss2.J64256b 6-7. Section 3.

Virginia Military Institute Archives Catalog

John J. Clarke Civil War Papers, Collection No. MS-0112

Washington & Lee University, James G. Leyburn Library Special Collections & Archives

Randolph T. Shields Collection. Collection no. WLU-Coll-0243, 1862–1920.

Coupland Page. *Reminiscences of the Battle of Gettysburg.*

BOOKS, PERIODICALS, PUBLISHED STUDIES

Acken, Gregory, ed. *Service with the Signal Corps: The Civil War Memoir of Captain Louis R. Fortescue.* Nashville: University of Tennessee Press, 2015.

Alexander, Edward P. "Artillery Fighting at Gettysburg." In vol. 3 of *Battles and Leaders of the Civil War.* Edited by Robert U. Johnson and Clarence C. Buel, 1884–1888. New York: Thomas Yoseloff, 1956.

—. "Colonel E.P. Alexander's Report of the Battle of Gettysburg." In vol. 4 of *Southern Historical Society Papers.* Richmond: James E. Goode, 1877.

—. "Letter from General E.P. Alexander, late Chief of Artillery, First Corps, A.N.V. to J. Wm. Jones, March 17, 1877." In vol. 4 of *Southern Historical Society Papers.* Richmond: James E. Goode, 1877.

—. "Longstreet at Knoxville." In vol. 3 of *Battles and Leaders of the Civil War.* Edited by Robert U. Johnson and Clarence C. Buel, 1884–1888. New York: Thomas Yoseloff, 1956.

—. *Military Memoirs of a Confederate: A Critical Narrative.* New York: Charles Scribner's Sons, 1907.

Allan, William. "Memoranda of Conversations with General Robert E. Lee." In *Lee: The Soldier.* Edited by Gary Gallagher. Lincoln: University of Nebraska Press, 1996.

Alleman, Tillie Pierce. *At Gettysburg; or What a Girl Saw and Heard of the Battle: A True Narrative.* 1888.

"Angular Size Calculator," https://www.1728.org/angsize.htm.

Archer, John M. *Culp's Hill at Gettysburg: "The Mountain Trembled."* Gettysburg: Thomas Publications, 2002.

Aughinbaugh, Nellie E. *Personal Experiences of a Young Girl During the Battle of Gettysburg.* Privately published, c. 1926.

Bachelder, John B. *Descriptive Key to the Painting of the Repulse of Longstreet's Assault at the Battle of Gettysburg* Boston: John B. Bachelder, 1870.

Bandy, Ken and Florence Freeland. *The Gettysburg Papers.* 2 vols. Dayton, OH: Morningside Press, 1978.

Bartky, Ian R. "The Adoption of Standard Time." *Technology and Culture* 30, no. 1 (Jan. 1989).

Batchelder, Samuel Francis. "The Washington Elm Tradition." In *Bits of Cambridge History.* Cambridge: Harvard University Press, 1930.

"Battle of River's Bridge." In *South Carolina Encyclopedia.* https://www.scencyclopedia.org/sce/entries/rivers-bridge-battle-of/

Bernstein, William J. *The Delusions of Crowds: Why People Go Mad in Groups.* New York: Atlantic Monthly Press, 2021.

Bibliography

Black, John Logan. *Crumbling Defenses: or Memoirs and Reminiscences of John Logan Black, Colonel C.S.A.* Edited by Eleanor D. McSwain. Macon, GA: The J.W. Burke Company, 1960.

"Borough of Gettysburg, Pennsylvania, USA – Sunrise, Sunset, and Daylength, July 1863," Time and Date. https://www.timeanddate.com/sun/@4558191?month=7&year=1863

Bower, Dr. Gordon H., John B. Black, and Dr. Terrence J. Turner. "Scripts in Memory for Text." In *Cognitive Psychology* 11, no. 2 (April 1979).

Brown, J. Willard. *The Signal Corps, U.S.A. in the War of the Rebellion.* Boston: U.S. Veteran Signal Corps Association, 1896.

Buie, David. "Carroll Yesteryears: Builder of Antrim in Taneytown Had Long Career in Carroll and Kansas." Historical Society of Carroll County, Aug. 23, 2020. https://hsccmd.org/23-august-2020-builder-of-antrim-in-taneytown-had-long-career-in-carroll-and-kansas/.

Busey, John W. and Travis W. Busey. *Confederate Casualties at Gettysburg: A Comprehensive Record.* 4 vols. Jefferson, NC: McFarland & Co., Inc, 2017.

"Inspirational Quotes." Leonora Carrington. https://www.leocarrington.com/quotes-citas.html.

Casey, Silas. *Infantry Tactics, for the Instruction, Exercise, and Maneuvers of the Soldier, a Company, Line of Skirmishers, Battalion, Brigade, or Corps D'Armee.* 2 vols. New York: D. Van Nostrand, 1862.

Ceremonies Connected with the Inauguration of the Mausoleum and the Unveiling of the Recumbent Figure of General Robert Edward Lee, at Washington and Lee University, Lexington, Va., June 28, 1883. Richmond: West, Johnston & Co., 1883.

Cheney, Newel. *History of the Ninth Regiment, New York Cavalry, War of 1861 to 1865.* Jamestown, NY: Martin Merz & Son, 1901.

Chlebowski, MD, Susan M., and Catherine Chung, MD, et al. "Confabulation: A Bridge Between Neurology and Psychiatry?" *Psychiatric Times* 26, no. 6 (May 25, 2009), https://www.psychiatrictimes.com/view/ confabulation-bridge-between-neurology-and-psychiatry.

Coco, Gregory A. *A Vast Sea of Misery: A History and Guide to the Union and Confederate Field Hospitals at Gettysburg July 1 - November 20, 1863*. Gettysburg: Thomas Publications, 1988. Reprinted in 2017 by Savas Beatie.

Coddington, Edwin B. *The Gettysburg Campaign: A Study in Command*. New York: Charles Scribner's Sons, 1968.

Coddington, Ronald S. and Dave Batalo. "Fallout from the Johnston Reconnaissance." In *Military Images* 36, no. 3 (Summer, 2018).

Cooksey, Paul Clark. "Around the Flank: Longstreet's July 2 Attack at Gettysburg." In *Gettysburg Magazine*, no. 29 (July 2003): 94.

Coxe, John. "The Battle of Gettysburg." In vol. 21 of *Confederate Veteran*. Nashville: S.A. Cunningham, 1913.

Craft, David. "Address of David Craft." In vol. 2 of *Pennsylvania at Gettysburg*, edited by John P. Nicholson. Harrisburg: E.K. Meyers, 1893.

Cullum, George W. *Biographical Register of the Officers and Graduates of the U.S. Military Academy at West Point, N.Y., from the Establishment, March 16, 1802 to 1890*, vol. 2, 3rd ed. New York: D. Van Nostrand, 1868.

Cutrer, Thomas, ed. *Longstreet's Aide: The Civil War Letters of Major Thomas J. Goree*. Charlottesville: University Press of Virginia, 1995.

Davis, Rev. Nicholas A. *The Campaign from Texas to Maryland*. Richmond: Presbyterian Committee of Publication of the Confederate States, 1863.

De Peyster, J. Watts. "A Military Memoir of William Mahone, Major-General in the Confederate Army," *The Historical Magazine* 2, no. 2 (June 1870).

Desjardin, Thomas. *These Honored Dead: How the Story of Gettysburg Shaped American Memory*. De Capo Press, 2003.

Dickert, D. Augustus. *History of Kershaw's Brigade*. Dayton, OH: Press of Morningside Bookshop, 1973.

Durborow, I.N. "The Big Battle." *National Tribune*, Dec. 8, 1892.

Early, John C. "A Southern Boy's Experience at Gettysburg." *Journal of the Military Service Institution of the United States* 43 (Jan–Feb. 1911).

Bibliography

Early, Jubal A. "A Review by General Early." In vol. 4 of *Southern Historical Society Papers*. Richmond: James E. Goode, 1877.

—. "Address of General Jubal A. Early." Address at the third annual meeting of the Survivors' Association of the State of South Carolina, Columbia, SC, Nov. 17, 1871. Charleston, SC: Walker, Evans & Cogswell, 1872.

—. "The Campaigns of Robert E. Lee." Address before Washington & Lee University, Virginia, Jan. 18, 1872. Baltimore: John Murphy & Co., 1872.

—. "Reply to General Longstreet." In vol. 4 of *Southern Historical Society Papers*. Richmond: James E. Goode, 1877.

—."Supplement to General Early's Review. – Reply to General Longstreet." In vol. 4 of *Southern Historical Society Papers*. Richmond: James E. Goode, Dec. 1877.

Early, Jubal and William Mahone. *A Correspondence Between Generals Early and Mahone, In Regard to a Military Memoir of the Latter*. 1871.

Ege, Thompson Prettyman. *History and Genealogy of the Ege Family in the United States, 1738–1911*. Harrisburg: Star Printing Co., 1911.

Elmore, Thomas. "Revelations of a Confederate Artillery Staff Officer: Coupland R. Page's Reminiscences of the Battle of Gettysburg." *Gettysburg Magazine*, no. 54 (January 2016).

Eminent and Representative Men of Virginia and the District of Columbia of the Nineteenth Century. Madison, WI: Brant & Fuller, 1893.

Floyd, Steven A. *Commanders and Casualties at the Battle of Gettysburg: The Comprehensive Order of Battle*. Gettysburg Publishing.

Ford, Dominic. "Equation of Time." In The Sky, https://in-the-sky.org/article.php?term=equation_of_time.

Forster, R.H. "Address of Maj. R.H. Forster." In vol. 2 of *Pennsylvania at Gettysburg: Ceremonies at the Dedication of the Monuments Erected by the Commonwealth of Pennsylvania to Mark the Positions of the Pennsylvania Commands Engaged in the Battle*. Harrisburg: F.K. Myers, 1893.

Frassanito, William A. *Early Photography at Gettysburg*. Gettysburg: Thomas Publications, 1995.

Freeman, Douglas Southall. *Lee's Lieutenants: A Study in Command*. 3 vols. New York: Charles Scribner's Sons, 1942–1944.

Fremantle, Arthur. *Three Months in the Southern States: April–June, 1863*. New York: John Bradburn, 1864.

Gallagher, Gary W., ed. *Fighting for the Confederacy: The Personal Recollections of General Edward Porter Alexander*. Chapel Hill: University of North Carolina Press, 1989.

—. "If the Enemy is There, We Must Attack Him: R.E. Lee and the Second Day at Gettysburg." In Gary W. Gallagher, ed., *The Second Day at Gettysburg: Essays on Confederate and Union Leadership*. Kent, OH: Kent State University Press, 1993.

—. "Jubal A. Early, the Lost Cause, and Civil War History: A Persistent Legacy." In *The Myth of the Lost Cause and Civil War History*. Edited by Gary W. Gallagher and Alan T. Nolan. Bloomington: University of Indiana Press, 2000.

—. *Lee the Soldier*. Lincoln: University of Nebraska Press, 1996.

Gettysburg National Military Park Commission. *Annual Reports to the Secretary of War 1893-1901*. Washington: Government Printing Office, 1902.

Gilham, William. *Manual of Instruction for the Volunteers and Militia of the Confederate States*. Richmond: West & Johnston, 1862.

Gilmor, Harry. *Four Years in the Saddle*. New York: Harper & Bros., 1866.

Golay, Michael. *To Gettysburg and Beyond: The Parallel Lives of Joshua Lawrence Chamberlain and Edward Porter Alexander*. New York: Crown Publishers, Inc, 1994.

Guelzo, Allen C. *Gettysburg: The Last Invasion*. New York: Alfred Knopf, 2013.

Hall, Hillman A., W.B. Besley, and Gilbert G. Wood. *History of the Sixth New York Cavalry*. Worcester, MA: The Blanchard Press, 1908.

Harman, Troy. "Gettysburg: Robert E. Lee Reconnoiters Little Round Top, July 2, 1863." April 2020. https://www.youtube.com/watch?v=ltD1j48qdYM

Haskell, Frank Aretas. *The Battle of Gettysburg*. Democrat Printing Co.: Wisconsin History Commission, 1908.

Hayes, Patrick, ed. *The Civil War Diary of Father James Sheeran: Confederate Chaplain and Redemptorist*. Washington, D.C.: The Catholic University of America Press, 2016.

Heitman, Francis B. *Historical Register and Dictionary of the United States Army.* 2 vols. Washington, D.C.: Government Printing Office, 1903.

Hess, Earl J. *Civil War Infantry Tactics: Training, Combat, and Small-Unit Effectiveness.* Baton Rouge: Louisiana State University Press, 2015.

Hill, D.H. "McClellan's Change of Base and Malvern Hill." In vol. 2 of *Battles and Leaders of the Civil War.* Edited by Robert U. Johnson and Clarence C. Buel, 1884–1888. New York: Thomas Yoseloff, 1956.

"Historiography." *Merriam-Webster Dictionary,* https://www.merriam-webster.com/ dictionary/historiography.

Hoke, Jacob. *The Great Invasion of 1863; or, General Lee in Pennsylvania.* Dayton, OH: W.J. Shuey, 1887.

Hood, John Bell. *Advance and Retreat: Personal Experiences in the United States and Confederate States Armies.* New Orleans: G.T. Beauregard, 1880.

—. "Letter from General John B. Hood, June 28, 1875." In *Southern Historical Society Papers,* vol. 4. Richmond: James E. Goode, 1877. Reprinted in 1990 by Broadfoot Publishing.

Hoopes, John W., ed. "The Confederate Memoir of William M. Abernathy." In vol. 2 of *Confederate Veteran.* Sons of Confederate Veterans, 2003.

Jones, J. William. "Gettysburg - Longstreet vs. Lee." *New York Sun,* Dec. 10, 1895.

—. *Life and Letters of Robert E. Lee: Soldier and Man.* New York: Neale Publishing Company, 1906.

—. *Personal Reminiscences, Anecdotes, and Letters of Gen. Robert E. Lee.* New York: D. Appleton and Col, 1874.

Jones, Terry L., ed. *Campbell Brown's Civil War.* Baton Rouge: Louisiana State University Press, 2001.

Buehler, Fannie J. *Recollections of the Rebel Invasion and One Woman's Experience During the Battle of Gettysburg.* 1896.

Jorgensen, Jay. "Edward Porter Alexander, Confederate Cannoneer at Gettysburg." *Gettysburg Magazine,* no. 17 (July 1997).

Kershaw, Joseph. "Official Report of General J.B. Kershaw." In vol. 4 of *Southern Historical Society Papers*. July–Dec., 1877. Reprinted in 1990 by Broadfoot Publishing.

—. "Kershaw's Brigade at Gettysburg." In vol. 3 of *Battles and Leaders of the Civil War*. Edited by Robert U. Johnson and Clarence C. Buel, 1884–1888. New York: Thomas Yoseloff, 1956.

Krick, Robert E.L. *Staff Officers in Gray: A Biographical Register of the Staff Officers in the Army of Northern Virginia*. Chapel Hill: University of North Carolina Press, 2003.

Ladd, David L. and Audrey J. Ladd, ed. *The Bachelder Papers: Gettysburg in Their Own Words*. 3 vols. Dayton, OH: Morningside House, Inc., 1994.

Laino, Philip. *The Gettysburg Campaign Atlas*. Revised and Expanded edition. Trumbull, CT: Gettysburg Publishing, 2015.

Laney, Cara and Elizabeth Loftus. "Eyewitness testimony and memory biases." In *Noba textbook series: Psychology*. Edited by R. Biswas-Diener and E. Diener. Champaign, IL: DEF publishers, 2020, http://noba.to/uy49tm37

Law, Evander M. "The Struggle for 'Round Top.'" In vol. 3 of *Battles and Leaders of the Civil War*. Edited by Robert U. Johnson and Clarence C. Buel, 1884–1888. New York: Thomas Yoseloff, 1956.

Lee, Fitzhugh. "A Review of the First Two Days' Operations at Gettysburg and a Reply to General Longstreet." In vol. 5 of *Southern Historical Society Papers*. Richmond: Johns & Goolsby, Jan.–June 1878.

Lee, Robert E. "General Lee's Final and Full Report of the Pennsylvania Campaign and Battle of Gettysburg." In vol. 2 of *Southern Historical Society Papers*. Richmond: Rev. J. William Jones, D.D.,1876.

Lee, Capt. Robert E. *Recollections and Letters of General Robert E. Lee*. New York: Doubleday, Page & Company, 1904.

Leon, Carlos. "An Architecture of Narrative Memory." *Biologically Inspired Cognitive Architectures* 16 (April 2016).

Linde, Charlotte. "Memory in Narrative." In *The International Encyclopedia of Language and Social Interaction*. 1st ed. Edited by Karen Tracy, et al. Wiley & Sons, 2015.

Loftus, Elizabeth. *Memory: Surprising New Insights into How We Remember and Why We Forget.* Reading, MA: Addison-Wesley Publishing Co., 1980.

—. "The Reality of Repressed Memories," *American Psychologist* 48, no. 5 (May 1993).

Long, Armistead Lindsay. *Memoirs of Robert E. Lee: His Military and Personal History.* London: Sampson Low, Marston, Searle, and Rivington, 1886.

—. "Letter to Jubal Early, April 5, 1876." In vol. 4 of *Southern Historical Society Papers.* Richmond: James E. Goode, 1877.

Longstreet, James. *From Manassas to Appomattox: Memoirs of the Civil War in America.* Philadelphia: J.B. Lippincott Co., 1896.

—. "Lee in Pennsylvania." In Philadelphia Weekly Times, *The Annals of the War.* Philadelphia: The Times Publishing Co., 1879. Reprinted in 1974 by Civil War Times Illustrated.

—. "Lee's Right Wing at Gettysburg." In vol. 3 of *Battles and Leaders of the Civil War.* Edited by Robert U. Johnson and Clarence C. Buel, 1884–1888. New York: Thomas Yoseloff, 1956.

McAden, Marie. "Battle of Rivers Bridge State Historic Site Preserves Civil War Battlefield." https://discoversouthcarolina.com/articles/rivers-bridge-state-historic-site-preserves-civil-war-battlefield

McLaws, Lafayette. "Gettysburg." In vol. 7 of *Southern Historical Society Papers.* Richmond: Rev. J. William Jones, D.D., 1879.

—. "Longstreet at Gettysburg." In *Philadelphia Weekly Press.* 3 parts. Feb. 15, 22, and 29, 1888.

McPherson, James. "American Victory, American Defeat." In *Why the Confederacy Lost.* Edited by Gabor S. Boritt. New York: Oxford University Press, 1992.

Macrobert, Alan. "Time in the Sky and the Amateur Astronomer." *Sky & Telescope,* July 18, 2006. https://skyandtelescope.org/astronomy-resources/time-in-the-sky-and-the-amateur-astronomer/.

Maeva, Marcus, ed. *The Documentary History of the Supreme Court of the United States, 1789–1800.* 8 vols. New York: Columbia University Press, 1985–2007.

Maurice, Frederickm, ed. An Aide-De-Camp of Lee: *Being the Papers of Colonel Charles Marshall Sometime Aide-De-Camp, Military Secre-*

tary, and Assistant Adjutant General on the Staff of Robert E. Lee, 1862–1865. Boston: Little, Brown, and Co., 1927. Reprinted in 2000 by University of Nebraska Press as *Lee's Aide-De-Camp*.

Moyer, H.P. *History of the Seventeenth Regiment Pennsylvania Volunteer Cavalry*. Lebanon, PA: Sowers Printing Co., 1911.

Murray, Jennifer M. *On a Great Battlefield: The Making, Management, and Memory of Gettysburg National Military Park, 1933–2013*. Knoxville: The University of Tennessee Press, 2014.

Murray, R.L. *E.P. Alexander and the Artillery Action in the Peach Orchard*. Wolcott, NY: Benedum Publishing, 2000.

Musselman, Curt. "In the Footsteps of the Topographical Engineers." *Professional Surveyor Magazine*, Dec. 2011. https://archives.profsurv.com/magazine/article.aspx?i=71028.

National Park Service. "These Honored Dead: The Battle of Rivers Bridge and Civil War Combat Casualties." https://www.nps.gov/articles/these-honored-dead-the-battle-of-rivers-bridge-and-civil-war-combat-casualties-teaching-with-historic-places.htm#:~:text=Rivers%20Bridge%20was%20one%20of%20the%20first%20historic,open%20daily%20from%209%20a.m.%20to%206%20p.m.;

Nevin, Alfred. *Men of Mark of Cumberland Valley, PA 1776–1876*. Philadelphia: Fulton Publishing Co., 1876.

Oates, William C. "Gettysburg - The Battle on the Right." In vol. 6 of *Southern Historical Society Papers*. Richmond: Rev. J. William Jones, D.D., 1878.

Oeffinger, John C., ed. *A Soldier's General: The Civil War Letters of Major General Lafayette McLaws*. Chapel Hill: University of North Carolina Press, 2002.

Pendleton, William N. "Personal Recollections of General Lee." Address delivered at Washington & Lee University, Virginia, Jan 19, 1873. In *Southern Magazine* 15 (1874).

Pfanz, Harry W. *Gettysburg: The First Day*. Chapel Hill: University of North Carolina Press, 2001.

—. *Gettysburg: The Second Day*. Chapel Hill: University of North Carolina Press, 1987.

Pfarr, Cory M. *Longstreet at Gettysburg: A Critical Reassessment.* Jefferson, NC: McFarland & Co., 2019.

Piston, William Garrett. *Lee's Tarnished Lieutenant: James Longstreet and His Place in Southern History.* Athens: University of Georgia Press, 1987.

Polley, J.B. *Hood's Texas Brigade: Its Marches, Its Battles, Its Achievements.* Dayton, OH: Press of Morningside Bookshop, 1976.

Powell, David A. "A Reconnaissance Gone Awry: Capt. Samuel R. Johnston's Fateful Trip to Little Round Top." *Gettysburg Magazine,* no. 23 (July 2000).

Purifoy, John. "Battle of Gettysburg, July 2, 1863." *Confederate Veteran* 31, no. 11 (Nov. 1923).

Reardon, Carol and Tom Vossler. *A Field Guide to Gettysburg: Experiencing the Battlefield through Its History, Places, and People.* Chapel Hill: University of North Carolina Press, 2013.

Richardson, James D. *A Compilation of the Messages and Papers of the Presidents, 1789–1897,* vol. 6. Congress, 1899.

Ross, Fitzgerald. *A Visit to the Cities and Camp Camps of the Confederate States, 1863–64.* Edinburgh: William Blackwood and Sons, 1865.

Ross, Michael and Fiore Sicoly. "Egocentric Biases in Availability and Attrition." *Journal of Personality and Social Psychology* 27, no. 3 (1979).

Sanger, Donald and Thomas Hay, *James Longstreet: Soldier, Politician, Officeholder & Writer.* Gloucester: Peter Smith, 1968.

Sauers, Richard Allen. "John B. Bachelder: Government Historian of the Battle of Gettysburg." *Gettysburg Magazine,* no. 3 (July 1990).

Scott, Douglas D. and Richard A. Fox, Jr. *Archaeological Insights into the Custer Battle: An Assessment of the 1984 Field Season.* Norman, OK: University of Oklahoma Press, 1987.

Sears, Stephen W. *Gettysburg.* Boston: Houghton Mifflin, 2003.

Sickles, Eugene and David Berman. National Register of Historic Places Nomination Form for Adams County Courthouse (1974).

Small, Abner R. *The Sixteenth Maine Regiment in the War of the Rebellion 1861–1865.* Portland, ME: B. Thurston & Co., 1886.

Smith, James Power. "General Lee at Gettysburg." A Paper Read Before the Military Historical Society of Massachusetts, April 4,

1905. Richmond: R.E. Lee Camp, No. 1, Confederate Veterans, 1905.

Smith, Karlton. "To Consider Every Contingency: Lt. Gen. James Longstreet, Capt. Samuel R. Johnston, and the Factors That Affected the Reconnaissance and Countermarch, July 2, 1863." In *The Most Shocking Battle I Have Ever Witnessed: The Second Day at Gettysburg: Papers of the 2006 Gettysburg National Military Park Seminar.* National Park Service, 2008.

Smith, Timothy, ed. *Farms at Gettysburg: The Fields of Battle: Selected Images from the Adams County Historical Society.* Gettysburg: Thomas Publications, 2007.

Sorrel, G. Moxley. *Recollections of a Confederate Staff Officer.* New York: Neale Publishing Co., 1905.

Southwick, Dr. Steven M., et al. "Consistency of Memory for Combat-Related Traumatic Events in Veterans of Operation Desert Storm." *American Journal of Psychiatry* 152, no. 2 (1997).

Steiner, Bernard C. *Life of Reverdy Johnson.* Baltimore: The Norman, Remington Co., 1914.

Stevens, C.A. *Berdan's United States Sharpshooters in the Army of the Potomac.* Reprinted in 1984 by Press of Morningside Bookshop.

Stevens, Jonathan W. *Reminiscences of the Civil War.* Hillsboro, TX: Hillsboro Mirror Print, 1902.

Strider, Robert Edward Lee, ed. *The Life and Work of George William Peterkin.* Philadelphia: George W. Jacobs & Co., 1929.

Strouss, E.C. "Address of E.C. Strouss." In vol. 1 of *Pennsylvania at Gettysburg*, edited by John P. Nicholson. Harrisburg: E.K. Meyers, 1893.

Styple, William B. *Writing & Fighting the Confederate War: The Letters of Peter Wellington Alexander, Confederate War Correspondent.* Kearny, NJ: Belle Grove Publishing Co., 2002.

Swinton, William. *Campaigns of the Army of the Potomac: A Critical History of Operations in Virginia, Maryland, and Pennsylvania from the Commencement to the Close of the War, 1861–5.* New York: Charles B. Richardson, 1866.

Tagg, Larry. *The Generals of Gettysburg: The Leaders of America's Greatest Battle.* Campbell, CA: Savas Publishing Co., 1998.

Bibliography

Taylor, Walter H. "The Campaign in Pennsylvania." In *Annals of the War*. Philadelphia: The Times Publishing Company, 1879. Reprinted in 1974 by Civil War Times Illustrated.

—. *Four Years with General Lee: Being a Summary of the More Important Events Touching the Career of General Robert E. Lee, in the War Between the States.* New York: D. Appleton and Company, 1878.

—. "Memorandum by Colonel Walter H. Taylor, of General Lee's Staff." In vol. 4 of *Southern Historical Society Papers*. Richmond: James E. Goode, 1877.

—. "Second Paper by Walter H. Taylor, of General Lee's Staff." In vol. 4 of *Southern Historical Society Papers*, vol. 4. Richmond: James E. Goode, 1877.

Teaching American History, teachingamericanhistory.org

Teague, Charles. *Gettysburg By The Numbers: The Essential Pocket Compendium of Crucial and Curious Data About The Battle.* Gettysburg: Adams County Historical Society, 2006.

Templeman, Eleanor Lee. "Benjamin Hallowell, Dedicated Educator." In *Arlington Historical Magazine* 2, no. 3 (Oct. 1963). http://arlingtonhistoricalsociety.org/wp-content/uploads/.

Thomson, Orville. *From Philippi to Appomattox: Seventh Indiana Infantry in the War for the Union.* Self-published, n.d. Reprinted in 1993 by Butternut and Blue.

Thompson, Allen R. "In Defense of Captain Samuel Johnston." *Gettysburg Magazine*, no. 61 (July 2019).

—. "It Was the Intention to Defend the Place: John Reynolds and the Decision to Fight at Gettysburg." *Gettysburg Magazine*, no. 65 (July 2021).

Tower, R. Lockwood, ed. *Lee's Adjutant: The Wartime Letters of Colonel Walter Herron Taylor, 1862–1865.* Columbia: University of South Carolina Press, 1995.

Tremain, Henry Edwin. *Two Days of War: A Gettysburg Narrative and Other Excursions.* New York: Bonnell, Silver and Bowers, 1905.

Trivers, Robert. *The Folly of Fools: The Logic of Deceit and Self-Deception in Human Life.* New York: Basic Books, 2011.

Trudeau, Noah Andre. *Gettysburg: A Testing of Courage.* New York: HarperCollins, 2002.

Tucker, Glenn. *High Tide at Gettysburg*. Indianapolis: Bobbs-Merrill Co., 1958. Reprinted by Konecky and Konecky.

—. *Lee and Longstreet at Gettysburg*. Bobbs-Merrill, 1968. Reprinted in 1982 by Morningside.

United States Department of the Interior. "Adams County Courthouse." In *National Register of Historic Places Inventory - Nomination Form*. National Park Service, June 20, 1974.

—.Cultural Landscape Report for Gettysburg National Military Park: Record of Treatment. 2018.

United States War Department. *Instructions for Field Artillery*. Washington, D.C.: Government Printing Office, 1863.

—.*List of Staff Officers of the Confederate States Army 1861–1865*. Washington, D.C.: Government Printing Office, 1891.

—. *The War of the Rebellion: A Compilation of the Official Records of the Union and Confederate Armies: Official Records of the Union and Confederate Armies*. Washington, D.C.: U.S. Government Printing Office, 1880–1901.

Wade, John Donald. *Augustus Baldwin Longstreet: A Study of the Development of Culture in the South*. New York: The MacMillan Company, 1924.

Wainwright, Charles S. *A Diary of Battle: The Personal Journals of Colonel Charles S. Wainwright*. Edited by Allan Nevins. New York: De Capo Press, 1998.

Walker, R. Lindsay. "Letter from General R. Lindsay Walker." In vol. 5 of *Southern Historical Society Papers*. Richmond: J.W. Jones, 1878.

Walker, Charles D. *Biographical Sketches of the Graduates and Eleves of the Virginia Military Institute Who Fell During the War Between the States*. Philadelphia: J.B. Lippincott, 1875.

Webster, Noah. *An American Dictionary of the English Language*. Springfield, MA: George & Charles Merriam, 1862.

Welsh, M.D., Jack. *Medical Histories of Confederate Generals*. Kent, OH: The Kent State University Press, 1995.

Wert, Jeffry D. *General James Longstreet: The Confederacy's Most Controversial Soldier - A Biography*. New York: Simon & Schuster, 1993.

—. *Gettysburg: Day Three*. New York: Simon & Schuster, 2001.

West, John C. *A Texan in Search of a Fight: Being the Diary and Letters of a Private Soldier in Hood's Texas Brigade*. Texas: Press of J.S. Hill & Co., 1901. Reprinted 1994 by Butternut and Blue.

Wittenberg, Eric J. *The Devil's to Pay: John Buford at Gettysburg: A History and Walking Tour*. El Dorado Hills, CA: Savas Beatie, 2018.

Wolchover, Natalie. "How Far Can the Human Eye See?" *Live Science*, May 7, 2012, https://www.livescience.com/33895-human-eye.html?msclkid=0ac86ebdd0cb11eca00ec5cc6cf82a15

Woods, James A. *Gettysburg July 2: The Ebb and Flow of Battle*. Gillette, NJ: Canister Publishing LLC, 2012.

NEWSPAPERS

Alexandria (VA) Daily State Journal
"To Contractors," June 10, 1872.

Alexandria Gazette
July 24, 1852.
Feb. 15, 1858.
July 7, 1868.
Aug. 17, 1868.
June 16, 1870.
June 12, 1871.
"The Late Thomas J. Moncure," Aug. 28, 1912.

Alexandria Gazette and Virginia Advertiser
June 24, 1859.
Jan. 15, 1861.
"Negro Games," Aug. 22, 1866.
"Property Sale," March 14, 1868.

Baltimore Sun
April 15, 1870.
"Monument to Gen. Lee," Oct. 31, 1870.
Sept. 17, 1880
"Death of Col. William Proctor Smith," Aug. 29, 1895.
Aug. 27, 1912

Brooklyn Daily Eagle
"After the Correspondents," Jan. 22, 1864.

"Swinton and West Point," June 18, 1866.

Sept. 17, 1880.

"A Visit to Gettysburg: Brooklynites, New Yorkers and Philadelphians Invited Guests of Mr. John Russell Young," May 31, 1894.

Burlington (VT) Daily Free Press

April 12, 1853

Charleston (SC) Daily Courier

"General R.E. Lee's Birthday - Address of General Jubal Early," Jan. 26, 1872.

Charleston (SC) Mercury

"From Gen. Lee's Army - The Battle of Gettysburg," July 16, 1863. Reprinted from *Richmond (VA) Dispatch.*

"The Great Battle of Gettysburg," July 23, 1863. Reprint from *Savannah (GA) Republican*, July 19, 1863.

"The Pennsylvania Campaign, - A Review of Its Movements and Results," July 28, 1863. Reprint from *Savannah (GA) Republican.*

"Meeting of the Colored People at Columbia - Addressed by General Wade Hampton, Hon. E.J. Arthur and Others," March 20, 1867.

"General Longstreet and His Position," June 24, 1867.

"General Longstreet and the Doctrine of Force." Reprinted in *Knoxville (TN) Daily Free Press*, July 2, 1867.

Cincinnati (OH) Enquirer

July 25, 1877.

Columbia (SC) Daily Phoenix

"Gen. Longstreet Speaks," March 28, 1867.

The (Fredericksburg, VA) Daily Star

"In Memoriam: Thomas Jefferson Moncure," Sept. 2, 1912.

Edgefield (SC) Advertiser

"General Longstreet with a New Vocation," Jan. 31, 1866.

(Frederick, MD) News

Dec. 14, 1885.

The Free Lance (Fredericksburg, VA)

"Delegate Thomas J. Moncure," July 13, 1901.

Bibliography

Hull (East Yorkshire) Packet; and East Riding Times
   "The Standard Time," Nov. 27, 1857.
Knoxville (TN) Daily Press
      "General Longstreet and the Doctrine of Force," July 2, 1867.
         Reprinted from *Charleston (SC) Mercury.*
Leavenworth (Kansas) Weekly Times
      "Time," March 9, 1876.
Memphis (TN) Bulletin
         "Rebel Generals," July 10, 1863. Reprinted from *St. Louis (MO) Republican.*
Memphis (TN) Daily Commercial
         "The Army of the Potomac," May 5, 1866. Reprinted from *The New York Times.*
Memphis Public Ledger
      "General Longstreet's Position," July 8, 1867.
Nashville Union and American
         "Gen. Beauregard on the Situation - He Counsels Submission," Mach 30, 1867. Reprinted from *New Orleans Times,* March 26, 1867.
New England Farmer (Boston)
      July 6, 1861.
New Orleans Crescent
      "The War in Virginia," June 13, 1866.
New Orleans Republican
         "Longstreet at Gettysburg - Letter from General McLaws - Pendleton's Statement Reviewed," Aug. 10, 1873.
New Orleans Times-Democrat
      June 28, 1882.
New Orleans Times-Picayune
      "Oration by Hon. Thomas J. Semmes," Oct. 23, 1870.
New Orleans Times
      "Views of Prominent Men Solicited," March 17, 1867.
      "General Longstreet on the Situation," March 19, 1867.
      "The Situation. The Views of Eminent Men. Letters from Gen. Longstreet, Judge Campbell, and Hon. Christian Roselius," April 7, 1867.

"The World Upside Down," June 6, 1867.

"General Longstreet," June 8, 1867.

"Letter From Gen. Longstreet," June 8, 1867.

New York Daily Herald

"Southern Reconstruction - The Power and the Programme of Secretary of Stanton," March 20, 1867.

(New York) Daily News

Dec. 14, 1885.

New York Sun

Perry, Leslie J. "Lee and Longstreet: Which Was Responsible for the Gettysburg Defeat?" Nov. 10, 1895.

Jones, J. William. "Gettysburg - Longstreet vs. Lee," Dec. 15, 1895.

New York Times

"White Sulpher Springs," Aug. 25, 1877.

"Battle of Gettysburg: Gen. Longstreet's Part In It." Partially reprinted, Nov. 5, 1877.

New York World

May 28, 1893.

Norfolk Virginian

"Meeting at Williamsburg - Respect to the Memory of Lee," Oct. 19, 1870.

Opelousas (LA) Courier

"The Longstreet Picnic in Texas," May 12, 1866. Reprint from the *Galveston (TX) News.*

Philadelphia Times

"Again at Gettysburg: Confederate Generals Visit the Scene of the Historic Conflict," April 29, 1893.

"Gettysburg's Field: The Visit of the Union and Confederate Generals," April 30, 1893.

"Making War History: Second Day of the Remarkable Reunion at Gettysburg," May 1, 1893.

Portsmouth (OH) Daily Times

"What the Rebels Accomplished in the Maryland Raid," July 23, 1864.

Raleigh (NC) Weekly Sentinel

"General Longstreet and His Position," July 9, 1867.

Richmond (VA) Dispatch

"From Gen. Lee's Army - The Battle of Gettysburg." Reprinted in *The Charleston (SC) Mercury,* July 16, 1863.

"A Northern History of the War," May 2, 1866.

August 7, 1869.

"Disabilities," April 30, 1870.

"The Death of Gen'l Lee - A Day of Mourning in Richmond," Oct. 14, 1870.

Dec. 20, 1870.

Feb. 28, 1871.

"Jackson's Widow - Correspondence with Acting Mayor Meredith, - Visiting Military," Oct. 26, 1875.

"Funeral of the Late Colonel John G. Clarke," Sept. 18, 1880.

Richmond (VA) Times

"Biography of Thomas Moncure," June 12, 1901.

Rutland (VT) Weekly Herald

"Miscellaneous Items," Dec. 1, 1864.

Savannah (GA) Republican

"The Great Battle of Gettysburg," July 19, 1863.

"Letter from the Army - Hagerstown, July 7, 1863," July 22, 1863.

"Letter from the Army - July 13," July 23, 1863.

"The Pennsylvania Campaign - A Review of Its Movements and Results." Reprinted in *The Charleston (SC) Mercury,* July 27, 1863.

Shreveport (LA) South-Western

"General Longstreet," June 19, 1867.

"Gen. Robt. E. Lee is Dead," Oct. 19, 1870.

Staunton (VA) Spectator and General Advertiser

"Casualty List," July 28, 1863.

"The 'Washington and Lee University," Nov. 8, 1870.

"Death of Col. Wm. Proctor Smith," Sept. 4, 1895.

(Staunton) Valley Virginian

"Richmond and Allegheny Railroad," Dec. 16, 1880.

(Louisiana) Times-Democrat

June 28, 1882.

Times (London)

Aug. 18, 1863.

Vicksburg (MS) Times and Republican

"Death of Gen. Robert E. Lee," Oct. 14, 1870.

Virginia Gazette

June 13, 1777.

Washington, D.C. Evening Star

"Auction Sales," June 29, 1864.

Yorkville (SC) Enquirer

"The Confederacy: The Dying Hours and Struggles - The Nobility of Lee - The Hopelessness of the Struggle - A Thrilling Account by an Impartial Observer," Nov. 30, 1865.

MAPS

Bachelder, John B. *Gettysburg Battlefield.* New York: Endicott & Co., 1863.

Bachelder, John B. *Map of the Battle Field of Gettysburg.* 1883. Set of 3.

Warren, G.K. *Battle Field of Gettysburg.* 1876. Troop Placements by Bachelder. Plate 13, 4:00 p.m.–4:30 p.m.

1858 Adams County, PA Wall Map.

1858 Frederick, MD County Wall Map, Library of Congress.

INDEX

ACKNOWLEDGMENTS

FIRST AND FOREMOST, I THANK MY FAMILY: MY WIFE AMANDA, for putting up with trips to Gettysburg, long weekends looking at documents and writing the manuscript, and for always believing in me and this project. My kids, Ben, Emme, and Ethan, for sacrificing weekend and evening time while Dad pored over old documents on the computer and for the company in roaming around the battlefield. My parents, for encouraging my love of history, instilling a healthy sense of skepticism, and being my first copy editors.

Steven Floyd and Scott Brown, thank you for the immeasurable contributions during discussions, battlefield walks, and reviewing the many drafts of the manuscript. The book is significantly improved by your insights, suggestions, and questions and I am forever indebted for that. Thanks for making me answer questions without leaving any loose ends, and for the company exploring the many interesting and enlightening paths and rabbit holes which I wouldn't have otherwise traveled. Your ability to produce sources is nothing short of uncanny.

Many thanks to Philip Laino, not only for his wonderful maps, but for the many suggestions and patience that made both the maps and manuscript better.

John Heiser offered invaluable assistance at the Gettysburg National Military Park Library and Research Center. Thank you for your quick, always polite, and invariably thorough answers to any and all questions Gettysburg-related.

I owe many thanks to David Batalo, for his very generous use of the photograph of Samuel Johnston.

I also need to thank Colin Zimmerman, for always making me prove my point; Ralph Siegel, for his always honest and helpful critiques of the thought process as it was being worked out and for the general editing pointers; Chris Army, for his always ready answers for my minutia inquiries and for helping find the answers when neither of us had one handy; and Jay Jorgensen, for his initial interest in my study of Sam Johnston and the kindness and opportunities ever since. Thank you to Rob Gibson for the incredible cover photo of the Round Tops.

Thanks to the staff at Gettysburg National Military Park Library and Research Center, Fairfax County Courthouse, Kentucky Historical Society, University of North Carolina–Wilson Library, Maryland Historical Society, South Caroliniana Library at SCU, Tennessee State Archives, Emory University, and the Daughters of the Confederacy, for the incredible professionalism, helpfulness, kindness, and promptness in fulfilling archive requests.

A general thanks is owed to the National Park Service and American Battlefield Trust, for preserving the field as much as it is. Walking the ground is invaluable to an understanding of the battle and why the decisions that were made were made.

Finally, but certainly not least, thanks to Roger Williams, Aleigha Kely, and everyone at Knox Press and Post Hill Press for their assistance in turning the manuscript into a book and for all the guidance along the way.

Acknowledgments

Any errors in the book, as there most certainly will be, are entirely my own. Many thanks to everyone who assisted in the thought and editing process for catching the ones that, due to your efforts, *didn't* make it into the final work.

ABOUT THE AUTHOR

Photo by Bobby Bates

ALLEN R. THOMPSON IS A PRACTICING ATTORNEY IN NEW Jersey, where he lives with his wife and three kids. His writing focuses on reevaluating primary source materials to examine the standard interpretations of historical subjects, from legal doctrines to historical events. His articles have appeared in the *St. Thomas Law Review* and *Gettysburg Magazine*.